THE STEWART EARLS OF ORKNEY

In Memoriam
Stewart James Anderson, 1983–2003
David Alexander Robertson Anderson, 1915–2005

The Stewart Earls of Orkney

PETER ANDERSON

JOHN DONALD

First published in Great Britain in 2012 by
John Donald, an imprint of Birlinn Ltd

West Newington House
10 Newington Road
Edinburgh
EH9 1QS
www.birlinn.co.uk

ISBN 978 1 904607 46 5

Copyright © Peter Anderson 2012

British Library Cataloguing-in-Publication Data
A catalogue record for this book is available on request
from the British Library

Typeset in Arno by
Koinonia, Manchester
Printed and bound in Britain by
Bell and Bain Ltd, Glasgow

Contents

Illustrations

MAPS

All drawings and maps are by the author, and all photographs are reproduced courtesy of the author.

Preface and Acknowledgments

This work has its foundations in two previous books, *Robert Stewart, Earl of Orkney, Lord of Shetland* (Edinburgh, 1982) and *Black Patie: the Life and Times of Patrick Stewart, Earl of Orkney, Lord of Shetland* (Edinburgh, 1992). Both were published by John Donald Publishers Ltd through the excellent offices of John Tuckwell to whom I remain extremely grateful. The first work began life as my doctoral thesis, completed under the supervision of Professor Gordon Donaldson. His influence still hovers over the whole enterprise. He took an interest in the book on Robert Stewart as the next stage after the thesis, but also looked over that on Patrick in detail, inviting me to his home in Dysart for a day to discuss his comments. He died not long after the appearance of *Black Patie* but, poignantly, his literary executor John Ballantyne made me a present of his review copy of the book, complete with the markings of what he called his 'correcting pencil'. This is the copy I have used in the preparation of the present work. I was also reminded of his helpfulness when Brian Smith, who had also studied under him, cast a critical and painstaking eye over the first completed draft of *The Stewart Earls of Orkney*.

This opus, undertaken at the invitation of Birlinn as the successors to John Donald, constitutes the culmination of well over thirty years of work on the subject, pursued during the leisure moments of a similar period in the employment of the National Records of Scotland, formerly the National Archives of Scotland, formerly the Scottish Record Office. No doubt it will not be the last word to be said on the Stewart earls – not even the last word to be said by me – though I certainly do not intend to produce a revised edition any time soon.

My efforts had their origin in my first interview with Professor Donaldson in the early summer of 1974. I was proposing to enrol to do research, and I needed some guidance on procedure, as well as suggestions for a subject, preferably something associated with the Northern Isles. Professor Donaldson was well known as a son, or at any rate grandson, of the north himself, and thus particularly qualified to point me in the right direction. As it turned out, his knowledge of history in general – northern, Scottish, British, European – was encyclopaedic, but he wrote extensively on the Northern Isles, particularly Shetland, which he loved with a passion.

His suggestion of the Stewart earls rather surprised me. This was as much a product of my own ignorance as anything else, but it had simply not occurred to me that these apparently wicked individuals, Robert and Patrick Stewart, on whom all the previous scholars had had strong opinions, had never found someone prepared to take them on their own terms, study precisely who they were, what they did, and why they enjoyed, if that is the word, such a poor estimation. Nevertheless this was, as Donaldson pointed out, no more than the truth. Although he himself had written a fascinating volume called *Shetland Life under Earl Patrick*, he was interested more in the picture of Shetland society presented by the Shetland Court Book of 1602–4 than in the story of the earls themselves. We decided on Robert Stewart, the first of the earls, and he told me to get cracking. Since I was working part-time but had no more than the five-year maximum for delivery of any PhD student, I needed to be 'well begun' before enrolling officially. This I did the following year, in the autumn of 1975.

The studies made steady progress, enlivened by the fortnightly seminars where Donaldson brought all his postgraduates together to review and discuss their findings – David Caldwell, later of the Royal Scottish Museums, on guns and armaments; Norman Reid, now archivist of St Andrews University, on the Wars of Independence period; Pat Dennison on burgh history; Helen Bennett on early knitting; and others. Latterly we had Professor Geoffrey Barrow as co-supervisor as he prepared to succeed Donaldson as Sir William Fraser professor, and finally I was put through the mill in my oral examination by these two, with my external examiner Dr Barbara Crawford, now the doyenne of northern studies in Scotland, being particularly rigorous.

This was in 1980, and now came the possibility of finding a publisher. I was naturally pointed, as we all were in those days, in the direction of John Donald, and particularly 'John', that is to say John Tuckwell, who was to be responsible for seeing both *Robert* and *Black Patie* through the press. Gordon Donaldson suggested that John Donald would probably be interested, not in the thesis as such, but in a combined volume on Robert Stewart and his son – in short, something like the present work. Surprisingly, this was not the case; John was prepared to take the volume in its current shape. Our discussions were interesting, since he mentioned that he had recently turned down a proposal for a biography of Archbishop Sharp, by Julia Buckroyd. I am not sure nowadays how many Scottish school pupils will have heard of Sharp, the covenanting renegade who paid for his mitre by being assassinated on Magus Muir, near St Andrews, and who is butchered anew each year during the university's Kate Kennedy procession; nevertheless he seemed to me a much more 'mainstream' figure in Scottish history than an illegitimate son of James V who inveigled his way into becoming earl of Orkney. (Dr Buckroyd's book did eventually come out under the John Donald imprint.)

The key words were Orkney and Shetland. The reading public of those islands form an unashamed captive audience, with an insatiable appetite for works on all aspects of the islands; this became clear to me later, when I found myself signing copies of both books at most unexpected moments. I recall walking up Hillside

Road in Stromness on the way to my parents' house when a near neighbour, Eric Flett, a retired butcher, came out of his house, book in hand, and asked me to sign it there and then, in the street.

The next stage was to rewrite the thesis in book form and, helpfully, Dr John Stuart Shaw, a colleague from the Scottish Record Office (SRO), sent me a copy of a review of a John Donald product on the hunting forests of Scotland, which criticised it roundly for being no more than a thesis dressed up. This was perhaps the main criticism of the firm at a time when all Scottish research graduates sought to be John Donald's bairns. There is an irony here because, although I took this point to heart and rewrote the whole work, at this distance when I read it again in preparation for this work, it still reeked of thesis. This I hope I have corrected. *Robert* came out in 1982, and I sought to ensure that copies of the book were available in time for a conference on Birsay which was held in Orkney in that year. For that reason I was able to get a specimen dustwrapper and had unbound signatures made up into a volume by Donald Campbell, one of the SRO's conservators, so that I could at least show it to the conference delegates. As it happened, John Donald delivered, and Tam McPhail, the Stromness bookseller, was in business at the conference, but I still have my special copy, without finishing titles on the spine, and with my own scribbled annotations accumulated over the years. This too is the version I have used while preparing this work.

Now came *Black Patie*. *Robert* sold well enough to make a profit (John Donald worked on the basis of a share of the profits to the author, not a royalty) and John Tuckwell was very supportive of the idea of a follow-up. I thought of it as finishing the job, though present developments have shown that this was not to be the case. The progress of the writing of *Black Patie* brought new elements into play. One – though I am ashamed to admit it – was my first visit to Shetland, in 1984, two years after *Robert*'s appearance. It is true that, with a young family and being only recently promoted to branch head level in the SRO, I needed a research grant to make the trip, but it must be strange for an outsider to find how little the two archipelagos care about each other, so that someone writing on matters which concerned both groups of islands, had never actually visited one of them. Of noteworthy Orcadians, George Mackay Brown only visited Shetland twice; Joseph Storer Clouston, author of what was until recently the standard history of Orkney, never went there at all. How can you understand the history of the north without visiting one of its most important cultural areas?

I spent a week or so working in the Shetland Archives, as well as drawing and sketching and touring the islands in the company of the Shetland archivist, Brian Smith, before returning south via Orkney. I had known Brian from his early days as an archivist in the mid 1970s, when he came down to the SRO to receive his training baptism of fire from the then deputy keeper, the formidable John Bates. Brian and I had been regularly in touch since, and this was to continue. Over the years he has produced helpful criticism of things I have sent to him, and his stream of seminal articles have added greatly to all our understanding of what was going on in former centuries. He has crowned this with a comprehensive survey of the manuscript, with detailed comments, some witty, some critical and astringent, some encouraging. It was in the early 1980s too that I met someone else who proved enormously helpful. This was John Ballantyne, whose contribution to our knowledge of the records of Shetland has been astonishing, culminating in the *Shetland Documents* volumes, edited with Brian. Until they were published, Shetland had nothing to rival Storer Clouston's *Records of the Earldom of Orkney*. What John and Brian produced is truly extraordinary, and edited to a very high standard of modern scholarship and comprehensiveness, supplanting such previous works as Balfour's *Oppressions*.

In a work such as this, with two books being distilled into one, it has been necessary to provide some changes of emphasis, and certain elements have had to be reduced, if not done away with altogether. *Robert* ended, and *Black Patie* began, with chapters on their general reputations and, particularly in the case of Patrick, of the legends, in some cases extravagant and ludicrous, surrounding their names. Much of this has been left out, and I would refer anyone wanting further information to the two original volumes, which are still available in larger libraries, and occasionally on the open market. There is also considerably less on the provision for Robert and his half-brothers in youth, and more on their early adulthood. Instead, I have sought to tell the story of Orkney and Shetland from the *impignorations* of 1468–9 through the era of the Stewart earls to the finish in 1614, and at the same time to look at the milieu that created, sustained and to some extent thwarted, these men.

I must acknowledge with gratitude the assistance provided by the British Academy, whose grant enabled me to visit Shetland on two occasions for concentrated research in the archives there, and the Shetland Arts Trust for financial assistance in the publication of *Black Patie*. I am also indebted to a wide number of other individuals. Particularly important among these have been my colleagues of the staff of the Scottish Record Office / National Archives of Scotland / National Records of Scotland, in particular: successive Keepers of the Records of Scotland – John Imrie, Athol Murray, Patrick Cadell and the present incumbent, George Mackenzie, as well as my former colleague in the archives Dr Frances Shaw, herself an authority on the north and west, and Fr John McInnes who, as a former member of staff and a very able member of my class on Scottish Handwriting, unearthed the original rebels' bond of association of 1614 from a dreadful mixter-maxter of sweepings from the Justiciary Court floor, and brought it to me with a well-justified feeling that it might be significant. There are also Ms Alison Fraser, now recently retired as archivist of Orkney Council; Professors Richard Fawcett and Denys Pringle, both former members of the staff of Historic Scotland; Dr David Caldwell of the National Museum of Scotland and Mr Angus Konstam of the Royal Armouries for expert advice on architecture, ordnance and instruments of torture respectively; the members of the Orkney Field Club, the Orkney Folk Festival and the Scottish

Society for Northern Studies, for invitations to give lectures which enabled me to try out parts of my work on them; the staff of the National Library of Scotland, Glasgow University Library and the National Archives at Kew (formerly the Public Record Office in Chancery Lane); the earl of Moray, the duke of Roxburghe and John and Wendy Scott of Gardie for permission to quote from items from their muniments; Mr R N Smart, then keeper of muniments, University of St Andrews; Mr Peter Leith, his daughter and my cousin the late and much lamented Mrs Anne Leith Brundle, and the late Miss Joan Heddle for helpful discussion and ideas. I must also acknowledge the invitation of Mr Hugh Andrew to produce this work, and his colleagues Mairi Sutherland and Nicola Wood for their support in it.

Place-names cited in the text have to some extent been brought into line with the modern Ordnance Survey spelling rather than given in in the forms found in Hugh Marwick's books on Orkney farm- and place-names, though his work remains invaluable in other ways. For Shetland, the main authority outside the OS has been John Stewart's *Shetland Place-names*. Personal names have been modernised wherever possible, and sums of money are in Scots currency unless otherwise stated, though in Orkney and Shetland there was a tendency to use any legitimate currency that came to hand, such as the yopindale, the angel noble and the dollar, as well as, occasionally, sterling. The meaning of these is explained either in the text or in the glossary. Any errors with regard to these matters and any other mistakes of any kind whatsoever are my responsibility alone.

My final acknowledgement is to the islands of Orkney and Shetland and their people, whose ancestors appear in the pages of this book. My first memories of life are in Orkney, and my family and ancestral links with those islands are very strong, but in the course of my research I have come to know and better appreciate Shetland, those more rugged islands with their especially strong memories of the Stewart period.

Now read on.

PDA
Linlithgow, 2011

Abbreviations

Abbrev.	Abbreviates
ADCP	Acts of the Lords of Council in Public Affairs, 1501–54
ADC & S	Acta Dominorum et Sessionis
Adv. Ms.	Advocates' Manuscript
APS	*Acts of the Parliaments of Scotland*
B. of C. & S.	Books of Council and Session
BL	British Library
BUK	*Book of the Universall Kirk of Scotland*
Cauts	Cautions
Chrs	Charters
Coll.	Collection
Comm. Ct	Commissary Court
CSP	*Calendar of State Papers* (*Scottish, Domestic, Foreign, Spanish*)
Ct Bk	*Court Book*
d	pennyland
Edin.	Edinburgh
Edin. Tests	Commissariot of Edinburgh Register of Testaments
ER	*Exchequer Rolls of Scotland*
Extr.	Extracts
GR	General Register
GUL	Glasgow University Library
HMC	Reports of the Royal Commission on Historical Manuscripts
Inv.	Inventory
Inventaires	*Inventaires de la Royne Descosse, Douairiere de France*
IR	*Innes Review*
JR	*Juridical Review*
Kirkwall Chrs	Charters and other Records of the City and Royal Burgh of Kirkwall
Lawbs	Lawburrows
microf.	microfilm
Misc.	Miscellaneous, miscellany
Min.	Minute

Ms.(s)	Manuscript(s)
Mun.	Muniments
NLS	National Library of Scotland
NRS	National Records of Scotland (formerly National Archives of Scotland, formerly Scottish Record Office)
O & S	Orkney and Shetland
OA	Orkney Archives
ODNB	*Oxford Dictionary of National Biography*
OLM	*Old Lore Miscellany of Orkney, Shetland, Caithness and Sutherland*
OSR	*Orkney and Shetland Records*
POAS	*Proceedings of the Orkney Antiquarian Society*
Pres.	Presentations
Prot. Bk	Protocol Book
PRS	Particular Register of Sasines
PSAS	*Proceedings of the Society of Archivists of Scotland*
RCAHMS	Royal Commission on the Ancient and Historical Monuments of Scotland
Recs	Records
Reg.	Register
Reg Cauts in Susps	Register of Cautions in Suspensions
Reg. Pres.	Register of Presentations
REO	*Records of the Earldom of Orkney*
RMS	*Registrum Magni Sigilli Regum Scotorum (Register of the Great Seal of Scotland)*
RPC	*Register of the Privy Council of Scotland*
RRS	*Regesta Regum Scottorum*
RSS	*Registrum Secreti Sigilli Regum Scotorum (Register of the Privy Seal of Scotland)*
SBRS	Scottish Burgh Record Society
SCHS	Scottish Church History Society
SHR	*Scottish Historical Review*
SHS	Scottish History Society
NRS	National Archives of Scotland; formerly NRS (Scottish Record Office)
SRS	Scottish Record Society
STS	Scottish Text Society
TA	*Accounts of the (Lord High) Treasurer of Scotland*
TDGNHAS	*Transactions of the Dumfriesshire and Galloway Natural History and Antiquarian Society*
TNA	The National Archives (London); formerly PRO (Public Record Office)

Genealogical Tables

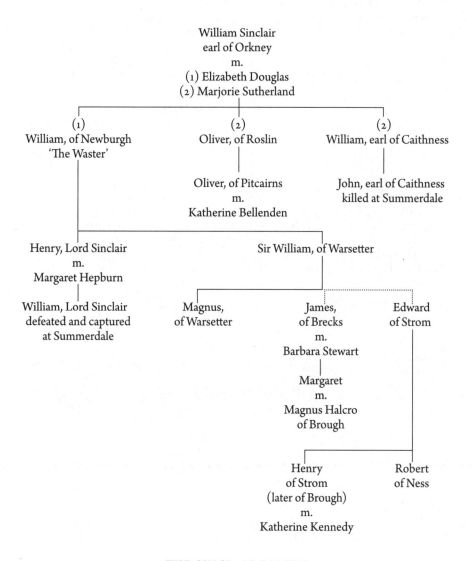

William Sinclair
earl of Orkney
m.
(1) Elizabeth Douglas
(2) Marjorie Sutherland

(1)
William, of Newburgh
'The Waster'

(2)
Oliver, of Roslin

(2)
William, earl of Caithness

Oliver, of Pitcairns
m.
Katherine Bellenden

John, earl of Caithness
killed at Summerdale

Henry, Lord Sinclair
m.
Margaret Hepburn

Sir William, of Warsetter

William, Lord Sinclair
defeated and captured
at Summerdale

Magnus,
of Warsetter

James,
of Brecks
m.
Barbara Stewart

Edward
of Strom

Margaret
m.
Magnus Halcro
of Brough

Henry
of Strom
(later of Brough)
m.
Katherine Kennedy

Robert
of Ness

THE SINCLAIR FAMILY

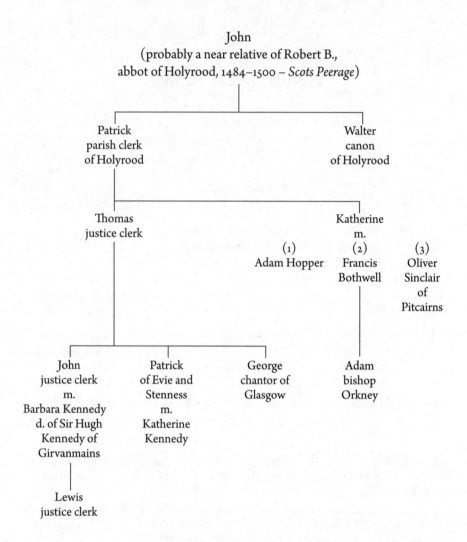

THE BELLENDEN FAMILY

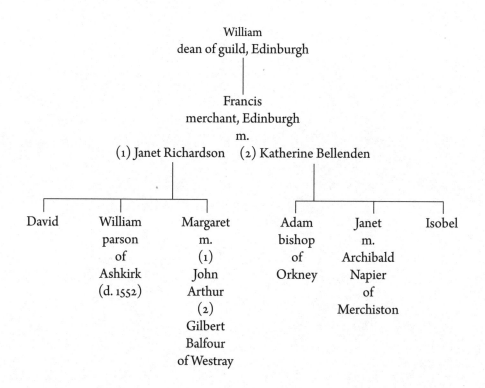

THE BOTHWELL FAMILY

1

The Islands under the Pole

On 5 April 1541, James V wrote to the pope, Paul III, recommending Robert Reid as bishop of Orkney. Robert Reid's diocese, which also included Shetland and temporal lands in Caithness, was referred to as 'the scattered isles in the polar ocean'.[1] Among the reasons the king gave for putting forward a strong, able and trusted royal servant for this post was that the neglect of previous bishops had led to the unsatisfactory observance not merely of the true religion, but also of the laws, 'for there the episcopal authority usually comes next after that of the king'. While it is never wise to place implicit trust in James's submissions to the pope – we will shortly encounter his letters seeking ecclesiastical preferment for his illegitimate sons – this reference to the position of the bishopric in the islands is an expression of a longstanding attitude of Scottish kings to the question of political power there. It also gives an opinion on islands that, uniquely among Scottish kings, he had actually visited.

The Norse line of the earls of Orkney foundered in complex circumstances in the early thirteenth century, and from 1232 their successors – the Angus and Strathearn lines and, most importantly the Sinclairs who, in the person of the first Earl Henry, became earls in 1379 – had strong Scottish connections. Nevertheless it was probably the bishopric that was the first Northern Isles institution to be subjected to strong continuous Scottish cultural influence. In 1384 the Great Schism within the papacy saw Christendom split between the rival pretensions of Rome and Avignon, with Scotland and Norway following Avignon and Rome respectively. Some, therefore, have suggested that Robert Sinclair, the first Avignon bishop of Orkney, might have been responsible for Orkney following Scotland's lead towards Avignon, thus initiating the obscure shift of allegiance from the metropolitan of Nidaros (modern-day Trondheim) to that of St Andrews a century later.[2] However, this seems premature; more recent evidence indicates that ecclesiastical Orkney remained under Norway until after Orkney and Shetland became *de facto* Scottish in 1468–9. During the Schism, Rome and Avignon each appointed three Orkney bishops.[3]

1 *Letters of James V*, ed. R. K. Hannay and D. Hay, Edinburgh 1954, 423.

2 *Letters of James V*, 118; O. Kolsrud, *Den norske Kirkes Erkebiskoper og Biskoper indtil Reformationen, Diplomatarium Norvegicum*, xviib, Christiana (Oslo), 1913, 300; *Diplomatarium Norvegicum*, vii, 475.

3 *Fasti Ecclesiae Scoticanae Medii Aevi* (SRS), ed. D. E. R. Watt and A. Murray, Edinburgh, 2003, 321.

But there was another, more important factor for declining Norwegian influence – the extreme weakness of the country, politically, economically and ecclesiastically. The whole period from 1380 until the death of the regent Margaret in 1412 was one of great uncertainty. There was royal minority for much of the time; the treaty of Stralsund with Denmark in 1370 gave a near monopoly to the merchants of the *Hanse* at the expense of native traders; and the treaty of Kalmar of 1397 robbed Norway of much of her political identity.[4] A major contributory factor to this had been the Black Death, which had ravaged the country about 1349–50; only one of the Norwegian church's bishops survived it, and as late as 1371 the archbishop of Nidaros complained to the pope that the pest had reduced the number of priests from about 300 to 40 or fewer.[5] The results of such a disaster, on top of political weakness, was to take centuries to overcome.

This possibly explains the appointment in 1418 of a Scot, Thomas Tulloch, as bishop by Pope Martin V, the first unrivalled pope after the conclusion of the Schism,[6] as well as the apparent paradox of Tulloch's co-operation with the king of a united Scandinavia, Erik of Pomerania, while at the same time bringing about important developments in favour of Scottish influence within his diocese. Erik trusted Tulloch sufficiently to place 'all the Orkneys' (presumably all the earldom and royal land in the islands) in his charge during later disputes with the Sinclair family, by then in the ascendant,[7] yet Tulloch was responsible for the substitution, in Orkney at least, of Scots for the native Norn tongue in legal and administrative documents,[8] and under his influence and that of his successor the influx of Scottish churchmen became so strong that in Orkney 'we can say with fair certainty that not only was there not a single Norse ecclesiastic after 1450, but not even a native of the Orkneys or Shetlands'.[9]

Once the example of Scottish appointment had been set, it became a practice extremely difficult to break. Although Thomas Tulloch undoubtedly co-operated with King Erik, the control of Nidaros over the bishopric of Orkney became so tenuous that when Orkney was named as owing allegiance to St Andrews in 1472 (only three or four years after political control had passed to the kings of Scots), the change seems to have gone unnoticed in Norway. By 1525 the archbishop of Nidaros had no idea how the Norwegian church had come to lose the see of Orkney and employed a representative, Zutpheldus Wardenberg, visiting Rome on other business, to try to find the answer.[10] The only document Wardenberg

---

4 K. Gjerset, *History of the Norwegian People*, vols I–II, New York, 1927, ii, 24, 41–2.

5 Gjerset, *History of the Norwegian People*, ii, 13.

6 *Fasti*, ed. Watt and Murray, 327; this view is strengthened by the date of Tulloch's provision, 1418, which suggests that he succeeded the Norwegian rather than the Scottish incumbent.

7 *REO*, 31, no. xiv; B. E. Crawford, 'The Fifteenth-century "Genealogy of the Earls of Orkney" and its Reflection of the Contemporary Political and Cultural Situation in the Earldom', *Mediaeval Scandinavia*, x (1976), 163.

8 H. Marwick, *The Orkney Norn*, Oxford, 1926, p. xxii.

9 A. W. Brøgger, *Ancient Emigrants. A History of the Norse Settlements of Scotland*, Oxford, 1929, 184.

10 *Letters of James V*, 118–19.

found explicitly subjecting Orkney to St Andrews was the bull elevating the latter to metropolitan status; however, in addition he found 'the statement in preceding bulls that Orkney was in Scotland, and immediately subject to the apostolic see, not previously *suffragan* [see glossary]'. The last clause in this is a clear description of the Scottish church, since from 1192, with the bull *cum universi* of Celestine III, till 1472, it had had 'special daughter' status from the Holy See, without a metropolitan of its own.[11] Scottish influence had therefore taken over the bishopric by default.

Nevertheless, it seems likely that when Scottish kings acquired power in the islands after 1468–9, their attitude to the bishopric was formed not by its effectiveness in propagating Scottish culture in the islands but, paradoxically, the example previously set by Norway of co-operation between crown and bishop.[12] The Scottish kings' efforts to exert executive power through the bishopric enjoyed mixed fortunes, but were employed as late as 1605 with the appointment of Bishop James Law and the subsequent collapse of the Stewart earldom, right at the end of our story.

But if the usefulness of the bishop to the crown in Norwegian times had impressed the kings of Scots, this was far from the case with the earldom. Though held for over two centuries by Scottish families who took a very active part in Scottish as well as Norse affairs, the earldom had remained a small but strong semi-independent entity, its rulers frequently following their own path in international politics. The kings of Norway had sought on several occasions to clarify their relationship with the Orkney earls and to curtail their independence of action. At his accession in 1379 as the first of his line, Henry Sinclair had to agree to avoid undue familiarity with the bishop, and not to 'raise or begin any war, litigation or dissension' that might cause damage to Norway; that he would not violate any truce concluded by the king with other countries; that he would keep his hands off the royal lands in Orkney; and that he would not construct castles or other fortifications in the islands without permission.[13]

It was of little use. Earl Henry duly built the massive castle of Kirkwall, which will come to figure prominently in our story, and in the years following the links between the earl and the rulers of Norway continued to atrophy. There is no evidence for example that Henry's son, the second Henry (predecessor of William, third and last of the Sinclair earls) ever received an official grant of his earldom, or had any significant contact with Norway or Denmark.[14] A similar approach was taken when Erik of Pomerania withheld recognition of the young Earl William; instead, administration was placed in the hands of the bishop. This approach worked no better; Thomas Tulloch was unable to take any real measure of control,

11 M. Lynch, *Scotland; a New History*, London, 1991, citing M. O. Anderson, *Early Sources of Scottish History, AD500 to 1286*, Edinburgh, 1999, i, 599; M. O. Anderson, 'The Celtic Church in Kinrimund', *IR*, xxxvii (1976); W. F. Skene, *The Chronicles of the Picts and Scots*, Edinburgh, 1867, 151.

12 Crawford, 'The Fifteenth-century "Genealogy"', 163.

13 *REO*, 26, no. xi.

14 Crawford, 'The Fifteenth-century "Genealogy"', 163.

and the outcome, rather than a strengthening of royal power, was a squabble among members of the Sinclair family, in which the late Earl Henry's brother-in-law, David Menzies of Weem, notorious in island history as an oppressor, emerged as the most successful.[15] King Erik recognised realities and made a formal grant of authority to Menzies, who already possessed it in practice.[16] This was to prove a significant precedent. In the end William Sinclair succeeded as earl through the intercession of King James II of Scotland, after a wait of fourteen years, and when King James's son, James III, gained control of the islands for himself, it was clear that the Scots had not been impressed by the relative weakness of King Erik in the face of the strength of whoever established undisputed power in the islands.

The story of how James III gained control of the islands – first Orkney in 1468, then Shetland the following year – has been told in a great deal more detail elsewhere than we need to do here. King Christian I of Denmark, seriously short of funds, pledged his estates and royal powers to James III, king of Scots, in lieu of dowry for his daughter Margaret.[17] For the next two centuries, there were periodic attempts by Denmark to invoke the redemption provisions in the treaty, though the absence of Norway as an independent polity, the Danish kings' preoccupation with more pressing matters elsewhere and the determination of the Scots to hang on to what they had long desired, meant that the former overlords of the islands became minor characters and noises off.

But this was in the future. For now James had to extend his power in the islands, and to do this he in effect made himself earl of Orkney. In 1470, two years after the pledging, James abolished the independent earldom by compelling William Sinclair to part with it in exchange for land at Ravenscraig in Fife.[18] As we shall see, this certainly did not mean that the Sinclair interest in Orkney and Shetland came to an end, and Earl William did far better out of his *excambion* with the king than might have been supposed.[19] Moreover, Earl William's long-standing preparations for a crown takeover, and the considerable concessions he secured, indicate that he had long thought royal intervention inevitable. In February 1472 the earldom of Orkney and lordship of Shetland were annexed to the crown, with a proviso that they were not to be alienated except to legitimate offspring of the monarch.[20]

Having established direct control over the earldom lands, James embarked on a policy of leasing them, presumably together with the royal estates, to *tacksmen* for administrative purposes. Significantly, the first two of these tacksmen were bishops, William Tulloch and Andrew Pictoris, who held the lease successively from 1474 to

15 Crawford, 'The Fifteenth-century "Genealogy"'; *REO*, 36, no. xviii.
16 Crawford, 'The Fifteenth-century "Genealogy"', 163.
17 W. P. L. Thomson, (*The New*) *History of Orkney*, Edinburgh, 1987, 199–202.
18 *RMS*, ii, no. 996.
19 B. E. Crawford, 'The Earldom of Orkney and Lordship of Shetland: a Re-interpretation of their Pledging to Scotland in 1468–70', *Saga Book* (Viking Soc.), 1969, xvii, 156.
20 *APS*, ii, 102.

1488.[21] The policy of employing bishops to enforce royal sway, though it enjoyed a greater measure of success than it had under Norway, was to be increasingly challenged by a man clearly bent on restoring what the Sinclairs had lost. This was Henry, Lord Sinclair, grandson of Earl William. He first appears some time before June 1484, and five years later becomes undisputed tacksman of the lordship lands, though not until after the king's death.[22]

His moves in this game were constantly countered by the crown. The king's first gambit, on 31 March 1486, was the erection of Kirkwall into a royal burgh, strengthening the municipality by the usual privileges, the award of substantial tracts of surrounding land, the unexampled grant of custody of the cathedral building, all with virtually no reciprocal payment from the burgh.[23] The measure was chiefly aimed at reinforcing Kirkwall's position within the islands, freeing it from the possible control of any local magnate and putting it in possession of the largest fortifiable building in its area outside the castle.

It was not until the death of James III and the succession of his youthful son that Henry Sinclair, on 29 May 1489, finally supplanted the bishop as tacksman, the office carrying with it the judicial offices of *foud*, justice and bailie, as well as custody of Kirkwall Castle. The very next day, it was hedged round by identical grants to Patrick, earl of Bothwell, Sinclair's brother-in-law, and John Hepburn, prior of St Andrews, Bothwell's uncle.[24] This odd arrangement was perhaps intended as a counter-move to Henry's unwelcome progress. Also oddly, the grant was for 13 years, (19 years was the usual period) suggesting a reluctant recognition by the crown of a state of affairs that had existed for six years or so. At the same time Bishop Andrew, who had been unsuccessful in fighting off Lord Sinclair's encroachments into the royal lands, was strengthened in 1490 by the erection of his own lands into a *regality*[25] and five years later by the transfer to his possession of the island of Burray, previously part of Lord

21 *ER*, viii–ix.

22 He is first mentioned, in the exchequer accounts of 1484: as *firmario . . . dominiorum* [*Orchadie et Schetland*] (*ER*, ix, 233) and the following year as renter of the lordships of Orkney and Shetland *sub reverendo patre Andrea episcopo eiusdem* (*ER*, 306). In 1486–7 the accounts bear no name (unlike all the previous years from 1474), but again in 1488 Henry Sinclair is styled 'intromitter'. Finally, in 1489, he became undisputed tacksman himself. (*RMS*, ii, no. 1842). Several points regarding the events of this time indicate the expected unwillingness on the part of the crown to contemplate this last appointment.

23 The charter was on a *blenche ferme* basis, the *reddendo* being four merks annually, if asked; *Charters and other Records of the City and Royal Burgh of Kirkwall*, ed. J. Mooney (Spalding Club), 1952, Kirkwall, n.d., 1–28. The difference this gift made to the burgh's relations outside the islands was slight. Kirkwall did not appear independently on the exchequer rolls and it sent no burgh commissioners to parliament for two centuries.

24 *RMS*, ii, no. 1844–5. It was never acted upon, and though this was not to be the last time that an earl of Bothwell was to have a connection with the Northern Isles, later examples were to show that major Scottish nobles without family or other links in the islands could rarely be induced to take an interest in them

25 *RMS*, ii, no. 1974; B. Smith, 'In the Tracks of Bishop Andrew Pictoris of Orkney, and Henry Phankouth, Archdeacon of Shetland', *IR*, xl (1989).

Henry's *tack*,[26] a grant ratified by the king on declaring his majority in 1498[27] and excluded from the earldom lands in subsequent renewals of the tack.[28]

Despite these attempts to limit his power, Henry Sinclair retained his position until his death in 1513, whereupon the tack passed to his wife Margaret, the earl of Bothwell's sister, with the judicial powers that had accompanied it taken up by his brother, Sir William Sinclair of Warsetter.[29] Not for more than half a century, till the time of James V and Robert Reid, did a bishop again figure prominently in events in the islands; instead, judicial and administrative powers remained in the hands of members of the Sinclair family. Royal attempts at containment were threatened seriously during James IV's latter days and collapsed completely on his death.

To consolidate his power, Henry Sinclair lost no time in compiling what was to be the first of two rentals, completed in 1492.[30] In it he included all the land in Orkney controlled by the Sinclairs – the earldom and royal land held in tack, the *udal* and the *conquest*, as well as land that paid *skat* to the bishop, but Henry was careful not to carry to dangerous lengths any aspirations he may have had to all this territory, and the bishop skatlands were not represented in the second of his rentals, completed in 1504.[31] In March 1502 he was charged to make no impediment to Bishop Andrew, confirmed in his lands and regality after the king's general revocation on coming of age,[32] and in June of the same year he was ordered to cease from *intromitting* with lands and teinds of the bishop.[33] These were probably no more than formal procedures, and in his later years, Henry Sinclair strove to maintain good relations with the crown. An attempt in 1502 by the Danish king to present his own nominee to the archdeaconry of Shetland, to the prejudice of the Scottish candidate, met with no success.[34] Henry Sinclair spent much time in the south, and when he died it was at Flodden in the service of the king.

Henry's death brought about a serious split within the Sinclair family. While his widow inherited his tack, their son William was passed over on the grounds of youth, and real power lay with Henry's brother, Sir William Sinclair of Warsetter.[35] This division marked the beginning of a major source of strife and dispute that was to rumble on for decades, well into the Stewart era. So long as Sir William was alive, the islands remained relatively quiet. On his death, some time after July 1522,[36]

26 *RMS*, ii, no. 2232.
27 *RMS*, ii, no. 2414.
28 E.g. in 1501 (*RSS*, i, no. 681).
29 J. S. Clouston, *History of Orkney*, Kirkwall, 1932, 284.
30 Hugh Marwick Papers, NRS GD1/236/1.
31 H. Marwick, *Orkney Farm-names*, Kirkwall, 1952, 194
32 *Rentals*, i, 1–101.
33 *RSS*, i, no. 787.
34 *RSS*, i, nos 755, 76.
35 *RSS*, i, no. 848.
36 Date of last extant reference to Sir William during his life-time (*REO*, xlii, no. 94; Edin. Comm. Ct Recs: Reg. Tests, NRS CC8/8/5).

conflict flared up. On one side was Henry's son William, now of age and seeking his birthright; on the other were Sir William's sons, his legitimate heir Magnus of Warsetter, but also the illegitimate Edward of Strom and, most important of all, the formidable and dangerously unstable James of Brecks. The murderous struggle that ensued was to culminate in the last pitched battle to be fought on Orcadian soil, at Summerdale in the hills of Stenness in the summer of 1529.

In piecing together what happened, we have to be mindful that most of what we know derives from William, Lord Sinclair himself in the wake of disaster;[37] however we have to do our best with what is much the most detailed account. When we do, we arrive at the following chain of events. Lord Sinclair, with royal approval, sought to hear courts and administer justice in Kirkwall in Easter Week, mid-April 1528. According to him, he and his party were set upon at night outside Kirkwall Castle by a band led by James and Edward Sinclair. In the struggle, James's own nephews, John, Nichol and David Sinclair, were killed, together with seven of Lord Sinclair's servants, despite surrendering their weapons and begging for mercy on their knees. He, in fear of his life, surrendered the castle and fled from the islands. The following May he secured further royal letters ordering his enemies to return the castle to his control, and charging the most prominent of the Sinclair kinsmen John, earl of Caithness, to support him, with force if necessary. David Lawrie, the hapless official given the task of formal implementation, was disarmed and imprisoned, leaving Lord Sinclair with no alternative to force of arms.

He and Earl John invaded Orkney on 7 June 1529.[38] We know their motives, and those of their opponents, but it remains difficult at this distance in time to work out exactly how the invaders hoped to achieve their objectives. In a direct military attempt to retrieve the castle of Kirkwall one might have expected a landing at Scapa and a march northwards up the valley towards Kirkwall. Instead, the invaders landed to the west, in Orphir – certainly an earldom centre, though by this time an ancient one – probably in Waulkmill Bay. They progressed northwards, along the west side of the Loch of Kirbister, and over the saddle in the hills beyond. It was here at Summerdale, on the downward slope, that the two sides met. The result for Lord Sinclair and the earl was humiliation, rout and reprisal. The Orkney and Shetland forces, led by Sinclair of Brecks, attacked with such ferocity that within the first few minutes the earl was killed with 30 of his followers, with 100 more Caithness men cut down as they fled for their boats. When they reached the sea, the pursuers were still not satisfied, and stormed the boats with the same ruthlessness they had shown in Kirkwall the previous year. Twenty-two crew members were dragged ashore and executed on the tide mark, their bodies stripped and left to be washed away.

All was not over. The Orkney and Shetland Sinclairs were determined to extirpate opposition. Three weeks or so later, they hunted down fugitives who had sought sanctuary in various churches, notably in the conquest heartlands of Sanday,

37 *REO*, 57–63, no. xxv.
38 *REO*, 57, no. xxv.

dragged them out naked and killed them. Magnus Sinclair, son of Sir David Sinclair of Sumburgh, was beheaded by Edward Sinclair of Strom at his brother's command, with three of his followers. Seven other men of Shetland who had come to support Lord Sinclair were cornered in a barn and dispatched. In July, Sinclair of Brecks went to Shetland, where he beheaded the *lawman*, as well as three young boys whose masters had excited his displeasure. Others he hanged, in person. By the end of the bloodbath, the total killed numbered 300 or more. Lord Sinclair's own son, William, was a captive of James Sinclair of Brecks and died in custody, despite his father's invoking of royal letters to free him. Lucky survivors escaped to Norway and England, reduced to begging in order to survive.

This was Lord Sinclair's account which, whatever his understandable point of view, clearly presents a picture of merciless ferocity that goes well beyond the exaggeration found in documents of this kind, and retains some ring of truth regarding events which, as we will see, were long remembered. The sheer scale of the rout and massacre suggests that Sinclair of Brecks was a formidable opponent and a dangerous enemy, savagely aggressive and inspiring the same demeanour in his followers. Lord Sinclair spoke to the king of him as acting, from his first appearance in Orkney as 'kingis-like, as he war ane king in thai partis and like as thar war na law, king, nor justice in this realme, in hie contemptioun and lytlying of your grace's autoritie, and in evill exampill to utheris to do siclyke and this remane unpunischit'.[39]

Older writers, like Storer Clouston, have blamed Lord Sinclair for the course of events, presenting a picture of a high-handed Scot attempting to lord it over the islanders. It is true that three years before Summerdale, on 13 February 1526, Lord Sinclair was charged by the lords of council to give up the bishop's palace in Kirkwall to Robert Maxwell, the new bishop.[40] This has been taken to mean that he had seized the palace as a means of enforcing his will,[41] but it was in fact merely a legal formality. On the other hand, the previous year the Scottish exchequer had remitted to Lady Sinclair £80 of her usual tack dues because of the depredations in Orkney of Sir William Sinclair's sons (as well, incidentally, as those of the English in Shetland, an ongoing problem in both archipelagoes at this period).[42]

The Clouston interpretation has excited the imagination, and romantic indignation, of Orkney writers ever since. The incongruous picture (from Holinshed)[43] of the saintly Magnus appearing on the horrific field of Summerdale is snapped up with relish – 'Thus, led by their saint and the stout James Sinclair and his brother, the Orkneymen for the last time fought and won a pitched battle on their native soil.'[44] Treating James Sinclair's stand as essentially patriotic is understandable,

39   *REO*, 57, no. xxv.
40   Acta Dominorum Concilii, xxv, 203.
41   Clouston, *History of Orkney*, 285.
42   *ER*, xv, 152.
43   *REO*, 60; R. Holinshed, *Chronicles* (1587 edn), ii, 439 (see bibliography concerning online version).
44   Clouston, *History of Orkney*, 290; and 'The Battle of Summerdale', *Old Lore Miscellany*, ii (1909), 95–100.

and it is an interpretation that has drawn support from elsewhere.[45] In reality the facts present a family quarrel in which the island faction was led by a commander so ruthless and ferocious as to be unbalanced, as subsequent events were to show. Lord Sinclair on the other hand, despite being described by Storer Clouston as 'rash and violently inclined', was to bequeath to his descendants, for the rest of the century and beyond, no more than an increasingly plaintive and ineffectual series of complaints, seeking what the main line of Sinclairs had lost, repeating them every time political opportunity arose.[46]

Summerdale terminated Lord Sinclair's claim to any sort of control in Orkney, whether in the earldom and royal lands but, more significantly, the *conquest lands*, which should indeed have fallen to him by right of succession.[47] The actions of James Sinclair and his followers – refusal to allow Lord Sinclair's messenger to execute his letters, armed resistance to his attempts to assert his rights – were hardly short of treasonable, the more heinous for their effectiveness; yet little action was taken. In November 1530, an ineffectual attempt was made to interest the earl of Moray in the islands by putting him in place of Lady Sinclair as lessee but, like the earl of Bothwell before him, he did nothing, and no action of any kind was taken after 1531.[48] During that period, James Sinclair is to be found acting as 'Justice' of Orkney.[49] There is no reference to any judicial appointment, either by the crown or the tackholder, and in a complaint against him for piracy in March 1535 by Thomas Miller, an English merchant, he is merely styled 'subject'.[50]

He was, however, clearly in charge. This was no doubt the result of his military success, but by 1535 he was becoming more powerful still as a consequence of a new growth of favour towards him at court, with a complete about-turn by a government that had hitherto supported Lord Sinclair, albeit unenthusiastically, but now countenanced the total rehabilitation of James Sinclair of Brecks, giving him recognised control of the island administration. On 17 June of that year he was legitimated,[51] knighted and he received a charter of the islands of Sanday and Stronsay.[52] The legality of this charter has been doubted and it was certainly a very odd grant,[53] but these gifts taken together constituted evidence of a decisive new policy by the crown.

45 W. C. Dickinson, 'Odal Rights and Feudal Wrongs' (*Viking Congress*, 149).

46 B. E. Crawford, 'William Sinclair, Earl of Orkney, and his Family: a Study in the Politics of Survival', *Essays on the Nobility of Medieval Scotland*, app., 252.

47 *The Scottish Correspondence of Mary of Lorraine*, ed. A Cameron (SHS), 1927, 85.

48 *RSS*, ii, no. 766; ADC & S, xliii, f. 32r. In August 1531 he protested to the Lords of Council that the Lady Sinclair's accounts, which had been faithfully rendered annually since her husband's death should 'in no way prejudice him in his feu and heritage of the same'. We know of no other actions.

49 *REO*, 216, no. cx; 219, no. cxiii.

50 *RSS*, ii, no. 1665.

51 *RSS*, ii, no. 1697.

52 *RMS*, iii, no. 1479.

53 *REO*, 220n.

As in the case of Henry Sinclair, formal recognition of James Sinclair's position in the islands was accompanied by the proffering of guarantees to other interests. Lord Moray faded from the northern background, and Lady Sinclair's tack was continued for a further seven years on 15 July 1536.[54] In February the following year, Kirkwall's burgh charter was renewed,[55] and James Irving of Sebay was granted a confirmation, in feudal form, of his rights to his udal estates. The reason given for the confirmation of Kirkwall's charter was that encroachments had affected 'the yearly rents and profits of all their common good . . . as well as their quoys, rights of patronage, prebendaries . . . detained and withheld from them by some of the inhabitants within the said island [Mainland] of Orkney'.[56] Previous writers have seen in this an attempt by the crown to curb episcopal power and to head off islanders' displeasure which would be awkward in a determined attempt by Denmark to redeem the islands.[57] However, there are other points to be considered. In the first place, a knighthood and a grant of land seem more than would be necessary to signal mere tacit recognition of James Sinclair's position. Secondly, if we look for anything that might explain this sudden favour, it becomes clear it coincides with the growing influence at court of another member of the Sinclair family, James V's favourite, Oliver Sinclair of Pitcairns, who had used his position to interest his master in the situation in Orkney.

Oliver Sinclair was a cousin of both Lord Henry and the late earl of Caithness, During the 1530s, he had become close to James V, and by 1536 he was sufficiently in favour to be included in king's marriage-expedition to France of that year. Shortly afterwards he replaced Sir James Hamilton of Finnart in the king's esteem.[58] In 1538 he shared with James Kirkcaldy of Grange the *wardship* of the heir of the late earl of Caithness.[59] It cannot be coincidence that this rise at court was paralleled by the progress of his cousin James from outlaw to knight and crown tenant, and the appointment of James's brother Edward as one of his sheriffs depute in 1541[60] as well as by the strained relations between him and Lord Sinclair in the 1540s.[61]

Sir James Sinclair did not enjoy the benefits of his cousin's ascendancy for long. The picture Lord Sinclair presents is of a ruthless and choleric strongman, vindictive and vengeful. According to Adam Abell, a contemporary observer, Sir James Sinclair was knighted by a king who took a cynical view of how to settle matters in the far areas of his dominions, by recognising a local warlord who would have equally merited a hanging. But behind Sinclair's forbidding face may have lurked a truly

54 *RSS*, ii, no. 2088.
55 Kirkwall Chrs, 1–28.
56 *REO*, 220, no. cxv.
57 *REO*, 220, no. cxv.
58 G. Donaldson, *Scotland, James V–James VII*, Edinburgh, 1971, 58, 60.
59 *The Scottish Corresp. of Mary of Lorraine*, 47.
60 Clouston, *History of Orkney*, 293; Strom in return gave Oliver Sinclair a *bond of manrent* (Acts & Decreets, NRS CS7/1, f. 208.)
61 *The Scottish Corresp. of Mary of Lorraine*, 85–6.

troubled individual. Abell's story is that after James returned to Orkney, he received legal letters from the king. Their import is unknown, but the effect on his mind was catastrophic, and without warning he became seriously mentally deranged. During a court hearing, he suddenly stood up from the bench and began dancing, 'castand gamuntis' – performing leaping movements which are to be found among dances of the period, but in this case evidence of some kind of mania. It took force to restrain him. He retired home but could not sleep. At dawn, he placed his ring under his wife's pillow, together with the royal letters that had so troubled him. He then rose and left the house, where he repeated his earlier capering, hauling peats from a peatstack; throwing them about, he ran to a 'ane fowll deip dub' – probably a pond filled with outflowings from the midden – and threw himself in. After further antics, he tore off his clothes and ran to a high crag above the Gloup of Linksness where he threw himself to his death.[62]

Various explanations have been suggested for Sinclair's ghastly end.[63] Adam Abell, as an Observantine friar, took a pronounced moral tone, seeing what happened as a judgment. Others have seen Sinclair as sensing human justice – for example a realisation by the king that he had been duped over the status of Sanday and Stronsay, which were not mere *sheep holms*, as he had understood.[64] The terms of the charter suggest that this is not the case, but in reality neither divine nor human reasons can answer the question, which can only have lain within Sinclair's own unfathomed mind. It was left to the king himself, guided no doubt by Oliver Sinclair, to pick up the pieces. In the meantime, administration of justice was quietly carried on by Edward Sinclair, James's brother, while old Lady Sinclair continued to make her exchequer returns. James Sinclair's estate was forfeited on the grounds of his suicide, though later granted to his widow, and there was some attempt to restore to Lady Sinclair revenues he had appropriated. In an effort to calm everything down, William and Edward Sinclair were compelled to conclude a bond of *manrent* imposing peace between them, and Edward, together with 30 other named followers, were pardoned for their part in the mayhem of 1529. King James then decided to take a hand in person.

This extraordinary course of events ushered in a new, and equally brief, stage in this turbulent period in the north. In the early summer of 1540, King James embarked on the first royal circumnavigation of his dominions, with a magnificent seaborne train of 16 vessels, his own fitted out for a 'luxury cruise'.[65] He was almost certainly accompanied by Oliver Sinclair, as well, possibly, as William, Lord Sinclair. James was probably more exercised by his perennially troublesome islands to the west, and he may have regarded Orkney and Shetland as an irritation at best but, influenced

62 A. M. Stewart, 'The Final Folios of Adam Abell's "Roit or Quheill of Tyme": an Observantine Friar's Reflections on the 1520s and 30s', *Stewart Style 1513–1542*, 233–4.

63 For discussion of these, see Thomson, *History of Orkney*, 241.

64 *REO*, 220; Clouston is sceptical and attributes it merely to tradition.

65 Donaldson, *James V–James VII*, 58.

by his favourite Oliver, he spent six weeks on the islands.[66] He was entertained by Bishop Maxwell, during which time the peculiar situation of the Northern Isles, both the political troubles of the previous decades, and current matters of law and administration, were clearly discussed. If William Sinclair was indeed involved, it is clear that Oliver had by far the greater influence on the king. On 20 April 1541 Oliver was granted a commission of sheriff in the islands, together with Lady Sinclair's tack of the crown lands. The appointment of a sheriff, as opposed to a lawman, meant that some steps from Norse towards Scots legal procedure had been made, though wholesale replacement was still 70 years off. Nothing was said of the conquest lands, but it seems highly likely that these quietly came into Oliver's hands too. In the same month of this grant, James was petitioning the pope on behalf of Robert Reid as a new and reforming bishop of Orkney, his application informed by what he had been told on his visit.

There are several elements coming together here: the king's desire to establish real control throughout his dominions, especially in the far-flung north and west; secondly his desire to protect what his forebears had won from the occasional attempts of the Danes to retrieve them; and thirdly Oliver Sinclair's desire to secure his hold on the Sinclair estates in the islands. In a letter to Mary of Guise of 23 November 1543 his wife, Katherine Bellenden, speaks of 'our native rowmes quhilk my husband and his surname hes brukit thir thrie or four hundreth yeiris'.[67] This is an explicit statement: that Sinclair regarded himself as having rights by *kindly* (longstanding, virtually hereditary) tenancy.[68] Though Oliver Sinclair enjoyed lands in Scotland, it was the Northern Isles that his wife was thinking of. Oliver Sinclair is to be found playing a part in northern affairs right into the 1560s – though in fact his direct power there was not to last long, as the political wheel spun yet again and he too, like William Sinclair before him, was trying to reclaim losses.

Oliver Sinclair's tack of the crown-controlled lands in Orkney and Shetland was significantly different from its predecessors, embracing 'all and sindrie our soverane lordis landis and lordschippis of Orkney and Shetland' and, as we have seen, probably including the conquest lands as well – everything not pertaining to the bishop or the udal proprietors. The tack duty payable amounted to 3,000 *merks* per annum, well over four times that paid by his predecessors,[69] and essentially the sum later to be paid by the Stewart earls. Up to now, James had not really been aware of what he possessed. He had placed a price of only £1,000 on the earldom as part of the proposed dowry of Madeleine de Valois, his first wife. He had been favourably impressed with Orkney, both in its fertility and in the momentary peace brought by

---

66 There is even a folk-legend of his time there; see E. W. Marwick, *The Folklore of Orkney and Shetland*, London, 1975, 150–2.

67 *The Scottish Corresp. of Mary of Lorraine*, 47.

68 For discussion of the implications of a statement such as this, citing a case involving questions of tenure in which similar phraseology is used, see G. Donaldson, *The Scottish Reformation*, Cambridge, 1960, 40.

69 See *RSS*, ii, nos 2088, 4856.

the end of the Sinclair feuding. As a monarch notorious in his desire to maximise income,[70] James was not going to spare even his favourite.

Oliver Sinclair's tack dated from 20 April 1541, and was for a period of three years, later extended to five.[71] In another departure from previous practice, his judicial powers were couched in Scots terms; he was designated justice, sheriff, admiral and bailie, marking, as Clouston points out, the 'end of the old order of *Lawmen* and *Roithmen* and the appearance of Sheriffs and Suiters of Court instead; the replacement of the Norse machinery of justice by the Scotch (though the actual laws administered remained as before)'.[72] He was also made constable of Kirkwall Castle. The award was not hedged round with the previous limitations, though this was perhaps because the crown had already restricted the tacksman's power of alienation in an act of 1540.[73] In any case, there was a countervailing force in the recently appointed Bishop Reid, former abbot of Kinloss.[74] But the need for such limitations would in any case have been short-lived. Oliver Sinclair, at the head of James's army against the English, was routed and humiliated at Solway Moss and, with the king's ensuing breakdown and death on 15 December 1542, his brief period of power in the north was over. He been in control for little over a year, had rendered two accounts to exchequer[75] and appointed two deputes, Sinclair of Strom and James Redpath[76] He had, apart from the royal visit itself, been an absentee but, as became clear, he had drawn on his revenues in some measure during the time he had been allowed.

The queen dowager, a woman of ability as she was later to show as regent, was quick to take charge of the island estates as her widow's portion. In 1543 she granted the tack to the earl of Huntly,[77] and possession of Kirkwall Castle to one of her French followers, a M. Bonot, who was to remain governor, sheriff and commissioner for at least 15 years.[78] About the same time she ordered the compilation of the first known account of the cash value of the islands' *victual* yield.[79] This assessed her total income from Orkney at £9,750, from Shetland at £4,210. From this, she was able to gain a shrewd picture of Oliver and his dealings, which had left him with

70 J. Cameron, *James V: the Personal Rule 1528–1542*, East Linton, 1998.

71 *RSS*, ii, nos 3989, 4856.

72 *REO*, 63n.

73 *RMS*, iii, no. 2233.

74 *RSS*, ii, no. 3974.

75 *ER*, xvii, 523; xviii, 3.

76 Clouston, *History of Orkney*, 293.

77 *The Scottish Corresp. of Mary of Lorraine*, 46n.

78 *The Scottish Corresp. of Mary of Lorraine*, 109 and n; no. xlix. He held a court there as late as 22 June 1558. Little is known about him or his administration. He probably visited France in 1554 (*Balcarres Papers*, ii, 250) and the following year he made unspecified allegations against the comptroller, Villemore, which set him at variance with another of the queen dowager's officers in Orkney, the chamberlain William Moodie (*The Scottish Corresp. of Mary of Lorraine*, 399).

79 A. L. Murray, 'Sir John Skene and the Exchequer, 1594–1612', *Stair Society Miscellany One* (1971), 141–2.

liabilities of about 3,000 merks. She accused him of owing 'greit soumes'.[80] Lord Sinclair now looted one of Oliver's ships, on the pretext that Oliver had denied him his land rights in Shetland despite royal orders, an act that had done him such hurt that, in the words of his letter to the queen, he 'may nocht do your grace service nor yit defend my ane place quhilk wilbe the distructioune of all Fyfe it beand wone' – a reference to Ravenscraig Castle, the Sinclair stronghold near Dysart, and its defensive importance against the English attacks of the period. In retaliation Oliver, on 14 May 1544, spoiled the ship *John Williamson* of Kinghorn, on its way from Orkney to Leith with a cargo belonging to his cousin.[81]

It took Oliver Sinclair at least a decade to extricate himself from these problems. He came to an agreement with the earl of Huntly on 21 May 1544,[82] whereby he was allowed access to the fruits that he was due from his former lands, in exchange for payment of 3,400 merks. Sinclair of Strom and Redpath were appointed factors to expedite this, and were still at work as late as December 1549.[83] Oliver's problems were eased by his delivery to Huntly of land round Dysart which he had acquired in litigation with Lord Sinclair. This last was in turn partially settled in an agreement of 29 July 1546, when recompense for the cargo of the *John Williamson* was exchanged for the lands of Boreland, north of Dysart.[84] Two days later Oliver raised further funds by granting a bond to Lord Borthwick.[85]

The earl of Huntly appears to have taken more interest in the Northern Isles than the members of the Scottish aristocracy who had preceded him. In Katherine Bellenden's letter to Mary of Guise he was reported as intending to go north in person. There is no evidence he actually did this, but he did appoint a constable for the castle of Kirkwall, Alexander Jameson,[86] and he was interested and influential enough to guarantee Jameson's assistance to Oliver, as well as that of the foud of Shetland. However, he rendered no accounts, and his tack seems to have been a dead letter from 1546 until early 1555 when he and his wife, in royal disfavour, renounced all interest in the islands.[87]

For the next decade and a half the administration put in place by the dowager seems to have carried on with little incident, though some of what we know indicates common themes. She used her revenues to reward loyalty, granting an annual pension of £100 to Robert Carnegie of Kinnaird in 1538. Three years later a herald was sent to Denmark to inquire about the Danish king's intentions concerning Orkney and Shetland 'with gud writyngis of contentation of all besines without ony promes', evidence of the renewed activity between Scotland and Denmark on

80 *The Scottish Corresp. of Mary of Lorraine*, 46.
81 *RMS*, iii, no. 3275; *The Scottish Corresp.of Mary of Lorraine*, 85–6.
82 Acta Dominorum Concilii et Sessionis, xxi, 160.
83 *REO*, 236, no. cxxvi.
84 *RMS*, iii, no. 3275.
85 Acta Dominorum Concilii et Sessionis, xxi, 159.
86 Acta Dominorum Concilii et Sessionis, xxi, 160.
87 *ADCP*, 638.

the question since the latter country had revived it in 1549.[88]

In the mid-50s endemic problems from outside were a particular nuisance. Government ships and troops had to be sent to counter one of the periodic attacks on Orkney by the men of Lewis.[89] The English too were active in the area, again not a unique instance. Relations between Scotland and England remained uneasy in the period, but these doings were as much local as national. In 1535 a complaint had been made by James V that English fishermen bound for Iceland had been in the habit of spoiling the North Isles of Orkney and taking inhabitants for 'sclavis, servandis and presonaris'. In 1525 they had laid Shetland waste.[90] Now in 1555 a group of 200 'utterlie hereit [harried]' the North Isles of Shetland and threatened to do the same in Orkney.[91] Like the attacks from Lewis, this was a chronic problem, which was never solved during the period. Forty years later the explorer Martin Frobisher, making his final landfall before setting out to find the North-West Passage, was to experience the continuing fear of English ships when he landed in Kirkwall Bay to take on water. The populace fled, and it was with difficulty that he and his men persuaded the Orcadians that their intentions were innocent. Perhaps the best response to English aggression against the islesmen was the victory (until recently unsung, but surely closer to Storer Clouston's romantic picture of Summerdale than that battle itself), at Papdale on 13 August 1557. Orkneymen under the old warrior Edward Sinclair attacked a landing party from an English naval force that had been sent into the area 'to annoy the Scots', and to protect the home-coming Iceland fishing fleet.[92] In the exchange, about 500 Englishmen were killed or drowned, including three captains, and the admiral, Sir John Cleere of Ormesby, himself lost his life when his boat overturned as it was being pulled off.[93] In the person of his brother, the ghost of James of Brecks still walked.

Administratively, the most significant developments of this time occurred within the bishopric. In 1545 Robert Reid drew up a new and elaborate constitution for his cathedral, and added significantly to the structure of his palace (Bishop Reid's Tower is a familiar landmark in Kirkwall today), but he was an absentee after 1550 leaving his constable, Thomas Tulloch of Fluris, in charge as constable. Tulloch was to have a stormy passage, with 'murmurs and quarrels' among the bishopric tenants and charges of tampering with the weights for the receipt and delivery of victual.[94]

88 *The Scottish Corresp. of Mary of Lorraine*, 353; G. Goudie, *The Celtic and Scandinavian Antiquities of Shetland*, Edinburgh, 1904, 216.

89 *CSP Spanish*, xiii, 19; *The Scottish Corresp. of Mary of Lorraine*, 353.

90 *ER*, xv, 152.

91 *The Scottish Corresp. of Mary of Lorraine*, 399.

92 W. L. Clowes, *The Royal Navy: a History from the Earliest Times to the Present*, vols I–VII, London, 1901, i, 473.

93 *CSP Spanish*, xiii, 320; Jo. Ben., 'Descriptio Insularum Orchadia'. *Macfarlane's Geographical Collections* (SHS), iii (1908), 319.

94 Tulloch of Tannachie Muniments (calendar description only), NRS GD107.

This issue too would be a recurring, and somewhat dreary, theme in island affairs, carrying on long after the end of our period.

On 15 September 1558, Robert Reid died, in mysterious circumstances, at Dieppe, while returning from negotiations on the queen's marriage. The scene was now set for the formal appearance of the first major player in the main act of this drama. Adam Bothwell was appointed bishop on 2 August the following year.[95] The bulls of his appointment were brought from Rome by another noteworthy figure, his brother-in-law, Gilbert Balfour.[96] During the vacancy, a gift of the *temporalities* of the bishopric had gone to a third major participant, the bishop's cousin Sir John Bellenden of Auchnoull, *justice clerk*.[97] Bellenden never set foot in Orkney, but he was to prove balefully influential over time, both personally and through his brother Patrick, who would also in time become a major northern figure.

The new bishop was not wholly a stranger to Orkney, having been there in 1555, on an unknown errand, with William Moodie, later his chamberlain.[98] Moreover, his family connections with those who had or were to have abiding interests in the north were strong indeed. So closely connected are the Bothwells, Bellendens and Balfours with each other and with the Sinclairs, both by family relationships and by the lands they held in the south, that it seems certain that Bothwell's appointment was secured through family influence and, as we shall see, all had major connections with the temporal lands of the abbey of Holyrood. Adam Bothwell's mother was the wife of Oliver Sinclair, who held Whitekirk of Holyrood, the sister of Bellenden of Auchnoull who was shortly to hold Broughton of Holyrood[99] and the mother-in-law of Gilbert Balfour. Bellenden and Balfour now found a new interest in Orkney and Shetland, and Sinclair a renewed one.

Adam Bothwell arrived in Orkney in the spring of 1560, accompanied by Gilbert Balfour and his brother John.[100] They immediately got into dispute with Thomas Tulloch, for various 'cruel actions' on their part, as well as taking property away from Tulloch's house in Kirkwall.[101] Litigation regarding this was to drag on for the next five years,[102] but much more important for the future, indeed causing unrest for the rest of the century, was the series of charters of bishopric land Bothwell now issued, beginning on 30 June 1560. Gilbert Balfour received enormous estates in Westray and also land in Birsay, the heartland of the bishopric estate – Marwick, Birsay Besouth, Skelday, Fea and others.[103] William Moodie the chamberlain

95 *Fasti*, ed. Watt and Murray, 329.
96 *RMS*, iv, no. 1668.
97 *RSS*, v, no. 589.
98 *TA*, x, 284.
99 *RMS*, iv, no. 1385.
100 G. Donaldson, 'Bishop Adam Bothwell and the Reformation in Orkney', *SCHS*, xiii (1959), 89.
101 Tulloch of Tannachie Mun. (calendar description only), NRS GD107.
102 O & S Papers, NRS RH9/15/75.
103 *RMS*, iv, no. 1668; Roxburghe Mun. (NRA(S) survey no. 179, no. 130). On the same day that Balfour received these grants he granted Bothwell in return an obligation. Its tenor remains wholly obscure,

received Orkney bishopric land in his native county of Caithness,[104] and two lesser followers, John Cullen and John Brown, were granted land in Weyland and Papdale respectively, in the parish of St Ola.[105]

Oliver Sinclair now reappeared in Orkney. On 20 September, accompanied by the Balfours, he witnessed a charter by his stepson the bishop to Duncan Scollay and his wife of the lands of Work in St Ola. In the document he was styled sheriff of Orkney, presumably on the authority of his grant of nearly 20 years before.[106] The arrival of Bothwell and Sinclair provoked a quick reaction elsewhere in the north. On 17 July 1560 a contract was concluded between the earl of Caithness and Magnus Halcro, *chantor* of Orkney, in which Magnus, with 13 named followers, accepted the earl's protection, in return for assistance 'gif it sall happen the said noble lord to invade the cuntre of Orknay in prosecution of his auld ennymeis'.[107] This is clearly a reference to the old enmity, still very much alive, between the two wings of the Sinclairs – Lord Sinclair and the earl of Caithness on the one hand, and the Warsetter Sinclairs, now represented by Oliver, on the other.[108] The idea of Sinclair's influence on Bothwell's appointment, first conceived in the light of their family connection, and given further credence by Sinclair's joining the bishop in the north, is given final confirmation in the bishop's response. On 20 October 1560, clearly feeling threatened by the Caithness–Halcro contract, he granted a charter to Oliver of the lands of Eday, in return for Oliver's defence 'contrare quhatsumevir invadaris'.[109]

The Caithness menace proved short-lived, but very soon Bothwell had to face trouble from a different quarter within his family network. He was at odds with the influential Bellenden of Auchnoull, who was demanding pensions from the bishopric. On 5 December 1560 he wrote to his brother-in-law, John Napier of Merchiston, appointing him as a mediator, together with his neighbour the laird of Roslin (another Sinclair), Oliver (designated 'the schiref') and Alexander King,

---

though its existence is noted on several occasions (O & S Papers, NRS RH9/15175; Roxburghe Mun., bundle 811). It probably referred to the Birsay lands, since Adam Bothwell later undertook to give it to Robert by an agreement tying up the loose ends of the excambions, 1569. Balfour of course retained his Westray estates, while his Birsay lands were (as will be seen) granted to Bellenden of Auchnoull, who in turn gave them to Robert. Balfour is once referred to as 'of Birsay' (*REO*, 263, no. cxlviii).

104 Abbrev. of Chrs of Kirklands, NRS E14, i, 107.

105 Abbrev. of Chrs of Kirklands, NRS E14, i, 70, 205. Cullen was a Leith merchant who retained interests in his home town (Edin. Comm. Ct Recs: Reg. Tests, 16 April 1588, NRS CC8/8/18); Brown, too, was probably a Scot. Unlike Gilbert Balfour, however, neither had actually arrived with the bishop – indeed both had been in Orkney for at least ten years (*REO*, 236, no. cxxv; 241, no. cxxix). There is no evidence to connect them with Oliver Sinclair's short-lived regime, though links with Sinclair would help to explain Adam Bothwell's generosity towards them. Cullen's wife was Agnes Balfour, a fact that might suggest a relationship with Gilbert Balfour, though nothing more.

106 *REO*, 263, no. cxlviii.

107 Sinclair of Mey Mun., NRS GD96/78.

108 Clouston, *History of Orkney*, 297.

109 Abbrev. of Chrs of Kirklands, NRS E14, i, 22.

one of his own *servitors*, 'anent sic differentis as ar happinnit betwix the justice clerk and me'. His cousin was stirring up trouble,[110] which came to a head the following February when a faction in Orkney attacked and occupied his house in Birsay, then lay in wait for him as he returned from a visitation 'to haiff alder slaine me, or taiken me'.[111] This was the story he told to Napier to enable him to 'mak answer' to representations to Lord James Stewart on the matter 'be aine of the Sinclairis'.

Gilbert Balfour was said to have been involved,[112] though the leaders of the bishop's would-be attackers were Henry Sinclair, younger of Strom (later of Brough), and Robert Sinclair of Ness, sons of Edward Sinclair the Summerdale veteran, to whom Bellenden of Auchnoull had 'maryet . . . twa sisteris'.[113] Henry was the true leader, and it was he whom Bothwell challenged. Henry countered by submitting to the bishop 18–20 petitions on matters concerning religion – specifically Bothwell's 'mutatioun' of it – in other words the reformation in Orkney. The bishop showed these to the sheriff (in this case, we must suppose, the boys' father Edward), who advised him to reply formally. This Bothwell refused to do until the house at Birsay was returned to him. Henry's father told his son and his followers that they were fools who did not know what they were doing, and that he would not permit the hearing of mass. It was clear that father and sons were divided on the new religion, but old Edward was anxious for some kind of accommodation. In spite of his support in this instance, he did nothing to stop Bothwell's further humiliation at the hands of his opponents. Knowing the bishop to be ill in his chamber, they arranged the saying of mass and marrying 'certaine pairis in the auld maner' at the 'scheik' of the door – this after the bishop had 'cloisset my kirk dorris and thoilet na mes [mass] to be said thairin sensynne'.[114]

If, as the bishop was convinced, Bellenden was behind the activities of Henry and Robert, religion was not the only bone of contention. The two Sinclairs had among their followers 'gret nomber of commonis quhem thai pat in beleiff to leiff frelie, and to knaw na superiouris in na tymis cumyn'. The Sinclairs, it is being suggested, had convinced their followers that liberation from the overlordship of the bishopric would mean something akin to udal tenure, with no superior on the feudal pattern. How this squared with maintenance of the old religion is anyone's guess. If indeed they offered this illusion as an inducement, it certainly would not have suited Bellenden, but then neither, one supposes, would the confrontation with the bishop on the purely religious issue, hence perhaps Edward Sinclair's castigation of his sons. Later evidence supports Bothwell's suspicion of Bellenden's intentions, while Bellenden was relying on the Sinclairs to foster local grievances

110 M. Napier, *Memoirs of Napier of Merchiston* (Letters of Adam Bothwell), Edinburgh and London, 1834, 66–7.

111 Napier, *Napier of Merchiston*, 68.

112 O & S Papers, NRS RH9/15/175.

113 Only one of the sisters has been identified, Katherine (P. D. Anderson, *Robert Stewart, Earl of Orkney, Lord of Shetland*, Edinburgh, 1982, app. 4.

114 Napier, *Napier of Merchiston*, 69.

on religion and land, without being particular as to detail. It was a storm in a teacup, and by 25 March the bishop had regained possession of his house.[115]

Bothwell had other troubles too. He and Gilbert Balfour were 'continualle at debait' because 'I wald not geiff hym all that I haid quhill I get mair'.[116] At the same time, further problems were caused by the antipathy between the bishop and the former bishopric constable and chamberlain, Tulloch of Fluris. This involved counter-claims by both parties, the bishop seeking to recoup certain of Tulloch's intromissions with the bishopric revenues[117] and Tulloch litigating on the grounds of 'actions of *spuilyie* and other cruel actions' against him and his brother by the bishop and the Balfours.[118] These lawsuits were not finally resolved until April 1565.[119] Bothwell saw Tulloch as another of Bellenden's agents in Orkney and as being in league with Henry Sinclair.[120]

By 20 April 1561 Bothwell, who had had enough, was aboard ship in Kirkwall Roads awaiting fair wind and weather for France to lay his problems before the queen herself. James Alexander, Bothwell's chamberlain, wrote to the laird of Merchiston, requesting that he approach Bellenden and the other lords of session to arbitrate on the 'mater' between Tulloch and Bothwell.[121] Tulloch's plight had not impressed John Kincaid of Warriston,[122] a relative of the bishop and intended protégé who had come with expectations of succeeding Thomas Tulloch as chamberlain and constable, but refused to remain in Orkney as long as the bishop tolerated the inter-ference of Balfour, who would give no account of what he had been up to with the bishopric revenues. Bothwell's inability to make good his promises to Kincaid may have been due to Balfour's opposition, either for general reasons of self-interest, or for other, more particular reasons. On 25 April 1561, shortly after the bishop's depar-ture, Francis Bothwell, treasurer of Orkney and a relative, wrote to his 'Darrest Antt', Janet Bothwell, Lady Merchiston, chiding her for revealing secrets that he had given her regarding 'sum thyngis anentis sum personis towart thair misbehavar towart my lord', but which she had shown to her sister Margaret, Balfour's wife, who 'wrait agane heir despitfullie and causit cummaris [trouble] to be amang us.'[123]

The treasurer went on to reiterate to Janet Bothwell the appeal for her husband to work on the bishop's behalf in the Tulloch affair. The appeals of James Alexander and Francis Bothwell for the use of Napier's influence on the justice clerk, when the bishop himself suspected Tulloch of acting on Bellenden's behalf, illustrate Adam

115 G. Donaldson, 'Bishop Adam Bothwell and the Reformation in Orkney', SCHS, xiii, 91 *et seq.*; Napier, *Napier of Merchiston*, 70–1.
116 Napier, *Napier of Merchiston*, 65.
117 Court of Session Recs: Acts and Decreets, NRS CS7/31, ff. 67, 206, 384.
118 O & S Papers, NRS RH9/15/75.
119 Acts and Decreets, NAS CS7/31, f. 384.
120 Napier, *Napier of Merchiston*, 69.
121 Napier, *Napier of Merchiston*, 72.
122 *REO*, 342–3, nos ccxx–ccxxi.
123 Napier, *Napier of Merchiston*, 75.

Bothwell's unenviable position. To this had to be added the trouble with Balfour and further, the fact that he and his servants were unable to trust even members of his own family. Besides Janet Bothwell's inability to keep a secret, and of her sister to refrain from using it 'despitefullie', it was also necessary to give the laird and lady of Merchiston differing accounts of what was happening in the north. Their estrangement had led the bishop to offer spiritual counsel to his sister in the past,[124] and even though her influence on her husband was being sought, some differences seemingly remained. When Alexander wrote to Lady Merchiston giving Kincaid's reasons for leaving Orkney, another letter of the same date that he wrote to her husband stated that Kincaid had 'rafussyt to remane in this cuntra, for quhat I caussys I kna nane'.[125] In view of this, it is easy to see why Bothwell, after an energetic and exceedingly frustrating year in Orkney, should make his way to France and the queen in search of a solution.

He was absent for a year or so, during which the disputes continued. In the autumn of 1561 the bishop's supporters, led by Francis Bothwell and supported by Edward Sinclair, brother of the laird of Roslin, Magnus Halcro of Brough and Nicol Chalmers, with ten companions, burst from the castle of Kirkwall in murderous pursuit of Henry Sinclair of Strom and William Moodie, though both survived.[126] Edward Sinclair was shortly to receive from Oliver Sinclair the latter's lands in Eday.[127] Magnus Halcro, despite his previous contract with the earl of Caithness, had since changed his coat and abandoned his opposition to the Warsetters. This change of heart eventually culminated in his marriage in about 1563 to Margaret Sinclair, daughter of the late Sir James Sinclair of Sanday.[128]

Adam Bothwell accompanied Queen Mary on her return to Scotland on 19 August 1561.[129] The following summer, shortly before returning to the islands, he concluded the first of a number of agreements intended to resolve his complicated financial problems. On 4 June 1562 he and Bellenden came to an arrangement concerning the latter's claims to pensions from the bishopric,[130] and agreed on the sum of 400 merks annually, so long as the bishopric remained burdened with two other pensions, of 600 merks to Lord John Stewart, granted 21 years before, and 300 merks to Archibald, Lord Ruthven. Half their value would accrue to the justice clerk if the bishopric was relieved of them. Bothwell, it seems, had no objection in principle to the pensions, only to the extent of the demands. He was not prepared 'to geif over that thing suld be my supple in time of neid, and that otheris weill deserving suld bruik efter me'. His representations to the queen may have had their effect, since Bellenden's demands had been reduced by well over half in their agreement.

124 Napier, *Napier of Merchiston*, 65–6.
125 Napier, *Napier of Merchiston*, 73.
126 *Criminal Trials in Scotland*, vols I–III, ed. R. Pitcairn, Edinburgh, 1833, i, 413.
127 Sinclair of Mey Mun., NRS GD96/95.
128 Clouston, *History of Orkney*, 297.
129 Donaldson, 'Bishop Adam Bothwell and the Reformation in Orkney', 91.
130 Court of Session Recs: Acts and Decreets, NRS CS7/31, f. 64.

Matters with Bellenden had been settled, but there was still Balfour to placate and, in keeping with the incestuous nature of these dealings, Bothwell was represented by Bellenden and Balfour by his brother, Sir James Balfour of Pittendreich.[131] Balfour had to hand over his lands in Birsay in return for a payment of 1,000 merks, prior to their transfer to Bellenden himself. By a second, curious, agreement, dated 30 June 1564, Bellenden agreed to lease the Birsay lands to Bothwell, his own superior.[132] It is likely, however, that this arrangement was simply intended to add to Bellenden's Orkney income by granting him tack duty from lands to which he retained a legal title, but with little responsibility for them – in other words virtually a simple pension. At the same time, now that he and Sir James Balfour had tidied up the legal loose ends, the justice clerk began to receive the 300 merks per year due to him from the late Lord John Stewart's pension, for the collection of which Balfour had been responsible.

It was thus obvious that the first agreement – the 'articles convenit upon' by Bellenden and Sir James Balfour in March 1564 – was in part intended to pave the way for the second, which took the form of a *decreet arbitral* by Maitland of Lethington, the queen's secretary. The two documents went a long way to clarifying the bishop's position in relation to both Balfour and Bellenden. It was agreed to forget past 'rancor' and 'controversies' between Balfour and Bothwell, particularly concerning the taking of the latter's house in Birsay, Gilbert was to pay all arrears from his tenure of the lands in the parish, and the bishop was to 'releif and skatheles [free from harm] keep' Gilbert at the hands of Thomas Tulloch, whose litigation against both parties continued. The June agreement attempted to set limits to the justice clerk's intromissions with the bishopric, limiting them to the arrangements for the Stewart and Ruthven pensions and the Birsay land settlement, nor was the payment of these pensions to prejudice the bishop's jurisdiction in the lands – in Rousay, Egilsay, Sanday, Deerness and Holm – from which the pensions were drawn. The only questions remaining to be settled after this were minor ones concerning past arrears, though interestingly the functionary charged with drawing up an account of these was Thomas Tulloch.

It is not always easy to follow the attitudes to one another of this small group of Scots who, for various reasons, had concerned themselves with the Northern Isles. Adam Bothwell felt himself plagued by the intrigues of his 'small frend' the justice clerk[133] and his partakers, but at the same time he maintained fairly strong personal links with him. Besides being Bothwell's business representative at this time, Bellenden was to be continually approached by Bothwell during the troubles that went on to beset him in the late 1560s. Even Bothwell's seeming belief that his cousin's activities threatened his very life could not apparently outweigh the family obligations between them. Balfour too was constantly pestering Bothwell

131 O & S Papers, NRS RH9/15/75.
132 Court of Session Recs: Acts and Decreets, NRS CS7/31, f. 64.
133 Napier, *Napier of Merchiston*, 69.

and interfering with his administration, but on his own account rather than that of Bellenden; he took no part in the justice clerk's schemes and in 1564 he was still on Bothwell's side in the litigation with Thomas Tulloch.

Bellenden sought only money from the bishopric of Orkney, and employed his unwilling cousin as a kind of personal forerunner of the *tulchan* bishops of ten years later – catspaws in milking the revenues of the old church. Balfour's activities were wholly different. His outlook, both then and later, was that of a soldier of fortune who was 'deeply and darkly involved in some of the most terrible happenings of his time'. Since his first arrival in the islands he had been constructing in Westray the massive fortress of Noltland; quite possibly his continual and impatient demands on his brother-in-law stemmed from the need to pay the skilled men and large workforce required. W. Douglas Simpson sees Noltland as clearly intended to be a hideout, its aspect being spare and military, with little domestic influence in its structure and nothing in its design to impinge on the field of fire of its sixty-one *falcon*-sized gunloops. Gilbert Balfour did not merely seek income from Orkney; he sought the sanctuary of strength in isolation. Simpson states that the more he looks at Noltland the more he is 'convinced that it was built for a man with a bad conscience – for a man with fear in his heart'.[134]

Although Adam Bothwell was in the Northern Isles each summer until 1566, his period of continuous administration was over. His problems concerning the bishopric, however, were not. For the islands, the mid-1560s were to be a time of anarchy and incident, at the end of which would appear a man who would cause more 'cummer' to bishop Bothwell, a man who would dominate the islands for thirty years – Robert Stewart.

134 Simpson, 'Noltland Castle', *Spalding Club* (1952), 144.

2

Of Undoubted Promise

Robert Stewart was born in the spring of the year 1533.[1] His father was the king, James V; his mother was Euphemia, 24-year-old daughter of Lord Elphinstone. We know nothing of their liaison. The timing might suggest that Robert was conceived some time in the course of spectacular entertainments laid on for the king by the earl of Atholl around 1532; but, however resonant a picture this might present of a king who liked to enjoy himself, all must remain conjecture.[2] The relationship between Robert's parents did not last. Margaret Erskine, lady of Lochleven, had borne the king the future earl of Moray two years before and she retained as much of James's faith as he was prepared to give any woman, since he was to seek her as his queen as late as 1536.[3] Like the other mothers of James's illegitimate sons, Euphemia Elphinstone was little more than a passing fancy, while Margaret Erskine remained, in Lindsay's words to the king, 'the Lady that luffit yow best'.[4]

Euphemia, whose son Laurence by her future husband, John Bruce of Cultmalindie, was to feature prominently in the careers of both Robert and his son, was one of nine known mothers of James V's illegitimate children, and one of three for whom evidence of support survives.[5] Robert Stewart had six known half-brothers of royal blood; the survivors, his companions in youth, were James *senior*, son of Elizabeth Shaw, born about 1528; James *secundus*, son of Margaret Erskine; and John, the offspring of Elizabeth Carmichael. Their earliest years were spent close to their mothers,[6] but James had important plans for his four young by-blows

---

1 Anderson, *Robert Stewart*, app. 1.

2 R. Lindsay of Pitscottie, *The Historie of Scotland* (STS), 1899, i, 335–8. While Pitscottie dates these to 1529, evidence in the treasurer's accounts, cited by Balfour Paul, suggests that they took place in September 1532 (*TA*, vi, p. xiii). Unfortunately, the latter writer also points out that the evidence does not permit the compilation of an itinerary for the king during the period of Robert Stewart's conception, or indeed during the whole of the years 1531–6.

3 *Letters of James V*, 320.

4 *The Works of Sir David Lindsay of the Mount*, ed. D. Hamer (STS), 1931, i, 104.

5 For a short analysis of the personalities involved, see Anderson, 'James V, Mistresses and Children', *ODNB* and Anderson, *Robert Stewart*, app. 2.

6 Christian Barclay had her son with her in 1533 and 1534 and had probably looked after him since his birth (*TA*, vi, 180, 196). Another unnamed son was stated in 1533 to be with 'Marioune Shaw', conceivably a relative of Elizabeth Shaw (*Ibid.*, 18). The closeness between Margaret Erskine and her son in after years

– following the example of his father with his own natural brother – namely their appointment to the *commendator*ships of the greatest monastic houses of Scotland, as these fell vacant. Essentially, they were to act as a conduit for diverting the incomes of these houses into the royal coffers. On 30 December 1534, he prevailed upon the pope, Clement VII, to set aside their defects of birth, standing in the way of ecclesiastical preferment.[7] The first major milestone in their advance in the spiritual army was their receipt of the *tonsure*, at the age of six. Each was then to be advanced to a major ecclesiastical dignity. In preparation for this, they left their infancy and fosterages behind and came to court, in new clothes specially provided by the treasury.[8] James *senior* came first, in December 1533, when he was in sight of his fifth birthday.[9] He received the *commenda* of the abbey of Kelso a little over a year later.[10] James *secundus*, born about 1531, became prior of St Andrews some time after 14 June 1538.[11] Towards the end of that year, the king approached Pope Paul III, Clement's successor, with a view to securing the abbey of Holyrood for Robert, at that time aged about five-and-a-half.[12] He became commendator of Holyrood on 18 August 1539.[13]

The pope's dispensation described the brothers as 'scolares' of the diocese of St Andrews. This was not purely a formal title. King James, again following the example of his father, provided an education for his sons to suit their high calling (his half-brother Alexander, archbishop of St Andrews, had studied under Erasmus).[14] Some time before November 1538, James, the seven-year-old prior of Kelso, arrived in St Andrews.[15] By May of the following year he was joined by his younger brother of the same name.[16] In June 1540, Robert and John came too.[17] They all lived in some comfort there, with servants held both in common and individually. John Cairns, in a black gown, doublet and bonnet made for him in 1539, was 'servitour to the Kingis grace sonis'.[18] Thomas Durie cooked for one of the Jameses, and Gavin Barbour was one of his servants.[19] Robert himself even had a minstrel to entertain him,[20] as well

---

suggests an early bond between them (M. Lee, *James Stewart, Earl of Moray*, New York, 1953, 18) and the same can be said of later relations between Robert, his mother and the family into which she married.

7 *Moray Muniments* (HMC), vi, 670.
8 E.g. *TA*, vii, 89, 265.
9 *TA*, vi, 181.
10 *Letters of James V*, 287.
11 D. Hay Fleming, *The Reformation in Scotland*, London, 1910, 116.
12 *Letters of James V*, 357.
13 *RSS*, ii, no. 3127.
14 R. L. Mackie, *King James IV of Scotland*, Edinburgh, 1958, 166.
15 *TA*, vii, 103.
16 *TA*, vii, 163–4.
17 *TA*, vii, 312–14.
18 *TA*, vii, 273–4.
19 *TA*, viii, 63–4.
20 *TA*, vii, 380.

as a servant called Thomas Carmichael,[21] perhaps a relative of the David and Robert Carmichael who were to serve him in later years.

As scholars of the diocese, the boys were no doubt tutored by members of the priory or cathedral clergy, first in their letters, then in more complex matters as their capacities were tested. It was admittedly not unheard of for individuals of such tender years to become undergraduates at this period,[22] but in fact only James *secundus* and John are recorded as having matriculated, and that not until 1545.[23] Perhaps this fact reflects the relative abilities of these two over their siblings. John, better known for his charm than his intelligence, was to die young but James, the future earl of Moray and regent, was to become a major player in the politics of his time. The treasurer's accounts of the period certainly indicate that these boys were maintained in some style,[24] but little more can be said. The presence of riding cloaks among their wardrobes might suggest that their time there was not only one of cloistered study. James *secundus* maintained close links with his family,[25] and indeed on 15 June 1543 Robert Douglas of Lochleven, husband of Margaret Erskine, James's mother, was accused of abducting his stepson 'furth of the . . . abbay [of St Andrews] quhair he was makand him reddy to cum with the remanent of his brether' to meet Arran, the lord governor.[26] In 1541, Robert's mother married John Bruce of Cultma-lindie.[27] Robert was eventually to become the guardian of Laurence, the child of that marriage,[28] and the activities of the pair were to be intimately connected for the whole of their adult lives. Periods of education must clearly have been interspersed with frequent visits to the family into which his mother had married, at their seat at Cultmalindie (now Cultmalundie), five miles west of Perth.

The monastic foundations to which James secured promotion for his sons were among the wealthiest in Scotland. As computed in 1561, in the aftermath of the Reformation,[29] the priory of St Andrews, not surprisingly, was the richest of all, with a minimum income of £12,500 per annum.[30] By the same criterion Holyrood was fifth in Scotland with an annual income of £5,600.[31] Kelso was seventh with £4,830.[32] It is difficult to discern any pattern in the allocation of benefices to James V's sons. James *secundus*, whose mother the king wished to marry did, it is

21 *TA*, viii, 93.
22 *Early Records of the University of St Andrews, 1413–1579*, ed. J. Maitland Anderson (SHS), 1926, pp. xxiv–v.
23 *Early Records of the University of St Andrews*, 252.
24 *TA*, vii–viii.
25 Lee, *James Stewart, Earl of Moray*, 18.
26 *ADCP*, 528.
27 W. Fraser, *The Elphinstone Family Book of the Lords Elphinstone, Balmerino and Coupar*, vols I–II, Edinburgh, 1897, i, 83.
28 Acta Dominorum et Sessionis, xxix, 80.
29 I. Cowan and D. E. Easson, *Mediaeval Religious Houses*, London, 1976, app. ii – Donaldson, 'The Income of the Scottish Religious Houses: The Sources', 199–200.
30 Cowan and Easson, *Mediaeval Religious Houses*, 82.
31 Cowan and Easson, *Mediaeval Religious Houses*, 75.
32 Cowan and Easson, *Mediaeval Religious Houses*, 59.

true, receive the greatest of the benefices, but the income of James *secundus*'s two abbeys of Kelso and Melrose was little short of that of St Andrews. On the other hand, and for no discernible reason, the income of Holyrood was about half that of the houses to which his two brothers were presented, and John's appointment was to the priory of Coldingham whose income was a mere £2,600,[33] albeit supplemented by a pension of 800 merks from the bishopric of Orkney.[34] Nor does the pattern of provision conform to the status of the boys' mothers; James *senior* and John were grandsons of minor lairds, James *secundus* and Robert of Lords Erskine and Elphinstone respectively. Nor, with the possible exception of James *secundus*, does the pattern reflect any particular preference for one mistress against another. The matter of just how this income was disposed of need not detain us here. What is clear is that, during the boys' minority, their father made appropriate allowance for each of them, and disposed of the rest of the income from their benefices as he saw fit. Only on his death, and their majorities, and finally the Reformation, did the problem of these revenues become crucial.

The avenue to the *commenda* of Holyrood was opened to the young Robert by the death of James Hay, bishop of Ross, and the king's decision that his successor should be Robert Cairncross, the noted royal adviser who was then commendator. In his letter of 15 December 1538, the king requested of Paul III that he declare the abbey vacant and grant the perpetual commendatorship to Robert, who was described as showing 'undoubted promise' despite being only in his fifth year.[35] The royal attention would be given to the fulfilment of that promise. In July the following year, Robert's co-adjutor was appointed in the person of Alexander Myln, abbot of Cambuskenneth, who was also to act in the same capacity for James *secundus*.[36] On 18 August 1539, Robert was admitted to the temporalities of the abbey.[37]

Alexander Myln was an 'outstanding' abbot of the old, pre-Reformation school.[38] Like Robert Reid, his near-contemporary and successor as president of the new College of Justice, he sought reform of the church by the revivifying from within of practice and organisation. Like Reid, his approach was essentially conservative, seeking revival of the church's energies by the overhaul of institutions (as Reid was later to do as bishop of Orkney) rather than re-appraisal of its religious priorities.[39] His main contribution to this was made during periods as clerk of the chapter of Dunkeld and as abbot of Cambuskenneth, before he became a full-time royal official. He took his position as administrator of Holyrood and St Andrews

33 Cowan and Easson, *Mediaeval Religious Houses*, 49.
34 *Letters of James V*, 423.
35 *Letters of James V*, 357.
36 *RSS*, ii, no. 3096.
37 *RSS*, ii, no. 3127.
38 Cowan and Easson, *Mediaeval Religious Houses*, 31.
39 See treatment of contrast between reforms in Orkney of Reid and Adam Bothwell in Donaldson, 'Bishop Adam Bothwell and the Reformation in Orkney', 85.

seriously. He prevailed upon the king to write to Rome on 5 June 1540 to secure for him permission to set the lands of Holyrood in tack,[40] a co-adjutor having no power under canon law to alienate heritage.

A contemporary picture of Myln[41] suggests a man of great spiritual worth as well as an able administrator, and it seems hardly possible that he took at face value the king's pretexts for his policy towards the abbeys as given in his letters to the pope. Kelso, for example, was in an exposed position and required a 'strong controlling power' for which the royal blood was necessary.[42] The desire to appoint one of his sons to the commendatorship of the priory of St Andrews arose out of James's being 'profoundly exercised about the firm foundations of the church in Scotland at an unhappy period'.[43] Coldingham was wanted for his son John to check 'dangerous communication of new doctrines unfavourable to the Roman see'.[44] However, it may be that Myln genuinely believed that royal appropriation of monastery revenues was no more than the price to be paid for the protection provided by direct royal control.

The possessions of the abbey of Holyrood, all acquired at a very early date from or through the agency of David I,[45] were concentrated in two areas. One, lying on the Solway coast around Kirkcudbright, consisted of the barony of Dunrod and the appropriated churches of Twynholm, Balmaghie, Kirkcormack, Kelton and Urr.[46] Much more important was the main group, which stretched in a crescent around Edinburgh from Airth in the west to Whitekirk in the east. It comprised the four baronies of Kerse, Ogleface, Broughton and Whitekirk, embracing the churches of Airth, Falkirk, Kinneil, Livingston, Carriden, Corstorphine, St Cuthbert, Liberton, Mount Lothian, Tranent, Bolton and Bara, and Whitekirk.[47]

At the heart of all this lay Broughton and the Canongate. Broughton was the barony whose jurisdiction extended over all the monastery lands around Edinburgh. The Canongate was the burgh that the Augustinian canons of Holyrood had founded by permission of King David, between their abbey and the

---

40 *Letters of James V*, 399–400.

41 *Commentary on the Rule of St Augustine by Robertus Richardinus*, ed. G. G. Coulton (SHS), 1935, 92.

42 *Letters of James V*, 279.

43 *Letters of James V*, 343.

44 *Letters of James V*, 426.

45 *Early Scottish Charters prior to AD 1153*, ed. A Lawrie, Glasgow, 1905, 116; *RRS*, i, 253.

46 I. Cowan, 'The Appropriation of Parish Churches', *An Historical Atlas of Scotland c.400–c.1600*, St Andrews, 1975, 37, 147; D. E. R. Watt, 'Appropriations of some Parish Churches by 1560', *Atlas of Scottish History to 1707*, Edinburgh, 1996, 368–9.

47 The best list so far found of the lands of Holyrood as they were around Robert Stewart's time is in a rent roll contained in the *Book of Records of the Ancient Privileges of the Canongate* (SRS, 1955), 40. It is undated but as it appears to show the lands entire, it must date from before 1587, when the church lands and baronies pertaining to the abbey were disjoined (*APS*, iii, 431). It is a somewhat confusing document in that several territories that pertain to the baronies are given the same separate itemised treatment as the baronies themselves, but it seems to be the most complete list available.

burgh of Edinburgh. Broughton had been elevated into a regality by David II,[48] and this jurisdiction extended over the other Holyrood baronies.[49] Nominally part of the barony of Broughton, the Canongate enjoyed a fair degree of autonomy. The monastery had renounced to the burgh the right of electing its bailies and council,[50] but the regality and barony court of Broughton also functioned as the Canongate burgh court.[51] Besides the Canongate, the barony of Broughton embraced the burgh of Broughton itself, on the road from Edinburgh to Leith, and the neighbouring lands of Pilrig and Inverleith; to the south lay the adjoining lands of the Pleasance and St Leonards; and ranged round the capital were the lands of Saughton, Bonnington, Wrightslands and others, as well as Slipperfield in the sheriffdom of Peebles.

The barony of Kerse had its centre between the lower reaches and estuaries of Carron and Avon; Kerse castle lay to the south of the meanders of the Carron about a mile from the Forth. Beyond the Carron lay the lands of Grange, Letham and Airth. To the east of the Avon were the church lands of Kinneil and Carriden. The barony extended from the Forth southwards to Falkirk where it bordered on that of Ogleface and the Livingston family's lands of Callendar. Whitekirk, the abbey's other and historic barony, lay on the North Sea coast a few miles north-west of Dunbar.

As commendator, Robert Stewart had major clients and followers. The Monteiths of Saltcoats, Kerse and Randyfurd were among them, as were the Bruces of Clackmannan, near-relatives of the Bruces of Airth.[52] Whitekirk had been in the possession of Oliver Sinclair of Pitcairns, the royal favourite since January 1539 and a major Orkney player.[53] His wife was Katherine Bellenden, sister of Sir John Bellenden, the justice clerk, and mother by a previous marriage of Adam Bothwell, later bishop of Orkney. The Bellendens were to acquire a strong interest in the lands of Broughton, which were ultimately erected into a temporal barony on their behalf. As we have already sketched in, these family connections were of great importance in our whole story.

Responsibility for the upbringing of the king's illegitimate sons rested ultimately with the king himself. On his death it was assumed by Arran, the lord governor, though the queen dowager also took some interest in the boys' welfare. In 1545, the year of their coming of age, James *secundus* and John matriculated at the University of St Andrews.[54] In August 1546 Robert and James *secundus* were present in

48 RMS, ii, no. 337.
49 See *Court Book of the Regality of Broughton and the Burgh of the Canongate*, 1569–73, ed. M. Wood, Edinburgh and London, 1937, where the regality of Broughton is sometimes referred to as that of Holyrood.
50 *Canongate Ct Bk*, p. viii.
51 *Canongate Ct Bk*, 1.
52 Armstrong, *The Bruces of Airth and their Cadets*, 29.
53 RSS, ii, no. 2857.
54 *Early Records of the University of St Andrews*, 252.

parliament,[55] and on 20 March of Robert's year of maturity, 1547, a letter was despatched in the queen's name to Edward VI of England requesting a safe-conduct through his realm for the young Robert in the care of John Hamilton, bishop of Dunkeld, with a retinue of 60 persons.[56] Robert's destination was 'the schools' in France, where it was thought expedient that he should be 'virtuously nourished, instructed and brought up in good letters'.

This journey through England was never made. The safe-conduct may only have been sought because the death of Henry VIII two months before might mitigate England's aggressive policy towards Scotland. English attitudes remained unchanged, the battle of Pinkie took place six months later, and Robert's journey was postponed until July 1548 when he departed by sea from Dumbarton with his sister. The application to the English king is noteworthy in that it was sent before any French marriage or consequent trip abroad was planned for the young Mary. It suggests that when John, James *secundus* and Robert accompanied their sister to France it was indeed for their education, or at any rate not merely to provide companionship for the young queen.

As a church dignitary, Robert had to be granted licence under act of parliament to leave Scotland, on 11 July 1548,[57] he being 'of fervent desyre and mynd to exerce his youtheid studying in lettiris, in gude maneris'.[58] Robert's immediate compan-ions, to whom the licence extended, were John Carmichael, parson of Invernochty, David Carmichael, vicar of Dunrod, Robert Carmichael and Andrew Callendar. Robert Carmichael was the young commendator's chamberlain (his brother James Carmichael was to administer affairs in his absence).[59] David Carmichael had been presented to his vicarage the previous year in what must have been one of Robert Stewart's first nominally independent actions,[60] and Andrew Callendar was to receive a tack of the lands of Bowhouse (in modern Grangemouth) soon after his master's return to Scotland.[61] Also among Robert's companions was James Stewart, son of the late abbot of Dryburgh.[62] During his time in France, it is possible that Robert studied with his brothers under Pierre Ramus, the noted French humanist scholar.[63] The latter was an 'old school friend' of Charles, cardinal of Lorraine, brother of Mary of Guise, and it would seem that the dowager was showing the same concern for her husband's sons as she did for their illegitimate sister Jean

55 *APS*, i, 466–79.

56 *CSP Scot.*, i, 3.

57 *RSS*, iii, no. 2849.

58 A. Fraser, *Mary, Queen of Scots*, London, 1969, 31; D. W. Doughty, 'The Library of James Stewart, Earl of Moray, 1531–70', *IR*, xxi (1970), 18.

59 Dumfries Writs, NRS GD179, box 3 'Pilrig Titles', 1506–1639.

60 *Charters of Holyrood* (*Liber Cartarum Sancte Crucis*), ed. F. Egerton (Bannatyne Club), 1840, 264.

61 *Chrs of Holyrood*,157.

62 Reg. Deeds, NRS RD1/1, f. 421.

63 See Anderson, *Robert Stewart*, app. 3.

whom she cared for 'almost as though she were her daughter'.[64] On the other hand there is no evidence that he did and, as we have seen, he did not matriculate with the other two. This, and his subsequent career, may well show that his forte was a sort of low treacherous cunning, rather than the higher intelligence shown by James and John. With James in particular, Ramus's thought may have had a real effect on the youngster; for Ramus himself, it resulted in his conversion to Protestantism and his later murder in the St Bartholomew's Day massacre. James's activities after the Scottish Reformation occurred about the time of Ramus's conversion, and suggest that the Frenchman's ideas made a lasting impression.

In the years following his return, Robert Stewart's life was that of a young sprig of the royal family. He was occasionally at court,[65] and was present at meetings of the privy council at Stirling in 1552 and at Perth the following year.[66] Up to now, the great abbey of Holyrood and its lands had been administered by others in his name, in earlier days with close scrutiny by Robert's father, anxious for revenue. Now, he was beginning to take the reins himself. Although he was never to enjoy the regard in which his brother, the future regent, was held, he was clearly beginning to form ideas on how to exploit the situation in which he found himself, though for the moment he was chiefly involved in the humdrum governance of Holyrood and interminable squabbles with his vassals and tenants, the stuff of any such administration. Not long after his return from France Robert Carmichael, his chamberlain, was ordered by the lords of council to hand over 'jowellis' of the abbey – copes, a chasuble, a cross, 'ane tystour [box] of silver ourgilt with gold', and other items. These had clearly been withheld as security for money owed Carmichael by Robert and others.[67]

The abbey of Holyrood itself had been in poor condition since its sack by the English in 1543, and now, ten years later, Robert secured money from the queen regent for its repair, in return for a tack of the fruits of the abbey. The past administration of the lands had also been neglected, since the same document stated that the patrimony had been 'hevelie' hurt by 'feus, long tacks and acquittances'.[68] Robert was also *ipso facto* superior of the burgh of the Canongate, and as such granted letters in 1554 permitting the crafts of *cordiners* and tailors to extend their powers to those of Leith, while the cordiners were in addition permitted to erect an altar to Saints Crispin and Crispinian, traditional patrons of workers in leather.[69] On 15 November 1554 Robert is to be found in Kirkcudbright, on Dunrod business.[70] The

---

64 R. Marshall, *Mary of Guise*, London, 1977, 73.
65 *RPC*, i, 469.
66 *TA*, xii, 13–14.
67 *RPC*, i, 473.
68 Court of Session Recs: Acts and Decreets, NRS CS7/6, f. 585v; ADCP, 619.
69 *Book of Records of the Ancient Privileges of the Canongate*, ed. Marguerite Wood (SRS), 1955.
, 27; *Chrs of Holyrood*, 290, 292.
70 *Chrs of Holyrood*, 159.

following year he contributed 500 merks to the *tocher* of his illegitimate half-sister Jean, betrothed to the son of the earl of Argyl!.[71]

Troubles with his vassals also obtruded. He was involved in an obscure dispute with Oliver Sinclair over Whitekirk. Difficulties over this, doubtless related to Oliver's other money troubles, caused Robert to have the lands apprised, and a charter granted to John, Lord Borthwick,[72] though Sinclair must afterwards have succeeded in redeeming the barony as he was still in possession as late as 1570.[73] Also noteworthy is a grant to the earl of Arran of the barony of Kerse on 1 October 1552, again a temporary manoeuvre regarding lands that were long to remain a pawn in Robert's complex affairs. Among the witnesses to the deed was Patrick Bellenden, of whom we shall see a great deal in the years to come.[74]

The evidence of Robert's life in his late teens and early twenties, derived mainly from his legal affairs, does not illuminate the growth of his character and political views, but events were taking place that would. In the winter of 1555–6, John Knox returned to Scotland for the first time since his exile after the siege of St Andrews in 1547 (which the young Robert and his brothers might well have witnessed). Among the members of the Scottish nobility whom he persuaded towards Protestantism – a major catch for the cause – was James the future regent, remembering his lessons in France.[75] For various political reasons, however, James remained for the time being an adherent of the queen regent. His change of heart when it came was to lay him open afterwards to charges of treachery but it constituted a very individual course of action.[76] Robert, significantly, followed his brother throughout. In August 1557, James, Robert and Lord Home conducted a raid into Northumberland on the regent's behalf.[77] The exploit was unsuccessful, the Scots having to withdraw in the face of the earl of Northumberland's forces. For the next eighteen months or so, James Stewart played a cautious game, but a growing belief that it was the regent's intention to crush Protestantism convinced him to act against her.

For his part, Robert remained close to the centre of affairs. He was reported to be departing for France in early 1558, doubtless to attend his sister's wedding to the Dauphin,[78] though he was back later in the year, being present in parliament in November.[79] He attended meetings of the lords of the congregation, though he does not appear to have played any important part in policy decisions. He was at Hamilton when they met Arran in September 1559, subscribing their letters to the

71 Reg. Deeds, NRS RD1/1, f. 123.
72 *Calendar of the Laing Charters*, ed. J. Anderson, Edinburgh, 1899, 157, no. 600.
73 *Canongate Ct Bk*, 132–3.
74 *Chrs of Holyrood*, 276, 288.
75 Doughty, 'Library of James Stewart, Earl of Moray'.
76 Lee, *James Stewart, Earl of Moray*, 26–39.
77 G. Ridpath, *The Border-History of England and Scotland*, London, 1776, 585–6.
78 Court of Session Recs: Acts and Decreets, NRS CS7/16, f. 285v.
79 *APS*, ii, 503.

regent,[80] and at subsequent gatherings at Stirling and Linlithgow. He witnessed the forcible entry of congregation forces into Edinburgh. He subscribed another letter to the regent on 19 October and was present at the siege of Leith and her 'deposition'. On 31 October, during a 'black week' for the congregation,[81] he earned himself an honourable mention in Knox's *History*.[82] The French had attacked and captured their heavy artillery on the road to Leith. Rumours that they had then penetrated as far as Leith Wynd, within uncomfortable distance of the town itself, caused the congregation's supporters to flee, Sir John Bellenden the justice clerk being among the 'feeble'. Argyll managed to stop the rout, and it was Robert who led the congregation's forces out of the West Port in a counter-attack. The following day he was on the Calton Hill as two pieces of artillery were mounted from which several shots were fired at the regent's besieged forces.[83]

Little more than a week later, however, he had changed sides and submitted to the queen regent.[84] Fortified Leith was proving too strong for the besieging forces, and French successes made the future of the reformers seem much less assured in November 1559 than a month before. His action was possibly the first evidence of the untrustworthiness that helps to explain later observers' uniformly poor opinion of him, beginning with Thomas Randolph, the English ambassador, who described his change of heart as 'shameful'. To be fair to Robert, Randolph was hardly an impartial observer, and the situation was in any case a complex one in which politics, religion and personal rivalries were intermingled. While Robert might have supported his brother as leader of the congregation, this did not guarantee similar feelings towards the Hamiltons, and he was no friend of the young Arran. Later too, he was to state that he had been unwilling to support the formal deposition of the regent on 1 October 1559, and thereafter became more and more disaffected from the cause of the reformers. The congregation's intended replacement of Mary of Guise with a committee in which two of the key positions were held by Châtelherault (James Hamilton, second earl of Arran) and his son could hardly be expected to appeal to Robert. On 8 February 1560, he gave evidence in the inquiry into the 'treason' of Arran, bearing witness to the participation of the earl in action in which he himself had taken a hand. Most notably he testified to having seen Arran append his signature to the letters that he had himself signed.[85] He said little regarding his own motives or views apart from an assertion that he had not wished to consent to the deposition of the regent.

At the end of March the English invaded Scotland. Robert went to Leith in a party including the French ambassador Henri d'Oysel, a major counsellor of the

---

80 *Report by De La Brosse and D'Oysel on Conditions in Scotland 1559–60*, ed. G. Dickinson (SHS Misc. IX), 119.
81 Lee, *James Stewart, Earl of Moray*, 53.
82 Knox, *History of the Reformation*, i, 260 (Dickinson edition).
83 *Report by De La Brosse and D'Oysel on Conditions in Scotland*, 120.
84 *CSP Scot.*, i, 267.
85 *Report by De La Brosse and D'Oysel on Conditions in Scotland*, 119.

regent, and remained there for some time during the English siege of the port.[86] By the second week in May, in a second volte-face, he had deserted Mary of Guise's forces. At the congregation's Leith camp on 10 May, he signed a ratification of the treaty of Berwick, whereby Elizabeth of England agreed to support the congregation.[87] The English generals regarded his change of side as of little military or political significance.[88] It is tempting to see Robert's change of heart as resulting purely from a further change in the military situation. The direct intervention of the English had brought enormous relief to the congregation, and the health of Mary of Guise was beginning to fail. The situation had changed in other ways too. If Robert had objected to the proposal to depose the regent, a clear challenge to the established order, then he may have been persuaded back to the congregation by the undertaking, in a bond signed at Leith on 26 April 1560, which under pressure from potential supporters,[89] emphasised obedience to lawful sovereigns.

Despite this shifty behaviour, Robert obviously still retained some standing in public affairs. He signed the letter from the lords of Scotland to Elizabeth thanking her for her support.[90] Despite his political manoeuvrings, his religious views do not appear to have changed, and in parliament in August he was described as 'one of those who had renounced popery'. He was stated to be among those to be sent in a special thanksgiving delegation to the English queen, and Randolph, in a letter to Cecil, hoped as much, though in the end nothing came of it.[91] In fact, after this, little is heard of Robert for about a year when, in August 1561, he was at Leith to meet his sister Mary on her return from France. Willing enough to play a part of sorts in times of active campaigning, or to append his name to an important document beside those of other notable men, he does not seem to have been thought worthy of any regard when it came to everyday administration in the delicate position in which Scotland found herself as a result of the victory of the congregation. But with his sister's return things changed, and Robert again comes into view, this time for an extended period, one which gives a more rounded picture of the character so far sketched in by events.

Queen Mary returned to Scotland in 1561, arriving on the morning of 19 August so suddenly, and after such a speedy passage, that of all the nobles only Robert was at Leith to greet her. He was joined 'incontinent upon the news' by his brother James,

86 A Diurnal of Remarkable Occurrents that have passed within the Country of Scotland since the Death of King James the Fourth till the year 1575 (Bannatyne and Maitland Clubs), 1833, 274.

87 J. Knox, History of the Reformation in Scotland, vols I–II, eds D. Laing, 1846–8; W. Croft Dickinson, 1949, i, 308.

88 CSP Scot., i, 407.

89 Donaldson, James V – James VII, 101; Aberdeen Burgh Recs, li, 322.

90 CSP Scot., i, 450.

91 CSP Scot., i, 460, 462; R. Keith, History of the Affairs of Church and State in Scotland, vols I–II, ed. J. P. L. (Spottiswoode Soc.), 1844, iii, 9 and n; CSP Scot., i, 466; CSP Scot., i, 470.

Châtelherault, and his son the younger Arran.[92] The three royal brothers – James, Robert and John – acted together in sympathetic treatment of their sister. James, despite his own reforming persuasion, put a stop to attacks on Mary's priests and placed them under the protection of John and Robert.[93] Robert's attitude to this policy is to some extent uncertain, as when the queen had a sung mass some weeks later 'one of her priests was well beaten for his reward by a servant of Lord Robert's,'[94] but since Lord James himself does not appear to have been altogether consistent in his treatment of Mary's chaplains,[95] it is doubtful whether this represents any serious difference of opinion between Robert and his brothers.

Already to some degree in the shadow of the abler James, he now seems to have been acting under the influence of John as well. The latter had followed a roughly similar path to Robert, though less prominently, in the events of 1559–60.[96] Now, in the autumn of 1561, the two brothers continued to act together. Robert supported John in continued opposition to the younger Arran, and the queen consulted John on obtaining guards to ward off a rumoured attempt by the unbalanced Arran to abduct her. He and Robert took turns to watch over their sister at Holyrood Palace.[97] In the dispute between Arran and Bothwell over the affair of Alison Craik, Arran's reputed mistress, Lord John was a leading supporter of Bothwell, his prospective brother-in-law, and 'this affinitie drew Lord Robert also to his assistance.'[98]

John seems to have appealed to the queen more as an entertaining companion, familiar with French ways, than as a political adviser; although he was involved in some public business, he was never at any time leader of a faction, or an initiator of policy. On 24 October 1561, Randolph reported to Cecil that Lord John had 'not least' favour with his 'leppynge and dansinge'.[99] On his sudden death, only two years later, his sister (notwithstanding his views on religion) was reported as saying that 'God took always from her those persons in whom she had greatest pleasure.'[100] Robert also sought the favour of the queen through his companionship. On 30 November 1561 the two brothers, with René d'Elboeuf, a Guise uncle of the queen, rode at the ring (a parlour form of jousting practice) for her entertainment. Two teams played; one led by Robert and dressed as women, and the other, in which d'Elboeuf was prominent, dressed as 'strangers, in strange masking

92 *CSP Scot.*, i, 547.
93 Knox, *History of the Reformation*, ii, 8; D. Calderwood, *The History of the Kirk of Scotland*, vols I–IV, ed. T. Thomson (Wodrow Soc.), Edinburgh, 1842–3, ii, 143.
94 *CSP Scot.*, i, 569.
95 *CSP Scot.*, i, 555.
96 *CSP Scot.*, i, 403. He was at first described as being of the queen's party in 1560 and received letters from her in January of that year, but had dealings with Elizabeth and the English in January and July 1560, and signed a ratification of the treaty of Berwick in May.
97 Calderwood, *History*, ii, 158.
98 Calderwood, *History*, ii, 164.
99 *CSP Scot.*, i, 563.
100 Knox, *History of the Reformation*, ii, 86.

garments'. Robert's 'women' won.[101] About this time, too, Robert gave his sister the gift of a sorrel gelding, an animal that she in turn gave to her ill-fated admirer, Pierre de Châtelard.[102]

Both Robert and John were seeking wives at this time. In October, Randolph reported that Robert 'consumethe' with love for Jean Kennedy, eldest daughter of Gilbert, third earl of Cassillis,[103] and in December both brothers were wed, within a fortnight of each other, John marrying a sister of the earl of Bothwell.[104] Robert's nuptials took place in Edinburgh at the lodging of the bride's kinsfolk. Brother James, newly created earl of Moray, was himself married less than two months later, on 8 February.[105]

The wives of Robert and John were women of character. Lord John's lady was described dryly by John Knox as 'a sufficient woman for such a man'.[106] Lord John, a man more noted for his charm than his capacity for action, later joined brothers Robert and James, on a *justice-ayre* in the north, apparently to avoid his wife's attempts to involve him in a personal feud with the Home family. The rigours of the northern trip killed him and he died at Inverness; his wife prosecuted the dispute herself, albeit unsuccessfully, in person at the head of her men.[107] In future years her 'madcap' son, Francis Stewart, was to receive the earldom of her attainted brother, the notorious James Hepburn, earl of Bothwell, and his path was to cross that of both Robert Stewart and his successor.

The other Jean, if not as doughty as Mistress Jean Hepburn, had already stood up for her rights under her father's will against members of her own family;[108] and her marriage to the first Stewart earl of Orkney was to be a difficult and argumentative one, calling from her the same resolute and litigious response. Randolph's comment on Robert Stewart's consuming passion for his bride could be regarded as a first genuine reference to the man's character – a dissolute and sensual one. His first recorded illegitimate child, a girl, must have been conceived barely fifteen months after his nuptials.[109] By late 1566, he had three lawful and three illegitimate children (though it is possible that one or more of the latter was born before his marriage).[110] He was to father at least ten natural children, and this may have been

101 Keith, *Affairs*, ii, 119–20.

102 Fraser, *Mary, Queen of Scots*, 204.

103 Keith, *Affairs*, ii, 132; according to Randolph (*CSP Scot.*, i, 563), Bothwell granted Robert land in Teviot-dale and the abbey of Melrose, but there is no corroboration of this – it would seem in any case more likely that John would be recipient of such a gift, perhaps in fulfilment of a marriage contract, though there appears to be no evidence for this either.

104 *CSP Scot.*, i, 563.

105 Lee, *James Stewart, Earl of Moray*, 97.

106 Knox, *History of the Reformation*, ii, 36.

107 Keith, *Affairs*, ii, 202; Ms History of the Homes, cited in *Scots Peerage*, vols I–IX, ed. J. Balfour Paul, Edinburgh, 1904–14, ii, 168–9.

108 Court of Session Recs: Acts and Decreets, NRS CS7/32, f. 133r and v; CS7/33, f. 226r and v.

109 *Inventaires*, 143–4.

110 *RSS*, v, no. 3101.

one of the factors that contributed to the marital disharmony of his later years.[111] The wider family relationships were also complex and acrimonious.

The marriage itself was nothing if not fruitful. Jean Kennedy spent much of the first decade of their marriage in pregnancy, bearing her husband five sons and three daughters. In order of birth, these children were Mary, Jean, Henry, Patrick (whose life story gives us the second half of this narrative), John, Robert, James and Elizabeth. The eldest trio, Mary, Jean and Henry, are first mentioned in November 1566 when Robert was granted a pension for their maintenance.[112] Mary was probably born within the first year of her parents' marriage, in late 1562.[113] Jean was next, born perhaps a year later, with her brother Henry arriving after February 1565, when his namesake Henry, Lord Darnley, came upon the scene. Patrick Stewart first appears on 27 September 1568, in Bishop Bothwell's charter to his father of the bishopric lands in Orkney.[114] (He may also be identified with the mysterious Thomas Stewart, entailed in the charter by Sir John Bellenden of Auchnoull to Jean Kennedy of 18 September 1568, but otherwise unknown.[115]) His actual birthdate is difficult to determine – perhaps between the summers of 1565 and 1566.[116] He was the first of a second identifiable group of four children. His brothers – John, James and Robert – were all born within a very short period indeed, less than two years from the first appearance of their elder brother and sisters. John Stewart, later master of Orkney, was the eldest, though he is mysteriously omitted from the documentation of the time.[117] He was followed by James Stewart, later Sir James Stewart of Eday and Tullos. The youngest was the later Sir Robert Stewart of Middleton.

Despite Robert establishing himself in Orkney, all his legitimate sons were educated in the south, and the evidence suggests that during his lifetime only the eldest, Henry and Patrick, came to the islands, though John and James both came to have landed interests there, at least after their father's death. Sir Robert of Middleton appears to have sought his fortune outside the islands altogether. The earl's lawful daughters brought their husbands Orkney concerns. Patrick, master of (later Lord) Gray, who married Mary on 20 July 1583 and at the time enjoyed great royal favour,[118] had been a *cautioner* for Bruce of Cultmalindie as early as 30 April 1577.[119] On 6 November 1586 Patrick, commendator of (later Lord) Lindores, who with his wife Jean was present at the making of his father–in–law's will, first appears

111 *Correspondence of Sir Patrick Waus of Barnbarroch,* vols I–II, ed. R. Vans Agnew (Ayr and Wigton Historical Historical Society), Edinburgh, 1887, 287–9.

112 *RSS*, v, no. 3101.

113 Bellenden Papers, NLS Adv. Ms. 22.3.14, no. 33.

114 *RMS*, v, no. 836.

115 *OSR*, 162, no. 78; Anderson, *Black Patie*, app. 1.

116 Anderson, *Black Patie*, app. 1.

117 *RMS*, v, no. 836.

118 *CSP Scot.*, viii, 34.

119 Court of Session Recs: Acts and Decreets, NRS CS7/68, f. 92.

in Orkney, and witnessed a tack by Robert to Thomas Swinton, an Orkney figure;[120] on 21 November 1591 he received land in Deerness from Patrick Stewart.[121] Elizabeth's husband, James Sinclair of Murkle, second son of John, master of Caithness, was appointed one of Robert's executors at the last.

Robert's illegitimate children fall into in two distinct groups. The earlier were in all likelihood born before Robert's departure for the Northern Isles and were to prove much more significant in their relationship with him, and later with Patrick as earl. Robert junior and the elder James (both mentioned in Robert's pension grant of 1566) disappear early from the record, but the other James and William remained to make their mark. James, old enough by 27 January 1587 to take part in an assize, must have been born in the same year as his legitimate brothers Patrick, James and John. He reappears again and again from 1584 onwards both as a witness to his father's transactions and in his own right.[122] William, later designated of Egilsay, had a chequered later career; in 1600 he was accused of murdering his wife, a Bellenden,[123] and by 1609 he was following in the footsteps of Gilbert Balfour as a colonel in Swedish service.[124] The second group of Robert's illegitimate children were those conceived with Marjorie Sandilands and other ladies with whom he sought consolation later in life, in estrangement from his countess.[125] Little is known of the daughters of Janet Allardyce and Janet Gray. Of the sons of Marjorie Sandilands, David died young, and George, of Eynhallow, although he held pieces of land in Orkney later erected into the tenandry of Brough, died without issue.[126] Edward on the other hand succeeded his brother and founded the family of Stewart of Brough.

Robert certainly seems to have been a man of prodigious sexual appetite. Beside the mothers of the bastards he acknowledged, it has been suggested that he was involved in other, even less savoury activities. In December 1588, before the kirk session of Elgin, one Helen Leslie, daughter of Mr George Leslie, parson of Mortlach, was accused 'for the conveying of certane wemen secreitlie as to pander to my lord of Orknay that he micht abuse thame and haue carnall copulatione with thame'. Helen denied this 'by her great aith, "or that scho knewe any sic filthie thingis be done"'.[127] For the cynical, this conjures up an extraordinary vision – a parson's daughter assembling a boatload of good time girls for Orkney, to delight his lordship and followers. Unfortunately, other than the commonplace that there tends to be no smoke without fire, little more can be said, though the sidelight on Robert's doings remains an interesting one.

---

120 Fea of Clestrain Mun., NRS GD31.
121 Balfour (of Balfour and Trenabie) Papers, OA D.2, box 27, bdl. 6.
122 E.g. 29 June 1586 (Craven Bequest, NRS GD106/78); 21 September 1586 (*RSS*, liv, f. 92*v*); 30 May 1587 (*REO*, 309, no. cxci).
123 *RPC*, vi, 93.
124 *Scots Peerage*, vi, 575.
125 F. Grant, *Zetland Family Histories*, Lerwick, 1893, 283.
126 PRS Orkney, NRS RS43/1, f. 2; printed *O & S Sasines*, 1.
127 *Records of Elgin 1234–1800*, ed. William Cramond, vol. 2 (New Spalding Club), Aberdeen, 1908, pp. 10–11.

Robert was to follow a clear policy of finding his natural daughters husbands among the more substantial proprietors of the Northern Isles, particularly Shetland – and not only for them, but for various of their cousins, his brothers' female children, both legitimate and illegitimate. Of his own natural daughters, Christian married John Mouat of Heogaland, Grizel married Hugh Sinclair of Brough and Mary became the wife of Laurence Sinclair of Gott.[128] Marjorie Stewart, daughter of Lord John, married first William Sinclair of Underhoull and then William Bruce of Symbister.[129] Barbara, lawful daughter of Robert's obscure brother Lord Adam Stewart, married Henry Halcro of Halcro, and is presumably the 'domina de Halcro' who erected her father's tombstone in the cathedral, and Mary, another niece, married John, son of Magnus Sinclair of Toab.[130]

During the upbringing of his eldest legitimate sons Robert, in accordance with common custom, placed them in the tutelage of others. In 1567 Henry Stewart was in the care of Bellenden of Auchnoull.[131] Fifteen years later, Patrick was under the supervision of a figure who was to play a major role in the lives of the Stewarts – Sir Patrick Waus of Barnbarroch, lord of session and ambassador.[132] Waus was to be a major source of counsel to Robert for the rest of his life. There were two reasons for this special relationship. There was a direct family link; Waus was married to Jean Kennedy's sister Katherine, and had strong connections with the family of Cassillis. He also acted for a number of years for Robert's half-brother Robert Stewart *secundus*, who became commendator of Whithorn in 1568. When this dignity was granted to Patrick after the second Robert's death, Waus became *yconomus* or administrator, as well as godfather and guardian, responsible for the young man's upbringing and education.[133]

During the first half of 1562, Robert remained in attendance on the queen, in Linlithgow, then Edinburgh and Stirling, whence he departed for Sutherland. His personal attendant was George Windram who, with others, received regular instalments from the treasury for expenses disbursed on Robert's behalf,[134] both for hospi-

128 Grant, *Zetland Family Histories*, 195, 277, 283.

129 Grant, *Zetland Family Histories*, 21.

130 RCAHMS *Inv.*, O & S, iii, 132; Anderson, *Robert Stewart*, 157; In April 1575 John Dick, an Edinburgh merchant and one of Robert's chief men of business, put the young Robert to 'bed and sculage' with Mr William Robertson, for £31 per annum (legal notebook of William Stewart, depute town clerk of Edinburgh, NLS Ms. 19312, ff. 144v–5r); *REO*, 304, no. clxxxvii; *OSR*, 196, no. 72.

131 Roxburghe Mun., bundle 1634, no. 11; Anderson, *Robert Stewart*, 60.

132 Reg. Deeds, NRS RD1/17, f. 336r and v.

133 Church Recs: Reg. Pres., NRS CH4/1/2, ff. 66v, 72r; Reg. Deeds, NRS RD1/34, ff. 278v–80v. Brian Smith has suggested that the name Patrick, unusual among the Stewarts, may have been chosen for him in honour of Barnbarroch. My own view has hitherto been that it resulted from a brief attempt to mend fences with the Bellendens, in particular Sir Patrick. Unlooked-for names usually have some significance in their choice, but little further can be said in this case.

134 *TA*, xi, 103, 110, 150–1; references to the queen's movements are taken from D. Hay Fleming, *Mary Queen of Scots*, London, 1898, 515–43.

tality[135] and payments to an apothecary for drugs during a brief illness. Gifts came from his waiting upon the queen; among them grand outfits – one made of black velvet, satin and taffeta, lined with blue and white *fustian*, embroidered with silver, with accompanying velvet belt, bag and bonnet, gloves and gilt *whinger*.[136] In return, Robert Stewart travelled widely on his sister's business. After his trip to Sutherland, possibly on a justice-ayre, he was sent in September 1562 to Edinburgh with eight large artillery pieces, shipped at Leith for Aberdeen, presumably in support of Mary in her struggle with the earl of Huntly and his son, who had risen in rebellion over religious differences within the Catholic side.[137] He was still in Aberdeen two months later and was thereafter in Dundee, Perth and Stirling,[138] accompanied by Windram and a colleague, William Mackeson, returning to Edinburgh by early February 1563,[139] then travelling to St Andrews to attend upon the queen, coming back to the capital two months later.

The support for the queen by her brothers was now recognised by honours and land. James and John both received titles on marrying.[140] James was invested as earl of Moray, in June 1563, with the lands of Cullaird, near Inverness.[141] John received the barony of Enzie, near Fochabers and briefly, towards the end of his short life, became Lord Darnley.[142] Robert, despite his military exertions, was not ennobled, though he was granted a charter on 16 June 1563 of the lordship and barony of Strathdon, Inverurie and Fetterletter, the lands of Cabrach and the lordship lands and barony of Cluny, all in the sheriffdom of Aberdeen.[143] By this time, however, he must already have set his sights on a much greater prize

On 25 July he was in Edinburgh.[144] Some months later, possibly in the second half of October he, Moray and Lord John all set off for the north, where they held justice courts.[145] They punished various thieves and murderers, and burned two witches in accordance with the new statute passed by parliament in June of that year,[146] one being 'so blinded by the devil that she affirmed "That no Judge had power over her"'.[147] It was now, at Inverness, that Lord John died. The cause of his

135 *TA*, xi, 251.

136 *TA*, xi, 107–8, 152–3, 173.

137 Pitscottie, *Historie*, ii, 178n.; Lee, *James Stewart, Earl of Moray*, 105–8.

138 *TA*, xi, 250–1.

139 Reg. House Chrs, NRS RH6/1904; *TA*, xi, 251.

140 Lee, *James Stewart, Earl of Moray*, 97; W. Fraser, *The Lennox Book*, vols I–II, Edinburgh, 1874, i, 420.

141 *RSS*, v, nos 1307–8.

142 There is no evidence for John Stewart's investiture as Lord Darnley, but he is so designated from 28 March 1563 (*RSS*, v, no. 1280) when he was appointed chamberlain, factor and bailie of the royal lands, barony and lordship of Enzie etc. (the lands of which he was ultimately granted a charter) and this remained his style for the rest of his life.

143 *RSS*, v, no. 1356.

144 Reg. House Chrs, NRS RH6/1919–20.

145 Keith, *Affairs*, 202.

146 *APS*, ii, 539.

147 Knox, *History of the Reformation*, ii, 86.

death is unknown, but given suggestions of poor health in his earlier life, it may be that he was never strong, and the rigours of a northern journey proved too much.

On 22 January Robert was mentioned in a report by the laird of Skeldon, newly home from negotiations in France, stating that among the 'fair words' given to the Scots by the French was the suggestion that the old band of Scots men-at-arms might be resurrected with Lord Robert as captain.[148] Nothing came of this. It shows that Robert was remembered in France, and was in some favour at the Scottish court; on the other hand, one is perhaps entitled to wonder whether he would have been suggested for this honour had brother John still been alive. In any event, Robert remained in Scotland.[149]

On 23 September 1564 the earl of Lennox, father of Henry Stewart, Lord Darnley, returned from exile to Scotland and stayed with Robert at his house at Holyrood, adjoining the abbey.[150] The arrival of Lennox marked the beginning of significant developments in Robert Stewart's life. There is no evidence up to this point of any particular friendship between Robert and members of the Lennox family, but the earl's lodging with him was only the first sign of a seeming closeness. In December, Robert was almost certainly in parliament in Edinburgh, when he received a grant of land that was to prove the most momentous of his life. This was a heritable *infeftment* of 'all and haill the landis of Orkney and Yetland, with all and sindrie yles pertaining thairto', with sheriffdom and foudry, following the queen's declaring herself to be of perfect age and the express dissolution in plain parliament of the islands' annexation to the crown.[151]

In February 1565, when Lennox's son, Henry Stewart, Lord Darnley, arrived in Scotland, he dined with Robert on one of the three days he spent in Edinburgh.[152] In the ensuing weeks a friendship grew up between the two; Robert, now in his early thirties, made a big impression on the 19-year-old Darnley. By March 20 Lennox had joined a faction whose members were characterised by Thomas Randolph as 'noted greatest enemies to all vertue'. Among this group, which included the earls of Atholl and Caithness and Lords Ruthven and Home, Robert Stewart was named. Randolph, unimpressed by Robert's conduct during the late wars, maintained his poor opinion. Already the previous year he had received details from Kirkcaldy of Grange of some of Robert's indiscretions (unfortunately transmitted in the bearer's words alone) and now, in the first explicit assessment of Robert's character by an observer, he described him as 'vain and nothing worth, a man full of all evil, the whole guider and ruler of my Lord Darnly'.[153]

The Lennox faction, with Darnley as a prospective husband for the queen, began steadily to acquire power at the expense of Moray, Arran, Argyll and their followers.

148 *CSP Scot.*, ii, 38.
149 Balfour of Pilrig Mun., NRS GD69/10; *Canongate Ct Bk*, 151.
150 *CSP Scot.*, ii, 77.
151 *APS*, iii, 254–6.
152 *CSP Scot.*, ii, 125.
153 *CSP Scot.*, ii, 75; Keith, *Affairs*, ii, 271–2.

Robert's support of the Lennox group marked a break with his brother. Darnley did not trouble to conceal his dislike for Moray. On one occasion in March 1565, when Robert showed him a map of Scotland, indicating Moray's lands and their extent, Darnley remarked that 'it was too much'. Moray heard of this and the queen counselled Darnley to apologise.[154] For Robert, joining the Lennoxes brought quick rewards. On 4 April, the day after his brother had departed from the court 'in deep perplexity',[155] he received a second charter of the Strathdon lands, erected into a barony and with other improved provisions.[156] On 6 May his charter of the Orkney lands was confirmed.[157] Nine days later King Consort Darnley, laden with new honours, knighted him (among others that 'never showede anye greate token of their vassallage').[158] On that day and again on 19 July he was included as an extraordinary member of the privy council.[159] It was at this time Robert showed his gratitude by naming his children Henry and Mary. On 11 May, according to Randolph, 'It is spoken that some other [besides Darnley] shall be called to greater honour – as the Lord Robert earl of Arcknaye . . .'[160] Just over a week later, Randolph reported, 'My Lord Robert . . . shall be (he says himself) earl of "Orknaye"'.[161] On 26 May the Orkney grant passed the privy seal, the *precept* to infeft him being given to his follower James Monteith of Saltcoats.[162]

But affairs at court were now to become difficult for Robert. By the beginning of July 1565 Randolph described him as 'nowe earle of Orknaye', though he was 'mislyked of the queen but keapt in by the Lord Darlye whom he serves with hys cape in hys hande'.[163] The English ambassador found Robert and Lord Fleming, a prominent courtier, on terms of such intimacy with the king that he had to address the last in their presence. This closeness to Darnley had hitherto paid dividends in fostering Robert's schemes in the north, but his baleful influence on the weak and arrogant king had set him at odds with his sister, and the acquisition of the earldom lands of the Northern Isles was not to prove as simple as he had hoped. Already, his plans were beginning to unravel. The formalities of the grant were never completed, though it continued for sixteen years to form the basis of Robert's title. At the beginning of 1566 Gilbert Balfour of Westray was made sheriff of Orkney, an office that had been part of Robert's grant.[164] Its Shetland equivalent, the *foudry*, went to William Murray of Tullibardine later the same year, on 29 July.[165] Meanwhile,

154 Keith, *Affairs*, ii, 275.
155 Lee, *James Stewart, Earl of Moray*, 135.
156 *RSS*, v, no. 2035.
157 *APS*, iii, 254.
158 Randolph to earl of Leicester, Minutes of Mar Peerage, 87, quoted in *Scots Peerage*, v, 614.
159 *RPC*, i, 335, 341.
160 *CSP Scot.*, ii, 157.
161 *CSP Scot.*, ii, 174.
162 *RSS*, v, no. 2078; Reg. House Chrs, NRS RH6/1992.
163 Keith, *Affairs*, ii, 301.
164 *RSS*, v, no. 2529.
165 *RSS*, v, no. 3014.

Robert's performance of the queen's business continued, and he set off for Suther-land, possibly on another justice-ayre.[166]

Behind Robert's problems lay the growing estrangement between the queen and her husband, sealed on 9 March by the murder in Mary's presence of her secretary, David Riccio. Robert, having returned from the 'Northland', was at his sister's table when the assassins burst in, but he took no part in what followed. Indeed, despite his close relations with the king, he seems to have been wholly innocent of any connivance in the killing of the unfortunate Italian, though Patrick Bellenden was among the gang, and pointed a cocked pistol at the pregnant queen.[167] As events were to show, Robert never wholly abandoned Darnley, but he ceased to be as involved in the king's doings as before. In fact, even before he supped with her in March 1566, his sister's actions towards him suggest that he may have been trying to mend relations with her. As early as November 1565, she had made him a gift of 4 ells of cloth of silver.[168] On 29 May he was authorised to command delivery of whoever was holding Riccio's horse; and when in May or June of the same year the queen made up her testamentary inventory in anticipation of the perils of childbed, she bequeathed him a richly jewelled cross.[169]

After the death of Riccio, Robert absented himself from court – and on his own, not royal, business. Shortly before 22 June, about the time of his sister's confine-ment in Edinburgh, he travelled west to settle a dispute between his servants and the followers of William, Lord Livingston over the lands of Carsegrange, which had recently erupted in disturbances in Falkirk. Both sides were ordered by the privy council to keep the peace, with Robert being told to stay in Stirling until the queen's next visit. Robert's followers in this were members of the Monteith family, who were to serve him long after he had surrendered the lands of which theirs formed a part. William Monteith of Randyfurd was his lieutenant in his appearance before the council, and it is very probable that the James, William and Patrick Monteith named as Randyfurd's men are the same individuals who two years later were to be involved in strife in Orkney while in Robert's service.[170]

Records for Robert's activities now are reduced to a commonplace account of Holyrood doings, for example a dispute with the Canongate burghers over the election of bailies.[171] His status at court continued to be recognised, but indicated how his position had declined in the short while since he had considered himself earl of Orkney in all but name. On November he received a privy seal grant of £990 and quantities of wheat, bere, oats and meal from the *thirds* of Holyrood for the education of Henry, Jean and Mary, his lawful children, and his bastards Robert

166 *TA*, xi, 464.
167 *CSP Scot.*, i, 23.
168 *Inventaires*, 158.
169 *TA*, xi, 507; *Inventaires*, 122.
170 *RPC*, i, 469; *TA*, xii, 13–14; *RPC*, i, 473.
171 R. K. Hannay Papers, NRS GD214/192.

and James. The reason for the grant was said to be that Robert had 'sustenit sic sumptious chargis and expensis besyde his labour, panis and travell in awaiting upoun thair hienes service in tymes bypast that he is nocht abill to continew langar in his former tryne and honourable convoy'.[172]

He was now comparatively isolated. The queen, who was lying seriously ill in Jedburgh at this time, was now wholly disgusted with the king, and no longer felt any need to tolerate his cronies, even her own relatives. She was not alone; Darnley was now heartily detested on all sides,[173] and his 'whole guider and ruler' did not find the political climate congenial. He had no dealings with his brother Moray who was now in firm control and did not shrink from imposing his will on his unpopular brother.[174] Worse was to come. On 10 February 1567, Darnley was murdered and Robert's fortunes reached their lowest ebb. His part in the murky doings before Kirk o' Field, like those of many others, is obscure. So far as can be judged, he was identified with none of the known factions, his sole connection with events being through the remains of his relationship with the king and queen. A week before the murder, according to a number of the sources for this episode,[175] the queen had brought Robert and her husband together 'and there confronting them never left to provoke the one against the other until in her own presence from words she caused them offer strokes',[176] hoping by this means to rid herself of her troublesome and unpleasant husband without herself becoming involved in murder. Only George Buchanan in his *Rerum Scoticarum Historia* states that Robert had foreknowledge of the plot and warned the king that his life was in danger. Darnley told the queen of this. Confronted with it, Robert denied it hotly, and the queen for good measure called in Moray, hoping that he also might perish in the ensuing violence.

The agreement between the sources suggests that there is at least a grain of truth in the story of an argument between Robert and Darnley, or at least plausibility for those who knew the relationships within the queen's circle. Mary is depicted as caring little who was killed in the struggle between Darnley and Robert, and relations between the latter two are shown to be frosty at best, though Buchanan's tale shows Robert still prepared to assist the hapless Henry. It is not disclosed why Robert was prepared to risk telling the ailing king of the moves against him in view of the fact – attested in this instance – that Darnley was notoriously unable to keep a secret; perhaps it was out of genuine regard.

Events in the ensuing months point to a collapse in Robert's fortunes. A privy seal letter to Robert, his half-brother Laurence Bruce of Cultmalindie, James Johnston of Elphinstone – a 'cousing' presumably a connection of his mother's – and two 'friends and servandis', Robert Leslie of Ardersier and John Stewart of Eildon,

172 *RSS*, v, no. 3101.
173 Lee, *James Stewart, Earl of Moray*, 173.
174 Lee, *James Stewart, Earl of Moray*, 177.
175 For an examination of these, see Donaldson, *The First Trial of Mary, Queen of Scots*.
176 Book of Articles, printed in G. Donaldson, *The First Trial of Mary, Queen of Scots*, London, 1969, 167.

permitted them to leave the country for France, Germany and elsewhere 'for doing of thair leiful erandis and besines' for five years.[177] Another, more significant, was the grant on 12 May to the earl of Bothwell of the same lands and jurisdictions in the Northern Isles granted to Robert almost exactly two years before, now elevated into a dukedom.[178]

But the circumstances of the time were volatile. Robert was still in Scotland on 26 April,[179] and by July had left Edinburgh, probably for the Kerse, to muster the Monteiths and others. When he returned on the evening of 15 July, he was 'well accompanied', and went to a meeting of the lords of council at the lodging of the earl of Atholl.[180] On witnessing this, the English ambassador, now Sir Nicholas Throckmorton, stated that 'Till now he has had no intelligence with them, but concurred with the Hamiltons'. This, the first evidence for several months of Robert's political stance, suggested that he had held to his allegiance to Mary throughout the aftermath of Darnley's murder but was now changing sides. Throckmorton was at that time acting under orders to sound out Mary's supporters and had concluded that not even the Hamiltons, hitherto her most prominent protagonists, were to be trusted in her cause.[181] Robert's meeting with the lords was an isolated incident in a career that was involved less and less in national affairs. He was not with his sister at Carberry Hill, nor did he carry his former support into any other form of direct action. On 11 September his brother gave him £100 from the treasury for some unnamed service, but that is all.[182]

On 24 July Mary abdicated. On 10 August Murray of Tullibardine and Kirkcaldy of Grange were sent in pursuit of the earl of Bothwell, who had left the country from Dunbar and made for his precarious duchy. They were accompanied by Adam Bothwell, bishop of Orkney.[183] On 27 July Robert was in the Canongate subscribing a pension to Balfour of Pittendreich of victual from the lands of Whitekirk, but from then on the meagre references to his whereabouts show him to be outside Edinburgh. On 14 August Throckmorton dined with the regent Mar, who was accompanied by his wife and several other ladies including the unescorted Jean Kennedy.[184] On 19 September Robert was represented by David MacGill in Edinburgh in litigation with George Towers of Inverleith over the teindsheaves of Inverleith and Wardie.[185] In fact, Robert was now planning the most vigorous and decisive action of his life. By 15 September the unsuccessful Kirkcaldy and his

177 RSS, v, no. 3387.
178 RSS, v, no. 3530.
179 RMS, iv, no. 2557; Reg. Deeds, NRS RD1/9, f. 157; T. L. F. Livingstone Papers (HMC), vii, 733; Reg. Deeds, NRS RD1/9, f. 157.
180 CSP Scot., ii, 354.
181 Lee, James Stewart, Earl of Moray, 203.
182 TA, xii, 74.
183 Donaldson, 'Bishop Adam Bothwell and the Reformation in Orkney', 98.
184 CSP Scot., ii, 383.
185 RPC, i, 571.

followers had returned empty-handed to Edinburgh.[186] A month and a half later, on 4 November, Robert Stewart was in Kirkwall, acting as sheriff and styling himself feuar of the lands and lordship of Orkney and Shetland.[187]

186 Moray to Throckmorton, *CSP Scot.*, ii, 394.
187 *REO*, 123, no. lvi.

3

A Princelie and Royall Revenew

Robert Stewart, at the height of his power as first of the Stewart earls, was to hold more than twice the amount of land and income in the Northern Isles than the Norse earls had enjoyed or than had been controlled, in various ways, by the Sinclairs. His hold on this was to prove precarious, but in time his son Patrick was also to inherit the same sort of influence and income, though he too found encroachments on his power and was responsible, ultimately, for its dissipation. With Patrick's fall and disgrace, arrangements in Orkney and Shetland changed utterly.

To see what all this meant, it is helpful to look at three indicators – extent, actual quantity of victual yield in modern units, and the quantity of cash at current values that this produced, in the light of previous or contemporary comparisons. The total extent of the assessed lands in Orkney amounted to 3670 *pennylands* (3,670d).[1] Of this, old *kingsland*, forfeited to King Sverrir of Norway by his defeated Orkney opponents after the battle of Florevåg in 1194, amounted to 673d or about 20 per cent of the total.[2] Situated largely in Rendall and the North Isles, it was these that the Danish king, Christian I, pledged to the king of Scots in 1468. The earldom lands, themselves divided into *auld earldom land* and *bordland*, had been taken from the Sinclair earls in 1470 by James III, and amounted to 336d or about a further 10 per cent.[3] These included large parts of Sanday, Stronsay and Westray, all of Hoy (as distinct from Walls), the southern part of South Ronaldsay, and the Mainland parishes of Sandwick and Orphir.

Conquest land which, as we have seen, had been acquired largely by William, last of the Sinclair earls, lay scattered throughout the islands, but with centres in the artificial creations of Warsetter, Paplay and Greenwall.[4] These amounted to 422d from an original total of 1,341d.[5] This collection had been carved out of the udal estates, those of independent smaller proprietors, whose obligations in tenure

---

1 Thomson, *History of Orkney*, 116.
2 Thomson, *History of Orkney*, 127.
3 W. P. L. Thomson, 'Fifteenth Century Depression in Orkney: the Evidence of Lord Henry Sinclair's Rentals', *Essays in Shetland History*, Lerwick, 1984, 137–8; Crawford, 'The Earldom of Orkney and Lordship of Shetland', 292–5.
4 *Rentals*, i, 11–15; ii, 10–12; Marwick, *Orkney Farm-names*, 89–90.
5 Thomson, 'Fifteenth Century Depression in Orkney', 137.

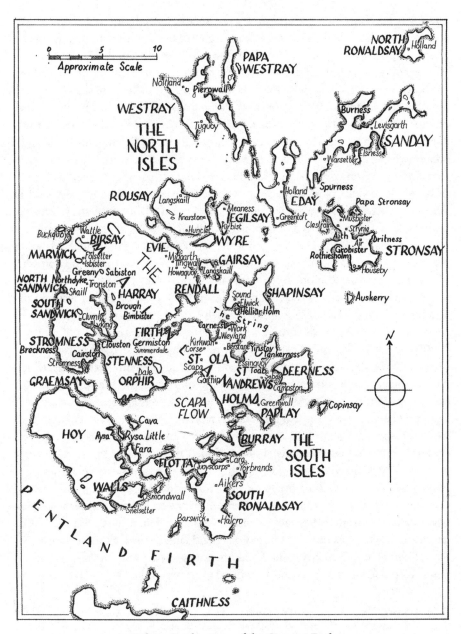

Orkney in the time of the Stewart Earls

and inheritance, in Norse tradition, lay not towards a superior, but to their own kinsmen. The latter had, in theory at least, rights of pre-emption in the buying and leasing of property, or redemption of land sold outwith the family.[6] Succession was by division among the children, the eldest son having first choice of the properties, a son's portion being twice that of a daughter. The udaller paid skat to the earl, but this had originally been a property tax, payable to the crown in the mother country of Norway; it was not a feudal tribute implying superiority, though it was sometimes seen as such.[7] These lands too were dispersed throughout the islands, some parishes having a great deal more than others. There were large concentrations in South Ronaldsay, Sanday and in the Mainland parishes of Harray, Stromness, the Sandwicks North and South (treated separately in the rentals), and St Andrews. There was no parish without any udal land at all, but in Westray, Stronsay and St Ola, all areas with large accumulations of other forms of property, its extent was very small indeed. The size of the holdings varied greatly. Much of South Ronaldsay was subdivided into small parcels, and the Germistons and Cloustons of Stenness held small plots in fractions of a pennyland. At the other end of the scale were families such as the Irvings of Sebay, the Groats of Tankerness and the Sinclairs of Tuquoy and of Essinquoy, whose political status was not unlike that of the feudatories that were later to be created on the bishopric lands.[8]

The largest collection of estates of all, however, was that of the bishopric of Orkney. In all, this amounted to over 1,000d.[9] The great centre was Birsay, which had the biggest concentration of any one type of property in the islands; almost the whole of the parish (excluding Marwick, which the rentals treat separately) was bishopric land. There were also possessions in Westray, St Ola, Evie and Stenness, Besides bishopric land proper, there was *kirkland*, lands bestowed as endowments on local churches and prebends. These included the estates of the archdeaconry and subchantry, the vicarages of Evie, Rendall and Stronsay, the chaplainries of St Ninian and St Mary and the prebends of St Katherine and St Augustine. Some of these endowments were extensive in themselves; the lands of St Katherine's *Stouk* were scattered through Westray, Stronsay, Shapinsay, Holm, Firth, Birsay, St Ola and Sanday.[10] The bishopric of Orkney also held land in the Caithness parishes of Reay, Dunnet and Canisbay[11] and, it has been suggested, in Strathnaver in Sutherland.[12] Its possessions in Shetland we will examine presently.

6 W. J. Dobie, 'Udal Law', *The Sources and Literature of Scots Law*, Edinburgh, 1936, 451–2; D. Sellar, 'Udal Law', *The Laws of Scotland; Stair Memorial Encyclopaedia*, Edinburgh, 1989, xxiv, 204–5; W. P. Drever, 'Udal Law', *Encyclopaedia of the Law of Scotland*, Edinburgh, 1933, xv, 327.

7 *Oppressions of the Sixteenth Century in the Islands of Orkney and Zetland*, ed. David Balfour (Maitland Club), 1859, 101.

8 'The Uthell Buik', Hugh Marwick Papers, NRS GD1/236/2.

9 *Rentals*, ed. Peterkin, ii.

10 *RMS*, vi, no. 1038.

11 Rose Papers, NLS Adv. Ms. 49.7.19, ff. 25r and v.

12 *Rentals*, ed. Peterkin, iii, 11.

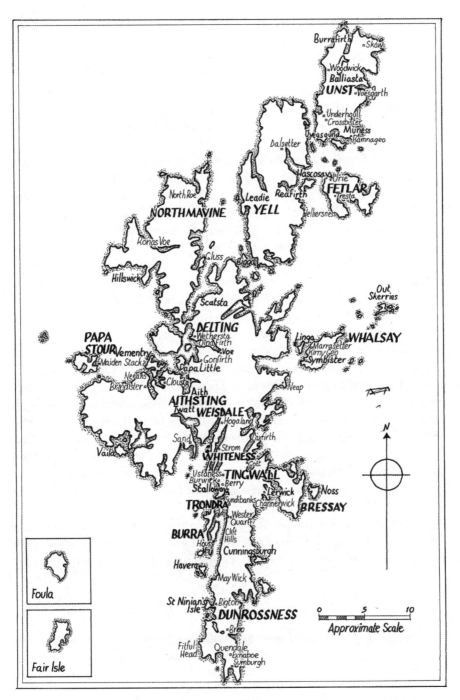

Shetland in the time of the Stewart earls

In Shetland the situation regarding all these classes of property was entirely different. The 'lordship lands' amounted to more than a quarter of the valuation of Tingwall, Weisdale, Northmavine, Dunrossness and Delting, scarcely less of Unst.[13] They appear to have included not only the Shetland equivalent of kingsland – which constituted a much smaller proportion of the whole skat-paying lands in the archipelago than those of Orkney – but a great deal more conquest land, the result of a similar campaign of acquisition by Earl William in Orkney, supplemented by a smaller quantity acquired by his natural son, David Sinclair of Sumburgh.[14] Though not the largest property, Sumburgh was of particular importance as a residence and administrative centre, remaining so throughout the Stewart era.

Bishopric estates were to be found in a large number of parishes, but were scattered in location and haphazard in extent. The main centres were in Dunrossness, Northmavine and the North Isles. There were the Shetland kirklands, which were also much less extensive than those in Orkney, but were not appropriated to cathedral prebends. They consisted only of those of the 'cannon and stallers of the cathedral', the lands of Asta, formerly pertaining to the prebend of St Giles of Asta, and those of the archdeaconry of Shetland, perhaps the most prestigious dignity within the see of Orkney after the bishopric itself.[15]

The udal lands, however, formed a much higher proportion of the whole than those of Orkney, and although they too varied very greatly in size, there were among them a number of constellations of property quite unlike anything in the more southerly islands, such as the lands of the 'lords of Norroway'. These derived from the division in the late fifteenth century of the large estate of the Norwegian magnate Hans Sigurdsson. They consisted of three parts, centred on the islands of Vaila (with 'Vaila Goods', the pertinents of the Vaila estate), Noss (and Noss Goods) and Papa Stour (with Papa Goods). In the sixteenth century only Noss Goods remained in Norwegian hands, at least on paper. The others, Vaila and Papa, were to become the permanent possessions of the Cheynes of Vaila and the Mouats of Heogaland.[16]

Unfortunately, the rentals of Shetland are neither as early nor as detailed as those of Orkney, so there are no figures for land value in Shetland to lay alongside those provided for Orkney by the rentals.[17] This makes it more difficult to mark out

---

13 1628 rental of Shetland (Exchequer Records: Orkney [and Shetland] Rentals and Accs, NRS E41/7); I am grateful to Brian Smith, archivist of Shetland, for a copy of the computer analysis of the rental from which these conclusions were drawn.

14 B. E. Crawford, 'David Sinclair of Sumburgh', *Scandinavian Shetland: an Ongoing Tradition?*, ed. J. R. Baldwin (Scottish Society for Northern Studies), Edinburgh, 1978, 5; *REO*, 421–5.

15 *RMS* v, no. 1045; Bruce of Symbister Papers, SA GD144/71/4.

16 Smith, 'Shetland, Scandinavia, Scotland, 1300–1700: the Changing Nature of Contact', *Scotland and Scandinavia, 800–1800*, 30–1. Frans-Arne Stylegar and Liv Kjorsvik Schei, 'Lords of Norroway'. The Shetland Estate of Herdis Thorvaldsdatter, *West over Sea: Studies in Scandinavian Sea-borne Expansion and Settlement before 1300*, Leiden, 2007.

17 In Shetland, extent was measured originally in merks, with a division into pennies imposed at a later date,

the value of the different types of estate. In Shetland the total extent of assessed land was about 13,500 merks, divided into crown land (rather over 3,000 merks), bishopric land (about 800 merks), kirkland (impossible to compute properly, but certainly well over 300 merks), and udal land, which thus amounts to about 60 per cent of the whole. The earliest complete Shetland rental extant is that of 1628 and, although it includes earlier material, nothing in it dates from before the beginning of the seventeenth century. If there was a previous rental – and it seems likely that the Stewart earls' *doers* were working from some now unknown source – it has not survived.

The first known account of the cash value of the islands' victual yield had been made at the behest of Mary of Guise, after she received the islands as her widow's portion in 1542, on the death of her husband, James V.[18] The total value of her income, already noted, stood at £9,750 for Orkney, £4,210 for Shetland. An attempt to derive equivalent sums for the time of Earl Patrick produces the figures of £11,600 and £5,400.[19] These values are only of limited usefulness in themselves. They do represent an increase in income of more than one sixth between the time of Mary of Guise and that of the Stewarts, and allegations of wilfully increasing the Orkney measuring weights were to be alleged against Robert in 1575 and against Bruce of Cultmalindie the following year.[20] On the other hand the sixteenth century was a period of general inflation throughout Europe, fuelled by population growth and the influx of Spanish silver from the New World. The increased number of mouths to feed drove grain prices up faster than those of manufactured goods.[21] When viewed against this background, the efforts to increase the yield of their estates by altering the weights, not only by the Stewarts but by Tulloch of Fluris and of Bruce of Cultmalindie, seem all the more avaricious. Unfortunately, however, without reliable evidence for the general state of harvests, statistics for sixteenth-century populations or even consistent means of deriving data, the real significance of price rises remains problematic.[22] An increase of one sixth in fifty years seems little enough if it is held to combine both general inflation and interference with the measuring instruments.

Mary of Guise's valuation appears to have formed the basis of the later account to exchequer, in 1587, of Sir John Maitland of Thirlestane, secretary at the time, and Sir Lewis Bellenden, though with a number of augmentations. More searching still was the examination by the 'Octavians', the eight officials appointed by James VI in 1595 to conduct a thoroughgoing reform of the royal finances. The Guise valuation

apparently in an attempt to introduce a more uniform unit than one that had come to vary considerably in value from place to place. The merk could have six, nine or twelve 'pennies the merk'. Only in Unst was there a consistent relationship of six pennies to the merk.

18 Murray, 'Sir John Skene', 141–2.
19 Anderson, *Black Patie*, app. 3,151–2.
20 *Oppressions*, 7.
21 J. H. Elliott, *Europe Divided*, London, 1968, 60–9.
22 Anderson, *Robert Stewart*, 32, 96–8.

was included by Clerk Register Skene in his 'Proposals for Resuming Crown Lands and Increasing Revenue', in which he referred to the lands of Orkney and Shetland as being set in *feuferme* for £2,073 6s 8d 'allanerlie', a meagre payment for £13,960 at prices half-a-century old.[23] In fact it was among the largest of such payments. Of the royal properties, only one – the royal hunting-ground of the lordship of Ettrick Forest – exceeded, by about £700, the earldom and lordship of Orkney and Shetland in *mails* paid into the royal coffers. Both sums were greatly in excess of any other. The earldom of Fife, for example, yielded little more than half as much; the earldom of Ross and lordship of Ardmannoch, previously granted to Darnley on his betrothal to Queen Mary, gave even less.[24]

The yearly payment of £2,073 6s 8d represented an initial valuation of 3,000 merks, with ten merks augmentation, contained in Robert's grant of 1564–5, together with a further 100 merks imposed at a later date. The alienation of the Orkney and Shetland estates, supposedly annexed indissolubly to the crown in 1472,[25] was representative of a besetting problem for the monarchy. During the recurrent minorities, large tracts of land had slipped out of its control. This had happened to the important earldoms of Strathearn and of Kintyre, and both James V and James VI in their time were concerned to retrieve their losses in youth.[26] Robert's acquisition of the lands of Orkney and Shetland in 1564–7, and of the earldom in 1581, both occurred at times when the political situation in Scotland was somewhat fluid. As his fortunes waxed and waned, there were re-assessments of the situation in the north, as the loss of crown land to unscrupulous elements became clearer.

In Orkney, by far the greatest proportion of the estate income came from grain and its products – malt, meal and *bere*. The *remainder* consisted chiefly of butter and oil – 16 per cent of the total – and a slightly lesser value in meat. In real terms of payment in kind, the income of earldom and bishopric comprised about 225 tons of *cost*, approximately the same quantity of bere, 100 tons of butter, 10 tons of fish oil, perhaps about 3,700 square metres of peats, just under 4,000 hens and about £460 in money.[27] The chief destination of much of this was markets on the east coast of Scotland where it could be converted into cash, though some was used to pay the servants of the estates and there were items, especially the peats and poultry, which were appropriated to the earl's own use.

Responsible for the ingathering of each parish's payments was a *tackman* – not a *tacksman* or leaseholder of the revenues, but a paid functionary.[28] From the

23 Murray, 'Sir John Skene', 141-2.

24 *ER*, xxiii, 27–30.

25 *APS*, ii, 102.

26 Murray, 'Sir John Skene', 126-7.

27 *Rentals*, ed. Peterkin, ii; for basis of weights, see Smith, 'Bismars and Pundars', *New Shetlander*, clxvi (Yule 1988), 6–7, citing O & S Papers, NRS RH9/15/169. For peats, see Smyth of Methven Mss, NRS GD190, box 42.

28 *REO*, 409n; Storer Clouston describes the distinction between 'tackman' and 'tacksman' as an arbitrary

islands and parishes, goods were generally transported to Kirkwall for export. Grain products were received at the *girnel*, butter at the 'butter booth', and then they were shipped out by independent skippers hired for the purpose. Meat – 'flesh' – appears to have been obtained and barrelled from different types of beast without distinction. Cattle and pigs were undoubtedly raised on the earldom lands, but the greatest number of references is to sheep. The Orkney sheep runs of the earldom, each with its own shepherd, were in Sandwick, Westray and Birsay. The shepherds were usually quite well paid,[29] though rather less was given to the sheepman of (South) Fara, who presumably did little more than keep an eye on the animals he ferried to Fara, Cava and Rysa Little; in Sanday at the end of the Stewart era, James Fea of Clestrain received a barrel of butter for pasturing the earl's sheep on the Holms of Spurness. Orphir men were paid by the tackman for *rooing* the sheep on the islands in the Flow, and those of Westray received a similar time-honoured payment. In Orphir, two *meils* of malt were 'allowit to the ferriboat', which, besides its general duties of serving the western South Isles, was presumably charged with ferrying the sheep. This ferry had a counterpart in Holm, presumably for the islands to the east of Scapa Flow, and there were ferries also working northwards and southwards from Burray, and from South Ronaldsay across the Pentland Firth.

Under the Stewarts, some of the fruits of the Mainland farms and other centres were taken direct to the earl's barn and peat yards, and had presumably done so under the old earls and bishop. Sandwick provided malt and meal for Skaill, and malt, meal, meat and peats for the Palace of Birsay. Peats came to the Palace of the Yards in Kirkwall from the commons of Rendall and of Holm and Paplay, and to the castle yard in Kirkwall from Harray.[30] The earldom lands in Sanday and the island of Burray gave rabbitskins as part of their rents, though there were rabbit warrens elsewhere, most notably at Birsay where, among a large establishment, there was a full-time *warrender*.[31] This official, besides keeping the warren, received remuneration for 'keiping and susteining of the kingis firrattis'. The ferrets may have enjoyed this rather curious royal patronage because the rabbit-meat they secured was used to feed the king's hawks, though there was much greater and better-known provision for them in the form of 'halkhenis'. The provision of hawks for the king had been a service in Orkney since the earliest days of Scottish rule, though the rental of 1595 specifically excluded hawk-hens from its calculations. Responsibility for the hens rested with one individual, who at the end of our period was John Hoy. Falconers visited Orkney each year in search of eggs, though payment for these

---

one, serving to distinguish between the two very different functions. However in the 1613 return the term 'tackman' is the one used.

29 Exchequer Records: Orkney [and Shetland] Rentals and Accs, NRS E41/3; the shepherd of Sandwick received over a third more in malt and meal than the estate officer of the parish.

30 Orkney [and Shetland] Rentals and Accs., NRS E41/3; the peats of St Ola were cut at the earl's expense and carted at the commons' expense.

31 Orkney [and Shetland] Rentals and Accs., NRS E41/3; the staff at Birsay included a shepherd, a peatman, a cooper and keepers of the park and of the horse.

came from the treasurer's accounts; provision was also made for a 'craig climmer', presumably a local man, who climbed the cliffs in search of eggs.

The rentals, with their emphasis on butter and grain and poultry, make it clear that the chief activity of the Orcadians was farming rather than fishing. The only contributor to the rental to pay in fish as such was Westray, which gave an undisclosed number of cod yearly among its revenues. Oil, the chief fish product given to the earl, was paid by some islands instead of butter, some in addition to it. The only Mainland parish to pay skat oil instead of skat butter was Stromness, where Hamnavoe, the modern port of Stromness, was one of the two main Orkney fishing centres. The other was Stronsay; in both, 20 visiting *doggers* lay each season.[32] Deep-sea fishing does not appear to have been an indigenous activity in Orkney, or even in Shetland, at this time, and the oil was provided from the humble coalfish, rather than the cod and *ling* that were the intended catches of the large visiting fleets.

In Shetland, butter and oil provided about 40 per cent of the total money value, closely followed by *wadmel* at about 30 per cent, the rest being made up by ship tolls, *wattle* and parish oxen and sheep. The process for converting it into cash was quite different from that of Orkney. Most of the butter and oil, collected by the *underfouds* under the supervision of the earl's chamberlain, was sold to visiting merchants, mainly German, but also from England, Scotland and the Netherlands.[33] With wadmel, the Stewart earls leased out their rights to lesser landowners. The responsibility for the measurement of victual payments for skat and other dues rested with the *lawrightman*, who had custody of the measuring instruments – the *cuttell*, for measuring wadmel, the *bismar* for weighing out butter, and the *can*, for measuring oil – and who also carried out the actual assessment.

Oil was the chief fish product even in Shetland. Natives undoubtedly did catch cod and ling, and in 1608 Patrick was to conclude contracts with the inhabitants of Dunrossness, and with the Orcadians of South Ronaldsay, Hoy and Walls, for receipt of all their catches, including 'ling and keilling'.[34] Even in these, however, oil was mentioned as an important element, and much of the deep-sea fishing appears to have been carried out by others, whence the earl derived an income from licences, rather than by Shetlanders or Orcadians who might have paid skats or mails in the form of dried or salted fish. On 9 September 1580 Robert concluded a contract with the Fife coast burghs – Crail, Pittenweem, Anstruther Easter and Wester,[35] and Patrick renewed it in September 1594.[36] These gave the fishermen liberty to fish, build houses and stores for drying and packing their catches, and buy necessaries

32 Court of Session Recs: Acts and Decreets, NRS CS7/175, ff. 242v–8v.
33 H. D. Smith, *Shetland Life and Trade*, Edinburgh, 1984, Chap. 2.
34 G. Donaldson, *Shetland Life under Earl Patrick*, Edinburgh, 1958, 50–1; Reg. Deeds, NRS RD1/180, ff. 348r–52r.
35 Reg. of Deeds (Books of Council and Session): 1st series, NRS RD1/20, ff. 347–9.
36 Reg. of Deeds, NRS RD1/46, ff. 381r–83r, printed *OSR*, i, no. 76.

from the local inhabitants. Fishing operations were on a much larger scale than in Orkney. There were well over 100 vessels involved, 30 at Ronas Voe and 90 at the Ness, the biggest centre of all, and they paid a good deal more for the privilege.[37] In 1613 the Fife fleet was joined by 18 doggers from Fisherrow, with their 'cost syd men' – the ones who stayed ashore; in 1604, the Fife men had brought 37 brewers to keep the fleet supplied with beer and ale.[38] The Scottish fleets were not the only visitors. The Dutch had established a base for herring fishing in Bressay Sound (the beginnings of Lerwick), and the English, though perhaps more interested in the distant waters around Iceland, did occasionally fish in the area.[39]

Despite the disparity between the records of Orkney and Shetland, it is still possible to use the rentals of both to calculate, at least approximately, what the figures contained in them mean in actual victual yield in modern units. The *lispund*, which was used as the unit of grain measure in Orkney, and of butter measure in both Orkney and Shetland, was equivalent to a *tron stone*, or 1 stone 8 lbs 1 oz (marginally under 10 kilos). In Orkney the 1595 rental makes these quantities fairly easy to compute. In Shetland, since each penny yielded one sixth of a lispund for both skat (paid by all assessed persons whether tenants of the earl or not) and landmail, then a simple calculation can be made. In Shetland the cuttell, both the measuring instrument and unit of measurement for wadmel extended at this date to 21 inches,[40] and this can be used in the same way. In the case of butter measure for skat in Shetland each penny yields, not butter alone but equivalent measures of butter and oil. Thus six pennies yields three pennies each of butter and oil. In butter this means half a lispund. Oil measure is more difficult to compute, but it seems likely that the oil barrel is almost certainly the same capacity as that for butter.[41] If so, then a barrel holds 12 lispunds of butter or nine *bulls* (= 36 cans) of oil. One sixth of a lispund of butter is therefore equivalent to half a can, which is in turn equal to a Scots pint or imperial quart.

Shetland also contributed the time-honoured duties of *leanger* and *wattle*. Leanger had originally been a duty paid to the chamberlain 'as ane discharge of all dewties' – presumably when all other duties had been paid – and wattle had originally taken the form of hospitality for the foud. These had changed their nature over the years, but by the Stewart time wattle was paid in cash and leanger in wadmel at the same rate as skat and landmail. The total figure can be derived from a list in the 1628 rental. Peat measurement presents some difficulties. In Shetland there are few early references to peat, and the peat levy, with its fathom measure of 126.9 cubic

37 Court of Session Recs: Acts and Decreets, NRS CS7/175, ff. 242v–8v.
38 *The Court Book of Shetland, 1602–4* ed. G. Donaldson (SRS), 1954, 141–2; the names of most of the brewers suggest that they had come with the boats, but among them are a Leask, a Leith, a Halcro, two Sinclairs, an Irving and a Bruce. Of the whole group, eight were women.
39 *Ct Bks of O & S, 1614–15*, 65; Anderson, *Robert Stewart*, 124; *Ct Bk of Shetland 1602–4*, 106.
40 O & S Papers, NRS RH9/15/165, cited in Smith, 'Bismars and Pundars', 10–11.
41 Brian Smith takes this view: 'Bismars and Pundars', 6–7; personal discussion.

metres – three to four times as big as that of Orkney – may have been Patrick's own invention. Peats in Orkney are extremely difficult to calculate, since there was a wide variety of different fathoms in use in different areas,[42] yet the rental of 1595 makes no distinction and gives no measurement. If, however, the fathom was about 35 cubic metres, then the total for Orkney (just short of 106 fathoms) would be 3,710 cubic metres. For Shetland the total annual income in kind was something like 14 tons of butter, 240 gallons of oil, over 20 miles of wadmel, 10 oxen and 138 sheep.[43]

Another source of income consisted of fines from the court of Shetland and Orkney, whose extant record begins in July 1602. The laws of Orkney and Shetland were still a form of the Norse law established by the Scandinavian settlers, though deriving them from what we know of the *Gulathinglaw* of Norway, generally thought to be their main source, is difficult, not least because the Orkney and Shetland versions of the law display striking dissimilarities, both from the original and from each other. Their independence from Scots law was guaranteed by the parliament of Scotland as late as 1567. There was, it is true, some degree of assimilation to Scottish practice. The surviving court documents of Orkney, and the priceless Shetland court book of 1602–4, said to be the second oldest court book in the Scandinavian world, are all in Scots, as the language of administration had long been, and the general form seems similar to contemporary Scottish models. Nevertheless there are many significant differences in the law as practised, one of which, that relating to foreshore, even survives today. It is not intended to go into the system in detail here, since its implications become clear as the story of the Stewart earldom unfolds, but it is as well to sketch out some elements of it.

The Shetland court book, our main source for the whole of island law-giving, far from being a record of tyranny, as one might have expected given the Stewart reputation, gives rather the impression of a long-established legal system coming full-grown into our ken, and it seems likely that neither earl interfered in any significant way in a centuries-old process. What we meet are humdrum cases, one after another, of petty theft, defamation, assault, disobedience, swine-rooting (grubbing up by pigs of other peoples' land – a very common grumble) ordinances regarding payment of skat, landmail and dues by foreign merchants, all parading before the earl or his depute as they perambulate through the islands. Norse and Scots law seem to co-exist peaceably enough. Two suicides were *escheated* in the Scottish fashion without objection, while one woman in Yell was fined in accordance with ancient Norwegian law for delay in burying her dead.[44] The death penalty, though threatened on a number of occasions,[45] was used only once during 1602–4, in the

---

42 A. Fenton, *The Northern Isles: Orkney and Shetland*, Edinburgh, 1978, 214–15; for remarks on modern units equivalent to peat fathoms, see Anderson, *Black Patie*, app. 3.

43 Murray, 'Sir John Skene', 126–7.

44 *Ct Bk of Shetland*, 18, 56; 23, 58; 73; Donaldson, *Shetland Life under Earl Patrick*, 117.

45 *Ct Bk of Shetland*, 3, 8, 30, 31.

case of a sheep stealer – a familiar penalty for persistent offenders.[46]

Besides the court book, there is the extraordinarily detailed list of complaints of the Shetlanders against Laurence Bruce in 1577 for oppression in 1577, with its ample public 'probatiounis' for each charge, its talk of *grandrie* and *sculding, cowp bills* and *swine-rooting*, was evidence of the continuing vitality of the native system of law there. In addition there are *schownd bills*, the Norse equivalent of a testament. There are only a few, it is true, but they are interesting, particularly from a Shetland perspective, as a Norse survival wholly unknown in Orkney. They are couched in terms very similar to Scottish practice, but crucially include heritage as well as movables. This contrasts with the curious arrangements in Orkney, where there was during the period a commissary – the Scottish official charged with administration of testaments and movable inheritance – but there is no evidence at all that he ever practised. All the testaments of the period for Orkney, also a handful and including Earl Robert's own, are to be found in the register for Edinburgh. In Orkney, only a handful of court documents survive, but they do suggest a court routine of three diets per year – the *Herdmanstein* in January, a second in July, and the All-Hallow court in the late autumn, but the number of instances is so few that it is difficult to make any detailed analysis, though others have tried, and some instances will be examined presently.

All this made up the stuff of Robert's great adventure, in time inherited by his son. For someone described as 'vain and nothing worth', it seems an extraordinarily ambitious enterprise, particularly in his worsting of Bellenden and Bothwell, who one might think were abler men, and both of whom never forgave him, pursuing him by whatever means possible for the rest of his and their lives, invoking such support as they could. In the face of this and the looming disapproval of the king, Robert was never, to the end of his life, able to make his position finally secure.

He also had trouble closer to home. Jean Kennedy was to suffer much for her husband in furtherance of his affairs. Her initial marriage settlement would have derived from the lands of Holyrood. The exchange by her husband of these for the estates of the bishopric of Orkney, and the grant to her of a *liferent* right to the lands in Birsay, therefore involved her in the general acrimony with Bellenden and Bothwell. Later, Robert was to exchange the Birsay source for her income for that of estates in Deerness, Stronsay and elsewhere. These were in turn to be feued off by Robert during troubles that beset him in the 1580s, an issue that would cause serious difficulties after his death. This, and his dalliances in Orkney while the countess remained for the most part resolutely in the south, were to result in the breakdown of the marriage in Robert's last years, and bitter disputes after his death.

Jean Kennedy did not accompany Robert on his first trip north, and he wrote to Bellenden of Auchnoull shortly after his arrival, speaking of sending a ship for both her and the justice clerk. By May 1572 she was writing to Sir John Bellenden that she had just arrived in Arbroath from Orkney, after 'aucht dayis being veray

---

46 *Ct Bk of Shetland*, 18–19, 56; Donaldson, *Shetland Life under Earl Patrick*, 121.

seik upone the sey' since when she had spent the time pursuing Bothwell to resolve his differences with her husband.[47] Later, she was commissioned by her husband to negotiate with the regent regarding the thirds of Holyrood, and on 26 July 1574, in Edinburgh, she concluded a contract on Orkney butter with merchants Edward Little and Alexander Couston. The experience of a sea journey to Orkney had clearly been a chastening one, and she set foot in the islands again only once,[48] despite Robert's attempts to persuade her. She certainly remained very reluctant to do so. Years later, on 4 May 1584, Robert wrote to Sir Patrick Waus recognising the latter's efforts to induce the countess to travel north, 'for trewlie I am unable to sustene and furthbeir hir charges ony forther in thay partis'.[49] She in turn was complaining that, despite her efforts on his behalf, she received nothing from him for her maintenance, and Robert sought to refute this by enclosing with his letter a list of the sums of money he had sent her since his last return to Orkney, amounting to nearly £2,500. She seems to have spent most of her time in or about the capital, and she had a house in the Canongate, where the earl of Bothwell visited her in 1589.[50] The marriage remained fractious and, in the last months of Robert's life, she was suing him before the session for maintenance arrears and before the commissaries of Edinburgh for divorce on grounds of 'the filthie cryme of adulterie'. When he died she was quick to seek her just due from his estate.

47 Bellenden Papers, NLS Adv. Ms. 22.3.14, no. 19.
48 Bellenden Papers, NLS Adv. Ms. 22.3.14, no. 36.
49 *Barnbarroch Corresp.*, 287–9.
50 *CSP Scot.*, x, 39.

4

Ane Pretendit Heritabill Infeftment

When Adam Bothwell left Orkney in 1561 it brought to an end his only lengthy residence there. For the next five years, his visits were regular enough, but were restricted to periods of a month or two in the summer and autumn.[1] His immediate purpose in leaving the islands was to seek the queen's help against the importunities of Bellenden of Auchnoull, but he was glad to depart. When in 1567 attention was drawn to the fact that he had not dwelt permanently in his diocese for the previous six years, he ascribed this to the fact that he could not 'remain in Orkney all the year, by reason of the evil air and the weakness of his body',[2] and shortly before his departure his servant James Alexander described his master as 'mervallis seik and beleefit nocht to haif recuverit'.[3]

The bishop's decision to make only periodic visits to the islands robbed Bellenden of Auchnoull of a permanent, if reluctant, channel of influence there. In addition, the man whom Bothwell regarded as Bellenden's chief mischief-maker in the north, Henry Sinclair of Strom (latterly of Brough), died some time before 4 July 1563.[4] For these reasons a new figure appeared on the scene in Orkney – Auchnoull's brother, Patrick Bellenden. As a readier ally than the bishop – even to the extent of marrying Henry Sinclair's widow, Katherine Kennedy[5] – he received land and would receive office in Orkney. In Kirkwall on 12 July he was granted a charter by Magnus Halcro of Brough of 6d land in Stenness – Housequoy, Mekilquoy, Dowscarth and others.[6] At the same time he was, as we have seen, involved in dark events at court, and Gilbert Balfour's idea of the islands as a haven when affairs in the south became too hot may also have appealed to Patrick. He built no Noltland, but the 'Palace' of Stenness, a house standing near the kirk of Stenness, elaborate for its date and situation, may have been his work; it is said to have been possible to see ships in Hoy Sound from its upper windows, which seems

---

1 Donaldson, 'Bishop Adam Bothwell', 94.
2 Donaldson, 'Bishop Adam Bothwell', 99.
3 M. Napier, *Memoirs of Napier of Merchiston* (Letters of Adam Bothwell), Edinburgh and London, 1834, 73.
4 *RSS*, v, no. 1419.
5 NRS (microf.) RH4/35/388/41.
6 *OSR*, 135, no. 65.

unlikely given the local topography, but nonetheless suggests a large building.[7]

Patrick's charter included among its witnesses Gilbert Balfour and William Halcro of Aikers, one of the supporters of Magnus Halcro of Brough in his contract with the earl of Caithness of the same year, where Magnus, with certain named followers, accepted the earl's protection. *Precept* was given to Halcro of Aikers, and the *instrument of sasine* was witnessed by Magnus's brother Ninian Halcro and Nicol Chalmers, both henchmen of the Caithness contract, and by George and Thomas Bellenden. Also witnessing both charter and sasine was another notable newcomer to the northern scene – William Henderson, Dingwall Pursuivant. He almost certainly arrived with Patrick Bellenden, and was later stated to be Auchnoull's factor in Orkney[8] – a point that reinforces the view that Patrick had come to Orkney at least partly on his brother's behalf. Henderson continued to carry out his functions in the south as a royal messenger for some time after his first appearance in Orkney,[9] but later he and his brother Cuthbert were to settle in the islands and receive ecclesiastical charges and grants of land. William's tomb can be seen in St Magnus cathedral to this day;[10] his importance for the present discussion, however, lies more in his observation and reporting of events than any significant part he played in them.

Patrick Bellenden's first visit to Orkney was brief. Little over a month after the first reference to his being there, he was in Edinburgh. On 17 August he granted a bond to Gilbert Balfour for £1,000.[11] George Bellenden remained in the north, and was acting as sheriff depute in December 1563.[12] This visit was no doubt in preparation for negotiations the following year between the three notables, Balfour, Bothwell, Bellenden of Auchnoull, and their arbiters. At the same time, Auchnoull was seeking to extend his power through the acquisition of the lands in Stronsay and Hoy. Bothwell was in the north later in the year.[13] He was followed at the beginning of 1565 by Patrick Bellenden, who presided as sheriff in Kirkwall; James Redpath, Oliver Sinclair's appointee of a quarter-century before, was depute.[14]

This time Patrick's visit was longer. He was still in Orkney in April when he granted his brother an obligation of any money that might accrue in obtaining a charter of the bishop's lands of Evie,[15] though he was soon back in Edinburgh where, eighteen days later, he received the bishop's charter of the Evie lands as well as the island of Eynhallow, Berstan in St Ola and further lands in Stenness – Tormiston,

7 P. Leith, 'The Bellendens and the Palace of Stenness', *POAS*, xiv (1936–7), 41–4; see also the denouement of Walter Scott's *The Pirate*.

8 Roxburghe Mun., bundle 1634, no. 6.

9 *TA*, xi, 356.

10 RCAHMS *Inv.*, O & S, ii, 132.

11 Reg. Deeds NRS RD1/6, f.387.

12 Craven Beq., NRS GD106/259.

13 Sinclair of Mey Mun., NRS GD96/165.

14 *REO*, 118, no. liii.

15 Roxburghe Mun., bundle 1612.

Culston and Hobbister.[16] Whether at this time or later, it is also likely that he received the Stronsay and Hoy lands previously sought by his brother,[17] and he was further granted a charter of the lands of the subdeanery of Orkney, embracing subjects in Sandwick, Stromness, St Ola, Hoy, Walls and Kirkwall, as well as the manse of the vicar of Unst in Shetland.[18]

Patrick Bellenden quickly made his influence felt, and installed his followers in positions of influence, granting them parcels of land and *bailiary offices*. He also threw himself into the maelstrom of dubious dealings in northern waters. On 23 July 1566 Humierus Meager, a German merchant in Shetland, was attacked by a band of pirates, who said that they were acting in the name and authority of Patrick Bellenden.[19] Piracy, like the attentions of English and Highland invaders, was endemic in Orkney and Shetland throughout the sixteenth century, but the year 1566 was a period of particularly intense and interesting activity. Humierus Meager was by no means the only European trader to suffer. On 28 May Herman Schroeder was attacked at Whalsay Sound and his ship and *booth* spoiled, Segeband Detken and John Beling received the same treatment three days later at Uyeasound, and in succeeding weeks so too did Theodor Fogen, Johan Michel and Luderus Brummer.[20] Orcadians, too, had problems; on 1 September the ship of William Irving, son of James Irving of Sebay, was stolen from its mooring in Kirkwall Roads.[21]

Three groups of robbers were involved in these actions. Those accused of the theft of William Irving's vessel were a varied lot – Scotsmen from Leith, Burntis-land, Caithness and Crail, with English and French accomplices. Bellenden's alleged followers, the attackers of Meager, were a mixture of Scots and Orcadians – William Gifford, Robert Chalmers and Andrew Mowat from South Ronaldsay and John Roen, Peter Loch and John Piper. The third group, which had attacked merchants Schroeder, Fogen and Michel, Beling and Detken, consisted of James Edmiston, George Foggo, William Simpson, John Orr, George Black and their leader, John Blackadder. This last group contained some significant names, names suggesting that Patrick Bellenden was by no means the most important person whose seamen were involved in dubious ventures in those parts; but he clearly intended to be a major participant in the action.

On 24 September 1566 William Blackadder, George Foggo and John Orr were granted commission to search for 'pirattis, sey thevis, rubbaris, pilliaris, rebellis and malefactouris upoun the seyis' who had been active in the Orkney area,[22] possibly

16 *RMS*, iv, no. 1710.

17 *RPC*, ii, 409–10.

18 *REO*, 288, no. clxx.

19 *RPC*, xiv, 268; full modern transcript and details given in *Shetland Documents 1195–1579*, ed. B. Smoth and J Ballantyne, 115–18, no. 158.

20 *RPC*, xiv, 268 ; for further details of Detken's career, see Donaldson, *Shetland Life under Earl Patrick*, 60; RCAHMS *Inv.*, O & S, iii, 128, also 142, fig. 663.

21 *REO*, 375, no. ccxxxviii.

22 *RSS*, v, no. 3046.

in response to the complaints of William Irving and the German merchants. Blackadder was a servant of Bothwell, having acted on the latter's behalf since at least June of the same year.[23] Ultimately he was to be accused of the king's murder and to suffer torture and death for it.[24] Foggo and Orr were among those named as their attackers by the merchants in Shetland, and the leader of their group, John Blackadder (surely a relative of William), and James Edmiston, another of the band, also eventually suffered for Bothwell. Considering that Foggo and Orr, and probably the others as well, were seemingly prominent members of the class of persons they were supposed to be pursuing, it is hardly surprising that their commission was revoked a mere three weeks later on the grounds that it was being abused; they were prohibited from molesting anyone, natives or strangers, 'undir the cullour and pretense of the lettres of marque or sey brevis of the kingis of Denmark, Sweden or ony uther foreign prince' under pain of being accounted pirates.[25]

Events at court now brought a serious reverse to Patrick's plans. The Darnley match and the eclipse of Moray brought Sir James Balfour of Pittendreich, Gilbert's brother, to prominence, and he and Riccio became 'most potent in the Queen's counsels'.[26] Gilbert was appointed master of the royal household on 1 October 1565, and granted Patrick's sheriffship of Orkney.[27] On 17 June the following year he also received the lands of Thurrigar, Sorquoy and Barswick in South Ronaldsay, together with the Pentland Skerries.[28] Balfour of Pittendreich's rise coincided with the return to Scotland from France of James Hepburn, earl of Bothwell, in the autumn of 1565, and a year later he was active as a henchman of the earl.[29] But events were changing fast, in the turbulent climax to Queen Mary's personal rule in Scotland. Gilbert Balfour's attitude to events at court followed those of his brother. Pittendreich's involvement in the murder of the king in February 1567 is mysterious but deep. Gilbert and his brother Robert were also implicated, and a placard pinned to the door of the Edinburgh Tolbooth inculpating Bothwell, Pittendreich and others also stated, 'and if this be not true, speir at Gilbert Balfour'.[30] The Balfours were included in the queen's remission of Bothwell's crimes, but growing estrangement between Pittendreich and the earl, plus the steadily weakening position of both Bothwell and the queen herself, drove James Balfour into the arms of Bothwell's enemies. Brother Gilbert went with him. By the time Bothwell left Scotland for the last time, now briefly elevated to duke of Orkney at the behest of the queen, Gilbert Balfour had retired to Orkney and he denied the duke (Bothwell) the strongholds of Noltland

23   R. Gore-Browne, *Lord Bothwell*, London, 1937, 255.

24   Gore-Browne, *Lord Bothwell*, 395.

25   *RPC*, i, 481; A. F. Steuart, 'Gilbert Balfour of Westray', *Old Lore Miscellany*, iv (1911), 148; Gore-Browne, *Lord Bothwell*, 405; Reg. Deeds NRS RD1/9, f. 367; Roxburghe Mun., bundle 1634, no. 1.

26   P. McNeill, 'Sir James Balfour of Pittendreich', *JR*, v (1960), 6.

27   *RSS*, v, no. 2352.

28   *RMS*, iv, no. 1759

29   McNeill, 'Sir James Balfour of Pittendreich', 9.

30   Steuart, 'Gilbert Balfour of Westray', 148; Gore-Browne, *Lord Bothwell*, 405.

and Kirkwall, and probably assisted the Grange expedition that arrived shortly after in pursuit.

The expedition, in which bishop Adam Bothwell also figured prominently, came very close to intercepting Bothwell in Shetland, and might well have done so had Sir William Kirkcaldy of Grange not ignored the advice of his seamen. In attempting to intercept one of the duke of Orkney's vessels, his ship foundered in Bressay Sound on a submerged rock, named to this day the *Unicorn* after its victim. Bishop Adam, clad in armour, was last to leave the ship, and was compelled to exert all his strength in leaping into the crowded ship's boat, to the peril of its passengers. Their quarry in the meantime made his way overland northwards, enshipped in the North Isles, and made his escape.[31] On the expedition's unsuccessful return to Leith, the scene was now set for a major change in the history of the Northern Isles.

With the final defeat of the queen at the battle of Langside, following which Gilbert Balfour fled to Sweden, Patrick Bellenden was briefly able to re-assert himself as sheriff, but less than a month after his receipt of the Evie charter his growing power in the islands was brought to a halt. He lost the office of sheriff for good to the newly-arrived Robert Stewart. It was something he was never afterwards to recover, even though he was to make his home in the islands, found a dynasty of lairds, and live on into the following century, fuming with enmity towards the Stewarts.

Robert Stewart arrived in Orkney towards the end of October 1567, probably on the *Muryeone*, a 'hoy schip' acquired from two Dutch merchants, John Egburg and Broune Claus.[32] According to William Henderson in a letter to Auchnoull, Gilbert and James Balfour, as well as Laurence Bruce of Cultmalindie, received recompense, probably for services rendered in the enterprise.[33] David and James Bruce, presumably Cultmalindie connections, were granted pensions. Gilbert Balfour had been guaranteed Westray and Papa Westray 'als frely haldin of the said lord [Robert] as he halds Orknay of the Kyngs majestie', in return for yielding the sheriffship and the Kirkwall Castle keepership. All this was clearly reward for supporters and placating of possible opponents. Other minor characters were mentioned as being 'in Orkney'. Robert Campbell, Thomas Cumming and Thomas Sanderson were all men of the Canongate.[34]

According to Henderson, the winter of Robert Stewart's first year in the north was a grim one. The weather was so bad that he had great difficulty in shipping out

---

31 Gore-Browne, *Lord Bothwell*, 405.
32 Reg. Deeds NRS RD1/9, f. 367.
33 Roxburghe Mun., bundle 1634, no. 1.
34 *Ct Bk of the Canongate*, 3, 231, 402; a Thomas Cumming had been in Orkney since at least 1527 (*REO*, 208, no.civ) and was presumably the Thomas Cumming 'in Orkney' cited as father of Thomas Cumming accused in the Canongate Burgh Court of theft (p. 402). His reasons for being in the north were therefore much older than Robert's expedition and as open to speculation as those of John Brown or John Cullen.

to his master and mistress victual which was 'verray scars in thir pairtis this yeir',[35] and later he reported that 'god hes plagit this cuntrie with mony plagis this yeir, god for his gudness to put remeid thairto'.[36] To the unrest in nature, Robert added a fresh turbulence in the north. Nevertheless, Henderson noted, 'My lord hes bene deligent in the furthsetting of justice and hes put gud ordor and rewle in the cuntrie god gif him grace to continew'. On 1 November Robert had heard complaints by the 'puir commownis' who occupied the lands of the subdeanery of Orkney, about exactions by servants of the bishop and by Patrick Bellenden.

It is clear that Robert's 'furthsetting of justice' involved rooting out Bellenden's arrangements in the islands. Robert, according to Henderson, was 'myndit to do him na plesor', and Bellenden departed from Orkney 'in ane strange maner', protesting that Robert had 'evictit his friends and servands furth of thair rowmes and baily-eries' and his wife and children from their heritage, and had put John Houston in charge of the lands of the subdeanery.[37] Henderson denied these charges, except in the case of William Halcro [of Aikers] who, he said, had lost his bailiary of Firth and Stenness for dishonesty.

On 10 November, the earl of Moray, now regent, acting on reports that his brother Robert intended to intromit with the lands of the lordship and earldom 'under pretense of ane pretendit heritabill infeftment', issued an order discharging tenants and occupiers from paying their dues until the question of title had been decided.[38] Clearly Patrick Bellenden, with the ear of the regent, was attacking Robert at his weakest point, the shakiness of his title to the lands he had acquired. Both Robert and William Henderson stated to Auchnoull that Robert was 'veray heychly offendit'[39] at Patrick, but Robert was prepared for Auchnoull's sake to take him back as a vassal, and even to make him some recompense if he were prepared to admit that his declarations to the regent were based on 'sinister information . . . utherwys your lordship wil nocht think that I can forgif sic offence as he hes done to me'.[40] Later letters were to contain less veiled threats.

On 20 December, in view of the new circumstances, parliament officially recog-nised the separate laws of Orkney and Shetland.[41] At about the same time Robert intercepted certain of Bothwell's fleeing followers[42] including Edmund Blackadder and the laird of Beanston[43] who had been named as murderers of the king 'with

35 Roxburghe Mun., bundle 1634, no. 2.

36 Roxburghe Mun., bundle 1634, no. 3.

37 Roxburghe Mun., bundle 1634, no. 2; he was actually granted a charter of these lands on 23 March 1568 and infeft by proxy on 2 August the same year (REO, 288, no. clxx).

38 RPC, i, 589.

39 Roxburghe Mun., bundle 1634, no. 2.

40 Roxburghe Mun., bundle 1634, no. 5.

41 APS, iii, 41.

42 Selections Illustrative of the History of Scotland, mdxliii–mdlxviii (Maitland Club), 1837, 306.

43 Roxburghe Mun., bundle 1634, no. 6.

the hands' in company with Gilbert Balfour.[44] Robert threw them in chains and wrote to his brother regarding their disposal. Moray told him to liberate the ship and crew that had been carrying them, to hang the less important of Bothwell's men and send the leaders to Edinburgh. Six were sent south to face execution 'with greater solemnity'.[45] This use of his services did not imply recognition by the regent of Robert's rule in Orkney and Shetland, nor did an ordinance of the General Assembly of 25 February 1568 charging him to assist Gilbert Foulsie and James Annand, commissioners for the planting of kirks, and to maintain the collector of thirds.[46] Owing to Patrick Bellenden's activities, Robert stated that he dared not leave the islands 'wythout that my lord regent send me his wrytting to assuir me to cum and gang unmolestit in my body or possessioun of this cuntrie'.[47]

Robert now travelled about his new domain, accompanied by Henderson, Foulsie and James Alexander, commissary of Orkney. On 6 February he was at Burness in Firth.[48] A fortnight or so later he was at St Peter's Kirk, South Ronaldsay.[49] On 16 March he rode from Kirkwall, accompanied by Foulsie and Henderson, to the house of John Gifford at Gorn in Sandwick.[50] Already there was trouble brewing. The following morning one of his servants, John Brown, newly arrived in Orkney, went to morning prayers in the cathedral. When the service was over, he made to ascend the turnpyke stair to the *pends* (*triforium*) of the cathedral. The bishop's men, who were charged with guarding the building, warned him to leave, or they would fire on him. He, 'nocht knawand that it was kepit gaif thame sharp words agane and thocht that it was done in dispyt'. He went and told his colleagues in the castle. On hearing his story, a group of Robert's servants – James and Patrick Monteith, George Dundas, Thomas Robeson, Walter Bruce, David Scollay and William Sclater[51] – 'in ane angir ruschit' from the castle, in company with Brown. The bishop's men, seeing the latter coming towards them, shot Brown dead. Robert's men entered the cathedral and opened fire, killing in the process bishop's men Nicol Alexander and James Moir. The others fled, lowering themselves out of the building on a rope, leaving Robert's men in possession.

This at any rate was Henderson's story when he and Robert wrote to Bellenden of Auchnoull three days later.[52] About three o'clock on the afternoon of 17 March, on hearing what had happened, Robert had immediately returned the ten miles or so to Kirkwall, arriving after dark. When he heard the details he 'wald nocht pass to the castell nor suffir his servands to speik wyth him', but went to the house of

---

44 CSP Scot., ii, 321.
45 C. Nau, The History of Mary Stewart, ed. J. Stevenson, Edinburgh, 1883, app. ii, 149–50.
46 BUK, i, 134.
47 Roxburghe Mun., bundle 1634, no. 6.
48 REO, 286, no. clxix.
49 REO, 116, no. li.
50 Roxburghe Mun., bundle 1634, no. 3.
51 RSS, vi, 306.
52 Roxburghe Mun., bundle 1634, nos 3, 5.

Hugh Gordon and remained there two days, during which he made an investigation of the incident and conferred with the 'honest men of the cuntrie' about what
to do. When he and Henderson wrote to the justice clerk on 20 March, Robert left
the narrative to Henderson, who also wrote to Patrick Bellenden. Both emphasised
Robert's lack of responsibility. For Robert, the incident was 'chanceit by [without]
his expectatioun and sair aganis his will'. Robert himself explained that it had taken
place in his absence 'but ony motyve bot of suddantye'. Both noted Robert's desire
to make recompense, with particular regret at the death of Nicol Alexander, who
was 'ferd' of kin (i.e. in the fourth degree of kinship). Robert desired Henderson to
remind Auchnoull of 'the auld affectioun and kyndness that hes bene betuix him
and you and siklyk betuix him and your broder Patrik and how that ather of your
bairnis and his ar ferds of kyne quhilk suld move you to luf and favor wyth us', and
thus to use his good offices in the 'dress' of the matter.

At first sight these letters seem to sound a sincere note of regret. The incident in
the cathedral hardly served Robert's desire for respectability as ruler of the islands,
and could have jeopardised his further plans. He and Henderson now set these
out in their letters, though probably not for the first time. In Henderson's words,
Robert was 'bent to haif superiorite of this cuntrie alswel of the bishopryc as the
rest'. Robert himself stated that he intended to achieve this by 'the interchance and
cois [exchange] of . . . [the bishop's] leiffing and myne and of the lands of Birsay
with your self and my lands of the Kers'. The bishop was very unwilling and Robert
would deny the justice clerk nothing should he help him to effect this. Robert
amplified these thoughts in a further letter of 31 March, stating, 'I think my land of
the Kers is als gud as the lands of Birsay and lykwys the superiorite and the bailyerie
of the Cannogait to be als gud as the bailyerie of the bischopis lands of Orknay and
Yetland.' To satisfy Auchnoull he was prepared to 'augment' him with the bailiary of
Kers (in addition to that of Broughton) 'swa that ye haiffand thai twa bailyereis thair
is na man in Lowthean may do bettir service to thair prynce'.

There now arose further cause for difference with the regent. In his letter of 31
March,[53] Robert stated that he had been 'falsely dissavit' by one Robert Boswell
who had undertaken to transport the laird of Beanston, Bothwell's captured
follower, to Leith 'and not to suffir him to eschew', but had instead taken his captive
to the south coast of the Moray Firth and there put him and his followers ashore.
Two of Robert's servants sent 'to convoy' had assisted in this, and the regent was
'informit that thai ar eschewit be my moyane [influence]'. Boswell had also apparently taken Edmund Blackadder, for whom Gilbert Balfour was to answer, and
would not hand him over.

However, the issues that take up the letters of both Robert and William
Henderson – Robert's dispute with Patrick Bellenden, his desire for an excambion
with the bishop, the fighting in the cathedral – were much more clearly linked than
the early correspondence suggests. Robert's chief complaint against Patrick was

53 Roxburghe Mun., bundle 1634, no. 6.

that as a result of the reports he and his followers had given to Moray, the regent was not prepared to accept Robert's feu mails for Orkney – in other words to recognise his title to the islands. Patrick and his friends (among whom Robert named the earl of Morton) had accused him of acting out of hatred. This Robert denied, stating that his actions had been purely in the interests of justice, 'for I haif done na thing sen I came in Orknay be way of justice bot I will answer for it bayth befoir God and man'. The regent took Patrick's part, and in April 1568 sent Robert letters on Patrick's behalf.[54]

Robert feared that, as well as pouring poison in the ear of the regent, Patrick was planning direct action against him. Henderson's letter to Patrick immediately after the cathedral affair stated that Robert 'allegeis that ye ar the caus thairof for he is suirly informit ye haif tane up ane cumpany of suddarts [soldiers] and purpois to cum in this cuntrie in his contrar'. Eleven days later Robert spoke to Auchnoull of a bond consisting of Patrick and some Orkneymen intending 'to persew me in my body and to rute me and all myne perpetually furth of this cuntrie gif it may ly in thair power'.[55] Finally, in a letter of 1 June, Henderson named Patrick's followers as including Magnus and William Halcro, Gilbert Balfour and William Moodie.[56] Robert, by now on his first visit to his other islands of Shetland, wrote abandoning his disavowal of responsibility for the events in St Magnus. 'The hail motyve and occasioun of the takyng of the kyrk' was this: Magnus Halcro had written to kinsman William telling of the bond involving Bellenden, Balfour and Moodie, and stating that Patrick was 'feand' soldiers to come to Orkney, take the steeple and force Robert to leave the islands 'and this to haif bene the bischopis devys'. Robert, 'takand ane feir thairof, caused his servants to take the kirk, but 'it was by his wil or wytting that ony slawchter suld haif bene maid'. It was already noticeable that, although ostensibly regretful at the deaths of Moir and Alexander, Robert had not ordered his men to evacuate St Magnus.

Despite all this, Robert's relationship with Bellenden of Auchnoull appears to have remained fairly cordial and he was clearly anxious that it remain so. Robert was constantly seeking Bellenden's assistance in his cause, while Bellenden was fostering Robert's son Henry[57] (a function he may also have performed for Adam Bothwell in youth).[58] This relationship echoes that which Robert was to have with Sir Patrick Waus, his son Patrick's guardian, twenty years later.[59] Robert suggested more than once that, since he could not come south, Bellenden should come north, 'and gif ye wald cum be sey I suld send ane bark of my awin for you and my wyf togidder'. At the same time, presumably on account of the *kindly* obligation between

54 Roxburghe Mun., bundle 1634, no. 7.
55 Roxburghe Mun., bundle 1634, no. 6.
56 Roxburghe Mun., bundle 1634, no. 8.
57 Roxburghe Mun., bundle 1634, no. 11.
58 J. Spottiswoode, *History of the Church of Scotland*, vols I–III, Edinburgh, 1851, ii (bk iv notes), 73.
59 *Barnbarroch Corresp.*, 238–9.

Bellenden of Auchnoull and his brother, he constantly reassured the justice clerk of his willingness to receive Patrick, despite his continual complaints of ill-usage at the latter's hands. He was reluctant even in the face of the regent's representations to make any contract with Patrick, but was prepared to make one with Auchnoull in his brother's name.

During the winter of 1567–8, having returned from Shetland, Robert was politically marooned in Orkney and sought Auchnoull's influence on events. Auchnoull for his part may have been under the impression that he was replacing Bothwell with Robert as his channel of influence in the north. Bothwell had complied up to a point with his uncle's wishes regarding the feuing of bishopric estates, but was proving otherwise reluctant, and was in any case cutting something of a figure on the public stage in his own right. Robert on the other hand had shown no previous indications of ability and was later to be described as 'of no great judgment' – though he had power, military experience and ruthlessness – and was doubtless regarded as easier to manipulate. Unfortunately for Auchnoull, neither he, nor other observers, knew their man. What Robert may have lacked in intellectual ability, he more than made up for in sly and slippery cunning.

Nevertheless, he was becoming desperate. Henderson's June letter contained what amounted to threats. He stated that of those directly interested in northern affairs, Robert feared only Auchnoull himself, since he did not believe that the bishop could do anything without the justice clerk's agreement, 'and he wil lay the hail wycht on your Lordship gif ony inconvenientis cums to him thairthrow'. Robert, being unable to come south, was prepared to give authority to his Holyrood chamberlain, Adam Bell, to treat with the bishop and the justice clerk and to do anything reasonable asked of him, 'bot gif he persavis na thing bot regour usit aganis him he wil do all the displesor that he dow or may aganis the bischop and his partakars'. He was prepared to take stern action to preserve his right and title to Orkney, 'and all that wil pretend to depryfe him thairof he wil nocht spair to tak thair lyffis . . . and he is ane man that wil get money assistars and it is dangerous deilying wyth him'. With regard to Robert and the bishop, Henderson said, 'I pray God that they war fairly sunderit furth of utheris way . . . for I haif na hop of thair aggreance sa lang as thai ar macheit in ane rowme togidder.' He repeated the view that had been noted in the March letters that since the lives of those killed could not be 'recuverit', it was better to make recompense than to go to the full extremity of the law. The best solution was for the bishop to take satisfaction for what had occurred and to allow 'the cois talkit of befoir to pas fordwart to perfectioun'.

Robert had been charged to present the cathedral killers before the privy council, and had undertaken, but failed, to do so. On 11 June the bishop received a gift of his escheat for this.[60] Robert now had forfeiture added to his troubles, and Henderson's letter of June maintained an aggressive tone. However the situation was easing. By 8

July Robert was back in the Canongate,[61] and on 18 August he was in the procession to parliament.[62] On 17 September he and Bellenden of Auchnoull began the legal moves which were to add the bishopric lands to the earldom and royal territories of which Robert was obviously now regarded as undisputed feuar.[63]

Robert's mixture of threats and promises to Bellenden seem to have provided the desired result, and had convinced the justice clerk that it would be wise to make the representations to Moray for which Robert had been asking since November 1567. The rewards that Bellenden was to reap from Robert's plans make this seem all the more plausible. Moreover since 8 May, when the deposed Mary escaped from imprisonment in Lochleven, the regent had had more than enough to bother him, and it was unlikely that he would give any high priority to the squabbles in the Northern Isles.

In the months after the return of Grange and his men from the north, Bishop Adam had not enjoyed a happy time. The Kirk Assembly of 1568 censured him for his limited attention to his diocese in favour of acting as a judge of the Court of Session, 'the sheep wandering without a pastor'; of retaining Francis Bothwell, 'a papist', in his company; and of solemnising the marriage of Mary and Bothwell, this being 'altogither wicked'.[64] He was deprived of his functions in the ministry,[65] though he was restored again in July 1568 on agreeing to make public confession of his fault on the last of these charges.[66] In part his problems were political. Attention has previously been drawn to 'a general atmosphere of suspicion', which singled out Bothwell at a time when the king's party could not rely on its supporters, but equally we may see the influence of Lord Robert and, more particularly, of Bellenden of Auchnoull.[67]

Whatever Bellenden's involvement in Robert's going north in the first place, the correspondence from Orkney suggests that the excambion was in fact Robert's idea. Mentioned soon after his arrival, it was clearly part of his plan before he ever set off. The way in which Henderson described the plan to his master, the way in which Robert sought to interest Bellenden in it, enticing him by a promise of a second bailiary, suggest that the original notion did not come from the justice clerk. On the other hand, the evidence that Bellenden was broadly sympathetic to Robert's aims in going north makes it seem strange that he was not made aware at the outset of a large-scale scheme of such profit to himself. The correspondence is, of course, demonstrably misleading on certain points, and it is possible that the letters were framed to suggest Robert as the instigator. Certainly the somewhat sudden way

61 Ct Bk of the Canongate, 76.
62 A Diurnal of Remarkable Occurrents, 135.
63 OSR, 162, no. 68.
64 BUK, i, 112.
65 BUK, i, 114.
66 BUK, i, 131.
67 Donaldson, 'Adam Bothwell and the Reformation in Orkney', 99.

in which Henderson brought the subject up in his letter of 20 March, in writing to an important man directly affected by the plan and likely to be of paramount mportance in bringing it about, suggests that Bellenden must have had at least some prior understanding of what was going on. Whatever the truth, there is no doubt about Bellenden's major role in the consummation of Robert's schemes.

On 17 September Robert and Sir John concluded a contract whereby the latter was to receive the Kerse barony lands, in exchange for which those of Birsay, held by Bellenden, were to pass to Robert's wife, Jean Kennedy, in liferent, and Mary, his daughter, in *fee*.[68] The charter to Mary Stewart was dated the following day; it contained a provision whereby she was bound to resign her lands to her father on payment of 400 gold crowns.[69] Three days later Robert made some small grants regarding land in the Canongate and Gorgie,[70] his last recorded actions as commendator of Holyrood. On 27 September, Adam Bothwell's final defeat was signalled when, at Fastcastle, en route for York with the regent for the queen's trial, he subscribed a contract with Robert regarding their lands and revenues[71] and granted a charter to Robert of his lands in Orkney,[72] and another, probably at the same time, of the lands of Dunrossness.[73] At Ayton on the same day, a precept passed the privy seal for a letter to the bishop granting him the abbey of Holyrood, and appointing him commendator for life, reserving a £1,000 pension to Robert.[74]

According to Adam Bothwell's later testimony, when Robert arrived in the south he lost little time in exerting naked physical pressure to force him into acquiescence, something he was seemingly able to do with impunity. Robert 'violently intruded himself in his whole living, with bloodshed and hurt of his servants; and after he had craved Justice, his and his servants' lives were sought in the very eyes of Justice in Edinburgh'.[75] He was forced to take the abbacy of Holyrood 'for meer necessity'. The bishop was now as isolated as Robert had seemed not long before. He could get no support from the kirk. There was apparently no curb whatever on Robert's activities; James Monteith, a likely leader of those seeking the lives of the bishop and his supporters, was respited on 26 September for his part in the cathedral killings.[76]

On 30 September in Edinburgh, Robert subscribed the Orkney contract and charter. They were registered three days later, together with his contracts with Bellenden, that of 17 September, and another regarding bishopric lands in Shetland.[77]

68 *OSR*, 162, no. 68.
69 *OSR*, 162, no. 68.
70 *RMS*, v, no. 378; *Calendar of the Laing Chrs*, 210, no. 834.
71 Court of Session Recs: Acts and Decreets, NRS CS7/42, f. 340.
72 *RMS*, v, no. 836.
73 Court of Session Recs: Acts and Decreets, NRS CS7/42, f.347.
74 *RSS*, vi, no. xlii.
75 *BUK*, ii, 165–6.
76 *RSS*, vi, no. 505.
77 Court of Session Recs: Acts and Decreets, NRS CS7/42, f. 347.

The contract of 27/30 September was a massive document. The bishop would infeft Robert in liferent, and Henry, his son, in fee, in all the bishopric lands not already feued to Sir John and Patrick Bellenden, Gilbert Balfour, and others, and set a 19-year tack to Robert of *teinds* not already feued and in the offices of bailiary and justiciary of Orkney, Shetland and Caithness; he was to deliver to Robert the palace of the Yards and the castle of Kirkwall with its artillery; with the respective offices of keeper and constable, funded from the mails of Birsay; and he was to discharge all bonds of manrent so that Robert could do as he pleased.

The contract was not strictly one of excambion, or exchange, since no mention was made of Robert's reciprocal grant of the lands of Holyrood, but it did include a number of obligations on Robert's part. He would grant the bishop a pension of £500; he would transfer to him the title of his wife and children to a tack of the teinds of Broughton, Inverleith and Wardie, and set a tack of them to the bishop, beginning with crop 1568; he would assign to the bishop an obligation made to him some years earlier by James Johnstone of Elphinstone, for victual from the teinds of Elphinstone; he undertook not to intromit with his £1,000 pension of the abbey during the bishop's lifetime. This provision makes the excambion seem much more favourable to the bishop than has previously been thought; however, Robert's cavalier attitude to his other obligations to the bishop, as will be seen, to some degree nullifies this. He would pay any arrears from the bishopric lands from the crop of 1567, and would ensure that William Lauder, Bothwell's chamberlain, came to Edinburgh to account for his intromissions with crop 1567, with penalties; finally, he would forget 'quhatsumevir anger, hatrent or displesor' that he had conceived against Patrick Bellenden, Magnus Halcro and other designated followers of the bishop.

The arrangement was clearly in Robert's favour. He would decide on the remainder conditions of the charters, the feu duty and the *augmentation*, the latter two of which could be named in money, and 'other clauses and privileges' to be contained in the document *setting* to him the bishopric lands. The bishop was bound to renew the infeftment and the tack of teinds as often as required. Robert's payment for this, his *reddendo*, was to be the usual price or 'sic ressonable pryce of money as [he] sall think most expedient'. Bishop Bothwell was receiving in exchange only a part of the lands of the abbey of Holyrood. He had no control over the Kerse and Ogleface baronies that had been granted to Bellenden of Auchnoull, who was bailie of the regality of Broughton, the barony lands of which formed the major part of what the bishop actually received. Robert and the justice clerk had concluded a further contract in which Bellenden undertook to ensure that the bishop lived up to, and maintained, his undertakings under the main contract.[78]

Adam Bothwell remained in England throughout the York and Westminster conferences of churchmen, returning to Scotland in February 1569. His troubles were still far from over, indeed he seems to have added to them by contracting

78 Court of Session Recs: Acts and Decreets, NRS CS7/42, f. 347.

debts in England,[79] but his pastoral work in Orkney and Shetland was at an end. The benefice of which he now became administrator presented its own difficulties, and these make an interesting postscript to Robert's tenure of the *commenda* of Holyrood. In March 1570 it was stated that all the 27 appropriated churches of Holyrood, even important ones like Liberton or St Cuthbert's, were decayed to a greater or lesser extent. Some were so ruinous that 'none darre enter them for fear of falling', the abbey itself being especially bad in this regard due to weakness in the two main pillars; others were so far gone that they had been made into sheepfolds. Two of the kirks, Falkirk and Whitekirk, having a total congregation of 600 souls or thereby, had 'never heard the word twice preached, nor received the sacraments, since the Reformatione'. The physical decay, according to the bishop, was due to the fact that the churches had been pulled down by 'some greedy persons, at the first beginning of the Reformatione, which hath never been helped or repaired sensyne'.[80]

Robert, however, had left all this behind. The way was now open for him to consolidate his rule over the lands he had won. He was back in Kirkwall by 2 May 1569.[81] Some arrangements still remained to be made, but essentially his achievement was complete. There now began the first lengthy period of his rule in Orkney and Shetland.

79 Roxburghe Mun., bundle 1634, no. 21.
80 *BUK*, i, 162–3, 165–7.
81 Roxburghe Mun., bundle 1634, no. 9.

5

Terrable to All

Robert Stewart stayed in the north from the spring of 1569 till about August 1575, when he returned to open arrest by the Regent Morton in Edinburgh Castle.[1] During the first year, argument continued on matters relating to the two excambions. In fact Robert's relationship with Bishop Bothwell was never finally stabilised. Bothwell, acutely embarrassed financially, was trying to extract arrears from William Lauder, his former chamberlain, speaking of 'the evill willit selfischnes of my servandis'.[2] In fruitless frustration, according to Lauder, he locked the chamberlain in 'ane cauld fast hous . . . quhair was na fyre nor eisment', compelled him to sign accounts and obligations under 'fear of perpetual ward' and 'wanting of fire and gret cauld'.[3] In the end, Lauder had a notarial instrument drawn up repudiating the deeds he had subscribed, on the grounds of duress. Under the terms of their contract, Robert had agreed to help Bothwell in recovering these funds, and to make sure Lauder would come to account in Edinburgh. In fact he refused Lauder permission to leave Orkney for nearly a year, until October 1569,[4] when he virtually threw him on to the ship, 'sa suddanlie and haistelie . . . that he micht nocht get nowther his writtingis nor yit his clathis to bring with him thairon . . .'[5] On 8 July 1569 William Bothwell, another of the bishop's servants, returned from Orkney saying that Robert, while speaking 'fair wordis', had not allowed him to take up any of the bishop's dues,[6] and supposed that Robert had done 'na less' in Shetland. He had become 'terrable to all that is within that boundis'. In the meantime the bishop faced, as he said, being 'eittin up be my creditors'. When confronted by attempts to recover outstanding arrears of the thirds of Holyrood, also in terms of the contract, Robert replied 'put me to the horne quhen ye will ye sall get na thing of me'.

1 Roxburghe Mun., bundle 1634, no. 9; *The Historie and Life of King James the Sext*, 1565–96 (Bannatyne Club), 1825, 157.

2 Roxburghe Mun., bundle 1634, nos 13–18, 19–23.

3 *Prot. Bk Gilbert Grote 1552–73*, ed. William Angus (SHS), Edinburgh, 1914, 80; Donaldson, 'The Early Ministers of the North Isles of Shetland', *Shetland News*, 9 Sept. 1943.

4 Roxburghe Mun., bundle 1634, no. 18.

5 *Prot. Bk Gilbert Grote*, 80–1.

6 Roxburghe Mun., bundle 1634, no. 14.

Lauder was not the only servant of Bothwell to be causing his master trouble. James Alexander, now commissary of Orkney, would not render account without recourse to law.[7] Bothwell was at the same time seeking legal action against Robert himself. He hoped to send William Bothwell north with a court officer, so that he could '*poynd* and *strenye*' where necessary with 'scharp chargis to me Lord Robert till caus me be abayit and assurit of the restis'.[8] The bishop sought Bellenden's support. His letters implied that Bellenden was scarcely in a better position as a result of Robert's doings in Orkney and Shetland. 'Suirlie I am verray sorie that on ather syid we ar in that povertie that nather of us may help uther and your Lordships distress in that point is mair grevous unto me than my awin.'[9] Despite this and the bishop's urgings, citing the support of the Lord Lyon,[10] by 30 October 1569, the date of Bothwell's last extant letter,[11] the regent had refused to permit the granting of arms to a messenger.

Robert's response to the bishop's problems, according to a letter to Bellenden dated 5 June 1569, was that he was unable to take possession of his new lands because Bothwell refused to subscribe the titles he had had drawn up, insisting that these, most notably his charter of the lands in Shetland, caused a reduction of the rental.[12] This Robert denied. While it was true that the Shetland charter departed from past practice in having payments calculated in money rather than kind, he explained to Bellenden the commodities of victual in Shetland butter and wadmel, giving equivalent weights and sums of money. As far as he was concerned, the charter 'contenit the haill soume of the rental albeit the pryce of silver be sett less nor may be gottin for it'. What Robert was forced to admit was that while the money payment might not have been in 'diminution' of the rental, it might well be, and in the future almost certainly would be, in diminution of the profit. A victual feu would retain a value commensurate with current prices, whereas a money payment would decline in value with inflation, with no mechanism for adjusting the payments to compensate. Robert justified himself on the grounds that the practice of changing payments from kind into money was now widespread 'and gif that be ane caus to reduce my chartor all the few chartors in Scotland that had wont to pay victual and ar turnit in silver will reduce'.

Bellenden relayed these arguments to Bothwell. The bishop replied that Robert wished to 'haf me my aris obleist to pay him ten thowsand pund gif ony successors that I salhef sall maik actioun of reduction aganis him'. It would at the same time be necessary for the bishop's successors to raise such an action 'as . . . may be justifeit be na law and that onles thai do the samen thai will not haf watter kaill to leve

7 Roxburghe Mun., bundle 1634, no. 18.
8 Roxburghe Mun., bundle 1634, no. 19.
9 Roxburghe Mun., bundle 1634, no. 21.
10 Roxburghe Mun., bundle 1634, no. 21.
11 Roxburghe Mun., bundle 1634, no. 23.
12 Roxburghe Mun., bundle 1634, no. 11.

upoun'. He had consulted wise men who were sympathetic to Robert's interests but who yet thought that Robert's proposed 'evidents' were not legally acceptable, and had made out charters of his own leaving out Robert's objectionable clauses before he sent them north on Robert's ship.[13] By 30 October Bellenden had still not replied and Bothwell had to allow the ship to leave without his documents.

The wrangling continued until finally, on 28 February 1570, a detailed agreement was drawn up, seeking to settle virtually all the outstanding issues between Robert and the bishop, and there were many.[14] Robert was conceded his tack of the bishopric lands and in return was to furnish the bishop with a number of items: a copy of the tack, appropriately confirmed; the obligation by Gilbert Balfour of 30 June 1560; an *acquittance* for the delivery of the Palace of the Yards; the common seals, registers and titles to Holyroodhouse; warrandice on the Holyroodhouse thirds and other matters; ratification by Jean Kennedy of Robert's contract with the bishop in respect of her former tacks of Broughton, Inverleith and Wardie. In addition Robert had to return various intromissions with the benefice of Holyrood; teinds and other duties of Broughton; arrears for Orkney and Shetland; and sundries, such as delivery of some munition cakes of lead (for the manufacture of bullets) from the Palace of the Yards; He was also to fulfil his contractual promise to the bishop's followers – this time noted as Francis Bothwell, Patrick Bellenden and Alexander Kincaid – that they might 'leve in quietnes peciabilnes and securitie'.

The length and detail of the document and the number of major issues and simple loose ends that required to be tidied up showed Robert's carelessness of legal forms and an impatience to take control of his lands which had left Bothwell, and probably Bellenden too, in a very awkward position for over a year. Robert might complain of his own difficulties, but there seems little doubt that he was already acting as feuar *de facto* and was consequently in a far stronger position than the other parties to the contracts of 1568. Moreover, it seems certain that the drawing up of the agreement was done on the bishop's side. The extant version is merely a draft, but the marginal annotations beside each clause all suggest it was submitted at the bishop's behest to Robert's commissioners, who inserted appropriate comments. Robert consented to most of the conditions, though he argued about the manner of his submitting a copy of the tack of the bishopric lands, would not surrender Balfour's obligation, but simply exhibit it before a judge, and he objected to refunding the cakes of lead from the Palace of the Yards.

The grants of the lands of Orkney and Shetland and of justiciary and bailiary were finally subscribed in July 1572.[15] Bishop Bothwell had at last prevailed over Robert. The payments for the lands were in both cases couched in victual. The bishop was perhaps correct in suggesting that Robert's contentions seemed wrong-headed even to those who supported him. On the other hand, why was the bishop

13 Roxburghe Mun., bundle 1634, no. 22.
14 Roxburghe Mun., bundle 1634, bundle 811.
15 *OSR*, 178, no. 69; Exchequer Records: Abbreviates of Charters of Kirklands, NRS E14, ii, 146–9.

now striving so hard to settle with Robert when only a few months before, in what
he implied were dire financial straits, he was still holding out? The reason may lie
with the General Assembly. On 3 March 1570, only a few days after the date of the
draft agreement, the Assembly produced a list of accusations against Bothwell.[16]
Like those of 1567–8, these charges seem more the result of a political campaign
against him than genuine evidence of his shortcomings. Again he was accused of
neglecting his pastoral duties for a seat in the session, and being responsible for
the dilapidated state of the *spiritualities* of Holyrood. He answered that many other
ministers were judges as well, and that he had had neither the time to improve his
new living nor a commission to plant kirks in the bare year since he had returned
from England.[17] As in 1568, his answers to the charges appear to have been accepted
with little further comment.

Whatever the motives behind the prosecution of Bothwell, whatever the part
played in it by Robert Stewart or by Bellenden, the inclusion in the accusations of
exchanging the lands of his diocese for those of a layman were to be the last major
reference to the excambion, and the agreement of 28 February (of which no fair
or registered copy seems to exist) was to be the last word for the time being on
the complicated relations between Robert Stewart and Adam Bothwell. Although
Bothwell may have proved himself against his accusers, the complaint in his rebuttals that his bishopric had been wrested from him under duress went unheeded, and
Robert had thus achieved the greater part of his ambitions.

In late May and early June 1569 Robert wrote twice to Auchnoull from Kirkwall.[18]
His first letter sought clarification of Bellenden's position on his troubles with the
bishop. In the second, however (in which he mentions that he has sent Janet Livingston south to take his son Henry from the justice clerk's custody), he turned to
his fraught relations with Patrick Bellenden. The reasons that he and Auchnoull's
brother were 'sa lang sindry' lay, he said, at the door of his servant James Monteith, a
ringleader in the earlier unrest. Monteith had now been 'put fra' him, and he sought
the justice clerk's help in mending relations with Patrick. (The first part of this statement is a demonstrable lie, as we shall see.) If he proved 'the honest man to me [he]
sal find me to be ane gud maister'. He hoped too that Auchnoull would counter any
evil that Monteith might speak to the regent.

Shortly before Robert's second letter, on 2 June, Magnus Halcro of Brough had
addressed himself to the justice clerk, also from Kirkwall.[19] His letter confirms the
opposition to Robert mentioned in Henderson's letters of 1567–8. 'Angir and ane
impatient hart' were the reasons that he had written to Bellenden 'sen this blak
excambioun wes maid for my part thairin is mair hevyar nor I will expreme in

16 *BUK*, i, 162–3.
17 *BUK*, i, 165–7.
18 Roxburghe Mun., bundle 1634, nos 9, 11.
19 Roxburghe Mun., bundle 1634, no. 10.

wrett'. He had had no wish to change masters and his 'gud mynd and service sall nocht be changit fra my lord the bischop nochtwythstanding all biganis' and the fact that his troubles were 'onrecompensit . . . all that I have done and gif it war ane hundretht tymes mair I think it weill warit'. He had, he said, never had so much of any man's gear as he had had of Bellenden's; he would not be found the 'ingraat man . . . and sal nevir refuis eftir my powar your lordship's querrell and charge'. He sought Bellenden's assistance in a feared dispute with Robert. He told Bellenden that he had heard that Robert had been promised a feu of 10d land in Rousay – 5d each of Skaill and Westness – which lay *runrig* with his own lands of Brough.[20] If Robert were to take possession of this grant 'it will at schorttyme returne to my trublis and wrak for . . . it is nocht gud to me to be pertinar in *rig and rendell* wyth my Lord Robert gif your Lordship knew quhat is and apperantlie wilbe amang us'. If this grant could be stopped, he was prepared to make recompense to Robert 'wyth geir and service to his plesour'.

Patrick Bellenden, having heard of Robert's approaches to his brother, wrote to him from Dalquharran in Carrick on 24 July.[21] He told Auchnoull that he offered Robert thanks, but that his absence from Orkney was from fear of enemies, and that he hoped to go north as soon as he could leave his other affairs. He reminded Sir John of articles subscribed between him and Robert 'with mony utheris promissis', no part of which was yet performed, although he had sustained great loss as a result. This had to be redressed before he could make any promises of fealty to Robert. 'Tharfor my lord (sen ye ken the natour of the man and how oft he is able to brek promissis) I will refer sik suirtie as his Lordship sowld mak to me (quharof the sum is that I be restorit to my officis and rowmes that I bruikit of befoir and the articlis to be fulfillit war first maid endit as your Lordship knawis) to be endit and devysit be your Lordships self. . . . ' It was to be some years before a settlement, or at least the form of one, was to be reached between Robert and Patrick Bellenden, and both men were to suffer considerable changes of fortune before that time. For the moment relations remained sour and Patrick remained furth of Orkney. Later he was to attempt to take direct action against Robert. For the time being, he remained a malign presence in the background, and Robert was now able to pursue the consolidation of his success.

Bellenden and Halcro's discontents were those of two major victims of Robert's chief preoccupation of the period 1569–75 – confirming his grip on his estates and their administration, at the expense of any whom he saw as rivals. In particular, he persecuted the Halcros, the friends of the former bishop, and their connections. He also conducted a campaign against Gilbert Balfour, conveniently absent in the service of the king of Sweden, and his large estates in Westray. At Burntisland on 13 April 1573, the notary Gilbert Groat drew up an instrument at the behest of Patrick Thomson, skipper, and George Cockburn, burgess of Dundee, owners of

---

20 Granted to him by Adam Bothwell, 22 Oct. 1560 (*Prot. Bk Gilbert Grote*, 54).
21 Roxburghe Mun., bundle 1634, no. 15.

the ship *Marie Blyth*, and Robert Laird, a seaman.[22] Thomson had been at Pierowall in Westray the previous February taking on a cargo of bere from Balfour's tenants. Robert had ordered them to take the bere to Flanders (where he clearly had interests), instead of their intended destination on the Firth of Forth, although they knew it was not Robert's to dispose of. The *Marie Blyth* was to have been accompanied by the *Stilhert*, skippered by Robert Troup, but on the way it had been lost. Presumably Thomson and the others did as they had been commanded, but sought by the instrument to protect themselves from blame for actions carried out under duress. Nor was this his only action against Balfour; in a short time his seizure of Noltland Castle was to be the subject of litigation in Edinburgh.

The building of power developed steadily. Robert and his relatives began to take formal possession of their northern grants following the agreements of 1568–70. In 1569, Robert and his son Henry received Bothwell's charter of lands in Deerness.[23] On 30 June 1570 Jean Kennedy and Mary Stewart were infeft in Bellenden's lands in Birsay. In 1572, charters were subscribed granting Robert and Henry the bishopric lands in Orkney and Shetland and making them justices and heritable bailies.[24] As he consolidated, Robert began finding places for his followers. In April 1571 he signed a charter by Alexander Dick, provost of Orkney, to William Ferguson of a *tenement* in Kirkwall.[25]

Next came the conversion of Robert's northern income into liquid assets. On 26 July 1572, in Edinburgh, a contract was drawn up between his commissioners and Bellenden, still an interested party, for the sale of Orkney butter.[26] On 1 November, also in Edinburgh, three of Robert's longest serving followers, William Elphinstone, John Dishington and James Hay, concluded a contract with two Edinburgh burgesses, William Monteith and James Marshall, for the sale of 36 *chalders* of bere.[27]

Acting as one of the cautioners for Robert's servants in the contract was his half-brother on his mother's side, Laurence Bruce of Cultmalindie, who had been appointed foud of Shetland at an early stage of Robert's tenure in the islands.[28] And about six months later, on 18 April 1573, Bruce was again in Edinburgh, registering an obligation concerning his appointment by Robert as 'faude, schiref depute and chalmerlane' of the king's part of Shetland and as 'baillie justiciarie of the regalitie' of the bishop's part.[29] Bruce's career as laird in Shetland was to constitute a whole separate episode in Robert's story, and even more so that of his son. When Robert's

---

22 *Prot. Bk Gilbert Grote*, 81–2.
23 Roxburghe Mun., bundle 1634, no. 15, bundle 1625.
24 Roxburghe Mun., bundle 1634, bundle 1612.
25 *REO*, 344, no. ccxxii.
26 Roxburghe Mun., bundle 1612; stated to have been registered in the B. of C. & S., 29 July 1572, but not to be found.
27 Reg. Deeds, NRS RD1/10, f. 211; interestingly, this contract was subscribed by Robert's mysterious brother Adam – a rare sighting.
28 *Shetland Documents 1195–1579*, ed. Smith and Ballantyne, 183.
29 Reg. Deeds, NRS RD1/12, f. 130.

affairs came to be investigated a few years later, his actions were to be the subject of their own inquiry.

Robert then turned his attention to other limitations on his power. On 25 October 1569 he had himself made provost of Kirkwall,[30] magnanimously accepting the appointment because of the 'compassion, pitie, respect and consideratioun' he felt for the commonweal of the burgh and noting how its liberties were 'hurt clean contrarie changit and abuset be *extraniers* [strangers] quhilkis forstall and regrate the samen'. In enforcing the burgesses' commercial monopolies, he secured for himself two thirds of any goods escheat for violation of the privileges of the burgh and found outside its precincts. Robert's relationship with Kirkwall was not to be a happy one; in the seventeenth century, Provost Craigie was to state that Robert 'on pretence of distraining for a private debt' seized the town's charter-chest and destroyed its contents.[31] If this is true, it suggests that he was trying to strike at the central element in Kirkwall's standing in the islands – its status as a free and independent royal burgh.

Another area to which Robert directed his attention, while not perhaps the most remunerative to his grasping nature, was undoubtedly the most significant for his continuing evil reputation. It was a campaign against a whole class – the udal proprietors of Orkney and Shetland. In April 1574 he issued a charter to Magnus Clouston of land in Grimeston, Harray, and Kirbuster, Orphir, escheated from William Clouston, Magnus's father, for theft.[32] Two months later, during a visit to Shetland, Robert granted a charter in Yell to Walter Donaldson *alias* Smith of land in Hammer, Unst, formerly pertaining to Ola Anderson but escheat because the latter had 'depairtit out of this cuntrie to the pairtis of Noroway and hes remanit thair thir dyverse yeiris bypast but licence of me or ony utheris his superiouris he beand ane heritour within this cuntrie'.[33] The first of these actions is specially noted by Storer Clouston as seeing the beginning of a whole series of evictions 'for thift' that were in all probability corrupt. Clouston believed that what Robert was doing was not so much confiscating land outright as establishing a quasi-feudal overlordship by taking the land on a pretext – charges of witchcraft and suicide occur as well as of theft and unauthorised departure from the islands – and then regranting it to the same persons or close relatives with the addition of feudal obligations.[34] The examples he cites in support of this can easily bear another interpretation, which will be examined presently, but evidence of more than 50 such confiscations – more than 40 from Patrick Stewart's 1595 rental alone – certainly suggests a policy of asserting earldom control over udal land.

30 Kirkwall Chrs, 80.
31 J. Mackenzie, *The General Grievances and Oppressions of the Isles of Orkney and Shetland*, Edinburgh, 1836, 36.
32 *REO*, 135, no. lxi.
33 *OSR*, 195, no. 71.
34 *REO*, 311, no. cxciii and 313n.

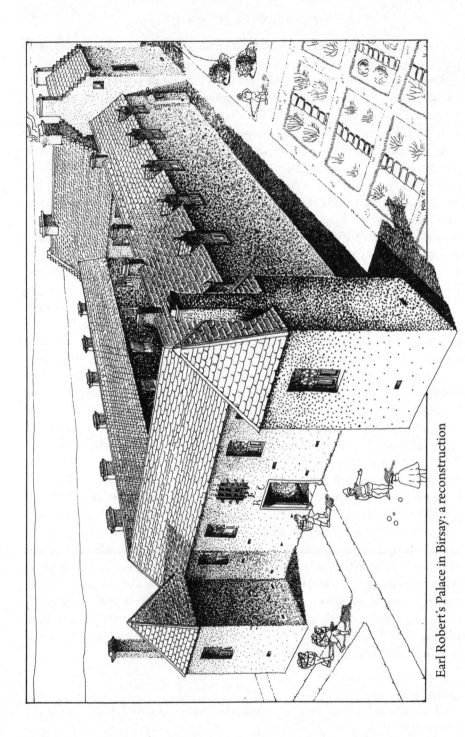

Earl Robert's Palace in Birsay: a reconstruction

This campaign of acquisition may in some cases have been part of Robert's strategy of amalgamation and reorganisation of all the territory that he had amassed. This included the erection of some large farms into *bus*. The term bu is common as a place-name in Orkney today and was in use as such in Robert's time, but in those days it was also a technical term denoting an assemblage of farms worked as one unit, and Robert was to apply the terms to the farms of Folsetter (in Birsay, about two and a half miles to the south of the palace), Corse (on the south-western outskirts of Kirkwall) and (as mentioned in Robert's testament) an unknown centre stated simply to be 'in Sandweik' but that is almost certainly the farm of Skaill, which by Patrick's time was described as being 'labourit in ane Bu', a status that was no doubt conferred by Robert. It is noteworthy that none of these farms, all of which are still thriving, bears the name 'bu' in modern times. The policy, however, was to be enlarged and expanded by Patrick.

Now came the symbolising in stone of Robert's power – his new palace at Birsay. It cannot have been long after his return to Orkney in 1569 that Robert began this project; and an inscription above the door, now lost, gives a date of 1574, presumably that of what was to be the first phase, and the opening of the building for the earl's use.[35] Birsay, since the days of Earl Thorfinn, had been the centre of the bishopric estates, Robert's greatest prize. It had hitherto been purely an ecclesiastical centre, the site of a bishop's palace, 'Mons Bellus'. The new building was an impressive country house, providing an alternative to his capital in Kirkwall, with its cathedral, its massively strong castle and bishop's palace, the old Palace of the Yards, refurbished and expanded 30 years or so before.

Built some yards to the north of Mons Bellus, there is some evidence that the new building quarried the old. A stone bearing the arms of Bishop Edward Stewart (c.1500–26) was found built into the walls of the new palace.[36] Masons' marks in the palace suggest that some of the same hands worked on Birsay as had erected Gilbert Balfour's Noltland Castle, different though the two buildings are.[37] If it was indeed built in two stages, construction of the first phase was probably around 1575, when Robert's progress faltered before his political difficulties. At that point the building consisted of a courtyard enclosed on three sides and protected to the north by a wall.[38] It comprised two storeys: the apartments of Robert and his immediate

35 RCAHMS, *Inv.*, O & S, ii, 9.

36 R. Rendall, 'Birsay's Forgotten Palace', *Orkney Herald*, 21 April 1959.

37 I am grateful for this and other information regarding Robert's palace to Professor Richard Fawcett, then of the Ancient Monuments branch of the Scottish Development Department, now Historic Scotland. At that time an official guide to the building was in preparation, and some of the remarks here derive from sight of the draft of this at the time. Unfortunately no published guide has yet been forthcoming.

38 The later north side, which eventually replaced the wall, has been attributed to Robert's son Patrick, but given Patrick's altogether grander architectural ideas, it seems more likely that Robert built it as well, possibly during the second half of his life in Orkney and Shetland, in the 1580s.

household on the upper floor, with domestic offices and servants' quarters beneath. The great hall and principal chamber was in the south range overlooking the main approach to the palace (this 'gallery' was later superseded by a great hall included in the later additions to the north side). Family and major guest rooms were probably on the east. The upper floor of the west range housed a further gallery, illuminated by large windows down each side, and was presumably one of those rooms later described as decorated by scripture histories painted on the ceilings, such as 'Noah's Floud', 'Christ riding to Jerusalem' and others, appropriately labelled.[39] The lower floor of the west range consisted of a series of self-contained lodgings, probably accommodation for Robert's more important servants. The kitchen and related domestic rooms were on the east side. It is not possible from the remains of the palace today to assign a function to every room, but we do know from written evidence that the palace also contained, as might be expected, a girnel, a brewhouse and several 'lach sellars', besides other chambers.[40]

Local tradition has it that sea birds' eggs were demanded from the populace for mixing with the mortar in building the palace. This is popularly thought of as an example of Stewart oppression, and the manner of its levying may indeed have been oppressive, but the actual use of eggs in this way was common practice. Eggshells mixed in the mortar aided its binding qualities, and yolk would be used for the tempera of the painted ceilings. More importantly, these details, together with discovery of glazed tiles among the palace ruins, and the cut mouldings decorating a fireplace in the south-west tower, indicate some sophistication in the treatment of the principal apartments and a much more civilised building than its near contemporary, Noltland Castle. It has been described as 'perhaps the earliest residence built by a subject which had an essentially domestic character as opposed to a fortified house'.[41] Certainly it was much pleasanter than Balfour's brutal pile, though it should be said that the house retained defensive capabilities. Among the very few openings at ground level were gunloops, which allowed handguns to be pivoted across a wide field of fire; and the projecting towers flanking the entrance and at the north-east corner permitted defenders to rake the walls with their shot. It was to be attacked only once, in 1614. Its capitulation, as we shall see, had more to do with the irresolution of its defenders than any military weakness in the building.

The building was also surrounded by a complex of buildings and other features. To the south of the palace lay what remained of the old bishop's house. The building may to some extent have escaped the cannibalisation that was its ultimate fate since it survived the construction of Robert's palace as one of the structures among the barns and stables marked in early plans and drawings. Between these and the palace lay the church of Birsay, which was thus rendered almost an integral part of the whole, perhaps employed informally as the earl's private chapel.

39 J. Brand, *A Brief Description of Orkney, Zetland, Pightland Firth and Caithness*, Edinburgh, 1701–3, 31.
40 RCAHMS *Inv.*, O & S, ii, 10; *POAS*, xxiii (1888–9), 303–5.
41 Donaldson, 'Stewart Borders', *The Stewarts*, xix, 20.

Running along the east front, and south towards the burn of Hunto, lay a series of gardens – flowers, herbs, kale and 'plants'. To the east and north-east of these lay cornfields. Parallel to the west range of the palace, next to the kirkyard, lay several massive peat stacks, each the length of the palace itself. To the north-west of these lay the 'north coninger', one of two rabbit warrens to north and south along the coast. These, beyond their primary function of furnishing rabbit-meat, probably doubled as golf links; certainly Robert's servants were ordering golf-balls from Edinburgh in the 1580s.[42] Golf was not the only pastime for Robert and his house-hold. Archery butts lay alongside the flower and herb gardens, and a bowling green lay east of the avenue from the main gate to the burn of Hunto to the south.

Besides the details of the building itself, effort was made to provide the new work with a fitting situation. It can be seen for some distance around – from the Brough of Birsay itself, from the eastern approaches on the Kirkwall road and from the Brae of Harpasa to the south, on the road from Stromness. The last of these can still be appreciated, with the bridge over the burn of Hunto leading to the main avenue which in turn leads the observer direct to the main entrance, though the road through Birsay village now swings round the palace to the left rather than straight to its door. Looking at this from the other direction, and imagining Robert leaving his palace on a journey, he would cross the bridge, and come to a junction; a westward turn took the earl to Cairston (Stromness) by way of Sandwick, going eastwards led to Harray, and thence to Kirkwall. More locally, the road through the peat yard forked at its northern end and one branch led through the north coninger to Buckquoy (the Birsay minister's glebe)[43] and the Brough. The other ran to the more northerly corn fields, under the windows of the hall and adjacent reception chamber added by Robert on the north side of the palace, probably in the 1580s. Further roads branched from this and led through the north coninger to Skippigeo, where the earl's boats lay moored or beached.

The whole suggests that even if Robert's building enterprises lacked something of the high, though costly, taste of those of his son, they nevertheless constituted a fitting centrepiece to his pretensions in Orkney and Shetland. There seems little doubt, in fact, that Birsay, or at least that part of the parish between the north-west end of the Loch of Boardhouse and the sea, formed the heartland of the estate of the Stewart earls. Besides the palace, there was the Bu of Folsetter nearby. Shortly after the 1568 excambion with Auchnoull, the area came to be called 'The Barony', a name it still bears today. There is no concrete evidence of it ever having been formally erected into a barony, but Jo. Ben, writing about 1590,[44] stated 'Birsa baronia dicitur', and Robert was granted the curious subsidiary title 'knycht of Birsay' when he was invested as earl in 1581.[45] The special status of Birsay in the earl's dominions

42 *Barnbarroch Corresp.*, 23 November 1585, 340.

43 H. Marwick, *The Place-names of Birsay*, Aberdeen, 1970, 60–1.

44 Jo. Ben., *Macfarlane's Geographical Collections*, iii, 309, 320; for discussion of a possible date for Jo. Ben's writings, see note by A. W. Johnston, *OLM*, i (1908), 300–3.

45 D. Moysie, *Memoirs of the Affairs of Scotland* (Bannatyne Club), Edinburgh, 1830, 34.

was to persist right through to the end of the Stewart era, and may help to explain the particular support at the end given to Earl Patrick's desperate cause by the men of that area.

On 23 January 1574 the Herdmanstein court, the traditional January court in Orkney, was held in Kirkwall with full assize of 27 members.[46] Robert presided; it was not his first court in Orkney[47] but the first of which we have detailed evidence, albeit fragmentary. The court's proceedings seem unexceptionable; they concerned a dispute between Malcolm Ireland on the one part and his aunts Margaret and Marion Ireland on the other concerning the former's claim to the latters' 'sister parts' of unspecified udal land – by no means an uncommon type of litigation. Malcolm's case against Marion was deferred, and in Margaret's case judgment was given in her favour.

Perhaps because of the fragmentary nature of the evidence, these proceedings have aroused some speculation by previous historians of Orkney and Shetland, and A. W. Johnston and Storer Clouston spilled a fair amount of ink over their significance. The Herdmanstein court was admittedly of some antiquity, in Norway the *Hirðmannastefna*, the court of the king's *hirðmenn* or bodyguard, but for Johnston this meant that Robert's holding this simple court indicated that he 'attempted to revive all the prerogatives of the old Norse regime, and naturally would wish to have his *hirð* or bodyguard'.[48] As we have seen, Robert was not without pretensions regarding his status but, as Clouston points out, the one previous reference to the court, in 1438,[49] shows it functioning as an ordinary court, that similar courts had been held before Robert's arrival and that others were to be held by him afterwards. Sometimes designated 'Herdmanstein', on others the 'first heid court eftyr Yeuil', it was for Clouston the ordinary customary court. It is difficult to disagree.

Johnston's fanciful ideas derived from two points that he had noticed in the proceedings, which are indeed worthy of attention: the presence on the assize of two Shetlanders – Arthur Sinclair of Aith and Johne Morray 'in Yetland' – and various of the feuar's own followers. William Henderson, Patrick Monteith, John Caverton and William Ferguson were all present. Clouston explains the presence of the Shetlanders, not as members of Robert's bodyguard, but as 'suiters of court' – men discharging their obligation, as vassals, to take part in assizes (according to a Scottish practice that had grown up in Orkney during the century), thus indicating that they were already Robert's vassals. This view, however, seems somewhat legalistic. It seems more likely that Robert was simply using the presence of his followers to influence the assizes, should this be necessary.

Robert held a second court on 31 March 1574 in St Magnus Kirk in Birsay.[50] It was

46 *REO*, 134, no. lx.
47 G. Donaldson, 'Stewart Builders: the Descendants of James V', *The Stewarts*, xix, 116.
48 *REO*, 123, no. lvi.
49 *REO*, 71, no. xxx.
50 *REO*, 135, no. lxi.

explicitly one of double jurisdiction – 'sheriff court of Orknay and court of regalitie of the sammyn [strictly speaking of the bishopric] respective'. It is quite possible that this particular diet, which did not conform to the usual timetable of earldom head courts – January, June and November – was in fact following time-honoured former practice, in both time and venue, of bishopric courts. The assize in this instance consisted of eleven men, including James Kennedy, Robert's brother-in-law and the case, as in the previous court, concerned a dispute over land. Katherine Man was found to have the right to a pennyland in Skeabrae, Sandwick, against the claims of Magnus Sinclair of Skaill, who, as it happened, had been a member of the Herdmanstein assize and who was later to become Robert's nephew by marriage. The evidence is sketchy compared to the later Shetland court book under Patrick, but there is a suggestion that there was a routine, if rough, justice in the system after all, so long as it did directly not affect Robert's interests.[51]

One change that Robert did bring to the administration of justice in Orkney concerned the dates of the holding of head courts. These had originally been held in January (Herdmanstein), June and November (*Alhallo*), but after 1559 evidence for the June court disappears, and by 1579 there are indications that it was definitely not being held.[52] The reason for this, according to Clouston, was Robert's need to visit Shetland which, given the treacherous nature of the weather and the *Sumburgh Roost*, was best done in the summer. This is certainly borne out by the times of year of Robert's known visits to Shetland – in 1568, 1574, 1575, 1588 and 1589;[53] all were in the summer, and of those for which we have definite dates, two were in June and one in July. The Shetland court book of 1602–4 suggests that this practice was carried on by Robert's son Patrick.[54]

Robert's first visit, in 1568, saw him in Scalloway.[55] Scalloway was, and remains, a major harbour for the islands of Shetland, but at this date the capital of the earldom, if we may so term it, was in Sumburgh. Sumburgh was itself a considerable harbour, but as an administrative centre it is somewhat isolated, compared to the centrality of Scalloway, with its quick access to the east coast, and to the north and west up the valley of Tingwall. Robert may have built houses in both locations. The remains of the house of Sumburgh, plain but stout, still stand. Little, if anything, is known of anything Robert may have built in Scalloway, but Patrick was to move his capital there, dominated by his castle and surrounding estates, and the town remained the capital of Shetland for long after.

Robert's second visit, in 1574, was a memorable one. On 12 May two English merchant and fishing vessels, the *Michael* and the *Mynioun*, based in Southampton,

51 See the same kind of observation in Donaldson, *Shetland Life under Earl Patrick*, 10–11.
52 *REO*, p. lxxvi n; 144, no. lxvi; 145, no. lxvii.
53 Roxburghe Mun., bundle 1634, no. 8; *RPC*, ii, 409–10; Shetland Library Collection, SA D.11/189; *Barnbarroch Corresp.*, 420; Cunningham of Caprington Mun., NRS GD149/265, ii, ff. 1–8.
54 *Ct Bk of Shetland*, 34, 108.
55 Roxburghe Mun., bundle 1634.

were fishing off Shetland when they were set upon by Robert and his men, who took both ships to Scalloway, charged the merchants, led by John Crooke, Bernard Cartmyll, Thomas Demaresk and John Smith, with various 'invented' offences, and confiscated cargoes and ordnance worth nearly £350.[56] English fishermen had a dubious reputation in the area, though this was generally associated with the main fishing fleets rather than isolated individuals, but it may be that Robert was capitalising on local suspicion of the English.

A few weeks later, in June 1574, Robert held another court at Scalloway Banks, where he condemned to death Gilbert McCreath, Robert Ratter (a significantly Shetland name) and David, James and Norman Leslie for despoliation of a ship of Emden. They had boarded this vessel while it lay sheltering off Nesting, removed a dozen bolts of Holland cloth, 2,000 Spanish royals and the ship's tackle, then set the stripped craft and its crew to sea in bad weather, never to be heard of again.[57] If what McCreath and his men had done was barbarous, however, it was well matched by Robert, who forced their loot out of them by keeping them at the gallows-foot for two hours with the ropes round their necks before finally sparing them. During the same visit Thomas Boyne, one of Bruce of Cultmalindie's followers, was said to have slain Patrick Windram in Robert's presence; Boyne was imprisoned for six weeks, but afterwards freed and sent to Norway.[58]

Robert then probably returned to Orkney and remained there, but the following summer he was back in Shetland, where he presided over a sheriff court at Houss in West Burra, which heard a dispute between Henry Foster of Lunna and the heirs of the deceased James Sinclair of Houss over possession of the lands of Lunna.[59] The members of the assize included fewer of Robert's and Bruce of Cultmalindie's followers than one might have expected, given the later complaints regarding Bruce's henchmen; indeed the only such person seems to have been Hugh Gordon, the man to whose house in Kirkwall Robert had repaired after the cathedral shootings. Also present on the assize, however, were William Halcro of Aikers, an Orcadian with a difficult relationship with Robert; and the clerk of the court was William Henderson, now described as a notary.

In the dispute over Lunna, both parties submitted documents to Robert and his assize giving details of their respective rights. Robert and the assessors found these 'sa null be generalitie and als sa informalie maid they can nocht decerne thairupoun'. Perhaps this was evidence of dissatisfaction on Robert's part at the unfamiliar udal phraseology of the various titles; at any rate Robert preferred to put the case to the arbitration of a number of 'discreit men of judgment' to be chosen by the parties. It is intriguing therefore that, of the four arbiters chosen, three were individuals

56 *RPC*, ii, 654–60.
57 *Shetland Documents, 1195–1579*, 167; McCreath and company were still being pursued for this crime by Patrick Stewart nearly thirty years later (*Ct Bk of Shetland*, 47).
58 *Shetland Documents, 1195–1579*, 165.
59 Shetland Library Collection, SA D11/189.

whose presence we had cause to note earlier – Hugh Gordon, William Halcro of Aikers and William Henderson (the fourth was Andrew Mouat of Heogaland, a prominent Shetlander). The case was found in favour of Foster of Lunna, though he had to agree make a grant to his opponent, Arthur Sinclair, representing the heirs and widow of Sinclair of Houss, of the land under the house of Lye in Olnafirth, with a sum of money. There is no evidence or suggestion of injustice being done here, and no mention was made of this case in the Shetlanders' later complaints about the administration of justice in their islands. In fact there are later suggestions that Robert's law-giving was actually preferred to that of his brother-in-law.

Robert's reason for making this decision may have more than a little cynical. This was his growing need to enlist support in the islands against opposing forces, which were steadily massing at this time – forces consisting both of his personal enemies of past years and of humbler individuals with various grievances, large and small, against his and Bruce's administration. Soon Robert would be fighting for the existence of everything he had achieved.

On 23 January 1570, Robert's brother James, the regent, was assassinated in Linlithgow, and was succeeded six months later by the earl of Lennox. This resulted in civil war between the new regent and an alliance of the Marian groups – notably the Hamiltons, one of whom had been the hitman – and the followers of Maitland of Lethington. On 10 January 1571 Lennox ordered the arrest of one of Robert's ships, which had arrived in Leith from Orkney, and the delivery of its cargo to his 'captaines and men of weir' in Edinburgh, presumably to supply the troops engaged in the lengthy siege of Edinburgh Castle, held by Kirkcaldy of Grange.[60] Robert's old 'concurrence' with the Hamiltons (and dealings with Lennox and his son) had not been forgotten and Lennox was taking advantage of Robert's distance from the centre of affairs.

On 9 September 1571 Lennox was in turn killed at Stirling, and replaced shortly afterwards by John Erskine, earl of Mar. This development began an ominous train of events for Robert Stewart. The Regent Mar was not a politician, and real power rested in the hands of James Douglas, earl of Morton,[61] no friend of Robert, who had in the past accused him of making evil report of him to Moray on behalf of Patrick Bellenden. It is little wonder, then, that Patrick was soon seen to be on the move against Robert. On 10 June 1572 Sir William Drury wrote to Burghley that 'Patrick Pallantyne, brother of the Justice Clerk, who long has envied Lord Robert for dispossessing him of somewhat he enjoyed in Orkney, being supported by the earl of Caithness, is now for revenge prepared to essay the same', even to the point of military action.[62] Robert was making preparations for this and had gathered together 300 men. When he was called to account three years later, faced with this

60 Pitscottie, Historie, ii, 243.
61 Donaldson, James V–James VII, 165.
62 CSP Scot., iv, 322.

crisis and lacking support among the powerful in Edinburgh, it is significant that 1572 was given as the alleged year of the gravest of the crimes laid to his charge – that of treasonable approaches to Denmark.

In 1574, as the political situation changed, trouble began to build up for Robert Stewart. Patrick Bellenden and Gilbert Balfour both saw their opportunity and he faced litigation from both. Their causes went before the privy council. On 3 February it was heard that the Bellenden matter had been the subject of *horning* because Robert had not appeared to answer such things 'as sould have bene laid to his charge'.[63] He had ignored this, as his procurators before the privy council, John Sharp and Clement Little, had to admit. On 17 March the council heard that Robert had ignored instructions to hand over to Gilbert Balfour the 'house and fortalice of Westraw' with surrounding lands, and ignored a further summons.[64] Jean Kennedy, acting for her husband through Clement Little, stated that legal letters had been duly executed and obeyed, the castle 'left void' and the keys given to the pursuivant responsible for the execution. Robert's representatives stated that 'his summons of treason was alleged to have been 'purchest . . . upoun verie malice . . . and divisit to draw the said lord (Robert) furth of the cuntre, swa that sindry personis abydand opportunitie may in his absence interpryise and execute sic thingis as is abill to tend to his utter wrak and the greit hurt of the cuntre'. Despite this, Robert was willing to come south but was prevented by the severities of the season. It does not seem impossible to guess who the 'sindry personis' might be.

The regent – who since October 1572 had been Morton himself – accepted the supplication by Jean Kennedy regarding Balfour's lands in Westray, and further action was postponed until 10 June. Nothing further was heard of this matter, but Patrick Bellenden secured further letters from the privy council directing Robert to repossess him in his Orkney lands in Stenness, Hoy and Stronsay, and other territories in Shetland. The letters were dated 20 September, with repossession to take place within 15 days. On 13 October John Dishington explained to the council on Robert's behalf that formal repossession had not taken place owing to the continued absence of Patrick Bellenden.[65] Robert and Patrick were at loggerheads, and it would have required stronger action by the authorities to resolve their dispute. Robert was not prepared in the current circumstances to come south, where he would be isolated in the face of Bellenden and his allies. Bellenden, whatever the truth of the tale of his Caithness-backed expedition, was not prepared to make his way into Robert's territory.

The following year, 1575, saw a number of other occurrences involving persons with northern interests. By now Gilbert Balfour, who had been represented in his action against Robert by counsel, was in fact in prison in Sweden on charges of

63 *RPC*, ii, 332.
64 *RPC*, ii, 340–1.
65 *RPC*, ii, 409–10.

treason. On 26 June Morton wrote to King John of Sweden[66] and again on 4 August to Charles, prince of Sweden[67] on his behalf. The representations were to no avail, and Balfour was executed on 6 August 1576.[68] On 20 June the strangely shadowed history of Robert's brother Adam came to an end with his death in Orkney; his daughter, who had married an Orcadian, Henry Halcro, furnished him with a tombstone that can still be seen in St Magnus Kirk today.[69] Of the illegitimate sons of James V, only the two Roberts now remained.

The feuar of Orkney was now in increasingly serious trouble. On 19 January 1575 Laurence Bruce, William Elphinstone and others of his servants, presumably in the south on his business, were *warded* in the area of Edinburgh, Holyrood and the Canongate.[70] This was the first sign of determined action by the central government against Robert. By August of the same year, hardly a month after his visit to Shetland, he himself had submitted to ward in Edinburgh Castle.[71] How it was that he had been induced to come south, when he had been so careful before about leaving the islands where he felt himself safest, is unknown. Perhaps the restrictions placed on his chief servants, perhaps the continued absence of his wife from the islands, influenced him in his decision. Perhaps, as succeeding events may show, he had for the time being nowhere else to turn in his conflict with Morton and his followers and was forced to the desperate hope of building up support for himself in Edinburgh.

66 State Papers, NRS SP1/4/29.
67 State Papers, NRS SP1/4/30.
68 For details of Balfour's later career, see J. Dow, *Ruthven's Army in Sweden and Esthonia*, Stockholm, 1965.
69 RCAHMS *Inv.*, O & S, ii, 132; also plate 35, fig. 201.
70 *TA*, xiii, 93.
71 *The Historie of King James the Sext, 1565–96*, 157.

6

But ane Simple Sheriff

The attempts to bring Robert to book for his activities in Orkney and Shetland now began to gather momentum. On 16 December 1575 came the formal completion of a list of complaints 'Articles and Informations of the wrangus usurpation of the King's Majesty's authority and oppression committed by Lord Robert Stuart, feuar of Orkney and Zetland'. It was a grave indictment, comprising 33 separate accusations, several citing more than one instance and others quoting the same action as evidence of more than one crime, together with some subsidiary charges. These can be arranged under five heads: treasonable dealings with Denmark regarding the sovereignty of the islands; general oppression – banishment, unlawful imprisonment, confiscation of property, etc., aimed both at personal enemies and at the apparently innocent; piracy and conniving with pirates; exceeding his authority; and interfering with the native laws to his own advantage.

This list is usually associated with that concerning the actions of Bruce of Cultmalindie in Shetland, compiled fourteen months or so later. The connection is a reasonable one to make, given some obvious affinities in content and the juxtaposition of the printed versions in Balfour's *Oppressions* (now superseded as a text),[1] but it is important at the same time to note the significant dissimilarities between the two. These are obvious even at first sight, and become more so the more closely the two documents are examined.

The 1575 list concerns, or purports to concern, both Orkney and Shetland – the later deals with Shetland only. It was drawn up by individuals (they refer to themselves as 'we') whose identity is unstated but are plainly the known opponents of Robert, including those named at various points in the document. It deals entirely with Robert's activities, though some of the accusations against him were treated much more fully in the complaints against Bruce. In fact, it does not mention Bruce at all. The later document makes only three very general references to Robert and is the product of a much more formal procedure. It was drawn up over a fortnight

1 This work, *Oppressions of the Sixteenth Century in the Islands of Orkney and Zetland*, edited by David Balfour for the Maitland Club in 1859, was until 1999 the only printed source for both complaints, and underpins the summary in Anderson, *Robert Stewart, Earl of Orkney, Lord of Shetland*. All references here are now drawn from *Shetland Documents, 1195–1579*, ed. Smith and Ballantyne.

or so at Tingwall in February 1577 in the presence, on successive days, of the chief representatives of the commons of the districts of Shetland. The paper accusing Robert was no more than a simple catalogue by comparison. The Shetlanders' complaints were concerned solely with abuses of the legal and administrative system and oppression of individuals (these will be examined in detail presently); no mention whatever was made of the more serious charges aimed at Robert.

This contrast illustrates important differences between the situation in Orkney and in Shetland. Shetland, whose past history had rendered it relatively free from outside interference, reacted in a much stronger and more 'democratic' manner than Orkney to a rule that must have been at least as oppressive and arbitrary as Robert's own in Orkney, if the examples to be found, meagre in comparison, are any indication. The whole Shetland document, with its ample public 'probatiounis' for each charge, was evidence of the continuing vitality of the native system of law there. The 1575 document indicated none of this. Its source is unstated, but internal evidence strongly suggests Orkney origin; those islands, over the years much more of a cockpit for political conflict and change, produced a paper in which native influences surface occasionally, but are generally lost in a turmoil of other elements.

Underlying the manifest contrasts of form between the two documents were wide divergences in the nature and intentions of the forces behind them. In examining the 1575 list and attempting to determine its source, it is important to note the striking differences between the Orcadians and the Shetlanders named there. The Shetland complainants, though numerous enough, were generally the bearers of individual grievances against abuse of the law, some directly foreshadowing the detailed Shetland testimony of 1577. Robert Wishart, Walter Hill, Magnus McCreath and others had been fined for concealing one Matthew Sinclair, though the latter was not an outlaw.[2] Jacob Tait, Bartholomew Strang, Henry Spence, Peter Nisbet and their companions had been fined for contravening a new law against bringing home boats to Shetland.[3] All these Shetlanders appear only once in the 1575 document, though Strang, Spence, Nisbet and the law on importing boats are all noted later.[4] None had shown any previous political animus towards either Robert or Bruce.

It is clear that the 1575 charges were compiled by Robert's sworn political enemies. It was their obvious intention, not merely to seek legitimate redress at law, as the Shetlanders were to do, but to present Robert in the worst possible light, not simply as an oppressor, but as a traitor, a man guilty of the highest crimes against king and realm. The preambles of the 1575 and 1577 documents illustrate the different approaches. Both begin by describing themselves as 'complaints', but whereas the latter then merely notes briefly the circumstances of its own compilation (leaving the identity and evils of the villain of the piece to emerge through the steady accumulation of testimony), the former goes on to describe its contents as 'Articles

2 *Shetland Documents, 1195–1579*, 166, no. 31.
3 *Shetland Documents, 1195–1579*, 165, no. 19.
4 *Shetland Documents, 1195–1579*, 213.

and Informations' of Robert's usurpation of royal authority, and oppression' . . . quhilkis haill pointis and articles concernis the King's Majestie in speciall'.[5] The suggestion of treason recurs continually. The king's authority was being threatened by Robert's approaches to Denmark, his assumption of the royal powers of admiralty and justiciary, arresting of the king's officers of arms, banishing of 'our Sovereign Lords free lieges', disponing of benefices 'vacant at the King's Majesty's gift', and so on.[6]

It seems certain that leading Robert's enemies was the figure of Patrick Bellenden, possibly supported by his brother Sir John (though he had not long to live) and certainly by Adam Bothwell. At the back of these stood a more powerful enemy still, the Regent Morton. This formidable movement against Robert must have brought to life again many of the problems that had faced him in the winter of 1567–8. Unlike that time, no-one throughout Robert's incarceration ever voiced any doubts as to his actual title to his northern lands, but he was still forced into desperate measures. To aid his case, Bellenden enlisted Orcadians, all members of that constellation of faction and family that had supported Bothwell and Bellenden in the past[7] and thus had demonstrable political reasons for complaint. Magnus Halcro and his wife had been compelled to 'discharge and quitclaim [renounce] their heretage and possession', and imprisoned in the castle of Kirkwall and the Palace of the Yards, with others including his wife's Sinclair relatives – William Sinclair of Warsetter, Oliver Sinclair of Essinquoy, Hugh Sinclair of Strom. Within the walls, too, had been William Moodie, former treasurer of Orkney and later commissioner for the 1577 Shetland inquiry who, with his relative Magnus Moodie and John Gifford, complained of being arrested by night and ultimately banished. The Sinclairs had been particular targets. There was Edward Sinclair of Eday, son of Oliver Sinclair, the former tacksman, as well as the long-dead victor of Summerdale Sir James Sinclair, whose estates were confiscated on the grounds of his suicide, despite the lapse of time and the fact that all had been settled long ago.[8] Of the three Shetlanders mixed up in these events, two were Sinclairs – Ola of Brow and William of Voster.[9] Magnus Halcro's fears for the future under Robert, expressed in his letter to Sir John Bellenden of 2 June 1569, had been fully justified.

Despite the occasional presence of Shetlanders in the document, there are other reasons for supposing a specifically Orkney origin. There is the compilers' tendency to forget Shetland in their accusations. One passage accuses Robert of introducing law 'never received of before in Orkney', then cites among its evidence a law on the subject of 'swine-rooting' – the grubbing up by pigs of neighbouring crops – a legal concept only ever found in Shetland, regarding a chronic local nuisance. When it

---

5 *Shetland Documents, 1195–1579*, 162.

6 *Shetland Documents, 1195–1579*, 162–4, paras 6–10.

7 *Shetland Documents, 1195–1579*, 164, no. 8; 6, no. 12; 8, no. 23.

8 *Shetland Documents, 1195–1579*, 166, no. 27.

9 *Shetland Documents, 1195–1579*, 164, no. 8; 164, no. 12.

speaks of the extra revenue that Robert would derive from this enactment, it refers to its being 'taen up in Shetland, bye Orkney'.[10] Another example can be found in the charge of misusing the instruments for weighing victual rents, in Orkney's case the *bismar* and *pundlar*. In the complaints of 1575, this accusation mentions only Orkney, despite the misuse of the Shetland instruments being one of the most important of Shetland's grievances, treated at great length in 1577.[11]

One charge in particular leads to a curious anomaly, both in itself and in what later historians have made of it, and serves also to point up again the contrast between the complainants of Orkney and those of Shetland. This was that Robert was guilty of 'inbringing of new laws and consuetudes, forgit of the laws of Norway, never received of before in Orkney, and abrogation of the auld laws and statutes of the realm'.[12] The nearest Storer Clouston comes to dealing with this charge in his *History of Orkney* is to speak of 'Alteration of the old laws of the country (expressly guaranteed by the Scots Parliament) and the addition of new enactments; including the promulgation of an edict that none should leave Orkney and Shetland to make complaint against himself'.[13] The placing of this passage at the head of Clouston's list of the 1575 complaints, and the reference to 'old laws of the country', suggest that he is thinking of the same charge. However, he has completely reversed its sense. Robert was not being accused of alteration of the native laws, but quite the opposite – he was not ruling the islands according to Scots law. It is not without significance that Storer Clouston, in producing his version of the charge, detaches it from the original three examples cited in its support and substitutes another quite different charge from another part of the complaints.

Two particular charges are cited in support of the contention of abusing the law. The continual grumble about marauding pigs, obscure in the 1575 complaints, was dealt with in detail in the Shetland document. Ironically, the evidence there supports Clouston's accusation against Robert rather than that of the 1575 complaints – what Robert (or rather Bruce) was guilty of was an alteration of the law, not the inbringing of a novelty or an abrogation of time-honoured practice. The same can probably be said of the law governing sisters and their 'heid bull'; the background to this law is unknown, but it sounds like a change in the rules of inheritance, allowing females to retain possession of a bu or head farm in default of male heirs. This, too, was a simple alteration. But the purpose behind these examples was not to indicate that these alterations had taken place (however oppressive and unwarranted they may have been). Instead they were twisted to fit the charge that Robert was using exotic laws inbrought from Norway to the detriment of the 'auld laws and statutes of the realm'. 'The realm' in a document in Scots, drawn up by Scots and Orcadians with strong Scottish connections intending to seek remedy in a Scottish court,

10 *Shetland Documents, 1195–1579*, 163, no. 2.
11 *Shetland Documents, 1195–1579*, 15–37.
12 *Shetland Documents, 1195–1579*, 163, no. 2.
13 Clouston, *History of Orkney*, 301.

could only mean Scotland. The charge was obviously erroneous – Scots law had never been the law of the islands and the native legal system had in any case been guaranteed by the Scottish parliament only eight years before – but it presented the regent with a picture of Robert perverting the law of the realm, placed in immediate juxtaposition to the most serious of all the charges, that of dealing with Denmark. This was, of course, a quite different motive from that of the Shetlanders, whose grievances were essentially about gross abuse of their own (Norse) laws.

Another question, to which the complainants devoted much space, again with overtones of usurpation and for which other background details are available, was that of piracy. Robert was accused of 'partaking with the pyrattis, in furnising and reking thame to the sey in pyracy, with men, victuall and munitioun, and ressaving and mantening of their goods and gear reft in thair pyracie'[14] as well as granting them his *bond of maintenance*. He was accused of usurping the office of admiralty and 'sitting upon all seafaring actions', and was said to have condemned those accused on occasion but to have returned their prizes to them, despite his previous judgment.[15] Notable among these prizes were two English ships taken in Shetland, probably the ones already noted in Chapter 5 as having been attacked by Robert and his men in 1574.

The pirates involved, described as Robert's 'household men and feallis [adherents]', were named as Patrick and Edmund (Edward)[16] Blackadder, David Willie, David Cathcart, Robert Stevenson, John Hume, Matthew Aikman, James Crosby and Henry Balfour; Robert granted his bond of maintenance to 'the maist part' of these, as well as to Magnus Moodie.[17] Their prizes amounted to 'nine great ships laden with precious gear' totalling in value more than £100,000, as well as the two English vessels, noted separately, one of which Robert appropriated to his own use, returning the other to the pirates minus goods and guns. There is little doubt that these men were indeed in Robert's employ, and there is independent evidence of their piracy. On 12 July 1574, one Peter Fisher, a merchant seaman suspected of piracy and interrogated in Edinburgh as to his past career, stated that he had been in Scotland at the time 'Lord Robert of Orkney's ship was taken out of the haven of Burnt Island', when he was hired by Robert's men.[18] He had then sailed to Orkney in the *Andro* and returned south with Robert's wares in John Hume's ship. Less

---

14 *Shetland Documents, 1195–1579*, 163, no. 6.
15 *Shetland Documents, 1195–1579*, 163, no. 5.
16 Edward Blackadder is so called in the *Oppressions*, and also in *Shetland Documents, 1195-1579*, and examination of the original by staff of the British Library confirms this reading; however, all other references to him name him as Edmund.
17 References to Magnus Moodie and his relationship with Robert are conflicting. On the one hand he received Robert's bond of maintenance (*Shetland Documents, 1195-1579*, 163, no. 6); on the other he was among those pursued by night (*Shetland Documents, 1195-1579*, 8, no. 21). Robert had taken an interest in piratical activities by the Moodies before, but since William Moodie had been involved in the alleged bond against him in 1568, it is likely that Robert's relations with the Moodies were complex and uncertain.
18 *CSP Scot.*, v, 24.

than two months later he had been hired by Hume and James Crosby and sailed to Norway where they had captured a *hoy* laden with copper kettles and other cargo. This was taken back to Orkney where it was received from them by Edmund Blackadder.[19]

Both the Blackadders, Edmund and Patrick, were well-known figures in Scottish maritime circles, in all probability related to the William and John Blackadder active in northern waters in the earl of Bothwell's time. Both are noted many times in the records of the sixteenth-century admiralty court,[20] and there is evidence that Edmund in particular was notorious. There had been complaints made regarding him on 1 January 1570 and again on 23 March 1571, when Frederick II of Denmark had written to the Scottish king concerning a ship of Lübeck seized by 'Capt. Eideman Bleceter' and carried to Orkney.[21] This is especially interesting in view of the fact that Edmund Blackadder was stated by Robert in his letter to Bellenden of 31 March 1568 to be one of the earl of Bothwell's two captured followers whom he had sent south by order of Regent Moray. As mentioned earlier, the two had escaped, or had been permitted to do so, and Robert had expressed the fear that his brother the regent might suspect that this had happened with his connivance.

But by far the most significant of all the charges is the first named on the list – the only one noted by contemporary observers outside the islands.[22] In 1572 Robert was said to have directed Gavin Elphinstone, his master of household, and Henry Sinclair, his 'chalmerchyld', to go to Denmark 'with expres commissioun under his great seall and hand writt, to render to the king [of Denmark] . . . the supremacie and dominioun of . . . Orkney and Zetland'.[23] It was Elphinstone who made the journey and the Danish king, it was said, had sent back his confirmation and gift with one Hans Corsmay, from Bremen, enclosed in a bolt of Holland cloth, and deputed Lawrence Carness to be his lawman in the islands. Other evidence shows that Gavin Elphinstone had indeed visited the Danish court, claiming to represent Robert, and offering King Frederick II sovereignty over the islands. However, the only existing document concerning this mission is a letter dated 23 January 1574 which was apparently sent back in Elphinstone's own keeping.[24] Though definitely suggesting that Robert had made approaches to Frederick II, the letter is much less positive in its sense than the charge against Robert would suggest. It was issued by two royal officials rather than by the king himself, and although stating their

---

19 The printed version of this document gives Blackadder's name as Edward, but further examination of the original by officials of the National Archives at my request confirmed that this is a misreading of 'Edmond'.

20 *Acta Curia Admirallatus Scotiae, 1557–62*, ed. T. C. Wade (Stair Soc.), 1943.

21 *Reports on the Royal Archives of Denmark, and Report on the Royal Library at Copenhagen (46th Report of the Deputy Keeper of the Public Records, 1884–5)*, ed. W. D. Macray, app. ii, 23.

22 *The Historie of King James the Sext*, 157; Sir James Melville of Halhill, *Memorials of His Own Life* (Bannatyne Club), Edinburgh, 1827, 265.

23 *Shetland Documents, 1195–1579*, 162–3, no. 1.

24 *Reports on the Royal Archives of Denmark (46th Report)*, app. ii, 24.

willingness to discuss the problem of Orkney and Shetland, the Danes avoided the whole sensitive issue by questioning Elphinstone's credentials as Robert's representative.

The letter (which survives only as a copy in the Danish royal letter-book) bears a marginal note describing Elphinstone as a thoroughly untrustworthy scoundrel (*scurra et praestigiator improbissimus, Scotus natione, fuit*) and this, coupled with an understandable reluctance to endanger Scoto-Danish relations (there had been no approach to a Scottish government on the question of the status of Orkney and Shetland for fifteen years, nor was there to be another until 1585) at the behest of one relatively minor magnate, meant that there was no response. Elphinstone himself remains a mysterious figure; the only other reference to him in connection with Robert – a story that the latter issued him with a licence to fight a single combat with one Patrick Clark – comes from the Complaints.[25] However, he was not unknown to the Danes. He had been a messenger from Moray to the Danish king as early as August 1568,[26] and he was the subject of a letter from Lennox to Frederick II on 18 July 1570 interceding on behalf of Alexander Campbell and Archibald Stewart, who had been imprisoned in Denmark on allegedly false charges.[27] Among Campbell and Stewart's accusers, all of whom were described as being infamous in Scotland, was Gavin Elphinstone, who was said to have robbed his patron 'with whom he had lived honourably for some years'.

However, there is another side to this story. Brian Smith has suggested that Lawrence Carness's appearance on the scene may have formed part of a stratagem used on three occasions by two of the Danish kings, Christian III and Frederick II, in their quest to regain a toehold of authority in the islands.[28] It involved sending a lawman of their own to Shetland to exercise his powers there in defiance of Scottish claims. Understandably the kings of Scots were not amused, and each of these ploys ended in humiliating failure. Diplomatic efforts were no more successful, but were at least more dignified from the Danish standpoint and approaches continued to be made at intervals. But the significance of the 1575 attempt in particular was the suggestion in the Complaints that Robert had co-operated with it, indeed invited it. If Brian Smith's analysis is right, then we can say either that the initiative came from the Danish side independently, or that Robert's overtures provided Denmark with an opportunity to attempt a ploy that had been tried before, albeit unsuccessfully.

Just what Robert's men were doing in Denmark is difficult to say. Given the Danes' views on Elphinstone, they may even have wondered if Robert knew of this embassy conducted in his name; perhaps, although it seems highly unlikely, he was indeed innocent. At any rate it seems strange that nothing further is heard

---

25 *Shetland Documents, 1195-1579*, 9, no. 29.
26 *Reports on the Royal Archives of Denmark* (47th Report), 18.
27 *Shetland Documents, 1195-1579*, 19.
28 B. Smith, 'When did Orkney and Shetland become Part of Scotland?', *New Orkney Antiquarian Journal*, v (2011), esp. 52–6.

of Elphinstone the scoundrel. It may be, as his name suggests, that he was related to Robert through the latter's mother. Possibly he was indeed Robert's master of household, but by contrast to Robert's other important followers, for whom there is no shortage of further references,[29] he is never heard of again. One possibility, though it must remain speculative, was that Elphinstone was employed by Robert solely for the purpose of making overtures to Denmark on account of his previous experience of the Danish court. The same obscurity affects the characters of Hans Corsmay and even Henry Sinclair, undesignated as he is, is extremely difficult to identify.[30] Lawrence Carness's name suggests an Orcadian living in Denmark, and as such a promising candidate as an alternative lawman, similar to Gervald Willemsen, a Shetlander who had been sent to try the same trick, with equal lack of success, thirty-odd years before.[31] The name Carness is a telling piece of circumstantial detail, as is the picturesque story of the bolt of Holland cloth; the latter could be true, since secrecy would be essential even for such an inconclusive missive as Robert in the event received, but the references to Sinclair, Corsmay and Carness regrettably find no corroboration elsewhere. In the end we can only say that the allegation of dealings with Denmark may be true and that Robert felt himself reduced to this desperate throw to hold on to what he had acquired; but the Complaints, given their source, could be relied on to put the most sinister light on the whole business. Certainly, although Robert was undoubtedly in trouble at this time, nothing more was heard of this alleged treasonable activity, though there may have been another reason for this – the attitude of the Regent Morton.

Robert had had cause before to fear Morton's relationship with Patrick Bellenden, but the regent, though he clearly disliked Robert, was not disposed to show the rigour demanded by Bellenden and his followers. His attitude was largely, perhaps characteristically, venal. According to the anonymous author of *The Historie of King James the Sext*, Robert was 'in greate feare to be heighlie puneist . . . but the Regents opinion was rather to fyne sum weight of gold from him than utherwayis'.[32] When, in the end, Morton fell, the charges disappeared. It would, however, be entirely wrong to see the charges (and the other instances of Robert's misbehaviour) as being purely the inventions of his enemies, or their pursuit as entirely the result of Morton's desire to wring money from him. The author of King James's history was in no doubt as to Robert's participation in grave crimes, and the closer the investigation of the crimes specified in the Complaints, the more apparent it becomes that Robert was lucky to survive this period of his life.

29 See Anderson, *Robert Stewart, Earl of Orkney, Lord of Shetland*, app. 6.
30 There are several Henry Sinclairs noted in *REO*, the most eligible of whom, by date and family connections, is the spouse of Agnes, daughter of William Sinclair of Warsetter, who granted land in Graemsay and St Ola, 6 Feb. 1587 (308, no. cxc) to Malcolm Groat of Tankerness in exchange for tacks in Sanday granted by Robert. However, the identification of this Henry Sinclair with Robert's servant remains purely a guess.
31 Smith, 'When did Orkney and Shetland become Part of Scotland?', 52–3.
32 *The Historie of King James the Sext*, 157.

Ironically, it could be argued that under a different regent Robert might well have suffered the punishment he feared.

All this is not to say that Robert was not oppressive, or did not alter the laws of the islands; as we have seen, the 1575 list contains details to back up both these charges, though admittedly there are nothing like the graphic particulars about his activities that were to be offered later against Bruce. But although Robert was undoubtedly harsh, his accusers were less interested in complaining about this than in proving him guilty of treason. Although evidence pointing to this existed, those accusers in their anxiety included some ill-conceived charges that attempted to inflate simple misrule into something much graver. The result is an unorganised mish-mash of accusations of high felony, general abuses, specific crimes against particular people, and other matters. To these is added for good measure the third, the complaints of the Shetlanders, suitably amended to present Robert (instead of Bruce) as the villain. Some of the charges comprising this last group still bear traces of their separate origin, since unlike the other groups they prefigure the 1577 document. Robert's compelling the lieges to offer him 'bankettis and great cheer on their awin expenses' was to be 'preven with the haill country' (later it was, but with Bruce as the offender).[33] The 'compelling of the countrymen to pay to him their males, grassums [entry fees paid by holders of tacks] and rests [arrears]' instead of to the *comptroller* 'as the country will testify.'[34] In this case, unfortunately, nothing further was heard.

There does seem at least high cause for suspicion as to Robert's guilt with regard to the charges of oppression, piracy and 'sklent [crooked] dealings' with Denmark. It is when the other groups of charges are considered – those alleging that he acted beyond his authority and in usurpation of royal power – that problems arise. Robert was accused of: usurping royal power in taking up royal customs, mails and *grassums* formerly paid to the comptroller;[35] declaring himself to enjoy quasi-monarchic power in the islands – 'as free Lord and Heritor of Orkney and Zetland as the King of Scotland is in his own realm, or the Queen of England, or the King of France in France'; taking unto himself the powers of admiralty and justiciary; *disponing* the benefices of the islands 'vacant at the King's Majesty's gift'; and remitting and forgiving capital crimes such as slaughter, theft and piracy.[36]

Since these charges were never heard in court, it may be unduly legalistic to debate their competence in law, but in fact they raise issues about the whole nature of Robert's position in Orkney and Shetland as well as his own view of that position. Two questions could be asked. Firstly, to what powers was Robert entitled by virtue of his *heritable* infeftment? Secondly, what special rights, if any, did he have as superior, sheriff, foud, etc? The issue is complex. Robert's grant was unusual. Its heritable quality was virtually the only respect in which it differed from Oliver Sinclair's tacks of 1541–2, and its entry in the privy seal register in May 1565 stated

33 *Shetland Documents, 1195–1579*, 164, no. 10.
34 *Shetland Documents, 1195–1579*, 166, no. 26.
35 *Shetland Documents, 1195–1579*, 163, no. 3; 166, no. 26.
36 *Shetland Documents, 1195–1579*, 164, no. 9; 163, no. 5; 164, no. 14; 165, no. 17.

that it was in the same terms as Oliver's.[37] The appointments granted to Oliver Sinclair by the late King James had included the constabulary of Kirkwall Castle and those of justice, sheriff, admiral and bailie. These powers were broad enough to answer at least some of the usurpation charges.

The question of particular rights accorded to Robert by the islands' ancient legal arrangements is more difficult. Such rights would presumably be those traditionally pertaining to the earl, and Robert, whatever his pretensions, was not earl, a title that remained vested in the crown. However, the idea that the superior of Orkney and Shetland, whatever his status, had special powers, does appear to have some validity. Robert himself was certainly conscious of this; regarding escheats, for example, he wrote to Bellenden on 21 March 1569 that he was 'als frelie infeft with all eshetres of Orknay and Yetland as the kyng or quene mycht gif the samen'.[38] This was a power he was not slow to use.

Moreover, Norse law made specific provision for superiors of Orkney and Shetland acting in what amounted to the capacity of admirals. As it happened, the first recorded admiral in Scotland was Henry Sinclair, the earl of Orkney who died in 1417,[39] but Robert's precedent for acting as he did would seem to have lain more with the lawbook. As foud of Shetland, for example, he was fully entitled to exercise a maritime jurisdiction. The arguments in the case of the Southampton merchants, brought on 14 December 1577[40] illustrate this. Robert defended himself on the ground that the merchants' ships were in fact fitted out for piracy and had attacked one David Rusman in Scalloway. Other maritime powers of the foud were more concerned with the regulation of trade. In 1571 John Smith, one of the Southampton men, had received a cowp bill – a licence given to a visiting merchant enabling him to trade and laying down conditions[41] – but had not dealt in merchandise and had gone away four or five days thereafter. Later, in 1574, Smith had entered his ship and received a 'coip bill according to the maner and custom of the countrie'. The latter source, in addition to noting this undoubted evidence of the foud's authority over merchant shipping, gives strong support to the view that his jurisdiction extended also over fishing and other vessels. The case of McCreath and his followers illustrated clearly the confusion between the Scots and Norse views of this jurisdiction. Robert may have behaved wretchedly, but it seems rather hard that he should be blamed on the one hand for usurping power of admiralty and justiciary (as he was specifically in this instance) and on the other for sparing McCreath and his men punishment for their 'cruel deed'.

Besides authority similar to that of a Scottish admiral, Robert's legal position as sheriff and foud seem to have given him what amounted to justiciary powers. The

---

37 *RSS*, v, no. 2078.
38 Roxburghe Mun., bundle 1634, no. 9.
39 *Acta Curia Admirallatus Scotiae, 1557–62*, p. xiii.
40 *RPC*, ii, 654–60.
41 The cowp bill is mentioned in both the complaints against Bruce: *Shetland Documents, 1195–1579*, 237, f. 11r,) and *Ct Bk of Shetland*, 74.

Scottish justiciar's powers were indeed broader than those of the 'simple sheriff' that Robert was stated to be, traditionally dealing with 'supreme cognisances of all controversies of every kind'.[42] However, if Robert was a sheriff (and even by his grant alone he was surely more than that), he was hardly a simple one. The term 'sheriff' had been in use in Orkney and Shetland since Oliver Sinclair's tack of 1541. Sinclair's commission, however, completely ignored the legal set-up in the north, and as far as jurisdiction is concerned, it is difficult to imagine the term 'sheriff' being more than the name (employed at first in Orkney alone) for the senior legal official in what was still very much a Norse system. By the 1570s, the foudry of Shetland had also become a titular sheriffship,[43] but retained its old judicial powers right up to the abolition of Norse law in 1611.[44] The lawbook of Orkney and Shetland does not survive, but the commonest opinion is that it was a regionally modified version of the Gulathinglaw, whose provisions extended over the whole gamut of civil, criminal and maritime law.[45] Given this, and the strongly independent position of the Orkney earls in former times, it is difficult to imagine Robert's judicial powers being much less wide than those of a Scottish justiciar. Of the two examples cited in support of the charge against Robert, the McCreath case has been noted; the other concerned one William Wishart in Shetland, an otherwise obscure figure, who had been dead for a year before Robert's entry, but who was condemned in effigy and had his goods and gear confiscated in a manner similar to that of Sir James Sinclair of Sanday and the even longer-dead Sir David Sinclair of Sumburgh.[46]

The debate continues when other examples are considered from among these accusations. Rights to *wrack and waith*, for example, were not included in Robert's grant, and it was duly pointed out that he had nevertheless 'uptaken' these. This is a complicated question. Professor Donaldson, in his *Shetland Life under Earl Patrick*, talks of three senses of the term 'wreck'. Two of these, the simpler and more basic, covered driftwood and the washed-up carcases of marine mammals. Disputes about both are included in the charges against Bruce, though the complaints were against interference with a private rather than a royal right, a right analogous to the udal landowner's right to foreshore. However, in the third, widest, sense 'Wreck . . . was claimed as the perquisite of the king or of the Earl as his representative . . .'.[47] In this sense it is possible that Robert, conscious of his special position, was overplaying his hand.

42 Dobie, 'Udal Law', 451–2; Drever, 'Udal Law', 327; Sellar, 'Udal Law', 204–5; J. Ryder 'Udal Law', *The Laws of Scotland: Stair Memorial Encyclopaedia*, vols I–XXV, Edinburgh, 1987–9, xxiv, paras 301–16, editorial excursus, paras 317–29.

43 W. J. Dobie, 'A Shetland Decree', *JR*, li (1939), 1.

44 *RPC*, ix, 181.

45 K. Robberstad, 'Udal Law', *Shetland and the Outside World, 1469–1969*, Oxford, 1996, 49; Dobie, 'Udal Law'; Drever, 'Udal Law'; Sellar, 'Udal Law'.

46 *Shetland Documents, 1195–1579*, 165, no. 17; 166, no. 27.

47 B. Smith, 'A Note on Waithing and Waith', *Toons and Tenants*, Lerwick, 2000, 58–60.; Donaldson, *Shetland Life under Earl Patrick*, 54–5; see also Goudie, *Antiquities of Shetland*, 90.

The same may well apply to his taking up the 'royal customs, tolls and victual'[48] of Shetland and 'disponing the benefices of the country, vacant at the King's Majesty's gift and compelling beneficit men to set their benefices to him'.[49] Robert's position in the latter question was to be the object of some dispute in later years, but the accusation at this date is more interesting in respect to Robert's policy towards the clergy. St Ola, Holm, Unst, Nesting and Walls are all cited as examples. We do not have evidence for all of these, but it is true that 1573–4 saw something of an upheaval among the clergy of the Northern Isles. *Demissions* took place in Holm, Unst, Delting (including Scatsta), Dunrossness and Orphir.[50] Alexander Thomson, vicar of Dunrossness, was stated in the Complaints to have been assaulted as he came down from the pulpit by William Hume, a soldier.[51] Magnus Halcro of Brough was replaced as minister of Orphir in 1574, dying not long afterwards, probably in exile; his successor was Thomas Stevenson, formerly at Firth and Stenness. The same year William Moodie was translated from South Ronaldsay and Burray to Hoy and Graemsay, being succeeded in his former charge by Alexander Dick who, during his tenure, 'abundantly dilapidated his benefice'.[52] James Maxwell, vicar of Stronsay, also suffered at the hands of Robert's followers,[53] though he did not actually leave the islands until 1577, being succeeded by William Henderson the following year.[54]

These events reinforce the picture of a determined and dangerous man, extending his power into every sphere of activity in Orkney and Shetland – the earldom, the bishopric, the clergy (probably with special treatment for those who retained a sympathy for the departed bishop), the udal lands, the burgh of Kirkwall and the administration of justice by land and sea; and who believed himself to have a perfect right to do so. But whatever force Robert accorded to the special laws of Orkney and Shetland in justifying his position and actions, he scarcely regarded them as sacrosanct, and gave the islanders no cause to anticipate any respect for the old system if it conflicted with his interests. On the contrary, there are plenty of examples in the Complaints of alteration of the native laws, even though these were not brought together into a general accusation. Several have already been noted – the changes in the swine-rooting laws and in female rights of inheritance. The charge of altering the weights of the bismar and pundlar of Orkney suggests, simply by its curious omission of Shetland, that Orkney suffered the same rapacity as her neighbour. The act that none should bring home boats without Robert's permission has also been noted, but perhaps deserves some comment. In fact the corresponding allegation in 1577 was that Bruce had compelled those who brought boats and timber back

---

48 *Shetland Documents, 1195–1579*, 163, no. 3.
49 *Shetland Documents, 1195–1579*, 7, no. 16.
50 See H. Scott, *Fasti Ecclesiae Scoticanae*, Edinburgh, 1915–28, for Holm (vii, 217), Unst (vii, 298) and
    Delting (including Scatsta) (vii, 306).
51 *Shetland Documents, 1195–1579*, 164, no. 16.
52 Scott, *Fasti*, vii, 229.
53 *Shetland Documents, 1195–1579*, 164, no. 16.
54 Scott, *Fasti*, vii, 272.

from Norway to sell their purchases at fixed prices.[55] Robert and Bruce may have been seeking to control and profit from what was undoubtedly a brisk trade.[56] The Shetlanders who suffered complained that no such act had been passed or at any rate had not been intimated to them.

Robert's 'compelling the dogger boats and other fishers of this realm to pay to him great toll and taxis bye auld use and wont',[57] also found greater background detail in the Shetland Complaints, as did his 'making and setting of new takkis and gerssumes to the poor lieges, and compelling them to pay to him great soums of money far by the auld order of the country',[58] though of course Robert's personal responsibility for these oppressions remains doubtful, as it is with all Shetland complaints. The 1575 Complaints accused him of 'wrangous and false judgement and sentences against the King's Majesty's lieges . . . and causing his deputies thereafter to reduce and retreat the same, as he did to Andrew Mowat, Mr Robert Cheyne and Andrew Hawick of Skatsta'. The charge involved measures of corruption and extortion, since the alteration of the sentence was the result of a bribe given to Robert by Hawick of Scatsta. Although these individuals were Shetlanders, the nearest to a corresponding charge in the 1577 document was in fact something quite different. Here it was stated that after the feuar had passed through the Shetland parishes holding courts (presumably during mid-1574 or 1575), Bruce had recalled cases that Robert had remitted and forgiven.[59]

It was even stated that when the Shetlanders had complained about Bruce to Robert, the latter had 'of conscience' relieved his brother of the foudry of Shetland, on payment of 700 merks 'to relief us of his tirrany'.[60] It is indeed possible that Robert was compelled to curb the excesses of Cultmalindie. Shetland's relatively good opinion of Robert probably stemmed from his being present in the islands for a mere two to three months in the summer, and thus being seen as a relief from the villainous Bruce; but although as a result his reputation may not have suffered as much as in Orkney, the Orcadians on the other hand had still further reasons for detesting Robert's rule.

He took away 'suckin fra the auld vuthall mylnis of Orkney, quhilkis wer observit of befoir inviolate'.[61] This charge is interesting because it indicates a distinction between the position of mills in Orkney and in Shetland. In Shetland, the system seems to have been one of small-scale mills, individually owned;[62] in Orkney, the charge shows that already, before Robert, there were mills with *suckens* or jurisdictions compelling local producers to use a particular mill. In view of the general

55 *Shetland Documents, 1195–1579*, 165, no. 19; 237, f. 20v.
56 Fenton, *The Northern Isles*, 552–3.
57 *Shetland Documents, 1195–1579*, 163, no. 4.
58 *Shetland Documents, 1195–1579*, 164, no. 11.
59 *Shetland Documents, 1195–1579*, 200, no. 237.
60 *Shetland Documents, 1195–1579*, 88–9.
61 *Shetland Documents, 1195–1579*, 166, no. 32.
62 Goudie, *Antiquities of Shetland*, 247.

and substantiated charge that Robert was seeking superiority over the udal lands, one might have supposed that Robert was similarly seeking to introduce a Scottish system of *thirlage* to the mill; but in fact it appears that he was rather taking to himself the right to dispone already existing suckens.[63] The udal mills were presumably large mills serving udal estates – as in the case of James Irving of Sebay's mill.[64] Their monopolies seem to have been less rigid than those of their Scottish counterparts,[65] and their existence did not prohibit the building of individual mills, and although it appears udal mills did in fact have suckens, it seems from the evidence he cites that Irving of Sebay's mill monopoly was more a matter of circumstance than of law. However, Robert may have attempted to usurp whatever rights the udal mills possessed and to attempt to assimilate them to the feudal arrangements which his testament suggests applied to the mills on the earldom estates.

Further accusations, like some of the usurpation charges, suggest that Robert was exercising legitimate powers derived from the islands' own legal traditions. The reference to 'bankettis and great cheers' is one. As in other cases, the Shetland document fails to substantiate the charge against Robert, but demonstrates Bruce's guilt all too clearly. But if we assume that Robert also exercised this power, it certainly suggests the abuse of a genuine entitlement of the superior of Shetland in his legal and administrative circuits. It was also alleged that he 'gave licence to men to fight singular combats', the disputants in question being Ninian Dougall and Alexander Bewmond, George Wallace and William Cullen, Nicol Sinclair and Stephen Busbie, Gavin Elphinstone and Patrick Clark.[66] There are no further details and there are no precedents for such combats in the Northern Isles, but there remains the possibility that Robert derived this archaic idea from the lawbook. It may be that the island form of the old Norse code retained in its provisions the old Scandinavian idea of *holmganga*, notwithstanding its absence from what we know of the laws of contemporary Norway, and the fact that it had not been practised in the islands within living memory. A further charge was that he forbade ferries running without his passport, apparently making a special statute to this effect, and departure from the islands without permission. This obviously rendered complaint extremely difficult for Robert's accusers. Certainly there is a comparative dearth of documentary evidence regarding Robert's activities dating from the years of his first stay in the Northern Isles, as opposed to the period immediately before and after, and there are other indications that Robert did indeed pursue these practices. Even during his incarceration in Edinburgh, on 1 July 1576, he granted a licence to his servant, William Garrioch, burgess of Kirkwall, to travel within South Ronaldsay or any other part of Orkney and Shetland, to 'use merchandise'.[67] Unauthorised departure

---

63 Fenton, *The Northern Isles: Orkney and Shetland*, 397; this volume also contains an estimate of the number of mills in Orkney at this time.
64 *REO*, 99, no. xliv.
65 Fenton, *The Northern Isles: Orkney and Shetland*, 397.
66 *Shetland Documents, 1195–1579*, 166, no. 29.
67 NRS (microf.) RH4/35/388/41.

from the islands was of course the reason given for the escheat of Ola Anderson in 1574, and a similar complaint about forbidding departure was later made against him by Magnus and Gilbert Irving in 1587.

Finally there were allegations of oppression that were altogether free from the legal and other problems which have beset the attempts herein to examine the charges against Robert. His promises to the burgh of Kirkwall on becoming provost had gone for nothing; he forbade the burgesses to buy skins, hides, butter, oil and other wares without his leave, and gave permission to others to exercise liberties that should have been limited to the burgesses.[68] It was possibly at this time that he destroyed the burgh's charter chest. He was said to have brought in 'hieland men', traditional marauders in the area, to 'sorn, oppress and spuilyie' the country, especially the island of Graemsay, and prevented their pursuit on the grounds that they were his men.[69] It is not possible to identify these Highlanders though possibly Robert was simply giving his blessing to the time-honoured piracies of the Lewismen in return for tribute – or the incidents that specifically affected Graemsay, but it is significant that not long after this James Stewart, Robert's illegitimate son, appears as superior of the island.[70] As if the foregoing were not enough, the 1575 Complaints reserved 'special points' of oppression and other crimes which 'sall be very large, odious and fearful to be read', for such time as the particular complainers might be given free passage out of the islands; these protests give preliminary notice of the later 'particular complaints' of the Shetlanders.

The Complaints suggest that Robert was well aware of the unusual powers that the superiority of Orkney and Shetland gave him, both in the plenary jurisdiction given by the lawbook, and in the traditional freedoms of the former earls, which he seems to have felt himself permitted to exercise. The whole document indicates a legal problem regarding the government of Orkney and Shetland that unfortunately would not be solved at this time. It would pass through a second crisis in the 1580s, but not until the fall of Robert's son nearly half a century later would decisive institutional change put an end to the trouble.

On 31 January 1576 the privy council, in accordance with the complaints that the islands of Orkney and Shetland were 'havelie troublit hereit and oppressit be cumpaneis of suddartis and utheris brokin men . . . dependaris upoun Lord Robert Stewart', and also that the inhabitants were forbidden to leave the islands by sea or land, as the result of which they were 'abill to be allutirlie wrakkit and hereit for evir', charged those now acting in Robert's name to cease from hindering traffic in and out of the islands.[71]

---

68 *Shetland Documents, 1195–1579*, 164, no. 15.

69 *Shetland Documents, 1195–1579*, 166, no. 28.

70 James is stated in the *Scots Peerage* to have been implicated in Robert's trafficking with the Danes, though there is no evidence of this in *Shetland Documents, 1195–1579*.

71 *RPC*, ii, 482–3.

A fortnight later, a further complainer was heard, Nicol Oliverson, son of Oliver Rendall, udaller in Gairsay.[72] Nicol's father had died when he was an infant and he had been compelled, he said, to leave Orkney for Norway, where he remained for forty years. He had returned some time previously (ironically because he understood that he could get better justice in Orkney than formerly) to pursue his father's heritage before Lord Robert Stewart, and had obtained decreet against the alleged possessors of the lands. These were Magnus Halcro of Brough and his wife, and John Muirhead, to whom Halcro's wife had granted her lands about 1560.[73] Nevertheless, shortly afterwards, in Nicol's absence, Robert had entered one Isobel Brown in the lands; Oliverson stated that this was because Robert was trying to tempt him, as a 'strangeare wereit and beggarit in persute of his just heretage', into illegality by forcing him to steal the land. He would thus presumably have rendered himself liable to escheat. John Sharp, Robert's procurator, stated that an assize and precept of Robert's had possessed Oliverson of land in Gairsay, previously held by his father, but that a second had found that by 'the law and practik observit within ... Orknay in tymes past', he had no title, and that the lands pertained to Robert.

This suggests an example of the charge against Robert of pronouncing judgments and then causing his deputes thereafter to 'reduce and retreat the same'. Whether or not Robert's first judgment in Oliverson's favour was indeed 'wrangous and false' cannot really be judged, but what is interesting is that in the first instance the land was taken from its holders, persons with no love for Robert, and in the second a further assize reversed the decision of its predecessor and the land was not returned to Magnus Halcro but granted to a third party. This affair therefore supports the charges against Robert of controlling the assizes, of oppressing Magnus Halcro and others, and of finding excuses for escheating land-holders. Oliverson's case returned before the lords on 4 April 1576 and judgment was found in his favour.[74]

On 25 March Alexander Hay wrote to Henry Killigrew, the English diplomat, 'As to the poor man's suit against my Lord Robert, the time were very proper if any would take the pains to come and pursue it, for my Lord Robert is still in Edinburgh Castle, and no great hope of his speedy delivery.'[75] Robert was to remain in the castle for two years until August 1577, and in Linlithgow from then until the beginning of the following year.[76] During this time power in Orkney appears to have rested in the hands of Patrick Monteith, who is described as 'capitane of Kirkwall in Orknay'.[77] William Elphinstone is named as sheriff depute.[78] On 26 June Monteith and twenty-nine followers allegedly slew one Adam Dickson, servitor of Edward

72 RPC, ii, 488–9.
73 Prot. Bk Gilbert Grote, 53.
74 RPC, ii, 517–18.
75 CSP Scot., v, 622.
76 RPC, ii, 622, 669–70.
77 TA, xiii, 136.
78 RPC, ii, 576.

Halcro (possibly a brother of Magnus Halcro).[79] For this, they were summoned to Edinburgh in August to submit to the law in the tolbooth.[80] Elphinstone, who was named among those summoned, was put under obligation on 20 December 1576 to apprehend the criminals.[81] Shortly afterwards the escheats of Walter Bruce, Edward Tulloch in Widewall and William Gordon were granted to Henry Sinclair, son of Robert Sinclair of Ness, on account of this crime.[82] Most of these men were associated with Robert Stewart, though what Adam Dickson's perceived fault was, we do not know. In any event, Robert's power, though diminished, still had a long reach.

At the same time, moves were afoot against Laurence Bruce of Cultmalindie and his rule in Shetland. On 1 November the privy council took the decision to hear the Shetlanders' complaints against him and he was warded south of the Tay.[83] Eight days later William Moodie of Breckness and William Henderson were commissioned to undertake the inquiry.[84] On 4 February 1577, at Tingwall, as its name indicates the original site of the *thing*, or parliament of all Shetland, they began taking depositions.[85] The complaints against Bruce provide an extraordinarily detailed picture, not merely of vicious and arbitrary rule, but of the society that was compelled to suffer that rule – its customs, its law, its economy and its way of life. The document embodying these complaints is itself a unique product of Shetland law in action – but with a vengeance; what happened in these days has no parallel. Somehow it seems to have been possible to harness the Shetlanders' liking for public testimony, shown in the oath-system of the court book, to an extent without precedent or successor. For once the relative obscurity regarding conditions in Shetland is lifted, and the equivalent evidence for Orkney furnished by a handful of charters and court decrees is made to look sparse by comparison.

Popular feeling in Shetland was undoubtedly running high, and the commons turned out in great numbers to bear witness before the commissioners. On 4 and 5 February, 110 men from Tingwall, Whiteness and Weisdale came, on 8 February, 29 men from Bressay, and on succeeding days, 51 from Nesting and Lunnasting, 30 from Whalsay, 41 from Yell, 43 from Unst and so on, culminating on 21 February with over 120 from Dunrossness alone.[86]

There were several major areas of discontent. Most important was the measurement of victual payments for skat and other dues. In time past, the responsibility for the public assessment of these had rested with the lawrightman, who had custody of the measuring instruments – the cuttell, for measuring the coarse cloth wadmel, the bismar, for weighing out butter, and the can, for measuring oil – and who also

79 *RPC*, ii, 576; *RSS*, vii, nos 794, 825.
80 *TA*, xiii, 136.
81 *RPC*, ii, 576.
82 *RSS*, vii, nos 794, 825.
83 *RPC*, ii, 563.
84 *RPC*, ii, 616–18.
85 *Shetland Documents, 1195–1579*, 183.
86 *Shetland Documents, 1195–1579*, 193–4.

carried out the actual assessment. Each parish presented its contribution to a coherent overall picture of abuse.

In the first place, the lawrightman had in the case of most parishes been forcibly relieved of his duty of measuring the victual, and replaced by one of the laird's own choosing or, in the case of Bressay, by an unwilling delegate who was compelled out of fear to measure at Bruce's orders. Nicol Hardwall, David Tulloch and Erling of Bu, lawrightmen respectively of Delting and Scatsta, Northmavine and Dunrossness, all made specific complaints that they were not allowed to discharge their duties.

The measuring itself was abused, both in the weights and measures used and in the lack of scruple with which it was carried out. In Tingwall, Whiteness and Weisdale 70 cuttells[87] were taken to the *pack* of wadmel instead of the customary 60; in Bressay the figure was said to be 75 cuttells. The measuring cuttells were also defective. When Erling of Bu had brought 'twa sindrie cuttellis of just measour' to the measuring he was forbidden to use them, and publicly broke them, calling upon the commons to witness his action.[88] When individuals complained about the 'large and wrangus gripping of the hands that mett [the wadmel]', the laird's men 'wald giff thame ane straik on the hand with the cuttell to gar thaim lat it gang'. Another complaint elicited from Bruce the comment that the wadmel 'was na volvat [velvet]'.[89]

The bismar had been increased by one fifth, as had been already stated in the complaints against Robert. This meant that for every 12 lispunds weight taken of old, it was said that 15 were now exacted. Erasmus of Kirkabister, lawrightman of Bressay in the days when Ola Sinclair of Havera had been foud, stated that he had used a bismar made thirty years before by William Irving of Trondra with the consent of the commons. Bruce had refused to use this instrument and had had a new one made 'transmonting sax, sewin, or aucht merkis mair, betuixt the wecht [weight] and the hand that weyit, nor that auld just bismeyre was'. Magnus Reid of Aith had compared the laird's bismar with one used all his days by his father who had been lawman, and found it to be eight merks (one third of a lispund) out; David Tulloch, lawrightman of Northmavine, stated that he had been fined five dollars for saying that it was 'evil done' that he should not be allowed to weigh the commons' dues and that unjust weights should be used.

In constructing his bismar, Bruce was said to have sought out the biggest 'that was amang the Duchemen'[90] – the German merchant community – and had his made even bigger. The 'Dutch' weights and measures were themselves complained of, but it was affirmed by the men of the North Isles that this was due to greatly higher exactions that the merchants had had to pay Bruce since his entry. It had been the custom for a merchant's prices to be set by the foud and 'honest men', but the

---

87 The term 'cuttell' is in this case used as a measure of length rather than as the name of the measuring instrument. See glossary.
88 *Shetland Documents, 1195–1579*, 194.
89 *Shetland Documents, 1195–1579*, 188.
90 *Shetland Documents, 1195–1579*, 195.

laird now set these for himself and had greatly increased the prices of 'Duchemen and strangearis geir'. The prices of barrels of beer and of ryemeal bran had been increased by 25 per cent.[91]

The can for measuring oil had also been altered and the manner of its use perverted. In time past the capacity of the can should have been one forty-eighth part of a 'Bramer [Bremen] barrel', and it should have been filled by being set on flat ground and oil poured into it to the level of two plugs ('plouks') set in the can's sides. Bruce's can was between one thirty-fourth and one thirty-sixth of a barrel in capacity, without plugs, and was filled to overflowing while standing on a plank over a barrel so that the oil in the barrel was augmented by a cupful or more of surplus. The barrels had formerly been furnished by the fouds, or by the commons with recompense from the fouds. Now the commons were required by the laird to furnish the barrels without recompense.[92]

At the same time, in the case of both merchants and commons, the victual/money exchange rates had been altered. The *yopindale*, a silver coin, had previously been worth three *gudlings* (a victual measure equivalent to six cuttells of wadmel) when paying arrears. Now it was worth only two gudlings, though the merchants would still give the old rate. Likewise the value of the angel noble, an English gold coin, had dropped from six gudlings to five. In Northmavine, Bruce had compelled the commons to pay 24 *bawbees* Scots for each gudling owing, the gudling never having been worth more than six bawbees before. Among the merchant community the equivalences of both victual and money had changed. A gudling had previously been equivalent to eight cuttells of 'unblicht larrett' – unbleached linen (as opposed to woollen) cloth[93] – but was now worth only six cuttells; the merk of copper, previously equal to two shillings, was now equal to four shillings. These changes could have been attempts to compensate for inflation, but other evidence suggests that Bruce's chief aim was a simple amelioration of his income by manipulating his exchange rate. He was said to have given the merchants two gudlings for a yopindale when selling, but demanded three gudlings for the coin when buying.[94]

The second major theme running through the complaints was that of Bruce's maladministration of the native legal system doubtless, as was to be proved repeatedly, out of a complete disregard for local conditions. The courts, scheduled no doubt by a more southerly calendar, were held by Bruce at times that prevented the gathering of harvest. Bruce's men were introduced to the assize in force. The Bressay men alleged that at the previous Lawting at Scalloway, scarcely half the assize were countrymen, so that the latter could not make objection, though they did not agree with the assize's decrees. James Bruce, one of Cultmalindie's followers, was said to

91 *Shetland Documents, 1195–1579*, 198.
92 *Shetland Documents, 1195–1579*, 205.
93 *Shetland Documents, 1195–1579*, 198.
94 *Shetland Documents, 1195–1579*, 196.

have sat on an assize the previous year while still *unrelaxed at the horn* (this statement is incidentally an interesting example of how, even in Shetland, Scots legal terminology was quite familiar, and that James Bruce was technically disqualified under Scots law from any assize). James Bruce's fellow assizemen included Henry Bruce and Thomas Boyne. The last had been on the assize that tried the Southampton merchants in 1574; and was alleged in both sets of complaints to have murdered Patrick Windram, and also in the Shetlanders' testimony to have killed one Alexander Duff in Strathbogie. In Unst, Boyne and Henry Bruce were actually permitted to sit on an assize case where they also acted as procurators.[95] The case in question – involving the wife of Bartholomew Strang of Voesgarth – foreshadowed another which was to be the subject some months later of an investigation by a higher tribunal – the privy council in Edinburgh.

Boyne and Bruce also assisted the laird in the holding of grandrie[96] courts each year instead of septennially according to use and wont. Such courts were usually initiated by private inquest, but Boyne and Bruce not only 'gave up the faults' but sat on the assize as well. John Smith, officer, William Magnusson in Benston and William Garrioch were fined six dollars for a *tulyie* in the latter's house and were refused a copy of the decreet against them despite paying one and a half yopindales for one. In addition to the unwonted frequency of the court, there were also complaints against summary conviction there, and of the indictment being taken up by Bruce's clerks instead of by a general inquest of honest men. It was also alleged that the reason why Bruce was so keen to use the grandrie procedure so frequently was because of the powers given to him by that part of the procedure called *sculding*. Here the whole population of a *scattald* (the equivalent of a Scottish commonty) might be put to probation on the report of one person in a case where a crime had been committed by a person unknown. Each member of the population was accordingly put to an acquittance, and on the laird's refusal of three such acquittances from anyone, escheat would follow. No specific instance was cited, but notable among the complaints against Robert had been the allegation that Bruce's half-brother had fined Robert Wishart, Walter Hill, Magnus McCreath, Ola Cumla and Magnus Reid 'great composition' for the alleged 'resset [receiving]' of Matthew Sinclair.[97] This may refer to the same activity.

Bruce's interference with Shetland law did not apply only to court procedure. His interpretation and changing of the laws themselves also caused great outcry. The law on swine-rooting, included also in the case against Robert, was particularly notable.[98] 'Under pretence and cullour of nichtborhood', Bruce increased the penalty for allowing one's swine to damage a neighbour's land and crops to at least double its former value, from 40 bawbees to three yopindales, and charged

95 *Shetland Documents, 1195–1579*, 200.
96 *Shetland Documents, 1195–1579*, 200.
97 *Shetland Documents, 1195–1579*, 166, no. 31.
98 *Shetland Documents, 1195–1579*, 201.

this whether or not there was evidence or complaint, by virtue of an assize held by Thomas Boyne and 'strangers'. This penalty was levied on all swine-owners in Unst, Fetlar and Dunrossness; Yell avoided it by payment in advance of 32 dollars between its eleven scattalds; in Tingwall only Erasmus of Wadbister and Laurence of Hammersland kept swine, for which they had to pay a dollar between them. Delting, Scatsta, Burra, Trondra, Quarff, Gulberwick and Bressay all killed their swine except for Nicol Johnston of Cruster in Bressay, who had a cow taken and sold, though his pigs had done no damage. Swine-rooting was also considered as a charge under the grandrie procedure, contrary to law.

In the past a scattald paid five gudlings as a fine for 'breiking of nichtbourheid'. Bruce, however, compelled every man in the scattald to pay this sum. He also awakened a case originally brought ten years before under Ola Sinclair of Havera, concerning the theft of sheep, and fined each household five gudlings, including heirs of some of the original parties, now deceased. He insisted on conducting the *schownd* (the inquiry for the purpose of dividing a deceased's estate) and raised the charge for this from six shillings to one ox of the best quality. He fined all without respect of person or excuse for non-*compearance* at the Lawting, instead of merely the major landowners, and increased the fine from the two dollars of Ola Sinclair's time to three dollars and a gudling.[99]

In addition to preventing the lawrightmen from carrying out their function in the measurement of victual, he compelled them to give more than their due in fulfilment of one of their other duties, that of arranging transport for the laird and his servants. They and their parishioners were compelled to *flit and fure* more often than the customary three times a year, over far greater distances, and often without payment. The men of Tingwall complained that they had had to transport the laird, his servants and goods 'ferdar be twelf myle of see, nor ever thai was wount in uther Fowdis tyme to do'. In Walls and Bressay complaint was made that parishioners failing to turn up with horse or boat were heavily fined even if there was sufficient transport there for Bruce's purposes.[100]

Another familiar complaint was about Bruce's abuse of what was probably an accepted right, that of local hospitality. He had arrived in Shetland with 15–16 men, and never travelled with fewer than a dozen; he made no payment for his or their bed and board; and his reluctant hosts were compelled to make gifts to his master of household, cook and steward; the goodwife and her servants got no access to their cellar during Bruce's stay. In Nesting he billeted at the house of Margaret Reid of Brough (a figure represented in the complaints against Robert); when he and his men had drunk all her beer he compelled the transfer to her house of a half-barrel of beer from the dwelling of Thomas of Kirkabister, which Thomas had been keeping for Thomas of Grunnafirth.[101]

99 *Shetland Documents, 1195–1579*, 208.
100 *Shetland Documents, 1195–1579*, 209.
101 *Shetland Documents, 1195–1579*, 199.

Besides the main complaints, there remained a massive catalogue of individual dissatisfactions, which together occupy a large part of the document. Several of these were relatively minor, though undoubtedly vexatious to those involved: Nicholas Paterson of Crossbister in Fetlar and his friends complained that Bruce had taken a large piece of driftwood from them and fined them without due process; several persons had been fined for transgressing the act fixing the prices for imported boats and timber; a case of 30 years before, involving the mistaken marking of a lamb belonging to the vicar of Yell, was revived, and Henry Spence, whose servant had committed the error, was fined; Ola in Islesburgh was *poinded* for making oil from the liver of a basking shark, despite the fact that courts at Nesting had twice found him guiltless of any offence; Nicholas Paterson, seemingly a stout heart, had been warded and fined for stating to Henry Bruce that Bruce cared more for 'gear' than for his own soul. Nicholas of Cullivoe and Garth of Ulsta complained that they had been compelled to become joint underfouds of Yell for which they had had to pay considerable sums. Nonetheless they had been prevented from exercising their office and had been refused the return of their fees. Edward of Odsta, in Fetlar, had sought to avoid the office of foud altogether, but had had to pay Bruce an ox in compensation to escape his anger.[102]

There were perhaps three more important complaints in this miscellaneous group. Firstly, the commons of Fetlar stated that they had been banned by law from inshore fishing in winter, their main livelihood while weather prevented them sailing deep-sea (why this had happened was not disclosed), and twelve boats and crews had been fined five gudlings each for breaking this ban.[103] Secondly, Magnus Leslie of Aith in Bressay told of his eviction from his house with his wife, children and servants by a party of Bruce's followers under Thomas Boyne. Leslie's wife had given birth only eight days previously. Boyne and his company of 15 or 16 soldiers remained in Leslie's house for nine to ten days, wasting his entire meat, drink, fish, flesh, butter and cheese, after which they stripped the house so thoroughly that Leslie was forced to borrow necessaries from neighbours (the description of all the items removed constitutes the earliest detailed inventory of plenishings for either archipelago). To add insult to injury, Leslie was not permitted to return to his empty house until he had paid a twenty-dollar fine, and was ejected from a three year lease of a steading in Bressay that he had held (presumably through successive renewals) for the past 24 years.[104] Thirdly, Arthur Sinclair of Aith (in what was, with the possible exception of Magnus Leslie's story, the most detailed and best attested single instance of oppression in all the complaints against Bruce) spoke of an incident which, by its nature and in view of the other complaints that he made at the same time, indicated the culmination of a feud between him and Bruce.[105]

102 *Shetland Documents, 1195–1579*, 214.
103 *Shetland Documents, 1195–1579*, 212.
104 *Shetland Documents, 1195–1579*, 216.
105 *Shetland Documents, 1195–1579*, 217.

Arthur Sinclair, a former sheriff depute, is frequently found at the centre of Shetland, and occasionally Orkney, affairs.[106] It was he who put the articles to the commissioners specifying the Shetlanders' complaints, both general and particular; indeed, it seems very likely that Arthur was a leader of the native opposition to Bruce's activities. At the time of the incident in question Sinclair had just returned from a visit to Scotland, and the reception that Bruce had prepared for him on his return suggests that this trip had been the first major representation by the Shetlanders on their grievances. An ambush was laid for him on his way to Scalloway Banks. He was forewarned, the attack was scotched, and he made his way instead to Whiteness. That night the laird's men pursued him there, searching the houses of William Sinclair of Strom and Magnus How without success.

The indictment of Bruce and his administration concluded with a number of 'particular' complaints. Of special interest is an apparent attempt by Bruce to drum up support within Shetland in the face of the dangerous problems that were facing his half-brother and now himself. When he left Shetland, Robert Yule, his court clerk, toured the islands seeking signatories to a testimonial whose tenor is not described, but which must obviously have favoured Bruce. Those who had signed this document were described as 'ruid, rusticall, ignorant and barbar peple', largely illiterate, who had been persuaded to sign 'partlie be feir and minacing, partlie be ignorance'. They were easily persuaded to rescind their subscriptions.[107] In the reports of bismar abuses, Tingwall, Whiteness and Weisdale stated that Bruce in 1575 had halved the amount of extra weight he had been taking in the previous years from 30 to 27 merks per lispund (24 was the customary amount). Of his exaction of oxen and sheep it was reported that 'the Laird layde doune this last yeir, feirand giff he continewit in it that he would be complenit upon'. Bressay, Dunrossness and others concurred that he had not continued this levy in 1576.[108] It seems likely that Bruce had become anxious in view of the fact that many of the charges aimed at Robert, though quite possibly countenanced by him, were in fact more Bruce's immediate responsibility.

Finally, the whole commons of Shetland pleaded that in the light of their grievances, of the length of time they had suffered without redress, their poverty and consequent inability to make the long journey to Edinburgh and its courts, they should have an act of parliament appointing commissioners to come to the islands regularly and to try, and deprive if necessary, all officers of whatever degree.[109] This concluded a truly remarkable document, testimony to an extraordinary event, and an eloquent and convincing appeal against misrule. The Shetlanders had made what amounted to a desperate plea in defence of their way of life and sought the assistance of the government in Edinburgh in the preservation of it. It is unfortunate,

106 *REO*, 134, no. lx; 184, no. lxxxvi.
107 *Shetland Documents, 1195–1579*, 222.
108 *Shetland Documents, 1195–1579*, 206.
109 *Shetland Documents, 1195–1579*, 223.

therefore, that events in the capital were moving in a direction that would ensure that, beyond giving Bruce and his half-brother a fright and a temporary setback, no immediate remedy would be forthcoming, though perhaps the islanders would find themselves treated with more circumspection in the future.

7

Near about the King

During 1577 Robert's fortunes were at a low ebb. In the last quarter of that year, an English memorandum on Scotland's nobility described him as being 'very poor and of no great judgment, party or friendship'.[1] On 21 August Walsingham, in a letter to Morton, spoke of the 'great and good report' of the procurator for the Southampton merchants regarding the regent's 'honourable dealing' towards them; there was even mention of a commission by Morton compelling Robert to travel to Southampton to answer for his treatment of the merchants three years before.[2] This never came to anything, but on 14 December the case of Smith, Crooke, Cartmyll, Demaresk, also involving Thomas Holfurde, was heard by the Scottish privy council.[3] It was continued until 15 April next, with commission to Jerome Cheyne and Gilbert Foulsie to examine those who might know the truth of the matter.

Besides the weakness of his position in ward, Robert's 'poverty' at this time was due to Morton's demands. Robert was making increasingly generous offers to the regent, and to observers it must have seemed that liberty would come only with penury, if at all. The *Historie of James the Sext* speaks of 'the Erle [*sic*] with perpetuall making of offers, and the Regentis delaying answeris to caus him cum heigher in pryce', and later states that 'the said Erle wald have gevin layrge compositions to Morton to have bene fred, and mair nor all that, he offerit his eldest sone in pledge for his relief, to have been mareit to ane kynniswoman of Mortons, gratis, without any tocher; but nayne of thir tua offeris was acceptit at that tyme'.[4] Robert was, however, compelled to grant Morton an obligation for a sum in excess of 10,000 merks.[5]

Yet this was very much the worst that Robert was to suffer. Already in 1577 there were signs that the tide was beginning to turn in favour of his cause. Within days of the completion of Henderson and Moodie's damning investigations, Laurence Bruce was appointed to the office of admiral depute of Orkney and Shetland.[6]

1 *CSP Scot.*, v, 252.
2 *CSP Scot.*, v, 236.
3 *RPC*, ii, 654–60.
4 *Historie of King James the Sext*, 182.
5 *RSS*, viii, no. 297.
6 *RPC*, ii, 595.

On 24 April William Henderson presented the commissioners' findings,[7] and six days later Bruce agreed to make just reckoning of his intromissions as foud and chamberlain; yet within a month he was in Shetland waters, causing further trouble.[8] In August, even at the time of the English report that pitched his fortunes so low, Robert was relaxed under more open ward, enabling him to enjoy the more congenial surroundings of Linlithgow.[9]

Morton's position was becoming noticeably weaker; Robert had by this time found the ear of the young King James and was using this opportunity to full advantage. It was during the course of 1577, according to Sir James Melville, that Morton was apprised of the dangers of his great unpopularity with those about the king. These, it was said, could not be bribed as their astute young master would be too quick to notice inconsistencies in their behaviour. Notable among the king's followers were James Stewart, son of Lord Ochiltree – and the Lord Robert.[10] On 14 October, at Linlithgow, Robert resumed his Orkney dealings in a contract with Alexander Stewart of Scotstounhill for the sale of the duties of Orkney and Shetland of crop 1577, and on 30 January 1578 he registered a bond that permitted him to pass to Orkney and elsewhere, but undertaking to ward himself south of the South Esk at command.[11] On 7 February Patrick Bellenden was induced to conclude the agreement that Robert had long sought. In a contract of that date, Robert undertook to 'mentene fortifie and defend' Patrick in the peaceful enjoyment of his lands as a good lord and master, while Bellenden agreed to 'friendlie serve' Robert under pain of 6,000 merks.[12]

Robert's progress back to freedom could not even be halted by the disclosure of further characteristic behaviour by Bruce in Shetland. On 30 August 1577 Nicholas Salus and other owners of the English ship *Marie Galland* complained that Bruce had 'wrongously intromittit' with the ship while she had been lawfully fishing in Shetland waters.[13] On 5 November Bartholomew Strang of Voesgarth laid charges before the council that Bruce had compelled his wife to pay her *umboth* duties,[14] which he held in tack, three months before the correct term of payment while Strang was abroad, probably in Norway; that Bruce had stopped him from going to Norway the previous August; and had compelled him to ferry Bruce and 23 followers from Shetland to Dundee without payment.[15] Bruce offered no defence on the charge regarding the umboth duties or on the staying of Strang from going to Norway; he stated, however, that the transporting to Dundee had been willingly

7 *RPC*, ii, 630, 616–18.
8 *RPC*, ii, 648–9.
9 *RPC*, ii, 622.
10 Melville, *Memorials*, 263–4.
11 Reg. Deeds NRS RD1/16, f. 327.; *RPC*, ii, 669.
12 Court of Session Recs: Acts and Decreets, NRS CS7/71, f. 229.
13 *RPC*, ii, 630.
14 Goudie, *Antiquities of Shetland*, 179–80.
15 *RPC*, ii, 648–9.

done. The second day of December was set for the hearing of Strang's proof on the first charge and the following 24 March for Bruce's defences. However, of this case, as of that of the Southampton merchants, nothing further was heard.

Though granted permission to return north at the beginning of 1578, Robert did not re-appear there until nearly two years later, in November 1579.[16] For the moment he remained in the capital, enjoying considerable prestige. On 12 March 1579 he was present, for the first time in fifteen years, at meetings of the privy council.[17] In the summer he was involved in litigation before the council when John Stewart, constable of the castle of Stirling, was granted the escheat of Alexander Stewart of Scotstounhill, at the horn at Morton's instance for non-payment of 4,000 merks that he owed Robert, presumably in connection with the payment for Orkney and Shetland produce.[18]

Following his return to Orkney, Robert remained until some time before September the following year.[19] He held the All-Hallow court in November in St Magnus[20] and in January and February the Herdmanstein and *Wappenstein* courts in the Yards.[21] He also summoned a further court for March.[22] The main case was a dispute between Henry Fraser and others and Magnus Sinclair in Skaill regarding the lands of Swartabreck and Hawell in Toab, St Andrews. Magnus Sinclair's son John married Mary Stewart, Robert's 'brother dochter', and the assizes of January and February both had in their number a new face, Rany Elphinstone, presumably a relative of Robert's through his mother. Details of the relationship between Mary and Robert Stewart are unknown, but it is possible that Mary was another daughter of Adam Stewart and a sister of Barbara, Lady Halcro. On 17 May Magnus Sinclair resigned in Robert's hands his lands of Toab, and Braebuster, Deerness, in favour of his son John and in fulfilment of the marriage contract.[23] Earlier the same month Robert had granted Rany Elphinstone a charter of land in Hammiger, Cairston.[24]

Unfortunately, the whole records of Robert's law-giving are too meagre to support the accusation in the Complaints that he influenced decisions by threatening to pack assizes with his followers, even if we may think it likely. The charge may have been justified on occasion, but Robert would hardly be inclined to influence as a matter of habit the quotidian causes that passed before him as judge. Of the 105 individuals named as assizemen, ten were definitely followers of Robert – William Henderson, Patrick Monteith, John Caverton, William Ferguson, James Kennedy, William Halcro of Aikers (though his attitude to Robert remained for some time in

16 *REO*, 145, no.l xvii.
17 *RPC*, iii, 108, 120.
18 *RSS*, vii, no. 1988.
19 *CSP Scot.*, v, 512.
20 *REO*, 145, no .lxvii.
21 *REO*, 150, no. lxix.
22 *REO*, 153, no. lxx.
23 *OSR*, 196, no. 72.
24 *RMS*, v, no. 1l78.

doubt), Rany Elphinstone, Stephen Paplay, Malcolm Groat of Tankerness and John Dishington. Only two from this group – Halcro and Elphinstone – served regularly, though both Henderson and Monteith served in Robert's courts in other capacities. Of the rest, only 23 served more than once, though some, presumably trusted for their wisdom and experience, appeared from time to time – men like Oliver Sinclair of Isbister, William and Andrew Linklater, and Andrew Hourston, who had been bailie of Harray for ten years or so.[25] If Robert held head courts every year that he was in the north – two or more in Orkney, one in Shetland – this would amount to over 60 sittings, not including Bruce's courts in Shetland, or the courts held by Robert's followers in his absence. These comments concerning Robert's influence on the legal system, however, have so far concerned only head courts. The choosing of smaller groups, for example arbiters for courts of perambulation were, as will be seen, a different matter.

Other references to this time in the islands are few and miscellaneous. On 6 January 1580 Robert was charged to apprehend one Captain Clerk, who had been committing piracies on subjects of the king of Denmark and was said to have taken refuge in Shetland.[26] Some time in February he received royal letters of undisclosed import.[27] All this while, too, the Henderson brothers, William and Cuthbert, had been consolidating their own affairs in the islands. About June 1578 William had received land in Holland and Meil, North Ronaldsay,[28] and in July 1580 Cuthbert was presented to the vicarage pensionary of Rousay.[29]

On 15 September 1580, probably now south again, Robert was granted the escheat of Archibald Balfour of Westray, at the horn at the instance of Nicol Tulloch, vicar of Westray and Papa Westray, for non-fulfilment of a contract.[30] This marked the beginning of a period of real success for Robert, punctuated by examples of increasing influence and marks of favour. On 25 September, Sir Robert Bowes, the English ambassador, wrote to his masters Burghley and Walsingham saying that Morton, seemingly seeking to combat the fast-growing influence of Esmé Stewart, earl of Lennox, had consulted Robert and summoned Robert's nephew Francis, earl of Bothwell, in an attempt to raise 'a party in the house of Stewart'.[31] This is an interesting and curious statement, since Lennox was of course a Stewart himself; it may be that Morton was making an attempt, in the event unsuccessful, to weaken Lennox's position by splitting the Stewart family asunder. Robert was surely too close to the young king to contemplate any action that ran counter to the interests of Lennox, a royal favourite. Bowes wrote again on 7 October stating that it was Robert and others 'near about the king' who had furnished him with information

25 *REO*, 108, no. xlviii.
26 *RPC*, iii, 255.
27 *TA*, xiii, 254.
28 Sheriff G. H. M. Thom's Papers, NRS GD1/212/27.
29 *RSS*, vii, no. 2445.
30 *RSS*, vii, no. 2517.
31 *CSP Scot.*, v, 512.

regarding the king's marriage plans.[32] Nine days later, with the earl of Glencairn and the master of Mar, Robert was sworn a member of the privy council and was a regular attender during the next two months.[33] At the meeting of 24 December he was appointed keeper of the former seat of his more open ward, the palace of Linlithgow.[34]

Morton was arrested on 31 December. Some days before, at a hunting party with the king, Robert and the commendator of Inchcolm informed the former regent (no doubt with pleasure) of his imminent apprehension.[35] Whether out of bravado or disbelief, Morton made light of this. On 2 January 1581 he was warded in Edinburgh, and Robert, notwithstanding the news he had borne in advance to the regent, was named as among Morton's chief antagonists.[36] This tale-bearing – for such it seems – is reminiscent of Robert's alleged warning to Darnley as he lay at Kirk o' Field; on the other hand, the fact that Morton had only recently sought Robert's help against Lennox suggests that Robert had not allowed his hostility to Morton to appear too overt. On 11 January it was reported that 'friends of [Morton's] principal enemies' – including Robert – would be in Edinburgh 'to resolve for progress in the case against Morton',[37] One week later Morton was removed from the castle and taken across central Scotland to Dumbarton, accompanied by a group of unfriends among whom Robert was prominent. When Morton protested that he was willing to go wherever the king should choose to send him, but wished to pass in safety, it was Robert, according to one report, who replied that he would be as safe as his own heart provided his own followers did not set upon the party. Whatever Morton's faults, the picture of Robert and his allies accompanying their humbled enemy on the long road from Edinburgh to Dumbarton is an unedifying one.[38]

While Morton's star declined, Robert continued in the life of a prominent courtier, councillor, auditor of exchequer and palace keeper at Linlithgow.[39] On 16 January his son Patrick was granted a charter of the priory of Whithorn, vacant on the death of Robert's half-brother, Robert *secundus*.[40] Robert was now the last survivor of the sons of James V. He returned from the west to Edinburgh towards the end of January, and subscribed the Negative Confession (denouncing all kinds

32 *CSP Scot.*, v, 522.

33 16 Nov. (*RPC*, iii, 328); 19 Nov. (*RPC*, iii, 329); 26 Nov. (*RPC*, iii, 333); 3 Dec. (*Accounts of the Master of Works*, vol. I, 1529–1615, ed. H. M. Paton, 1957, i, 310); 7 Dec. or before (*Calendar of Border Papers*, ed. J. Bain, vols I–II, Edinburgh, 1896, i, 28; *CSP Scot.*, v, 545); 14 Dec (*RPC*, iii, 335).

34 *RPC*, iii, 337; *RSS*, vii, no. 2656.

35 *CSP Scot.*, v, 569.

36 Calderwood, *History*, iii, 483.

37 *CSP Scot.*, v, 580.

38 D. Moysie, *Memoirs of the Affairs of Scotland* (Bannatyne Club), Edinburgh, 1830, 29; Calderwood, *History*, iii, 484–5.

39 *RPC*, iii, 339, 340; *ER*, xxi, 120; *RPC*, iii, 341; *RPC*, iii, 342; *RPC*, iii, 344; *RPC*, iii, 348; *CSP Scot.*, v, 640; *RPC*, iii, 361.

40 *RMS*, v, no. 314.

of papistry at the height of a popish scare).[41] Twelve days later it was reported that Robert was to escort the king from Edinburgh to Linlithgow. It did not happen. To Thomas Randolph, the possible reason was reports that Robert, and indeed his wife, had been showing undue favour to the duke of Lennox, favoured by the king, but a controversial figure.[42] Robert's friendship with the king and his circle continued. He was appointed keeper of Blackness Castle, essentially a state prison associated with Linlithgow, and successfully sued Malcolm Douglas of Mains for the return of 'the great irne yett of the dungeoun' and other items..[43]

Morton remained in Dumbarton until 20 May when he was taken back to Edinburgh. During his trial on 1 June, Robert was mentioned in connection with the major charge against him, the rather curious one of responsibility for the death of King Henry 15 years before – 'and being accussit by the ministeris of the cryme, and quhatt knawledge he had thairin, he declairitt that Mr Archibald Douglas [Scottish ambassador to England] reweillit the same to him, the quhilk he wald reweill to the king; bot seing that Lord Robertt had gottin ane reward, he durst nocht reweill the same, and this was all that he knew in that turne'.[44] Robert's 'reward' had been that Darnley had told the queen about the plot against his person 'which had near hand cost him [Robert] his life'.[45] The day after this exchange, Morton was executed.

The great improvement in Robert's fortunes also benefited his family and servants. On 2 June 1581 Mary Stewart, Robert's eldest daughter, was granted 10,000 merks from Morton's escheat, part of a larger sum that her father had been compelled to grant the grasping regent.[46] William Elphinstone, certainly a family connection, was appointed a *sewar* to the king, his fee drawn from the surplus of Orkney teinds.[47] Thomas Boyne, Bruce of Cultmalindie's sinister follower, was the subject of two slightly puzzling references in the register of the privy seal; in one he was granted the escheat of his own goods, forfeit for not finding surety to underlie the law for the slaughter of Mark Vondroum in Shetland[48] and this naturally sounds as though he was benefiting from his master's new-found favour. However, a subsequent entry close by in the register granted his escheat to his son, Adam Boyne, in connection with the death of Patrick Windram, whose slaughter in Robert's own presence had been noted in the complaints against him.[49] Why both these entries were required is a mystery; but the similarity of the victims' surnames –Windram and Vondroum – might suggest divergent versions of the same episode.

---

41 *BUK*, ii, 515–18.
42 *CSP Scot.*, v, 629.
43 *RSS*, viii, no. 91; *RPC*, iii, 363, 364.
44 *A Chronicle of the Kings of Scotland* (Maitland Club), Glasgow, 1830, 135.
45 Hunsdon to Walsingham, 8 June 1581 (*CSP Scot.*, vi, 27–8).
46 *RSS*, viii, no. 297.
47 *RSS*, viii, no. 88. Later he was granted the escheat of the fruits of the subdeanery of Orkney: *RSS*, viii, no. 373.
48 *RSS*, viii, no. 37.
49 *Shetland Documents, 1195–1579*, 165, no. 22; *Oppressions*, 8, nos 22, 71.

On 28 August Robert finally realised his ambition. He was created earl of Orkney, lord of Shetland, 'knicht of Birsay' at Holyrood.[50] Two months later his heritable infeftment of 16 years before was confirmed,[51] and a month after that parliament approved its elevation into an earldom and lordship; his judicial powers were strengthened by the addition of the justiciary jurisdiction, derived from the bishopric, which he had so recently been accused of usurping. The only provision whose terms sounded in any way like a reference to what had gone before was the specific reservation to the crown of the 'grite customes of gudis and merchandice transportit furth of this realme'.[52] He also received a charter of the island of Cava.[53] This island is a poor, intermittently inhabited hummock among the South Isles of Orkney, and formerly pertained to the Grey Friars of Inverness. Robert's only interest in it may have been that it had more recently been granted to William Halcro of Aikers,[54] who had been a supporter of Magnus Halcro of Brough, and as such an enemy during Robert's early years in Orkney. Although after Magnus's death William actually served on Robert's assizes and had prudently altered his position, Robert may have wished to establish a superiority over him. William Halcro was never afterwards known to be disobedient to the undisputed superior and earl of Orkney.

At the turn of the year 1582 Robert returned to his new-won earldom, and on 4 March he is found writing from Kirkwall the first of his letters to Sir Patrick Waus of Barnbarroch.[55] Waus had stood *caution* for him at the time of his liberation from Linlithgow, and he was now addressed on the education of Robert's son Patrick.[56] Aside from this correspondence, with its details of Robert's family circumstances, evidence regarding Robert's first years back in Orkney, like that of his earlier visit, is meagre, so much so that one is reminded of the complaint against him of preventing protest by prohibiting exit from the islands. There are a number of general allusions to his political attitudes, albeit contradictory, in the complex affairs surrounding the visit to Scotland of Esmé Stewart, later duke of Lennox, his rivalry with the Hamiltons and the general suspicion as to his motives. A letter to the king of France from Castelnau, a French diplomat, placed Robert with Lennox's party,[57] whereas an English memorandum pronounced him neutral.[58] John Colville, Scottish politician and agent of the English, in writing to Walsingham, the English secretary of state, felt Robert to be among those favouring the English who, viewing Lennox

50 Moysie, *Memoirs*, 34.
51 *RMS*, v, no. 263.
52 *APS*, iii, 254–6.
53 *RMS*, v, no. 309.
54 24 March 1576 (*RSS*, vii, no. 530).
55 *Barnbarroch Corresp.*, 238.
56 *RPC*, ii, 669–70.
57 16 March 1583 (*CSP Scot.*, vi, 333).
58 *CSP Scot.*, vi, 159.

as essentially French, were suspicious.[59] Perhaps Robert was all of these things, depending on which way the wind was blowing. The unknown author of 'An opinion of the present state, faction, religion and power of the nobility of Scotland' describes him as 'a man dissolute in lyef; lyttle sure to any faction; of small zeale in religion'.[60] It had been a decade and a half since any observer had attempted to delineate Robert's character so directly, but it seems that little had changed.

Robert was in Edinburgh at the end of 1582, subscribing the precept ordering the removal of Morton's head from the Tolbooth.[61] His presence in the capital excited interest from diplomatic observers; but he was not present at council or other meetings, and by 11 September 1583 he had returned to the north. On that date, sitting in Birsay, he insisted on hearing a case between William Irving and Magnus Paplay concerning their yards in the burgh of Kirkwall.[62] In December William Irving of Sebay again figured in Robert's court, held in Linksness, for harbouring John Aitken, a notorious outlaw of long standing. Irving admitted the offence, but pleaded in mitigation his relationship to Aitken by marriage, and sought mercy on the grounds of his poverty.[63] Robert remitted his forfeiture in consideration of his 'good and thankful service'. The following month – January 1584 – Irving acted as procurator for Robert in an action before the earl's own deputes.[64] Robert's opponents in this case were William Irving's own brothers, Magnus, Gilbert and Edward. They were charged by a summons at William's instance to 'warrand extend and renew the charteris evidentis and utheris wraittis', granted by them to the earl in 1581, of the lands of Twinness, Messigate, Garth and Carabreck, all in St Andrews parish.[65] Before Robert's own appointed justices – John Dishington, John Caverton, Patrick Monteith and David Scollay – they stated in answer to query that they had made their former grant willingly and uncompelled, and they were ordained to 'warrand acquit and defend' Robert in the lands in all time coming. Since the existence of this case at all suggests that the Irving brothers were unwilling to furnish Robert with titles to the land, these were strange proceedings. It seems certain that Magnus, Gilbert and Edward Irving were unable to pursue their case in a court so strongly controlled by the earl. Magnus and Gilbert were to make strong representations to the king three years later regarding Robert's behaviour towards them,[66] but their brother William, Robert's creature, was granted these lands,[67] from which

59 *Papiers d'état relatif a l'histoire de l'Écosse au XVIe siècle*, vols I–II, ed. A. Teulet (Bannatyne Club), Edinburgh, 1851, ii, 499.

60 *Bannatyne Miscellany*, vols I–III (Bannatyne Club), 1827–55, i, 56.

61 *Extracts from the Records of the Burgh of Edinburgh, 1573–89* (Scottish Burgh Record Society), ed. R. K. Hannay and M. Wood, 1927, 1931, 262.

62 OA, D8/1/3/3; copies SA D16/388/41; NRS (microf.) RH4/35/388/41.

63 NRS (microf.) RH4/35/388/32.

64 *REO*, 155, no. lxxi.

65 *REO*, 155, no. lxxi; this was not the only land granted to Robert by the Irvings – Magnus and Gilbert Irving had granted him land in Sebay in which he was infeft 9 Sept. 1581 (*REO*, 303, no. clxxxvi).

66 *Oppressions*, 98.

67 Clouston, *History of Orkney*, 303.

they were unable to evict him until 1594, after Robert's death.[68] William was in addition strengthened in his tenure of the lands of Sebay by a court of *perambulation* which confirmed certain rights to peat-cutting and seaweed that he had taken upon himself.[69] Of an assize of 23 men, only eight were named in the decree, a group whose names read like a list of Robert's closest men; in addition to Dishington, Scollay and Caverton, there were William Gordon of Cairston, Laurence Bruce of Cultmalindie, William Halcro and, making his first appearance in the records, Robert's own natural son, James Stewart of Graemsay.

The proceedings against the Irvings were only the beginning of a concerted campaign against the udal proprietors of Orkney, in which the process of wresting land from its owners and granting it to one of their relatives, under conditions, was a point of policy. In March 1584 Magnus Sinclair of Toab, otherwise referred to as Magnus Sinclair in Skaill, was escheated for 'succeeding in his fatheris vyce for steiling and grippind the kingis landis and for with halding of certane outbrakis brokin furth upoun the kingis balk'.[70] His lands in Brabister, Hawell and Swarta-breck (the same that had been the subject of litigation before the All-Hallow and Wappenstein courts in 1579–80) were granted to his daughter-in-law Mary, Robert's niece. Another instance where a member of a udal family stood to gain from the oppression of the rest concerns the Halcros. Robert and his chamberlain, John Dishington, obtained letters against Janet and Katherine Halcro, daughters of Magnus Halcro of Brough, and Henry Halcro of that Ilk, his nephew, for arrears of landmails owed by the late Magnus.[71] These arrears had previously been sought from Margaret Sinclair, Magnus's relict, but attention had been transferred to his heirs and it was intended to *apprise* the lands of Brough. Representations were made by Rany Elphinstone and Roland Hamilton, the women's husbands, and by William Halcro of Aikers, regarding their rights in the lands. Judgment was found for the earl by an assize which, quite improperly, had Halcro of Aikers, an interested party, as its chancellor.[72] With his change of allegiance to the earl, his right to part of the lands of Brough was, not surprisingly, guaranteed.

This case marked the complete submergence of the Halcros of Brough. Robert's aim of acquiring their lands seems to have overridden all other considerations. One might have expected Rany Elphinstone, for example, to have received better treatment, or Henry Halcro, whose wife was Robert's niece. However, although the apprised lands of Brough were offered back to their former owners at a price, they were not present in court and the lands became Robert's personal property. The year 1584 was, in Storer Clouston's word, Robert's 'vintage' year for oppression of Orkney landowners, but 1585 saw further similar cases. On 19 January Robert

68 *REO*, 157n.
69 *REO*, 157, no. lxxii.
70 *REO*, 304, no. clxxxvii.
71 *REO*, 160, no. lxxiii.
72 Storer Clouston also suspects that this assize consisted in some measure of Robert's own servants (*REO*, 164–5n).

granted a charter to Jerome Tulloch, subchanter of Orkney, of land in Quholm, Bowbreck and Garson in the parish of Stromness, confiscated 'for criminal causes' done by Oliver Sinclair, heir to Alexander, last possessor of the lands.[73] On 20 February land in Stromness pertaining to the heirs of James and Henry Halcro was apprised for unknown reasons.[74] Nor were these the only moves against the Orkney landed; the regrants to udallers of previously confiscated land by Robert in September 1587[75] and the complaints of Magnus and Gilbert Irving in December the same year point to considerable further oppression. Gilbert complained of ejection from 9d land in Deerness and Holm, including Delday, Brecks, Midhouse, Hurtiso and Ocklester, and both rehearsed the familiar charges of removal of goods, compelling transport without payment, closing of ferries to prevent the carrying south of complaints, and the stripping of plenishings from the houses of escapees from the islands.

Storer Clouston sees all this as a matter of general policy of oppression on Robert's part, and the case of the Irvings certainly lends weight to that view. However, while accepting that control of the udal lands was one of Robert's aims in his various acts of harshness, another more direct reason may be detected. The Halcros of Brough, for example, suffered for the previous opposition to Robert of their relative Magnus, exacerbated by their probable involvement in the Complaints of 1575. Magnus Halcro himself was dead, but it is possible that the more obscure James and Henry Halcro in Stromness lost their lands for the same reason, and also that Magnus Sinclair of Toab suffered for Robert's enmity to the Warsetters, with whom Magnus apparently had a connection.[76]

But besides the evidence yielded by the regrants to udallers and the complaints of the Irvings regarding Robert's overbearing attitude to the independent land-holders of the north, both are, at the same time, signs that there had occurred yet another downturn in Robert's career, stemming again from changes at court; the first time for several years that Robert had been compelled to take note of court affairs. The first sign of this came on 30 August 1586 when M. Courcelles, the French ambassador, after a long conversation with one of Robert's servants, noted that three or four weeks before, a group of Englishmen had descended upon the island of 'Chetland in Orkenay' and carried away goods to the value of £30,000 Scots. Robert's man was indignant that despite this, and despite his allegation that the English had spoken slightingly of the king – calling him 'Jaquet', their pensioner – he had been unable to get satisfaction from the council. The latter had sent him away, telling him to 'inform himself particularly of those who had committed the disorder', and stating that the country's policy towards England could not be disturbed for the single reason of the ill-usage of his master.

73 REO, 305–6, no. clxxxviii.
74 REO, no. lxxiv.
75 REO, 311, no. cxciii and n; Storer Clouston Papers, OA D23, no. 159; Morton Papers, OA D38/1650.
76 REO, 468.

In view of this evasive and unsatisfactory reply, Robert's representative was to be sent to repeat his complaint to the king in person. Courcelles thought that he was unlikely to receive any greater satisfaction from the king than he had had from the council, since it was said that the king 'does not much like the . . . Earl of Orkney, saying that he only serves his own ends'. He was described in an English memorandum as a 'malcontent' (though to be fair, so also was the greater part of the Scottish nobility). His own behaviour towards the English was not exemplary and showed that he was still engaged in some of the activities that had been held against him in 1575. It was complained that on 14 March 1585 the *John* of Hull had been spoiled by 'Mounce Heneson', a Dane and 'one Knightson, a Scottishman'. The ship was then taken to Orkney and kept there by Robert. The ship, worth £140, was ultimately restored to its owners, but the cargo, worth £2,420, was retained.[77] 'Heneson' was almost certainly Magnus Heinason, a Faeroese hero, famous for having cleared the seas round his islands of the English pirates who proved so troublesome in Orkney and Shetland waters; Thomas Knightson is noteworthy, too, as a name that will be encountered again. In view of this incident, it is hardly likely that the king would look favourably on Robert's requests for recompense, or at least for the tactful ignoring of reprisals. Nor would his opinion have been rendered happier by Courcelles's impression that the earl intended to proceed with revenge on the English regardless. It is also probable that James was already aware of the growing discontent with Robert's government of the islands, which was shortly to be made public, while he was involved in delicate negotiations with Denmark, in which the ambiguous constitutional position of Orkney and Shetland loomed larger than he would have liked.

Negotiations had begun with Denmark in 1585 for James's marriage with the Princess Anne, and continued throughout this period, though they did not bear fruit until 1589, when the parallel negotiations on a French marriage were abandoned.[78] From the outset, the Danes had mounted their biggest diplomatic initiative for many years on the subject of Orkney and Shetland. Danish ambassadors were sent in June 1585, accompanied by Nicholas Theophilus, a doctor of laws, who treated the king to a trenchant discourse on the whole question.[79] This academic approach may have been calculated to be of special appeal to James, and it certainly caused the king to consider the matter critically. In 1586, James's old tutor, Peter Young, was sent to Denmark, and seems to have satisfied the Danish king on various points, but Courcelles stated that the Danish king pretended 'yf he match not one of his daughteres with the Scottishe kinge, to retire the Orcades'.[80] Six months later Courcelles wrote to his king saying that the seeking of favour with the king of Denmark was as much concerned with holding on to Orkney and Shetland

77 'Spoils committed by the Scots upon the English since 1581' (*CSP Scot.*, ix, 516).
78 D. H. Willson, *James VI and I*, London, 1956, 85–7.
79 Goudie, *Antiquities of Shetland*, 220–1.
80 *Courcelles's Negotiations in Scotland, 1586–7* (Bannatyne Club), 1828, 9.

as with marriage.[81] Robert, curiously enough, was reported by Courcelles to have rendered some assistance in Young's voyage to Denmark, since he was granted 2,000 crowns in connection with it, but, significantly, the king had made it known that he had not wanted this gift to be made and stated that it was done as a 'charity of the secretary'.[82]

In 1587, there began a full-scale attempt by Maitland and Bellenden to deprive Robert of his lands. Maurice Lee gives as the immediate reason for their campaign Robert's oppressive rule in the islands[83] but again, as in the case of Morton's prosecution of the previous decade, the motives of Robert's opponents were not unmixed. The king's standpoint has been noted, and we may perhaps date from this time a desire to see the Stewart earldom and lordship abolished once and for all, regardless of the character of the earl himself. Also, as Lee points out, Bellenden was far more active in the affair than Maitland, who seems simply to have lent moral support (he was the secretary who had rewarded Robert for his part in Peter Young's trip to Denmark and, since he preferred the French marriage to the Danish,[84] was presumably lukewarm, at least at this time, to the whole Danish adventure). Bellenden's motives, as one might perhaps have expected, were not wholly pure. On 20 April 1587 he wrote to Archibald Douglas concerning a tack of the subdeanery of Orkney that the latter had apparently granted to Bellenden's uncle, Sir Patrick Bellenden, during the king's minority. Sir Patrick had been 'secluded altogether' from this tack, and had sustained 'such damage as the whole of the benefice might be worth'; his nephew therefore hoped that Douglas would subscribe and seal a new tack to Sir Patrick.[85] This question of the subdeanery lands was indeed one of the long-standing causes of enmity between Robert and Patrick Bellenden, mentioned in Robert and William Henderson's first letters from Orkney in 1567–8, and Archibald Douglas had been the subdean of Orkney who had granted Bellenden the lands in a charter (not a tack) at that time).[86] In addition, Sir Lewis himself may have had a personal interest in the islands; as early as 10 June 1569 Robert had expressed fear that Sir John Bellenden had infeft his son in the lands of Birsay.[87]

This problem had been brewing for some time, and Robert knew it. The influence at court of his son-in-law, the master of Gray, was declining, and giving way to that of the secretary, Sir John Maitland of Thirlestane.[88] His support against Robert was successfully enlisted by Robert's old Bellenden enemies, in the person of Sir Lewis Bellenden, son of Sir John and last of the dynasty of Bellenden justice clerks. As he had done in the Morton crisis, Robert started casting around for allies

81 Courcelles's *Negotiations in Scotland*, 57–8.
82 *CSP Scot.*, viii, 639.
83 M. Lee, *John Maitland of Thirlestane*, Princeton, 1959, 160.
84 Willson, *James VI and I*, 85.
85 *Salisbury Papers* (HMC), vols I–XXIV, London, 1889, iii, 247.
86 *REO*, 288, no. clxx.
87 Roxburghe Mun., bundle 1634, no. 12.
88 Lee, *John Maitland of Thirlestane*, 108–9.

abroad. In 1586, he approached king and council, complaining about his losses through piracy. His envoy received no satisfactory answer to this complaint and entered into conversation with Courcelles in August that year. Courcelles related to d'Aisneval, a colleague, in such detail as to suggest that what had happened had been unusual, that Robert's representative had been at pains to emphasise the affection that Robert bore towards France 'with many expressions full of the good will that he bears to the service of his majesty'. The envoy even drew to Courcelles's attention to the fact that Robert was a pensioner of the king of France, 'although it was a long time since he had received anything' – presumably a reference to the earl's youthful days in France with his sister, the young queen. These overtures were clearly designed to counter his declining stock at court. Robert subsequently wrote from Kirkwall on 12 October 1586 to M. du Pré, a servitor of the king of France, thanking him for the goodwill shown to his servant, who bore the letter and would relate 'my intention touching some affairs which I have with your master the King of France.'[89] The outcome of Robert's intrigues is unknown, and notwithstanding the fact that the affair appears to have been handled with much greater discretion than his previous dealings with Denmark, nothing very decisive occurred. Of far greater importance was Robert's contact with Spain, through new allies in the pro-Spanish faction, the earl of Huntly and his own nephew, the earl of Bothwell. This, too, seems to have come from Robert's need to seek allies at home and abroad. As in the case of France, little happened at the time, but this connection survived the Maitland and Bellenden crisis and, as we shall see, led Robert and his followers into the affair that, more than any other single episode, gives dramatic colour to the closing years of his life

Notwithstanding the king's opinion and the moves by Bellenden, Robert appears to have come south in the spring or early summer of 1587 with every confidence. On 17 July he was one of the nobles who bore the honours to Parliament.[90] Only 16 days later, however, his troubles began; the question of presentations, already raised in the complaints of 1575, was explored in a parliamentary statement 'anent the benefices presentit be the erle of Orkney'. Robert was stated to have taken upon himself to dispone the provostry, chancellory, archdeaconry, chantory and other Orkney benefices as a result of a general clause in his infeftment concerning patronage. Despite the fact that a privy seal confirmation in 1581 of a gift by Robert to Thomas Gunn of the stallery of the Orkney treasurership had described him as 'undoutit patroun of the kirkis chaiplenreis and benefices foundit and erectit within' the king's and bishop's lands of Orkney,[91] it was decided that the earl had not and never had had any right of patronage over the benefices.[92] This was just the beginning; on 15 August the lands of the earldom of Orkney and lordship of Shetland

89 *CSP Scot.*, ix, 98.
90 *CSP Scot.*, ix, 452.
91 *RSS*, vii, no. 155.
92 *APS*, iii, 489.

were confiscated, on paper at least, and granted to Bellenden and Maitland.[93]

Within a month, on 4 September, Robert, in search of support in the islands, already seemed to be making some amends for his past activities. On that date several grants were made to 'gentlemen udallers' of 'uthall landis, quoylandis, and utheris heritages as wes evictit fra thame be his Lordships courtis of perambulationis and *ogangis* [inspections of boundaries] haldin thereupoun', subject only to a check by commissioners (including Halcro, Dishington, Bruce and Groat of Tankerness – practically a list of the members of some of the original perambulations) that the udal marches were not set to the detriment of king's or bishop's land. Three such regrants survive; to James and John Germiston, of land in Germiston, Stenness;[94] to James Corrigall elder and younger, of land in Corston, Harray;[95] and to Magnus Begg, Alexander Sutherland, Magnus and Thomas Davidson, of lands unspecified.[96] Storer Clouston interpreted these documents as evidence illustrating 'very clearly Robert Stewart's policy of converting the free and independent odallers into vassals holding their land in return for 'dutifull and true service'".[97] However, these grants, all of the same date, in exactly the same terms and all extracted from the sheriff and regality court book of Orkney, are unique. There is no other surviving evidence of udal land granted in this way. All of the other escheats of which we have knowledge were disponed either to a relative of the previous owner,[98] or to someone with no previous traceable connections with the property at all.[99] And if we look for a reason for this exceptional proceeding, it seems more than coincidence that Robert was in trouble at the time, and that there are no further examples of differing date to indicate a general policy. It is true that the day after these documents were drawn up, 5 September, William Irving of Sebay, again receiving favour from Robert, was infeft in land in Grotsetter, St Ola, its former owners having been evicted by decreet of perambulation, the precept emanating from Laurence Bruce and Patrick Monteith; however, the instrument followed on a charter by Robert (undated, as seems very common in instruments produced in Orkney), drawn up in all probability before the earl's troubles began.[100]

The date of these grants to the udallers suggests that Robert had returned rapidly to Orkney, to repel threats to his power. In the face of these he sought, and found, one particularly puissant ally – his own nephew Francis Stewart, earl of Bothwell, son of the late Lord John. On 22 September, the English diplomat Robert Carvill stated that Maitland and Bellenden were preparing three ships at Leith under the overall command of Patrick Bellenden who had undertaken to 'fetch' Robert from

93 *RMS*, v, no. 1354.

94 *REO*, 311, no. cxciii; O & S Papers, NRS RH9/15/76.

95 *REO*, 311n; Storer Clouston Papers, OA D.23, no. 159.

96 Morton Papers, OA D38/1650.

97 *REO*, 313n.

98 See e.g. 1–3 April 1574 (*OSR*, 193, no. 70); 20 Jan. 1592 (Scarth of Breckness Mun., NRS GD217/567).

99 See e.g. June 1574 (*OSR*, 195, no. 71); 20 August 1591 (Craven Beq., NRS GD106/81).

100 Misc. Papers, OA D8/3/1.

his dominions. The preparations were certainly formidable. The wage bill for the lead ship, the *Lyon*, indicates a skipper, 19 sailors (two were from Burntisland, probably seasoned Fife coast men). There was also a barber (presumably a barber-surgeon) with his 'furnest kyst', and generous supplies of meat and flour were laid in. Soldiers were enlisted, and horse to contact Patrick's prospective ally the earl of Caithness, always looking for a way to discomfit Orkney.[101] All this was backed by royal letters notifying the inhabitants of the revocation of Robert's grants and charging all between 16 and 60 to assist Bellenden in the event of a siege of the castle of Kirkwall, and charging Robert himself to render castle, palaces and steeple under pain of treason.[102] Various notables, including the earls of Huntly and Sutherland, Ross of Balnagown and Maclean of Duart, were charged to assist Patrick in 'repressing the disobedience and rebellion of Robert, late earl of Orkney'. Patrick Bellenden and his backers meant business.[103]

Robert in turn had not been idle. He had sent money to Bothwell to provide him with three ships, which were at that moment being fitted out at Dundee before they were sent north well-manned and appointed 'under color of *wafting* [protecting] the fishermen from the pyrates'.[104] Robert was seeking to duck any suggestion that he was treasonably opposing a government-backed expedition. Fortunately for him, the constitutional position was much less clear-cut than at the rebellions of the seventeenth century under Earl Patrick, and in any case Robert's enemies, whatever the legal position, were riven among themselves. At this time Richard Douglas, a relative of Archibald Douglas, ambassador to England, wrote to him noting the rift that was now developing between Bothwell and Maitland over the latter's part in the moves against Robert.[105] Robert in addition sought support in other quarters. He wrote on 12 October to Barnbarroch regarding the 'hasert and danger I stand into be the procedingis usit aganis me in this last parliament'. He understood that 'sindrie undir cullorit freindschipe and bluide intendit forder to truble and unquiet myne estait', and therefore sought Waus's help in making 'appoyntment' with the chancellor and justice clerk, an arrangement which the master of Caithness was apparently trying to prevent. He had also sought the assistance of his own son-in-law, Lord Lindores, husband of his daughter Jean.[106]

Despite this determined and effective response, Robert's position in Orkney and Shetland could never be the same again. He was never his own master, his title being under close scrutiny and eventually passing to his son in all but name. In February 1589 he had to pay Maitland 8,000 merks for his claim to half the bishopric and earldom lands of Orkney and Shetland.[107] The following month he satisfied

101 Roxburghe Mun., 723.
102 NLS, Adv. Ms. 35.5.1.
103 NLS, Adv. Ms. 35.5.1.
104 *CSP Scot.*, ix, 485–6.
105 Salisbury Papers (HMC), iii, 282.
106 *Barnbarroch Corresp.*, 410.
107 Reg. Deeds, NRS RD1/32, ff. 330v–1r.

the justice clerk with lifetime grants of Sir Patrick Bellenden's old lands of Evie and Stenness, and extensive guarantees of Sir Patrick's own rights, including assistance in the pursuit of some of his own followers.[108] To meet the cost of these agreements, he was forced to feu large tracts of land in Orkney and Shetland to his supporters. In April 1589 he granted a charter to Magnus Sinclair in Clumlie of the lands of Northdyke in Sandwick.[109] In August 1590 he feued the island of Papa Stronsay to his follower David Scollay of Tofts.[110] It was from Stronsay in particular that much of the feued land came; in 1590 grants followed of Aith and Grobister to Norman Bruce and of Huip to Malcolm Groat of Tankerness, with Elsness and Levisgarth in Sanday.[111] Edward Scollay, David Scollay's brother, became Edward Scollay of Strynie;[112] the family of Fea of Clestrain first appeared on the scene as feuars, when they were infeft in their leasehold lands of Clestrain and St Margaret's Quoy;[113] Hugh Sinclair received the lands of Houseby and the island of Auskerry;[114] and Margaret Bonar, widow of Robert's old servant William Henderson, had her tack of Musbister in Stronsay and Holland in North Ronaldsay superseded by a charter.[115] During the same period there were other smaller grants of lands including those whence derived the names of Gordon of Cairston and Kincaid of Yinstay.[116]

In his demands for cash Robert was not particular about the lands he was feuing off; Musbister, Clestrain and Strynie were among properties he had previously granted his wife, after she had relinquished her original marriage portion to suit his Orkney plans. It had only been after much acrimony in the late 1560s and early 1570s that he had persuaded her to accept them in exchange for the Kerse barony lands with which he hoped to placate Sir John Bellenden,[117] and his action now was to store up further trouble for his son. The grant to Norman Bruce, a figure otherwise unknown in Orkney, was in return for money lent to Robert by Bruce's uncle, the now deceased Robert Bruce of Clackmannan, an old Cultmalindie connection, in 1588. He had also borrowed substantial sums elsewhere. He had obtained 1,000 merks from another long-standing servant, William Elphinstone. In April 1591 he and Patrick borrowed more than £7,000 from William Monteith, John Dick, Katherine Stewart and Janet Fockhart, all merchants well versed in his affairs.[118] And he owed money to Francis, earl of Bothwell, for assisting in his troubles.[119]

---

108 Reg. Deeds, NRS RD1/34, ff. 105r–7r.
109 Craven Beq., NRS GD106/328; *RSS*, NRS PS1/62, f. 1lov; *RMS*, v, 1902.
110 *Rentals*, ii, 85.
111 *Rentals*, 84, 86; Smyth of Methven Papers Mss, NRS GD190, box 15; *RSS*, NRS PS1/62, f. 127r.
112 *Rentals*, ii, 85; *RSS*, NRS PS1/62, f. 125v.
113 *RMS*, v, no. 2191; Fea of Clestrain Mun., NRS GD31/4.
114 *Rentals*, ii, 87; *RMS*, v, no. 1994; Bruce of Symbister Mun., SA GD144/49/20/4.
115 *Rentals*, ii, 85; *RMS*, v, 1895.
116 *RSS*, NRS PS1/61, f. 104r; *REO*, 317, no. cxcix.
117 Anderson, *Black Patie*, app. 2, 150.
118 Reg. Deeds, NRS RD1/30, ff. 224r–5v; RD1/33, ff. 172r–3r; RD1/36, ff. 266v–8r, 450v–2r.
119 *CSP Scot.*, x, 482.

On 22 January 1589 Robert appointed commissioners to go to Shetland to set lands in feu and tack.[120] These were Arthur Sinclair of Aith, and an interesting and relatively new face on the northern scene, Michael Balfour of Montquhany. Sinclair had been an active supporter of Robert against Bellenden's invasion, and he and his son had already received charters of land in Burra, Dunrossness and St Ninian's Isle.[121] Michael Balfour of Montquhany represented a branch of his family senior to that which had settled in Orkney, being a nephew of the latter's founder, Gilbert Balfour of Westray. He had assisted Robert in his payment to Maitland,[122] and his presence marked an improvement, at least for the time being, in difficult relations between the Robert and the Balfours.[123] During the summer of 1589 Sinclair and Balfour made grants to Mans Olason and his wife of their six merks at Channerwick;[124] to Laurence Bruce of Cultmalindie of udal and kingsland in Northmavine;[125] to Laurence Sinclair of Gott of 40 merks in Dunrossness and Burra;[126] and to Andrew Gifford of Wethersta of various lands in Delting.[127] During the same period Robert himself granted to Jerome Umphray and his spouse nine merks in Outer Sand in Nesting confiscated for theft from Nicol Manson and Pol Williamson.[128]

The commissioners' work was completed by the autumn of 1589. Besides his fee, Balfour was paid £7,560 from the Shetland income to replace what he had paid Maitland on Robert's behalf, and a longstanding dispute over the Westray lands was settled.[129] The lordship estates of Shetland, briefly in Balfour's hands, were then granted to Patrick Stewart, master of Orkney. He was to have greater advancement than this. His father, for all his efforts, was a spent force. Robert's title to the lands of Orkney and Shetland, officially suspended in 1587, was still under investigation, and when it was regranted five years later it was in a different form – a form that effectively advanced his son to the dignity.

But Patrick was to experience his own difficulties. In December, he wrote from

120 Reg. Deeds, NRS RD1/32, ff. 230r–1r.

121 Gardie House Papers; Vaila Papers, SA D10/2/3.

122 Reg. Deeds, NRS RD1/37 , ff. 280v–2v.

123 Robert's previous relations with the Balfours had been uneasy, but from the mid-1580s the situation changed. Archibald Balfour got into financial difficulties (Court of Session Recs: Acts and Decreets, NRS CS7/82, ff. 273r–4r; CS7/93², ff. 373r–4r; Reg. Deeds, NRS RD1/20¹, pt 2, f. 392r; RD1/22, ff. 270r–1v) and his interest in Westray passed to Michael Balfour (Court of Session Recs: Acts and Decreets, NRS CS7/103, ff. 260r–1r). On 18 May 1589 the latter received from Patrick a grant of the Orkney island of Faray (North Fara) (O & S Papers, NRS RH9/15/264).

124 Shetland Documents, 1580–1611, ed. B. Smith and J. Ballantyne, 59, no. 138.

125 E. S. Reid Tait Papers, SA D.6/194.

126 Shetland Documents, 1580–1611, 62, no. 147.

127 Shetland Documents, 1580–1611, 63, no. 151.

128 Shetland Documents, 1580–1611, 61, no. 146. There were also charters of ten merks in Nesting to David Strang (Reg. House Chrs, NRS RH6/3020) and two merks there to Laurence Thomesone (O & S Sh. Ct Recs, NRS SC12/65/l/27).

129 Shetland Documents, 1580–1611, 65, no. 156. The charter by which this transfer was effected is of great interest as it includes the first ever complete list of the pro rege lands of Shetland, one which accords in all major respects with the 1628 rental (RSS, NRS PS1/60, f. 121v–3r).

Edinburgh to Barnbarroch, thanking him for his support against the 'manifest and inexpectit wrang quhilk undeservitly I sustene at the handis of the justice clerk, quha first preparit the way to cancelett my leving, nixt hes tane my plaice our my heid'. He accused Bellenden and Maitland of aiming at 'the uter exterminatioun of our raice'.[130] Bellenden, who was at that moment planning his uncle's abortive invasion, was seeking the downfall, not only of Robert, but also of his son. Patrick's particular weakness lay in disputes going back almost 20 years, over the estates of the priory of Whithorn. The priory had been founded in the twelfth century by Fergus of Galloway – the same Fergus who had granted to the abbey of Holyrood the Dunrod lands later enjoyed by Patrick's father.[131] In terms of wealth, it was of the second rank of religious houses. Its income in 1560 was said to be £2,540 annually, about half that of the larger foundations settled by James V on his older illegitimate sons – St Andrews, Kelso, Melrose, Holyrood – though comparable with that of the priory of Coldingham held by Lord John.[132] At the height of its fortunes this *Premonstratensian* house had three main centres of property – the church and barony of St Trinian in the Isle of Man, the church and lands of Kilcolmkill on the south coast of Kintyre, and the main cluster of estates and 20 appropriated churches lying along the Solway. These were located chiefly in the Machars parishes of Whithorn and Glasserton, but some parts were scattered as far as Clayshant and Toskertoun/Kirkmadrine in the Stoneykirk area of the Rhinns of Galloway, Gelston near Castle Douglas, Girthon south of Gatehouse of Fleet, and Borgue near Kirkcudbright.

With the exception of the lands in Man, all of this was still intact when Robert Stewart *secundus* appeared on the scene,[133] but there was also a rival claimant, William Fleming, a relative of Lord Fleming and nephew of Robert's predecessor. Fleming's claim prevented Robert from drawing the revenues of the priory for some years after his grant[134] and now, as soon as Bellenden of Auchnoull found a cause that would discomfit the Orkney Stewarts, the old troubles were brought to life again. In September 1587 Andrew Martin wrote to Barnbarroch seeking his assistance against Fleming who, through Maitland's influence, had secured an act of repossession of the estates. Martin had no very high opinion of Fleming's claim, believing that it had previously been declared null by the session 'sua I think the [Master] salbe in the less danger'[135]. Martin was right, and it was Waus's success in combating it that earned him Patrick's gratitude at the end of the year.[136]

130 *Barnbarroch Corresp.*, 411.

131 RRS, i, 253.

132 Cowan and Easson, *Mediaeval Religious Houses*, 55, 101.

133 B. Megaw, 'The Barony of St Trinian's in the Isle of Man', *TDGANHS* (3rd ser.), xxvii (1948–9), 173–82; A. McKerral, 'The Kintyre Properties of Whithorn and the Bishopric of Galloway', *TDGANHS* (3rd ser.), xxvii (1948–9), 183–92.

134 G. Donaldson, 'The Bishops and Priors of Whithorn', *TDGANHS* (3rd ser.), xxvii (1948-9), 147.

135 *Barnbarroch Corresp.*, 405.

136 Monreith Chrs, quoted in Donaldson, 'The Bishops and Priors of Whithorn', 147.

Unfortunately for Patrick, there was another long-standing problem over Whithorn concerning a tack of the priory revenues, granted about 1572 by Robert *secundus* to Alexander Stewart of Garlies, one of his chief vassals. Garlies had found great difficulty in drawing these, partly through the younger Robert's own obstructiveness, and partly because Morton as regent used the Fleming dispute as a pretext to draw the income for himself.[137] Garlies himself died very soon after Robert's own death in 1582,[138] but his family continued to pursue their claim. During the elder Robert's period of ascendancy in the early 1580s, Waus managed temporarily to buy off Garlies's nephew Alexander,[139] but in the troubles of 1587 the whole issue was re-awakened. Patrick and Waus had reluctantly to recognise the Garlies claim.[140] There was much argument about income, Patrick making urgent demands and Garlies complaining that 'of treuth the last silver ye gat fra me was of my awin silver and nane of your priorie; Nor yit had I never ane plak [four pence Scots]. . . of your benefeis, bot restand still in thair handis that suld pay it . . . gif ye be mekill behind I am sumquhat mair'.[141] In August 1589 Patrick enjoyed a minor success over arrears[142], but in February 1592, in need of cash, he sought to trade all claims on the priory with John Kennedy of Blairquhan, for a straight payment of £5,000.[143] This did not work. In July 1595, the Stewarts of Garlies, now represented by the curators of Alexander Stewart of Clarie, grandson of the original Sir Alexander, won their case.[144] Patrick's income was reduced to 500 merks a year – the original duty specified in the 1572 tack. He did not lose touch with his Whithorn vassals – he dined with a Stewart of Garlies in Edinburgh as late as 1606 – but he had no financial interest beyond what was to prove a somewhat paltry annual income.

On 16 December a royal commission to try Robert, 'lait erle of Orknay', was granted to the chancellor, the justice clerk and to Sir Patrick Bellenden, 'directed in the first instance' to the former two.[145] This was stated to be in response to the complaint by Magnus and Gilbert Irving mentioned earlier. Robert, it was stated, in addition to wresting large tracts of land from the Irvings, had stripped and demolished 18 houses, carrying away goods to the value of 400 merks; he owed Gilbert Irving £150 for the freight of 1,000 *deals* brought by him to Orkney from Norway and he had removed eight barrels of oil, worth £13 16s 8d each, from Gilbert's house (curiously, this charge was 12 years old, and thus dated from the old year of troubles, 1575).

---

137 Donaldson, 'The Bishops and Priors of Whithorn', 147.
138 Stewart died in January 1582 (Court of Session Recs: Acts and Decreets, NRS CS7/158, f. 81r).
139 Court of Session Recs: Acts and Decreets, NRS CS7/32, ff. 300v–1v.
140 Court of Session Recs: Acts and Decreets, NRS CS7/122, ff. 425v–6v.
141 *Barnbarroch Corresp.*, 419–20.
142 *Barnbarroch Corresp.*, 428–9; Court of Session Recs: Acts and Decreets, NRS CS7/118, ff. 249v–50v, 306v–8r.
143 Reg. Deeds, NRS RD1/33, ff. 445r–6r.
144 Court of Session Recs: Acts and Decreets, NRS CS7/158, ff. 80r–3v.
145 *Oppressions.*, 95–8.

Gilbert, in the face of refusal of redress and the stopping of the ferries, had been compelled to brave the perils of the Pentland Firth in December in a small fishing boat in order to make representations in the south; on his departure Robert had taken all his plenishings, goods, corn and cattle and put his children to beggary. Charged with his father to find caution and surety was possibly the favourite of all Robert's sons, James Stewart of Graemsay.

It was possibly at this time, too, that the king's attention was drawn to a supposedly treasonable inscription that Robert had had placed on a wall of his palace. *Robertus Steuartus filius naturalis Jacobi 5ti Rex Scottorum hoc aedificium instruxit,*[146] the text ran; while its literal meaning does suggest that Robert might have thought of himself as king of Scots, this seems rather far-fetched and it appears more likely that its form can be attributed simply to bad Latin. However, according to Brand, the king was displeased, and it seems reasonable to suppose that Robert's botched inscription and its possible meaning were simply one more cause of irritation to his nephew (who would have little sympathy with botched Latin at any time). This irritation perhaps made him the more willing to pursue an active policy against Robert through Maitland and Bellenden. In his endeavours to seek allies, Robert was compelled to adopt a more and more overtly political stance – namely to side with the chancellor's opponents, the pro-Spanish faction at court. In November 1586 he had been stated to be neutral on the question of whether Scotland should support England or France and to have been 'neutral in religion and parts before'.[147] A month later Don Bernardino de Mendoza, the Spanish ambassador, numbered him among those friendly to his country.[148] Now he was forced into open alliance with leading pro-Spaniards. His buying of help from Bothwell was followed on 30 December 1587 by his subscribing, in Kirkwall, of a *bond of friendship* with the earl of Huntly, in which he pledged himself to 'mentein, fortefie and assist' Huntly and his house against all opponents except the king.[149]

At the same time, there is evidence regarding Patrick, Robert's son – by now master of Orkney, on the death of his elder brother Henry – which suggests that the earl was not the only member of his family to suffer from the antagonism of Maitland and Bellenden, and that that antagonism (as far as Bellenden was concerned at least) sprang from motives more personal than the desire to right the wrongs of Orcadian landholders. Patrick Stewart's servant, Andrew Martin, wrote to an unknown addressee (possibly Barnbarroch) on 11 September 1587 stating that Lord Fleming had, through the agency of Maitland as secretary, obtained an act of repossession of the priory of Whithorn, which he now intended to enforce.[150] Martin sought his addressee's good offices in the matter. There had indeed been a

---

146 Brand, *A Brief Description of Orkney, Shetland, etc.*, 31.
147 *CSP Scot.*, ix, 169.
148 *Papiers d'État*, iii, 524–5.
149 Gordon Castle Mun., NRS GD44/13/7/30.
150 *Barnbarroch Corresp.*, 405.

long-standing dispute regarding possession of the priory of Whithorn,[151] but Martin understood that Fleming's father's title, upon which his son's claim was based, had been declared null by the lords and the last possessor, Patrick's uncle, Robert *secundus*, had been declared to have full title.

Patrick was thought by Martin to be returning to Orkney about Michaelmas (29 September), 'to remane at hame for keipinge the cuntrie'. On 12 December, however, he was in Edinburgh, writing to his foster-father.[152] In view of the fact that Maitland and Bellenden's persecution of Robert Stewart extended to his son and his lands at the opposite end of Scotland, it is scarcely any wonder that Patrick spoke of their pursuit of his father's life 'to the uter exterminacioune of our raice; and that but regaird to my bluid, my rycht, my friendschip and null offence committit be me athir aganis his maiestie or [the justice clerk]'. In view of this 'manifest and inexspectit wrang' (for which he blamed Bellenden without mention of Maitland), and in view of the reported preparations for sending a military force to Orkney, he therefore sought Barnbarroch's advice as a 'speciall' friend regarding which course he ought to follow 'as I have done the lyk to all my honourabill friendis'. He looked for an answer as he perceived 'they intend no delay in their entirprise'.

At first sight his perception would seem to have been correct. Richard Douglas, seeking a letter from the justice clerk which he wished to despatch to Archibald Douglas, waited in vain for three days, Bellenden being incommunicado, 'for he is so busily occupied with sending away men to Orkney with his uncle that he cannot get time as yet to write'.[153] The comptroller's accounts for the time indicated that the revenues for Orkney and Shetland were in the name of Maitland and Bellenden.[154] However, even at this juncture, when Robert seemed in the greatest danger, one observer at least saw the beginning of opposition to the royal officials' plans. A letter to Walsingham of 1 January 1588, author unknown, related the plan for Bellenden's expedition but noted, 'the Chancellar and the Justice Clerk rules all still as they please, but sudden will be their fall in my opinion, for they run a course even now will help them to it'. Though no-one was yet 'angry' with the plan against Robert, 'it will breed a further matter if they prevail, for the King is very well minded they should have the same'.[155] This last sentence suggests that the writer foresaw 'anger', presumably from the direction of Bothwell, which would be in direct opposition to the wishes of the king. The king's wishes are noteworthy; what we may see here is the first manifestation of a determination to end the Stewart earldom and re-annex the islands to the crown.

On 21 March 1588 Robert granted a bond of maintenance to William, Edward and Oliver Sinclair, sons of Sir Patrick Bellenden's wife, Katherine Kennedy, by her first

151 Donaldson, 'The Bishops and Priors of Whithorn', 147.
152 *Barnbarroch Corresp.*, 411.
153 *Salisbury Papers* (HMC), iii, 300.
154 *ER*, xxi, 325–6, 358, 390–1, 407–8.
155 *CSP Scot.*, ix, 532.

marriage to Henry Sinclair of Evie (the Henry Sinclair of Strom, later of Brough, encountered earlier);[156] this was ostensibly due to the damage that the Sinclairs' patrimony had sustained at Sir Patrick's hands during their minority. It was Robert's only recorded measure against Sir Patrick at this time, but it was significant enough. Henry Sinclair was never, so far as is known, designated 'of Evie' in his lifetime, and Patrick had obtained a feu of lands in Evie on 19 April 1565 from Bishop Bothwell. By that date Henry Sinclair had been dead for two years, and despite Patrick having acquired the land with the acquiescence both of the bishop and of Patrick's own brother, Henry Sinclair's erstwhile patron, Robert seems to have been contending, as justification for the occupation of Bellenden's lands, that they had in fact been Henry Sinclair's and had been reft from his heirs.

By now, however, the whole situation was changing. The letter to Walsingham of 1 January 1588 was the last reference to the proposed expedition to wrest the Northern Isles from Earl Robert. It does seem to have set sail and landed in Orkney, but clearly Robert's allies had honoured their commitments, and the hapless Bellenden had to withdraw in the face of their strength.[157] On 11 April, before a Convention of Estates, the provost of Lincluden and others 'of the wiser sort' succeeded in reconciling Bothwell with the chancellor and the justice clerk. The points of difference between these men were several, but noteworthy was the statement that Bothwell's enmity towards Bellenden 'proceeded from my lord Robert's cause for Orkney'.[158] After this meeting the danger was past. A letter of 23 May from the laird of Garlies to Patrick, master of Orkney, discussed arrears of the priory of Whithorn without reference to the Fleming threat,[159] and Mary Stewart, Robert's daughter and wife of the master of Gray, wrote to Barnbarroch on 27 May stating that her father was intending to go to Shetland to pick up his rents.[160] Obviously the earl no longer felt it necessary to remain in Orkney to 'keep the country'. The affair was not quite over yet. In December 1588 it was reported that the disappointed justice clerk had fallen out with the chancellor and his English friends and was 'discording' about Orkney.[161] Moreover, Robert does not appear to have escaped without making some placatory moves. On 24 June 1589, he granted Sir Lewis Bellenden a charter of the lands of Evie he had denied to Sir Patrick;[162] and it may be of significance that Robert's daughter Elizabeth was married, at an unknown date, to James Sinclair of Murkle, uncle of the master of Caithness who had been acting against the earl of Orkney during his troubles.

The only explicit reward that Robert granted his nephew Bothwell for restoring

156 NRS (microf.) RH4/35/388/41.
157 Roxburghe Mun., 723; *CSP Scot.*, ix, 485; NPS 1/57, f. 171v.
158 *Salisbury Papers* (HMC), iii, 317–18.
159 *Barnbarroch Corresp.*, 419–20.
160 *Barnbarroch Corresp.*, 420.
161 Fowler to Walsingham (*CSP Scot.*, ix, 655).
162 Roxburghe Mun. (NRA(S) Survey) no. 179, no. 132).

his quietness was to make him his heir in default of his own legitimate issue. This was, as Maurice Lee points out, little enough, as he had at least four lawful sons alive.[163] Bothwell in the remaining years of Robert's life was to show his displeasure.

Sir Lewis Bellenden died in 1591, but for some time before that his malign influence had waned, and there were marked changes for the better in Patrick's fortunes. He became lord of Shetland. Although the regrant of the earldom to him and his father did not take place until 11 March 1592 and made no mention of any particular elevation, Patrick had called himself 'P. Yetland' as early as November 1590.[164] This was not merely a courtesy title; he did receive a tack of the Shetland estates from his father. The terms of this grant do not survive, but the reason for it was explicit enough; it was for Patrick's 'interteynment . . . in court and in service with the king's majestie and for performing and doing of his effairs'.[165] Patrick's public position was growing stronger as his father's fortunes faded towards the end of his life. He was assured of a favoured position at court, and the regrant of the earldom, when it came, advanced him to the status of feuar. Old Robert still had a few months to live, but already Patrick was described as earl. In December 1592, during a return to the Northern Isles after his first period at court, he was designing himself 'Erle of Orknay, Lord Yetland and Justice generall of the samin'.[166] This description of him was echoed by Bruce of Cultmalindie and the other landholders who complained of him during that year.[167]

But the advancement in his fortunes was accompanied by difficulties elsewhere, deriving from a disastrous incident that occurred right at the beginning of his courtiership. In June 1590 he sailed south from Orkney to join his royal cousin, bringing with him 'his whole furnishing in money, jewels and movables'. On the way his ship was attacked by English pirates, led by Captain David Gwynn, a notorious and ruthless freebooter. He lost everything, to the extraordinary value of £3,000 sterling (£36,000 Scots).[168] Why he was carrying such an enormous sum on board – more than three times the money value of the earldom's annual income, half as much again as the total combined yearly wealth of earldom, bishopric and kirklands, remains something of a mystery. It seems unlikely that he was compelled to do so by the demands of court life. Perhaps we see here early evidence of his extravagance and irresponsibility. The calamity was compounded by his difficulties in obtaining compensation, as well as in raising ready cash to replace quickly what he had lost. In November 1591 he is found granting no fewer than four bonds to the merchant William Monteith in Leith, for a total of over 5,000 merks,[169] and it is against this background that the problems with his Whithorn income should be

163 Lee, *Maitland of Thirlestane*, 160n.
164 Gardie House Papers.
165 Court of Session Recs: Acts and Decreets, NRS CS7/170, ff. 166v–8r.
166 *REO*, 166, no. lxxv.
167 *Oppressions*, 101–3.
168 *Salisbury Papers* (HMC), iii, 96.
169 Reg. Deeds, NRS RD1/38, ff. 298r–302r.

seen. Less than a month after Patrick's humiliation, his father took reprisals against English fishermen in Shetland. Gwynn was imprisoned in England at the request of the Scottish ambassador, Archibald Douglas.[170] But there the matter rested; no charges were brought against Gwynn,[171] and the issue did not surface again until after Robert's death.

170 *RPC*, iv, 54.

171 There are no references to any such charges in *CSP Scot.*, and interrogations of one David Gwynn before the English High Court of Admiralty in August and November 1590 make no explicit reference to the robbery of the earl of Orkney (TNA HCA.l/42, ff. 185v–6r, 193r).

8

Robert's Last Years

When the danger of Maitland and Bellenden had passed over, Robert felt able to make two visits, albeit brief, to Edinburgh.[1] In the spring of 1589 he subscribed an Orkney charter at the Canongate, and in December 1590, this time accompanied by Patrick, he was reported to be departing from the capital. Though now well into his fifties, the earl was still vigorous, and on his return north he was soon on his way to Shetland for the summer.[2] Patrick's presence with his father in Edinburgh signalled that they had resolved their differences in Patrick's youth, and he was finally taking a more direct role in his father's affairs. The two had concluded some form of contract, and during Robert's absences in Edinburgh and Shetland, Patrick acted as 'administrator, guydar and governour' for him. On 18 May 1589, acting in this capacity, he granted a charter to Michael Balfour of Montquhany of the island and lands of North Fara. Robert himself actually signed this document.[3] On 22 June, a letter from Patrick to Barnbarroch confirmed his growing role.[4]

Robert's life remained the usual round of administration and charter-making. On 29 August 1588 he granted a charter to Jerome Tulloch, subchantor of Orkney, of land in Quholm, Stromness;[5] the deed was noteworthy in that the land involved had been escheated for 'thift', showing that Robert's former policies were continuing. A month or so later, at Kirkwall, he granted a disposition to Magnus Louttit of Lyking of land in Sandwick.[6] However, a chronological tracing of Robert's doings is less appropriate at this point than an examination of the different aspects of his activities against the background of momentous events in which Orkney and Shetland were to play a role of some importance. Such an examination greatly illuminates the nature of Robert's activities at this time.

There is little evidence that Robert interested himself in political affairs outside Orkney and Shetland, whether in Scotland or abroad, except in response to outside pressure. His overtures to Denmark and France in the 1570s were clearly related

1 Craven Beq., NRS GD106/338.
2 *Barnbarroch Corresp.*, 433.
3 O & S Papers, NRS RH9/15/264.
4 *Barnbarroch Corresp.*, 433.
5 *REO*, 314, no. cxciv.
6 *REO*, 314, no. cxciv.

to the growing menace of Morton. His chief external activity in relatively peaceful times was that of piracy, or at least the sponsoring of pirates. After the exploits of Edmund Blackadder and his henchmen, this continued in the late 1580s. On 12 November 1588 a merchant from Emden, Johan Hendrickson, complained to the privy council that, while travelling from Danzig to Bremen the previous July with rye and other wares, he had been intercepted off Norway by a ship with a Scottish crew led by George Peterson, a Fleming. His craft had been taken to Orkney, where all its goods were sold, and it was intended to dispose of the ship itself, which still lay 'at the bak of the toun of Kirkwall'.[7] Robert was represented in the case by John Caverton, and Bothwell appeared for his interest as admiral of Scotland. Peterson pled in justification that, being Flemish, he was a subject of the king of Spain, and he held a *letter of marque* to apprehend ships from the Low Countries, then in revolt against Spain. Hendrickson's counsel, Captain Robert Arnot, stated that his client was in fact a subject of the graf of Emden, who remained friendly to the king of Spain. The lords resolved to remit the matter to 'proper judges', presumably the admiralty court. Bothwell and Robert were ordered to return the ship to Hendrickson within ten days, and Hendrickson in turn undertook to make the ship available to any having right thereto.

On 9 July 1588, just eight days after the attack on Hendrickson, it was reported that one of Robert's ships – later named as the *Phoenix* – had been brought into port by 'some of Enchuissen' (Enkhuizen, on the Zuider Zee) in men o' war that guarded the Dutch herring fleet. It was said that the ship had fought with 'an Englishman'.[8] A fortnight later it was stated that 'the most part of seventy-two men' were to suffer death for piracy, the ship being suspected of 'many piracies'.[9] King James demanded restitution and satisfaction and threatened reprisals. In November Bothwell obtained interest in the ship from Robert and pursued the matter further, demanding back both ship and furniture.[10]

Robert was not the only Scottish noble with interests in freebooting in the North Sea; indeed he appears not to have been the only one to sponsor George Peterson. On 8 March 1589 William Asheby, the English ambassador to Scotland, wrote to Walsingham suggesting the stationing of a man o' war for the purpose of intercepting Peterson and an accomplice named Haggerston. They were acting on a letter of marque from the prince of Parma, commander of the Spanish forces in the Low Countries, and were said to be countenanced by Bothwell.[11] On 16 June the same year Asheby reported that Peterson was in prison in Edinburgh.[12]

But the intertwining of international affairs and seaborne skulduggery is best illustrated by an episode in which Robert's previous self-interested support for the

7 *RPC*, iv, 331.
8 *CSP Foreign*, xxii, 20.
9 *CSP Foreign*, xxii, 68.
10 *Salisbury Papers* (HMC), iii, 373.
11 *CSP Scot.*, ix, 706.
12 *CSP Scot.*, x, 105.

pro-Spanish faction, born of his need for allies against Maitland and Bellenden, played a part. The Maitland and Bellenden crisis was now past, but Robert's currying of favour with Huntly and Bothwell had not been forgotten, as he would soon be forcibly reminded. During the aftermath of the coming of the Armada and its defeat by the English, Robert made no move. Fleeing Spanish ships were first sighted off Orkney on 10 August 1588[13] and from then until the end of September unsubstantiated rumours flew round about a possible Spanish landing in the islands.[14] Spanish toing and froing around the islands, however, came from the need to run before the appalling weather rather than any intent to land. When at last a gravely damaged Spanish ship anchored and then sank off Fair Isle, Robert kept his peace. The ship was *El Gran Grifón*, flagship of the Spanish store and transport fleet. After a miserable month of starvation and cold on the island, Admiral Juan Gomez de Medina and his men were rescued by Malcolm Sinclair of Quendale and Andrew Umphray of Berrie, the latter of whom ferried the survivors to Anstruther.[15] The Stewart earls' interest in the ship did not take active form until nearly a decade later, when Patrick Stewart, by then earl, concluded a contract with William Irving to raise its ordnance.[16]

Robert's pro-Spanish intervention did not begin until a year or so later, in mid-1589 – he was not, for example, implicated in the letters written by various members of the Scottish nobility to the duke of Parma in February 1589.[17] To examine his involvement when it does come to light it is necessary to investigate a series of events that began on 5 January 1590. A Spanish *galleass* dropped anchor off Whithorn, causing much concern in government circles in the uneasy aftermath of the Armada. As Sir Richard Wigmore, an English diplomat, noted, 'the arryvall of this baable ... did greatly perplex the honestest and wonderfully distracted the dowtfull'.[18] The king being absent in Norway seeking the hand of the Princess of Denmark, it was the council, composed of counter-weighted groups from both pro-Spanish and pro-English factions, who despatched commissioners – including Sir Patrick Waus of Barnbarroch – to conduct investigations and bring the captain and pilot to Edinburgh for questioning. The primary intention of the interviews with the captain, Don Alvarez de Merida, and the pilot, Scotsman James Colville, was to find out the ship's intentions in visiting Scottish waters. The council never received a satisfactory answer to this question, but a number of interesting facts emerged.[19]

13   *CSP Scot.*, ix, 600.
14   *CSP Scot.*, ix, 602, 612; *CSP Spanish*, iv, 415, 425.
15   For details of this whole episode, see T. M. Y. Manson, 'The Fair Isle Armada Shipwreck', *The Scottish Tradition* (1974), 121–31; P. D. Anderson, 'The Armada and the Northern Isles', *Northern Studies*, xxv (1988), 42–57.
16   Irvine of Midbrake Papers, SA ref. D.13; NRS (microf.) RH4/388/35/41.
17   Lee, *Maitland of Thirlestane*, 181–2.
18   *CSP Scot.*, x, 242.
19   Cunningham of Caprington Mun., NRS GD149/265, ii, ff. 1–8.2

It was not the ship's first visit to Scotland. The previous summer of 1589, she had made for Dunkirk to rescue sailors stranded after the failure of the Spanish fleet. In all probability she went northabout, the English Channel having proved a dangerous place for Spanish ships. On leaving Dunkirk, she retraced her steps north to the Isle of May where her crew had enjoyed a day's hospitality from the laird of Barns, a follower of Bothwell, then to Orkney where they lay some time in Cairston Roads. On departure, they were caught by bad weather and, after running before the storm, they made landfall in Shetland, where they were 'weill interteynit' by Robert, who was on one of his summer visits. They then made their way home down Scotland's west coast.

The ship's cordial reception in Shetland is the more significant because, at about the same time, on 22 June 1589, Patrick Stewart wrote anxiously from Kirkwall to Sir Patrick Waus, concerned about the arrest in Edinburgh of George Peterson, the errant Fleming, in possession of a letter from Earl Robert to the prince of Parma. This letter, he said, might 'carrie sum Inconvenient and preiudice to my lord and me In cais the samen were not prevented be dealegente foirsycht'.[20] He said that the story of this letter mystified him, and that he found it 'uncredabill', but he asked Barnbarroch to find out more about it, though nothing emerged. In the course of whatever murky doings this suggests, Robert and Bothwell fell out, possibly because the intemperate Bothwell was suspicious that his uncle was, typically, seeking only to serve his own interests, and had as yet shown him no sign of gratitude for assistance in his troubles. In February 1590 Walsingham was told that Bothwell, in addition to other intrigues with Huntly and the Spaniards, was mounting an expedition, involving 360 men and two ships, to take Orkney with the intention of ensuring safe harbours for the Spanish 'in case they shall be dryven to come upon that coast as before they did'.[21]

Bothwell's threat may help to explain the part played by the earl of Orkney in the events that followed the arrest of the Spanish ship in 1590. Despite the fact that the council could establish no sinister motives, and in spite of the bond under which the captain and pilot had been brought to Edinburgh, Merida and Colville were imprisoned for entering the realm in a ship of war, refusing to surrender themselves to trial without condition, and making fortification within the realm without permission.[22] Bothwell was for a time denied the custody of the ship and men to which he was entitled as admiral, out of distrust of his intentions, though he ultimately received it, much to the annoyance of Sir Robert Bowes, English ambassador and longtime observer of Scottish affairs.[23] Colville the pilot escaped briefly, and the ship departed from Whithorn, but, lacking supplies, she surrendered again after

20 *Barnbarroch Corresp.*, 433.
21 *CSP Scot.*, x, 842.
22 *RPC*, iv, 830.
23 *CSP Scot.*, x, 840.

sailing round to the east coast.[24] On 4 March the king had sent strict instructions against any member of the council assisting the ship[25] and on 29 March Colville, by then recaptured, was sent to Denmark to explain himself to the king. (Colville was a cousin of John Colville, the minister, politician and English agent, whose aid Bowes sought to enlist in discovering the reason for the Spanish ship's visit to Scotland.)[26]

For some time the ship remained in Leith and interest in it waned. Attention shifted rather to the exploits of English pirates who were particularly active in their attacks on Scottish shipping at this time. Bowes was approached regarding a Captain Gwynn, who was 'chasing all Scottish ships between [King's] Lynn and Shetland'.[27] He had attacked three Kirkcaldy ships and six or eight others, and behaved with notable brutality, but he achieved particular notoriety early in June 1590 when he attacked and robbed Patrick Stewart. Three weeks or so later, the 'Spanish barque' put to sea again. The favoured explanation for her liberation was that unnamed allies of Earl Robert were helping him to seek recompense for the robbery committed on his son,[28] though it is also true that commercial interests were wary of actions that might harm their dealings in Spain.[29] Certainly Robert was reported to be exacting his own revenge at the expense of English fishing vessels in Shetland.[30] The Spaniards sailed south. On 22 June, off Hartlepool, they attacked no fewer than six small English coasting vessels. Three they left 'fleete emptie on the sea'; the other three, the *John* and *John Collingwood* of Lynn and the *John Sheringham* of Cley, were taken to Anstruther where the Spaniards arrived on 26 June.[31]

Here they spent some time negotiating with the Englishmen for their ransom. Shortly they fell into a dispute with the townsfolk of Anstruther in which one of their men was captured and two English boys rescued from their clutches. They took reprisals by executing some of the seamen, and by battening down the hatches on the *John Collingwood*'s crew and firing the ship, keeping the townsfolk at bay with muskets.[32] The same day they hoisted sail and departed, taking with them the two remaining English ships, and an accompanying *fly-boat* commanded by one Captain Rig and a brother of the laird of Barns. Of the English ships, the *John* had as its pilot George Peterson, whose release from prison had so irritated the English ambassador; the *John Sheringham* had on board 'one Knightson of Pittenweem' – certainly the Knightson who had been complained of by the English five years before for piracy involving Robert. Knightson indeed owned property in Pittenweem[33] but

24 *CSP Scot.*, x, 259–60.
25 *CSP Scot.*, x, 245.
26 Strathmore Papers, Bowes letter books, Glamis Castle; NRA(S) Survey no. 885, vol. E, 14.
27 *CSP Scot.*, x, 322.
28 *CSP Scot.*, x, 336.
29 *CSP Scot.*, x, 390.
30 *CSP Scot.*, x, 336.
31 *CSP Scot.*, x, 335, 345.
32 *CSP Scot.*, x, 346.
33 Pittenweem Writs, NRS GD62/158; *RSS*, v, no. 1669.

was to make his home in the north, serve as steward to Patrick,[34] and die there in 1622.[35]

They left Anstruther on 27 June, bound for Orkney.[36] By 11 July they were in Kirkwall, with 25 prisoners.[37] While the authorities in Edinburgh sought fruitlessly for a solution to what was now more of a domestic embarrassment than a cause for political alarm, the Spaniards were being 'feasted . . . greatly' by Robert,[38] but they were not idle. On 19 July, accompanied by William Stewart, another of Robert's illegitimate sons, they attacked four English fishing vessels off Fair Isle and took them to Kirkwall. They gave the *Jesus* of Scarborough to the earl in exchange for four cannon, the *Old Elizabeth* of Shields to an unnamed person in Kirkwall and the 'ship of Yarmouth pertayning to Wedow Harrison there' to the 'Captaine of Kirkwaie'. The *John Litster* of Newcastle was redeemed by Gilbert Foulsie, archdeacon of Orkney, for £50 at the request of her master. At the same time, negotiations proceeded on the fate of the Lynn cargo vessel the *John*, which was sold to James Dickson, Robert's servant.[39]

Robert Bowes in the meantime made strenuous efforts to seek relief for his countrymen, with little success. Thomas Gray in the *Lyons Whelp*, who had recently brought captured pirate ships into the Forth, undertook to make for Orkney, but, perhaps wary of the Spaniards' reputation, sailed to Berwick instead.[40] Bowes petitioned Maitland to see if he would influence Robert to apprehend the Spaniards. Maitland undertook to approach the king with a view to promising Robert that he would be allowed to keep the islands if he would stay the Spaniards and their followers in Kirkwall.[41] This answer is interesting insofar as it indicates that the dispute between Robert, Maitland and Bellenden, though officially unresolved, was not high among Maitland's priorities, but from Bowes's point of view it was a wholly empty promise. By the time real help seemed on the point of materialising – in the form of an English warship and pinnace – news had already reached Edinburgh of the Spanish barque's departure from the Northern Isles.[42]

Bowes had despatched representatives to Orkney, who kept him in contact with the Spaniards' activities there. On 24 July they had been engaged in selling corn, the cargo of one of the English merchantmen.[43] It was said that they had intended to massacre their prisoners but had been prevented from doing so by the Scotsmen in their company;[44] by mid-August, however, Bowes had heard that they had killed

34 Donaldson, *Shetland Life under Earl Patrick*, 66.
35 Orkney Tests, NRS CC17/2/1.
36 *CSP Scot.*, x, 346.
37 *CSP Scot.*, x, 353.
38 *CSP Scot.*, x, 364.
39 *CSP Scot.*, x, 195–6.
40 *CSP Scot.*, x, 364.
41 *CSP Scot.*, x, 364.
42 *CSP Scot.*, x, 397.
43 *CSP Scot.*, x, 369.
44 *CSP Scot.*, x, 369–70.

12 of the Englishmen and reserved the rest for slavery. The Scots had also failed to prevent them burning some of the English dogger-boats with both men and unsold fish aboard.[45] When the Spaniards finally left Orkney early in September, they apparently had three ships well fitted out, and had as pilots George Peterson and William Stewart.[46] The latter seemingly acted as pilot as far as the Western Isles, where at his own request he was put on board a Scottish ship bound for Leith. Despite contrary reports, Bowes later received triple confirmation of their departure from Orkney, from John Callendar, one of his representatives, from John Caverton, whom Robert had sent to Bowes, and from Robert's wife.[47] (The further history of the ship does not concern us here, though there is evidence that it was intercepted by English ships not far from its home port of Corunna (A Coruña) and taken back to England.)[48]

After the departure of the Spaniards, little more was heard of Robert's dealings with the Spanish faction, though there were again reports of Bothwell's intention to go to Orkney. On 9 March 1591 Bowes reported to Burghley that Robert's nephew was said to be going north to exercise his office of admiral, 'looking to draw . . . his uncle to profitable composition, or otherwise to take hold of some of his possessions in that isle'.[49] Later the same year Bothwell himself told Mary Stewart, Lady Lindores, that he intended to visit her father in Orkney, and there was a general rumour, which reached the ears of the king, that he proposed to take the 'castle and island' in order to 'pleasure' the king of Spain. The king was said to have sent a force against Bothwell, under the master of Glamis. The enterprise was, however, one 'which sundry think to have been to small effect or danger', Bothwell being thought much too weak to attempt such an adventure.[50]

On 4 April 1592, as a probable result of Maitland and Bowes's representations to the king,[51] Robert was charged not to give shelter to Spanish pirates reported to be entering Scottish waters bent on attacking English shipping.[52] On 14 September it was alleged that he was among those friendly to rebels in the pay of Spain,[53] but by this date there is no longer any evidence that Robert was in any way personally involved with Spain or her supporters.

While the Spanish barque's depredations were causing concern in Edinburgh, another old source of dispute, dormant for twenty years, came to life again. On 16 June 1590 Adam Bothwell obtained letters of horning against Robert, citing

45　*CSP Scot.*, x, 381.
46　*CSP Scot.*, x, 394, 399.
47　*CSP Scot.*, x, 397.
48　*CSP Scot.*, x, 434, 436.
49　*CSP Scot.*, x, 482.
50　*CSP Scot.*, x, 590–1.
51　*CSP Scot.*, x, 665.
52　*RPC*, iv, 739.
53　*CSP Scot.*, x, 665.

breach of the contract of excambion of September 1568, especially his undertaking to pay for the maintenance of the kirk, school and the Palace of the Yards; that he would pay the bishop a pension of £1,000 per annum; and that he would meet the cost of any of the pension from the Holyrood thirds that might be 'evicted' from his children, recipients hitherto.[54] This had left Bothwell deeply in debt. In light of previous dealings between Robert and the bishop, the official orders that the bishop received in the letters had a familiar ring. Robert was charged to fulfil the contract by proclamation at Edinburgh, the Canongate and Leith. Proclamation in Orkney was specifically excluded because 'thair is na officer that dar pas in thais pairtis of Orknay for geving of ony chairges to him or ony lettres . . . seing he ather takis thame and detenis thame captive or utherwayis causis thame to be retenit in the cuntrie and evil handlit and sufferis thame not to returne againe lyk as he hes detenit as yit John Adie our messinger . . . sua that thair dar na uther pas thair for feir of thair lyfe'. Bothwell, seeking funds from Holyrood for payment of royal ambassadors to Denmark, had sent John Adie to Orkney in July 1589 with letters of horning.[55] Robert offered Adie £1,300 in cash; and when the messenger stated that he had no power to receive money or thereby suspend the horning, Robert's procurator demanded redress against him for any further denunciations 'besyde the puneissment of his awin persoun'.

Four further attempts were made to execute letters between June and September 1590, the first being in presence of Patrick and his mother. Finally on 27 October Robert was denounced rebel. This did not, however, interrupt the final return to legality of his supremacy in the north. On 11 March 1592 he received a regrant of his lands in Orkney and Shetland,[56] though the charter was to Robert in liferent and to Patrick in fee, evidence that Robert's career was finally spent – he had not long to live – and Patrick was poised to take over. More significant, however, was the fact that the charter incorporated a ratification, passed by parliament just over a year later, of the earl's right of patronage of benefices within Orkney and Shetland 'and that na uther hes haid nor sall pretend richt thairto nochtwithstanding of quhatsumevir act statute or constitutioun made in this present parliament . . .' This was a complete overturning of the case against Robert with which Maitland and Bellenden had opened their campaign in 1587. Incidentally, the term 'foudrie' was not repeated in the document; Shetland courts had been referred to as 'sheriff' courts as early as 1572[57] but this was the first explicit recognition of the supplanting of the old Norse term.

Perhaps in view of his increased role, Patrick Stewart, master of Orkney, now started to use his title of lord of Shetland in official documents, and as such granted land in Deerness to his brother-in-law Patrick, Lord Lindores, on 21 November

54 O & S Papers, NRS RH9/15/102.
55 Prot. Bk Thomas Auchinleck, NRS NP1/36, f. 19v.
56 APS, iii, 589–90.
57 Dobie, 'A Shetland Decree', 1.

1591.[58] This change was not merely the adoption of a courtesy title after the English style, but may indicate a genuinely greater interest in Shetland than any ever evinced by his father, despite his regular visits. This would continue. As earl, his building projects would include the construction of Scalloway Castle, and he would administer the law there, either himself, or through his own deputes, notably John Dishington.[59] He would not rely on his father's client, his uncle Laurence Bruce, and it may be this supplanting of Bruce, in the position he had formerly enjoyed in Shetland, that in 1591 began the ill-feeling between the two men, which effectively lasted till the end of both their lives. On 3 April Thomas Bellenden, brother of Sir Lewis the justice clerk, stood caution in £2,000 for Patrick that he would not harm Bruce,[60] and on 21 January the following year Bruce protested to the privy council and obtained an execution of horning against Patrick.[61] This antipathy was to come to the surface quite often in the future and would be a significant factor in Patrick's final downfall.

Immediately after the regrant, Bothwell was granted a 'protestation' in parliament[62] recognising that this development should not prejudice the bishop's actions against the Stewarts, father and son. This brief document made particular reference to the relieving of Bothwell from payments from the thirds of Holyrood and, coupled with an 'exception' passed earlier in the same session,[63] gives a clearer idea of the nature of the bishop's complaints. The thirds of Holyrood had been set aside twenty-six years before for the payment of a pension to Robert's children, and by his contract with the bishop Robert had agreed to pay to his children any of the pension 'evicted' from them – should the church, for example, seek to add its own demands from the thirds. This had occurred in 1573 when it was ordained that the sum of £860 per annum should be set aside for the payment of stipends to the ministers of the abbey kirks, and the demands on the bishop noted in his letters of horning consisted largely of arrears of stipend. The purpose of the 'exception' was simply to excuse Holyrood from a general rise in demand from the thirds, but it indicates fairly clearly that it was the *warrandice* on the demands from the Holyrood thirds that Robert was refusing to meet. It is noteworthy, incidentally, that the warrandice had been disponed by the king and collector of thirds to James Stewart of Graemsay for the payment of £500 – perhaps more evidence that Robert was gradually transferring his responsibilities to his sons.

On 9 August 1592 Robert, having ostensibly made payment to the bishop, was granted letters of relaxation of horning.[64] Despite this, the subject was still alive

58 Balfour (of Balfour and Trenabie) Papers, OA D.2, box 27, bundle 6.
59 *Ct Bk of Shetland.*
60 *RPC*, iv, 605.
61 *RPC*, iv, 718.
62 *APS*, iii, 590–1.
63 *APS*, iii, 547–8.
64 Sheriff Thom's Papers, NRS GD1/212/38.

on 1 March 1597, more than four years after Robert's death.[65] By that time Adam Bothwell was himself dead and Robert's escheat had been granted to Mr Thomas Barclay, but it was only with difficulty that Earl Patrick was able to rid himself of the problem finally, probably some time in 1597.

Despite his shedding of responsibility, and probable failing health, some of Robert's activities remained characteristic to the end. On 20 August 1591 Alastair Banks and his wife were granted a tenement in Kirkwall from which Simon Cursiter had been evicted 'for thift'.[66] On 20 January 1592, Robert's servitor David Angusson received a privy seal gift of the escheat of his father, Stephen Angusson, at the horn at the instance of William Halcro of Aikers for *spuilyie*.[67] On 23 July following, David also received land in Sanday from Robert.[68] Some time before 24 November, Robert disponed lands in Lyking, Sandwick, to Margaret Craigie of Clumlie; this territory also had been evicted for theft.[69] Robert's other charters of the period were largely to familiars and relatives, perhaps in settlement of his affairs as the end approached. On 3 August 1591, at Kirkwall, he granted land in Yinstay to Alexander Kincaid, a former servant of Adam Bothwell who had been in his employ for some years.[70] Six weeks later he granted land in Weyland to Marjorie Sandilands, his mistress, and to Edward, one of her sons by him.[71] The following month James Fea received land in Clestrain, Sanday.[72] Towards the end of the year, in his last recorded action, he gave the lands of Housbie, in Stronsay, and the island of Auskerry to Hugh Sinclair of Brough, husband of his illegitimate daughter Grizel.[73]

This was the last charter by Robert for which details are available. In November, the earl was formally included in a general commission to the nobility and others to execute the acts against Jesuits.[74] Just over a year later, perhaps in anticipation of his father's death, Patrick directed a precept in which he designated himself earl of Orkney.[75] The last official mention of Robert Stewart during his lifetime occurred on 12 January 1593, when the comptroller received his feu mails.[76]

Robert Stewart died on 4 February 1593.[77] Two days before, lying in his chamber

65 O & S Papers, NRS RH9/15/104.
66 Craven Beq., NRS GD106/81.
67 Scarth of Breckness Mun., NRS GD217/567.
68 Traill Dennison Papers, OA D.144/9.
69 *REO*, 318, no. cc.
70 *REO*, 317, no. cxcix.
71 Reg. House Chrs, NRS RH6/3140.
72 Reg. House Chrs, NRS RH6/2191.
73 *RMS*, v, no. 1994.
74 *The Autobiography and Diary of James Melvill* (Wodrow Soc.), 1842, 304.
75 *REO*, 166, no. lxxv.
76 *ER*, xxii, 283.
77 Edin. Comm. Ct Recs: Reg. Tests, NRS CC8/8/30. J. Mooney reckoned that Robert might possibly have been buried in the cathedral (*The Cathedral and Royal Burgh of Kirkwall*, Kirkwall, 1943, 90). This seems reasonable, given the presence there of the tomb of his brother Adam, but the comprehensive list of St Magnus tombs in the RCAHMS Inventory makes no mention of a tomb for Robert.

at the Palace of the Yards in Kirkwall, he ordered notary David Arthur to draw up his will.[78] Present as witnesses were his daughter Jean and her husband, Lord Lindores; James Stewart of Graemsay, his natural son; Thomas Swinton, minister at Kirkwall; Walter Bruce, sheriff clerk and a servitor from Robert's earliest days in Orkney; and two Edinburgh burgesses, John Dick and David Pringle. Robert remitted and forgave 'all rancor and malice conceavit aganes' Patrick, 'heir present upoun his knes', praying him 'mast effectuallie to observe and keip the . . . contract quhilk wes maid betuix me and him'. The reference to 'rancor', while possibly a formality, was not without cause, as we have seen. Moreover Patrick was not named as an executor in his father's will, perhaps in anticipation of trouble that was indeed to ensue after his death. Robert's wife Jean Kennedy, countess of Orkney, was not mentioned at all, although he left bequests to his mistresses, Marjorie Sandilands, Janet Allardyce and Janet Gray.

Other provisions of the will involved Robert's servants, as might be expected. Most of these were relatively humble, since Robert's important followers – Patrick Monteith of the Fair Isle, John Caverton of Shapinsay, William Gordon of Cairston – had been given adequate rewards already in the form of land. The only exception was John Dishington, who was discharged of all his intromissions as chamberlain and sheriff depute, and was the subject of a clause seeking to ensure Patrick's ratification of his pension. Other grants were miscellaneous: Magnus Hourston, keeper of Robert's girnel, received a discharge of his intromissions with 'our victuall det'; William Twatt received a pension of one barrel of butter and six meils cost yearly from the lands of Twatt; a general clause ordained all Robert's servants to have their fees paid; and finally John Sutherland was left 'the auld shellop with hir haill furnettours'.

It was all in vain. Whatever the named individuals may finally have received, the will was to be set aside and Robert's testament and inventory were not registered until 26 May 1597, more than four years after his death,[79] and then as *dative* (i.e. in the absence of a will), with Patrick as sole administrator. Why this happened is not known, but it could easily be for the same reason as the late registration – the difficult legal position of Robert's estate, which could have rendered the whole will invalid.

Nevertheless the testament gives an interesting picture of the late earl's movable assets and their distribution. His livestock, meat, grain and other agricultural commodities were listed as lying in the five main centres mentioned earlier, all in Orkney. The main asset of the Bu of Corse was that of dairy cattle, of which there were 180 hogs totalling £95 in money value. Folsetter had £130-worth of assorted bovine stock.

Since Robert's main girnels were in Birsay and Kirkwall, there was little in the way of grain products in the barn and barnyard of Corse, and none at all in Sandwick

---

78 Morton Papers, OA D38/2238.
79 Edin. Comm. Ct Recs: Reg. Tests, NRS CC8/8/30.

or Folsetter. Kirkwall, although the livestock there consisted only of six 'fed oxen' and two horses – a brown hackney and an old grey called 'The Rumlar' – nonetheless had within its boundaries the widest range of Robert's movables, contained in the 'lardner', the girnel, the castle and (probably) the Palace of the Yards. The larder contained a total of seven and a half barrels of beef and 20 *marts* of fat beef, with an overall value of £70; the girnel contained three *lasts* of malt and two lasts one meil of meal, £264-worth; there were 12 fathoms (£24) of peats in the peat yard. The inventory of the castle contents, apart from a silver spoon and an eight-ounce piece of silver, both worth 50s, were armaments, including a brass cannon called 'the lapster' worth £200, two iron cannon and ten *hagbuts*. Notwithstanding the value of the brass piece, this seems little enough. The only luxurious-sounding items in the inventory are not assigned a home, but it seems likely that they were in the Yards. They consisted of two French saddles with harness, one covered with purple velvet, the other with dry leather, costing £70 together, eight pieces of 'auld tapestry' worth £150 and two 'fute' mantles, one of velvet, one of blue cloth, one wrought with *passments* of silk, the other 'bigaret' with velvet; these last were worth respectively £100 and £40. Despite the almost certainly luxurious outfitting of the Palace of Birsay, the goods recorded as lying there were largely agricultural. Besides the livestock, there were quantities of malt and meal in the girnel, three lasts of ale in the cellar, bere, oats and fat beef in the barnyard, and 14 fathoms of peats in the peat yard.

The sum total of the inventory of Robert's movable assets was given as £4,116 11s. This, in common with the totals of many inventories of this period, was something of an underestimate. It is probable, for instance, that Robert would have possessed more and better riding horses than are recorded here, the armaments of the castle seem rather meagre, and it is distinctly frustrating that there is no reference at all to the plenishings of the Palace of Birsay. It was left to Patrick and his mother, now the dowager countess, to conduct the arguments over the accuracy of all this.

The debts owed to Robert consisted of a long list of the mails and duties owing for the year 1592, amounting to £4,568 18s 10d, and giving a very detailed list of tenants, feuars and skat-payers of both earldom and bishopric lands of Orkney with the amounts they owed for crop 1592. Notable are the outstanding *multures* of the mills of Deerness, Holm, Lingro (St Ola), Birsay, North Sandwick, Sanday and South Ronaldsay, evidence that whatever Robert's intentions towards the udal mills, there were already many mills in Orkney over which he had superiority.

Robert's own liabilities, which amounted to £4,800, consisted firstly of £2,068 13s 4d owed to the crown and 1,700 merks owed to the crown collector of teinds. Then followed a long list of 'years fees' to individuals who had served Robert in some capacity – headed, interestingly enough, by 'Andro Mertene, gentilman', his son's detested servant, who was owed £100. The list, embracing 45 people, covered a wide spectrum of activities, including Alexander Strachan, John Murray and Rob Glass, wrights; John Kincaid and William Oswald, smiths; John Wallace and Mans

Lauchlan, slaters; Gilbert Boyd and Duncan Crawford, quarriers (the presence of these men suggests that extensive building work was still going on at Birsay); Robert Smith, bellman; John Stewart, stabler; Andrew Lyle, brewer; and Robert Walker, gardener at Birsay, as well as other lesser souls.

One striking feature of the list is the relative lack of Orkney surnames; only Wattie Towp (?Toab) and one 'Stannoquoy', carter, have definitely Orcadian names. It is probable that there were a good many more Orkneymen in Robert's employ than this would suggest; a number of non-Orkney surnames in the list were in the process of becoming common in the islands at this time – Banks, Cogill, Sutherland, Sclater, Traill – and their bearers may well have been islanders. A first name such as that of Mans Lauchlan suggests a native born of an incoming family. Moreover, among Robert's other servants (and indeed named elsewhere in the testament) were James Gloup, *grieve* at Folsetter, and one Scarth, barnman at Birsay. Nevertheless, those among Robert's servants of likely northern origin represent a mere sprinkling amongst the group as a whole. Of the 140-odd persons who can be traced as having served Robert in any capacity whatever during his life in Orkney, only a handful – 15 or so – seem likely to have been Orcadians.[80] With the exceptions of two Scollays, Edward and David, the three sons of the late Henry Sinclair of Strom, and persons of the questionable surnames of Smith, Sclater and Sutherland, all the names that occur more than once in the list of Robert's servants are Scots – Blackadder, Brown, Bruce, Crawford, Dickson, Dundas, Elphinstone, Henderson, Johnston, Kennedy, Kincaid, Lyle, Monteith, Morrison, Murray, Redpath , Robson and Stewart.

Robert's more important followers had origins that are easily traceable. The Monteiths – James, Patrick and William – all came from Saltcoats, in the Kerse barony lands of Holyrood, and first appear on the scene apparently as followers of William Monteith of Randyfurd, himself a henchman of Robert; in Orkney, Patrick Monteith became the most prominent, becoming sheriff depute and captain of Kirkwall Castle during Robert's absence in the 1570s. Some were fairly obviously related closely to Robert himself. Laurence Bruce's men, Henry and James Bruce, were presumably relatives. Walter Bruce, Robert's sheriff clerk for many years, was an illegitimate son of the laird of Clackmannan, and as such was related both to the Cultmalindie Bruces, Robert's relatives, and to the Bruces of Airth, Robert's vassals as commendator of Holyrood.[81] Of the Elphinstones in Robert's following, William was the brother of Lord Elphinstone and thus his master's uncle; presumably Rany and Gavin Elphinstone must also have had some family or 'friendly' connection. James Kennedy was Robert's brother-in-law, and Oliver Kennedy was presumably another kinsman in that direction. The Kincaids would seem to have had two separate origins; Alexander Kincaid had originally been a servant

---

80 Except where otherwise stated, all references for statements made in this passage are to be found in Anderson, *Robert Stewart*, app. 6.
81 Armstrong, *The Bruces of Airth and their Cadets*, 29.

of Adam Bothwell, as had been John Kincaid of Warriston, an earlier visitor to Orkney. William Kincaid the smith, however, is designated 'of Falkirk', and he and his brother John presumably came into Robert's employ through their connections with the barony of Kerse. The 'inner circle' of Robert's servants, those who were involved over a long period in his most important doings, were Thomas Auchinleck, John Caverton of Shapinsay, John Dishington, William Elphinstone, William Gordon of Cairston, Alexander Kincaid, Patrick Monteith of the Fair Isle, and two of the small number of prominent native Orcadians, Malcolm Groat of Tankerness and David Scollay of Tofts.

Of these, all but Auchinleck and Elphinstone were concerned in some capacity in Robert's campaign against the Irvings of Sebay. Auchinleck, Dishington, Caverton and Kincaid were all south on Robert's business at one time or another, and Monteith, as we have seen, was mixed up in some of Robert's more violent and disreputable activities. Both Elphinstone and Monteith acted as sheriffs depute during Robert's troubles in the 1570s and David Scollay was provost of Kirkwall when Robert demitted that office during his second period of tribulation, 1586–9. Both Monteith and William Gordon were at different times captain of Kirkwall Castle. The profusion of deeds in which these individuals figure suggests that they were seldom far from their master's side and, as their designations might indicate, any time spent out of Robert's company by Caverton, Gordon or Monteith was probably spent administering their own not inconsiderable estates.

Outside this group of regular and important counsellors was a larger number – perhaps 30-odd – of lesser lights. These in fact form more of a class than a clearly identifiable band of men, since their identities appear to vary at different periods of Robert's career. William Ferguson, for example, possibly arrived in Orkney with Robert in 1567, but disappears after 1574, as does James Kennedy, Robert's brother-in-law (both may have gone south with the disgraced Robert in 1575 and simply never returned). Thomas Knightson on the other hand, though serving both Robert and his son, does not appear on the scene till 1585. James Hay appears in Robert's affairs in 1572 (though he may have been in Orkney earlier) and disappears again after 1584. James Dickson, a servant of Henry Stewart, master of Orkney, appears only twice, in 1584 and 1585, though it is obvious from his letter to Andrew Martin in the latter year that he was indeed a permanent servant. It is Dickson who gives us our only glimpse in Robert's lifetime of another servant, David Moncreiffe, though the latter is known to have been alive in Orkney in 1614.[82] Dickson and Moncreiffe seem to have played golf together, one imagines on the links between the Birsay palace and the sea.[83]

Of this group, a handful remained with him throughout his time in the north. Walter Bruce was in Robert's service during the whole period 1567–93, and Thomas Robeson's period of employment was not a great deal shorter, ending about 1587,

82 REO, 382, no. ccxli.
83 Barnbarroch Corresp., 340.

perhaps simply as a result of his death. To this group, too, belongs a small number of individuals who were not servants of Robert in the strict sense and who never set foot in the Northern Isles at all – Robert's Edinburgh agents. These men, Alexander Couston, James Marshall, William Monteith and possibly Andrew Williamson, were responsible for transacting Robert's business in the capital, chiefly translating Orkney and Shetland produce rents into cash, but also witnessing legal documents and, in Williamson's case, purchasing a ship. Also in treating of this group of Robert's servants we may name those whom we know to have exercised specific functions under the earl; Gloup the grieve, Scarth the barnman, Magnus Hourston, keeper of the girnel, Robert Walker, the gardener at Birsay, and John Sutherland, skipper, who, being left an old ship by Robert in his will, may perhaps have been the latter's own personal shipman.

9

Ane Yoing Nobill Man of Good Expectation

Patrick Stewart was now undisputed earl of Orkney. Robert Stewart had been responsible for the earldom's existence, and held sway in Orkney and Shetland for nearly twice the length of time that his son was to do, but nonetheless it is Patrick who is the better remembered, or more notorious, in the popular imagination of present-day islanders. As Storer Clouston states, 'By a curious fate it is the name of "Pate" Stewart, Earl Robert's son and successor, that is still remembered in Orkney today as a symbol for oppression, while his father's stressings and even his very name are forgotten.'[1]

Patrick stayed with the king from mid-1590 until the autumn of 1592. During that time, besides his attendance upon his cousin, his chief preoccupation at court was the first of two unsuccessful attempts to find himself a wife. The object of his advances, or negotiations, was Jean, youngest daughter of the earl of Morton. By 11 March 1592 he was in communication with the earl, 'whereby it is deemed that the Douglases and Stewarts shall be wholly joined together.'[2] A fortnight or so later it was reported that the king 'for some respects has stayed the accord of marriage' between the two, but it was thought he would eventually agree.[3] By 6 June, however, the 'practice of some courtiers, as it is thought' had caused the engagement to be broken off.[4] Patrick left for the north shortly afterwards, and remained there for the next two years or so, when he returned to the capital to take part as a server to the king at the banquet celebrating the birth of Prince Henry. He became a member of the privy council and took part in its deliberations regularly from September 1594 until May 1595.[5]

His other great priority during these years was redress against the English pirates who had robbed him of his treasure. In January 1595, no doubt in response to Patrick's

---

1 Clouston, *History of Orkney*, 307.

2 *CSP Scot.*, x, 654.

3 *CSP Scot.*, x, 661.

4 *CSP Scot.*, x, 687; this was not the only occasion on which the king was to show great interest in a Morton marriage, and he was later to be extremely angry with the earl of Morton for ignoring the royal wishes in respect of one of his other daughters (*RPC*, iv, 506–7).

5 *RPC*, v.

appeal, King James raised the matter again in a letter to the English queen,[6] and this was followed by a mission to England on Patrick's behalf by James Learmonth of Balcomie. It had little success. Balcomie was unable to obtain redress before English judges, even though the notorious pirate, Captain David Gwynn himself was in court. Patrick, the 'yoing nobill man of good expectation', sought a commission to arrest all English ships that came to Orkney and Shetland until he obtained redress. By now 'one of the chamber and a great courtier', he procured this easily, but his success was short-lived. English diplomats George Nicolson and Roger Aston sought to have the measure set aside, arguing with both the secretary and the king himself that penalising English vessels would simply provoke counter-measures against the merchants of Scotland. They were successful, and Patrick's commission was stopped.[7]

Nevertheless, in January 1596 Patrick took the *Hope Well* of Dunwich, bound with wheat from Danzig to London, and detained her in Kirkwall. Nicolson and Robert Bowes both approached the king on behalf of the *Hope Well's* owner Mr Offley, a London merchant.[8] Patrick was peremptorily ordered south and told to make restitution.[9] He did this willingly enough, since King James also commanded David Foulis, one of the Scots representatives in London, to press again his demands for compensation.[10] This claim too achieved nothing, and in May 1599 the earl took further action. He became involved in a dispute between the king and the English, in particular Sir William Bowes, Robert Bowes's nephew and fellow diplomat, over the activities of Dunkirk pirates in Scottish waters. Bowes was protesting that two pirate ships had captured English vessels off Bamburgh and Fastcastle, and had been allowed to convoy them to Crail without challenge, in contravention of an agreement between James and the English queen. James, unwilling to provoke reprisals from Dunkirk, simply made excuses.[11] When Patrick, seeing an opportunity to ingratiate himself with the English, captured one of the Dunkirk boats and took her to Leith, James reproved him severely, set the ship free and gave her a safe-conduct, even though she was carrying English captives and booty.[12]

The English were not unaware of Patrick's motives, which were aimed, in George Nicolson's words, solely at 'the more favour . . . anent the piracy committed against him'.[13] By this time the old hurt had rankled for nearly a decade, and whatever short-term support he might offer to the English, he continued to regard Sir William Bowes with suspicion. On 22 June 1599, Bowes wrote that he had ridden out of Edinburgh that afternoon 'to take the air for my health'. He took great care to go

6 *Salisbury Papers*, v, 96.
7 *CSP Scot.*, xi, 576–9.
8 *CSP Scot.*, xii, 136, 148, 167.
9 *RPC*, v, 284–5.
10 *CSP Scot.*, xii, 188, 199, 215–16.
11 *CSP Scot.*, xiii, 481.
12 *CSP Scot.*, xiii, 494.
13 *CSP Scot.*, xiii, 497.

northwards 'to avoid the vain suspicion of my privy departure, but watch being had upon me more than 40 horse were suddenly out of the town spread over the fields after me'. Among them were Patrick Stewart and his brother John.[14]

Besides his attempts to seek compensation for his losses, Patrick became involved in a more intriguing attempt at wife-hunting. In December 1594 Colonel William Stewart of Houston went to the Netherlands, ostensibly as a royal emissary. Officially his aims were several. He had to bring back the final confirmation of the treaty of Bins, a treaty of mutual protection with the Netherlands, originally signed with the emperor Charles V. He was also to request advice and assistance in combating the Spanish party in Scotland, to the extent of money for 1,000 foot and 500 horse for six months.[15] Thirdly, he was to negotiate for a proposed marriage between Patrick, earl of Orkney, and Princess Emilia, sister of the Stadtholder, Prince Maurice of Nassau.[16]

According to one English observer, Thomas Bodley, Colonel Stewart was resented by the Scots resident in the Low Countries. The Scottish ambassador, Archibald Douglas, had visited him 'of purpose to ease his stomach of dislike of this coming thither of Colonel Stuart ... '; he thought the venture a lost cause, as was Patrick's proposed marriage.[17] Another prominent Scot, Colonel Murray of the Scots Regiment, told the Englishman that Stewart's embassy, though supposedly official, had in fact been pursued at his own request. The king of Scots was said to have no great liking for him, and his expedition was therefore funded either entirely by himself or in half shares with Patrick in return for his good offices with the Dutch princess.[18] Had there been any likelihood of this marriage becoming a reality, it would have been a glittering success for the earl of Orkney. Maurice of Nassau had made a European name for himself by his spectacular victories against the Spaniards. Whether it was realistic to expect such a proposal to be taken seriously, particularly without any sort of official endorsement, is another matter, and it is perhaps early evidence of Patrick's unrealistic arrogance and conceit. The flat response of the lady herself was that she had no wish to live so far away from her brother and kinsfolk; and in the Hague it was said that Patrick had 'no assurance of the Orcades because they have been claimed by the Kings of Denmark, and it was a late speech of the Queen of Scotland that she hoped her son should enjoy those Isles'.[19] Despite a brief period of optimism in May 1595, shortly before Stewart's return,[20] it became clear that his embassy had been a failure. All he had received from the Dutch authorities was the expected treaty ratification and a licence to transport arms and armour to

14 *CSP Scot.*, xiii, 505.
15 *CSP Scot.*, xi, 498; *Salisbury Papers*, v, 11o.
16 *Salisbury Papers*, v, 129.
17 *Salisbury Papers*, v, 110.
18 *Salisbury Papers*, v, 111, 167.
19 *Salisbury Papers*, v, 111.
20 *CSP Scot.*, xi, 589.

Scotland.[21] The collapse of this ambitious scheme was a great disappointment to Patrick, who had spent 'so much tyme and substance in vane'.[22]

The reference to Queen Anne's desire for the island estates was significant; it derived from a grant to her in August 1593, after the deaths of Robert and Bishop Bothwell, of the temporalities of the bishopric. This was to replace part of her dowry, the lordship of Dunfermline, whose revenues were nearly exhausted.[23] The outright loss of the Orkney bishopric revenues would have meant for Patrick a drop of nearly 50 per cent in income from what he might have hoped to inherit from his father, and it helps to explain his desire to win the queen's favour in a difficult game, fraught with danger for his relationship with the king. By early 1595 he was already receiving consideration from Queen Anne. In February, with her husband's consent, she appointed Patrick bailie of the bishopric lands of Orkney, the grant being backdated to the death of Adam Bothwell. This gave the young earl wide administrative powers, but also compelled him to pay her a yearly composition of 1,000 merks, and to lend an ear to her private schemes. Ever since the birth of Prince Henry in 1594 and the immediate consigning of the child to the care of the earl and countess of Mar, Queen Anne had been agitating for the return of her son; it was to be a bone of contention between the royal couple for many years. In March 1595 Patrick was with them at Stirling in company with the duke of Lennox, the earls of Argyll and Crawford, and Mar himself. The king confronted the nobles, offended by their support for his wife in the matter.[24] James was soon to issue a command forbidding Mar or his wife, in the event of his death, to give up the prince to the queen until he reached the age of 18.[25] The physical paroxysms that affected the queen whenever her wishes were rejected now manifested themselves, and on 7 June she lay sick at Linlithgow.[26] By 12 July she was 'something craised'. Her husband had tried to persuade her to move back to Stirling, away from the faction that he felt to be encouraging her; Patrick had in turn sought unsuccessfully to persuade the king to visit her.[27]

James, physically timorous, was not prepared to put himself among the queen's supporters, who might bring threats and other pressure to bear on him. This faction, consisting of Sir George Home, Walter Scott of Buccleuch and William Ker of Cessfurd, were said by Nicolson the English observer to be trying to find a more malleable protector for Prince Henry than the resolute Mar, one from whom direct custody of the child might more easily be obtained. The first choice was the duke of Lennox; Patrick was the second. According to Roger Aston the earl of Orkney, feeling himself 'behind hand . . . since his purpose failed in Flanders', had hung on

21 H. G. Stafford, *James VI of Scotland and the Throne of England*, New York and London, 1940, 138.
22 *Original Letters of John Colville* (Bannatyne Club), 1858, 175; *CSP Scot.*, xi, 683.
23 *RMS*, vi, no. 1572; *RSS*, NRS PS1/66, ff. 84v–6r.
24 *CSP Scot.*, xi, 549.
25 Willson, *James VI and I*, 117.
26 *CSP Scot.*, xi, 607.
27 *CSP Scot.*, xi, 608, 637.

at court, hoping to be awarded custody of the prince, as well as the governorship of the castle of Edinburgh, another of Mar's distinctions – 'Although he dissembled the matter with the King he was as deep in as the rest. I see nothing but that those whom the King most trusts soonest deceive him, looking rather to their own particular than the honour and preservation of him who has preserved them.' Like Patrick's Flanders purpose, the queen's efforts and those of her party came to nothing. On 20 August 1595 Patrick was still with the queen at Lindores, but was reported by John Colville to be on his way home at last, bewailing his losses and the failure of his elaborate schemes.[28]

By now there was between the king and queen 'nothing but lurking hatred, disguised with cunning dissimulation . . . each intending by sleight to overcome the other'.[29] Nevertheless Patrick's activities – the intrigues over the prince, the taking of ships in defiance of the king – seemed to have done little harm to his relationship with his royal cousin. On 25 March 1596, at the time of the *Hope Well* affair he had been with the king at his visit to the General Assembly,[30] and in June the same year he was noted by Robert Bowes as a possible member of an embassy to Denmark to negotiate a Protestant alliance against Spain. He was not in the end chosen, but was a regular attender at meetings of the privy council during 1596. The continuing royal favour was further indicated when the king attended his nuptials.

Patrick had at last found a wife. She was Margaret Livingston, daughter of Alexander, sixth Lord Livingston and, more significantly, the widow of Sir Lewis Bellenden. It was a union clearly intended to put to rest the old differences between the Stewarts and the Bellendens. The couple were married in the church of Falkirk on 17 August 1596 by the minister, Adam Bellenden of Kilconquhar, youngest brother of Sir Lewis, as well as his presentee to what was an old Holyrood living.[31] Two days later, a banquet in the couple's honour was held nearby at Lord Livingston's house of Callendar, and it was from there that the king, breaking his progress to the west, travelled to Dunfermline where his own wife had that same evening given birth to a daughter, Elizabeth, the future 'Winter Queen'.[32] After this, the details of their marriage are sketchy, and they had no children, though by an island woman, Marjorie Sinclair, Patrick had an illegitimate son, Robert, who was to play a major, if inglorious, role at the end of the story. Margaret Livingston, like her predecessor Jean Kennedy, felt compelled to act in support of her lord. She accompanied him to Orkney for an extended stay in 1597 and 1598. She was in Shetland in 1603 while Patrick was in London, and after Patrick's return the following year.[33]

What sort of picture do these details provide of the king's young gentleman and

28 *CSP Scot.*, xi, 683.

29 *CSP Scot.*, xi, 683; *Original Letters of John Colville*, 175.

30 *CSP Scot.*, xii, 176.

31 Edin. Comm. Ct Recs: Acts and Decreets, NRS CC8/2/41; Anderson, *Robert Stewart*, 6.

32 *CSP Scot.*, xii, 306.

33 Reg. Deeds, NRS RD1/29. ff. 32*v*–3*r*; RD1/71, f. 317*r* and *v*; RD1/180, ff. 315–16.

his position at court? The most important point is undoubtedly the royal favour, which persisted despite tiresome behaviour. Admittedly, such esteem as he was accorded did not extend to employment in matters of any great moment; he served James in the bedchamber or in the chase, rather than as a political adviser or envoy. On 1 March 1600 we find him hunting with the king in Teviotdale. During the trip a misunderstanding arose between the royal party and John Vevara, representative of Lord Willoughby, one of the English wardens of the marches. Vevara's party was watching that of the Scottish king from the English side of the border, and James became suspicious of what he believed to be its excessive size. The drawing of a sword by one of the Englishmen (said by Vevara to be entirely innocent) led to the 'ill taken' impression among the Scots that Vevara and his men had 'braved' the king. Patrick was of that group in the Scottish party who sought to offer provocation by hunting on English ground. They were thwarted by the lateness of the hour. Patrick exclaimed, 'Fie for two hours of day!'[34]

There was one episode where, apparently travelling on the king's business in a matter where he had little personal concern, Patrick's conduct earned a small compliment from James Melville, minister of Anstruther, and one that went beyond mere formal flattery. In September 1593, the crafts and burgesses of St Andrews had deposed their provost, the unpopular James Learmonth of Dairsie, and put in his place Captain William Murray. Learmonth's supporters, led by Michael Balfour of Burleigh, were extremely angry and gathered their forces to enter the town under arms. They were deterred by an assembly of townsfolk led by Lord Lindsay, Sir George Douglas and Andrew Melville, James Melville's uncle and rector of the university.[35] Murray remained provost for two years in the face of opposition from Burleigh and the Dairsie faction. In September 1595, however, Burleigh procured from the king the services of the earl of Orkney in reconciling Dairsie with Andrew Melville and the two ministers of the town. This Patrick did 'verie craftelie'. The reconciliation induced the people of St Andrews to change their provost again. Murray resigned willingly, 'perceaving the changeablenes of the peiple'.[36]

Patrick may have had an interest in the case through his connections with Dairsie's kinsman Learmonth of Balcomie, who had represented him in London in pursuit of his lost moneys; but the incident remains an obscure and local one, and the only example of Patrick being entrusted with a task on his own account, rather than in a group with others. He was not the subject of the sort of contemptuous comments that political observers had made about his father in earlier days;[37] but beyond the references to his 'good expectation', which was more a question

34 Salisbury Papers, x, 47.
35 C. J. Lyon, History of St Andrews, vols I–II, St Andrews, 1843, i, 425–6.
36 Melvill, Diary, 221; background to this episode is to be found in the unpublished MA dissertation by Louise A. Yeoman, 'Godly Revolution in St Andrews', University of St Andrews, 1988. My thanks are due to her for drawing her work to my attention.
37 Anderson, Robert Stewart, 45.

of favour than of promise, little was said about his character or capabilities. The overall impression is of a young man, perhaps of some charm, but arrogant and impulsive, capable of double-dealing, and loud among the hot-heads in the king's hunting-party. The wealth he had sought to bring with him on his first coming to court speaks of extravagance and love of display, and his pursuit of one of the most eligible brides in Northern Europe suggests a good conceit of himself.

As the sixteenth century drew to its close, evidence began to grow of his unpopularity. This was not the result of his behaviour at court, nor at first did it seem that his enemies were of his choosing – they were either inherited from his father, or came from within the ranks of his own family. Nevertheless it was in the 1590s that he first began, through his own efforts, to provoke the opposition that was to increase, steadily and massively, and ultimately engulf him. The most extraordinary aspect of this is that, despite doubts over aspects of his titles, his estates should have provided him with an excellent and dependable income, without the need to search, as he was so notoriously to do, for additional funds elsewhere. It was the unceasing rapacity with which he conducted this search that made foes of his natural vassals, the forces of government and in time the king himself. It is time to look at the sources of this slowly but inexorably growing animus.

At the end of the old earl's life, there were two groups of territory outwith his direct control: the lands feued out by Bishop Bothwell before his arrival in Orkney, and forced out of Robert himself at the end of the 1580s; and the private udal estates. Adam Bothwell's difficult episcopate had seen the alienation of more than half the landed property of the bishopric and kirks. Between this and subsequent transactions, a whole new class of feuars had been created in Orkney – the Eday Sinclairs (descending from Oliver Sinclair of Pitcairns), the Monteiths, the Bellendens, the Balfours, the Moodies. These lairdly families were to play an important, and in some cases crucial role in the story of Patrick Stewart's earldom and downfall, and their influence in the islands was to last for the next four centuries.

In Shetland the equivalents were the Cheynes of Vaila, the Mouats of Heogaland and, in particular and in conflict, the Sinclairs on the one hand, of Brough, Havera, Houss; and the Bruces on the other, of Cultmalindie and Symbister. As we have seen, Arthur Sinclair of Aith, a senior representative of the family of Houss, had led the opposition to Laurence Bruce in the 1570s as foud. The death of Henry Sinclair of Brough in 1563 had led to the minority of his son Hugh and a period of eclipse for that branch of the family, but in the early 1580s Hugh joined Sinclair of Aith and others in paying Robert, then newly created earl, the sum of £1,000 to remove Bruce from the office of foud.[38] Under Patrick, Brough and Cultmalindie were to fall into dispute with the earl and each other over rights to a tack of the wadmel of Shetland, possibly granted to both by Robert.[39]

38 *Shetland Documents, 1580–1611*, 16, no. 34.
39 Reg. Deeds, NRS RD1/32, ff. 216r–18r.

The Sinclairs' support for Robert, and their reluctance to implicate him in Bruce's misdeeds, a noteworthy feature of the 1577 Complaints, was further displayed ten years or so later, when Sinclair of Aith and Brough rallied to his standard against Sir Patrick Bellenden.[40] Nevertheless, the Sinclairs and the Bruces, perhaps conscious of Robert's manipulations, made efforts to improve their own relationship. Brough married Jean Bruce, sister of Andrew Bruce of Sandwick, William Bruce of Symbister married the widow of William Sinclair of Underhoull, and in 1589 Laurence's son Andrew was matched with Sinclair of Brough's daughter Margaret.[41] The last of these marriages in particular was not a success (Andrew Bruce divorced his wife for adultery with a piper's son from Kirkcaldy),[42] and relations between the Sinclairs and the Bruces remained difficult. But in the end it was not the Sinclairs who thwarted Bruce in his attempts to attain his former position. His plans came to naught in 1591 when Patrick became lord of Shetland.

Perhaps the most unexpected aspect of Bruce's period of actual rule in Shetland had been the lack of evidence of any attempt to amass territory. Only when he was stripped of his offices did he set out to build up landed interests for himself. This may be because of his affairs elsewhere; there were disputes over his Cultmalindie estates, near Perth,[43] and it could be that his ferocious milking of the Shetland revenues had been intended to put his finances in the south on a sound footing. In the 1580s however, he began to deal in landed property in Shetland. A favourite gambit was to buy up estates and then lease or pledge them again. He did this in Gluss in Northmavine, in Laxfirth and Scalloway which he *wadset* to Robert Cheyne of Urie, and in Delting where he leased back lands to Andrew Hawick of Scatsta.[44] On 6 February 1581 he was granted four merks in Symbister in Whalsay by Culben Ormeson; this was the first of a series of transactions which by 1587 had taken the whole 32 merklands of the Symbister estates out of Ormeson's hands.[45] Popular memories survive of the oppression by which he achieved this. Bruce is said to have taken a gun and pursued the unfortunate Culben, who only escaped by jumping on to a rock in Kirny Geo in Whalsay, and thence into a waiting boat. In October 1585 Bruce set the whole estate in tack to his 'weill belovit and trustie servitor' (according to tradition his nephew), William Bruce.[46] This title ultimately became permanent, and the Bruce of Symbister family also became notable in Patrick's Shetland.

40 *Ct Bk of Shetland*, 142–3.
41 *RSS*, NRS PS1/57, f. 171v.
42 Grant, *Zetland Family Histories*, 21, 277.
43 Court of Session Recs: Acts and Decreets, NRS CS7/52, ff. 245r, 347r and v.
44 Bruce of Symbister Papers., SA GD144/21/13; Vaila Papers, SA D.10/12; Reg. Deeds, NRS RD1/41, ff. 324v –6r.
45 *Shetland Documents, 1580–1611*, 14, no. 30; 15, no. 32.
46 *Shetland Documents, 1580–1611*, 32, no. 75.

Robert had rendered his last account to exchequer in January 1592.[47] From then on, each year until 1598, the familiar payment of £2,073 6s 8d appeared in the exchequer rolls.[48] Patrick's name was not explicitly mentioned in the rolls as his father's had been, but it was to him that any special instructions regarding the destination of the payments were directed. From time to time the king found the large revenues of Orkney and Shetland very useful, and employed them for various purposes. In 1593 Patrick was instructed to pay £400 to John Robertson, an Edinburgh merchant, to repay loans to the king, and £576 to David Murray, the king's master stabler, who had furnished the royal kitchens.[49] More importantly, he had to pay the entire sum for the years 1594–6 to John Arnot, deputy treasurer, as security for the money Arnot was spending on arrangements for the celebrations at the baptism of Prince Henry.[50] Arnot was soon to become one of Patrick's most important financial advisers – a thankless task, as it was to prove.

Despite this, and notwithstanding a very wide-ranging commission as lieutenant in the Northern Isles, Patrick's titles to his father's estates remained a matter of doubt for seven years after he became earl. Partly this was due to the unfinished business left by old Robert at his death – he was still being pursued by Bishop Bothwell over money due under the terms of their exchange of the Orkney bishopric and Holyrood abbey lands 25 years before,[51] and Patrick's mother was to object strongly to the provision made for her as a widow. More important was the attitude of the crown and its advisers to the whole question of Robert Stewart's wealthy lands, amassed at the crown's expense. Besides this was the examination by the *Octavians*, the eight officials appointed by James in 1595 to conduct a thoroughgoing reform of the royal finances as a whole. As late as 1597, two years after the start of the Octavians' programme of retrenchment, the king was still said to be intending to 'challenge the earldom of Orkney'.[52]

But in the final years of the sixteenth century, as Patrick settled affairs with his relatives and servants, the way was cleared for his formal succession to his father's lands. On 22 July 1598 Andrew Martin rendered in exchequer an account for £15,550 – seven and a half years at £2,073 6s 8d per year.[53] Although the annual payment for Orkney and Shetland had indeed been included in the accounts, it may be that, pending the settlement of the late Robert's affairs, the money was not actually paid over. Now it was. The doubts over Patrick's titles were beginning to dissipate. Two years or so later, during the same day that he was hunting with the king on the borders, there passed the seals his charter of the lands of the earldom of Orkney and

47 *ER*, xxii, 183–4.
48 *ER*, xxii, xxii, xxiii.
49 *ER*, xxii, 579–81.
50 *RPC*, v, 168.
51 Anderson, *Robert Stewart*, 125–8.
52 *RPC*, xiv, 612; *CSP Scot.*, xiii, 78.
53 *ER*, xxiii, 223–5.

lordship of Shetland. Some weeks later, on 15 May, he was granted a similar charter of the bishopric lands.[54]

The Octavians did not prevent the full recognition of Patrick as successor to his father, but in Orkney there was one important result of their activities. Their survey of crown finances was almost certainly the motive behind the compilation of the rental of 1595.[55] John Dishington, Patrick's deputy, perambulated the islands with his assistants, checking procedures, accepted methods of payment, weighing instruments and so forth. The rental was more detailed than its predecessors, and furnishes clear evidence of the earl's policies during the early period of his rule. Towards the end of that rule – during 1613 after he had lost all title to the lands – the rental was used as the basis for a massive statement of account, prepared by the servants of the king and the bishop.[56]

Patrick's financial difficulties meant that the early 1590s were a time of reorganisation and expansion on the Orkney estates. He redeemed the lands in South Ronaldsay leased by his father to Henry Halcro as a dowry for his niece Barbara, daughter of Lord Adam Stewart.[57] In 1593 he concluded a contract with Adam Moodie who received the earl's lands in Melsetter in exchange for estates in Osmondwall and Dounreay.[58] He bought up the lands of various prebends, those of St Ola in Deerness, St John in the parish of St Ola and some of the St Katherine lands in St Ola, Firth and Shapinsay. He acquired the subchantry lands in Birsay. Later the *teindsheaves* of the stouks of St Duthus and St Augustine were added to the rental.[59]

At the same time, if Bruce of Cultmalindie and his fellow udallers are to be believed, he sought to establish suzerainty over the whole udal lands of Orkney and Shetland. He did this, it was said, by ignoring the peculiar nature of udal tenure and arguing that they had 'fallen in nonentry', i.e. were forfeit due to the heirs' failure to take formal possession of them in the feudal manner. He sought thereby to establish a claim to any land for which no written title could be proved.[60] This was an obscure and short-lived crisis; Patrick's later activities suggest that if he had made such an attempt, it had been unsuccessful. He sought instead to buy up udal land piece by piece. One of his important aims was to augment the main centres of the Orkney estates built up by his father – Folsetter, Corse, Skaill – all of them on bishopric or kirkland. Among his acquisitions therefore were the St John's Stouk lands in Corse;[61] to this were added the lands of Newbigging, part of the prebend

54 *RMS*, vi, nos 1022, 1038; Reg. House Chrs, NRS RH6/3599.
55 *Rentals*, pt ii.
56 Exchequer Records: Orkney [and Shetland] Rentals and Accs, NRS E41/3.
57 *Rentals*, ii, 102; Craven Beq., NRS GD106/178.
58 *Rentals*, ii, 93.
59 Exchequer Records: Orkney [and Shetland] Rentals and Accs, NRS E41/3.
60 *Shetland Documents, 1580–1611*, 86, no. 198.
61 *Rentals*, pt ii, 24.

of St Katherine.[62] The subchantry lands in Birsay included Buckquoy, hard by the palace, which were added to a large number of small parcels of udal land. [63]

Later, when Patrick acquired his title to the bishopric lands, he was to continue his father's policy of creating new head farms (bus) on the estates as a means of administering the bishopric and earldom lands as a single entity. By 1595, he had augmented the Bu of Skaill and those of Westness in Rousay and Sound in Shapinsay.[64] He was also responsible for Shetland's only example of this property type – the Bu of Trondra, which we will examine presently. All, whether new or dating from Robert's time, were augmented with small additions. To Sound was added a pennyland from the St Katherine's Stouk lands in Elwick.[65] Sound was made the subject of special attention, being rerentalled in 1601.[66] Knarston and Langskaill in Rousay were leased to Edward and Henry Alexander respectively 'in form of ane bull'. And in the return of 1613, after Patrick's fall, the Bus of Sound and Skaill were given separate treatment in the accounts.[67] The addition of small udal properties to major centres of power is particularly noticeable in Birsay. In the Isbister district of Marwick, Patrick granted 2¾d land to Oliver Sclater in exchange for the lands of Wattle in Birsay, at the same time receiving ½d land from Henry Baikie for the lands of Tronston in Sandwick. In the bishop's lands in Marwick, he acquired three merks in Sabiston from Matthew Scollay and his brother, and in Birsay-be-South over 11 meils-worth of small lots, exchanged with various individuals.[68]

Patrick was perfectly prepared to make concessions where it was difficult to work certain land and where maintaining the traditional payment in the face of a low yield would result in work being given up altogether. The lands of Tingwall, Midgarth and Howaquoy in Evie, Air and Dritness in Stronsay, Bimbister in Harray, Gaitnip in St Ola and Hunclet in Rousay, were 'given down' – granted gratis, or at a lower value – 'because the lands was dear and like to be ley [fallow], to get the same laubourit' (he did the same in Shetland, reducing the rent of Rerwick in Dunrossness by a quarter).[69] The general picture is one of prudent estate management, with no obvious evidence of oppression. Patrick's servants, Dishington and the others, are putting structure to the vision of his dispiriting, yet somehow enterprising, father. To seek anything more sinister in the rental it is necessary to look at the escheats. More than 40 individuals are mentioned as having lost their land for one reason or another. Some of these forfeitures may date from Earl Robert's time, and there are some that were clearly entered in the rental after 1595; but there are no details of the former, and only seven or so of the latter, giving the impression

62 Rentals, pt ii, 23.
63 Rentals, pt ii, 54–5.
64 Exchequer Records: Orkney [and Shetland] Rentals and Accs, NRS E41/3.
65 Rentals, pt ii, 43, 47–9, 67, 111.
66 Rentals, pt ii, 111.
67 Exchequer Records: Orkney [and Shetland]Rentals and Accs, NRS E41/3.
68 Rentals, pt ii, 51–4.
69 Exchequer Records: Orkney [and Shetland] Rentals and Accs, NRS E41/17.

that the early years of Patrick's rule saw a systematic campaign of legal confiscation. Particularly suspicious are his activities in the district of Marwick, where no fewer than 11 persons were forfeited. Thomas and Robert Gyre, John How, John Linklater and one Heggrie were evicted for theft, Robert Gyre's sister for child-murder, Adam Moir, Andrew Merriman and Nicol Sclater and his wife for reasons unknown. The values involved were not great, Nicol Sclater's ¾d land being the largest, but with the numerous other small tracts that Patrick was acquiring there by lawful purchase, they suggest the use of escheat in the furtherance of policy.

There were tiny scraps of property acquired in other, less significant, parts of Orkney that were unlikely to be of any great use to the earl; their confiscation may have come by due process of law. The forfeiture of udal possessions for such reasons as theft, child-murder and suicide did not excite any protests that we know of, any more than the confiscations for suicide were to do in Shetland. Such opposition as was provoked by the changes wrought in the rental was duly noted down by Dishington. Quoysharps in South Ronaldsay was alleged by the 'uthell men' to have been 'wrongously taken from them' and Yorbrands there (now Brance) was 'alleged to be Kingis land, whereon the uthell men complain'. There were also in Sanday certain 'Tumails reddin by David Scollay and other honest men of the Isle ... whereof the commonis and occupiers for the most part refuse to make payment'. This refusal to pay up was more effective than one might have supposed. In the case of Yorbrands, the lands were still 'allegit be the uthelmen to be thair awin' in 1613, and no duty either on it or on Quoysharps had ever been paid.

After Patrick's formal infeftment in the earldom and bishopric estates, it seems likely that the acquisition of udal land in this way was put on a more systematic footing. In 1601 he had the 'Uthell Buik' drawn up. This was a list by parish of all the udal estates. It used distinctly feudal phraseology, describing the estates as 'fewit ... to the uthellaris thereof, thair aires and assigneys of na hiear degrie nor themselves ... payand thair scattis and deuties conform to the rentall'. There are indications that this was more through ignorance than malevolence. Both Robert and Patrick obviously recognised the distinctiveness of the udal lands, but simply lacked the vocabulary to describe them in other than feudal terms. They were not alone; even udallers who complained of Patrick in 1592 spoke of paying 'scattis callit in our language the feuduties'.[70]

Up to 1600 Patrick appears to have taken particular interest in Orkney, possibly because he had still to secure his rights there. After 1600 he turned his attention to Shetland, and set himself to guarantee and enlarge his revenues. He attempted to extend the lands around the new castle.[71] He directed his attention to his numerous other privileges and incidental sources of income – rights to wreck goods, to payments on entry and succession to property, to unmarked sheep. He compiled a new peat rental, whose terms were strictly enforced; in 1602 his courts ordered

70 *Shetland Documents, 1580–1611*, 86, no. 198.
71 *CSP Scot.*, xiii, 1007.

the parishioners of Dunrossness to deliver 24 Shetland *fathoms* – an extraordinary quantity, measuring about 3,045 cubic metres – to his house at Sumburgh, and two years later all the other Mainland parishes had to cut peats and deliver them to the new castle.[72] With both peats and *timmer* – he demanded oaths from the whole population of Scalloway clearing themselves of theft. He seems also to have pushed his rights to wreck goods beyond the spirit of the law. In July 1594 he was accused of plundering the Danzig ship *Ark of Noy* (Noah's Ark), while it was at Burrafirth in Unst for repairs. The whole vessel, its cargo and fittings, valued at over £30,000, were removed by the inhabitants, led by the underfoud, and Patrick's servants were then said to have disposed of it all.[73]

Another source of income consisted of fines from the court of Shetland, whose extant record begins in July 1602. Perhaps the most striking point about that record is the picture of normality that it provides, of a long-established legal system coming full-grown into our ken. Humdrum cases, one after another, of petty theft, defamation, assault, disobedience, swine-rooting; ordinances regarding payment of skat, landmail and dues by foreign merchants – all paraded before the earl or his depute John Dishington as they perambulate through the islands. There are no obvious signs of oppression, and Norse and Scots law seem to co-exist peaceably enough. Two suicides were escheated in the Scottish fashion without objection, while one Ingagar in Leadie was fined in accordance with ancient Norwegian law for delay in burying her dead.[74] The death penalty, though threatened on a number of occasions,[75] was used only once during 1602–4, in the case of the sheep stealer Christopher Johnson.[76] This calm picture is to some extent misleading. Professor Donaldson, who subjected the court to searching examination in his *Shetland Life under Earl Patrick*, points to it as 'inquisitorial and vexatious, and the fines a heavy burden on a community where cash was scarce'; the frequency of charges for defamation was due to the court being 'in part a mere money making device' rather than evidence of undue prickliness among the Shetlanders. There are also complex undercurrents to some cases that do not surface in the record, particularly those concerning the Sinclairs and the Bruces.

In 1604 the carefully detailed returns of Patrick's chamberlain Alexander Bruce began, possibly based on a new rental of Shetland.[77] In that year the earl bought up an extraordinary range of property and debts. In the first six months he acquired conquest lands. He brought the canons' lands within the rental, and the extensive property in the North Isles formerly pertaining to William Lauder was marked down for inclusion. As in Orkney, there was a mixture of *ad hoc* acquisition of

72 *Shetland Documents, 1580–1611*, 172, no. 378.
73 *RPC*, v, 195–7; W. F. Skene, *Memorials of the Family of Skene of Skene . . .* (New Spalding Club), Aberdeen, 1887, 164–5; Misc. Papers, NRS RH9/5/21.
74 *Ct Bk of Shetland*, 18, 56, 23, 58, 73; Donaldson, *Shetland Life under Earl Patrick*, 117.
75 *Ct Bk of Shetland*, 3, 8, 30, 31.
76 *Ct Bk of Shetland*, 18–19, 56; Donaldson, *Shetland Life under Earl Patrick*, 121.
77 Smyth of Methven Papers, NRS GD190, box 21.

Scalloway Castle

land by escheat, and deliberate enlargement of specific centres. On the one hand, Patrick confiscated three merks of land in Crossbister in Unst for theft and David and Andrew Forrester lost 12 merks in Whalsay.[78] On the other hand there were noteworthy transactions regarding Sumburgh and Scalloway.

He paid particular attention to the lands around Scalloway, which he clearly intended to be his new administrative centre, replacing Sumburgh. He bought two merks in Over Scalloway from David Forrester, probably earmarked for the castle and its surrounding policies. In terms of the accumulation of territory, he was actually more interested in the island of Trondra, whose north end was a short boat trip across the East Voe of Scalloway from the shores below the castle. He bought land there, as well as in Burra, the island to the south, from William Sinclair of Ustaness and Arthur Sinclair of Aith; the latter received extensive lands in North Roe as part of a large excambion.[79] He also swapped six merks of kingsland for the seven and a half merks of Herman and Thomas Magnusson at the north end of Trondra.[80] All this, which was plainly visible from the new castle, came to form the 'Bu of Trondra'.

These territorial manoeuvrings bear the mark of other, supportive, minds – most particularly, perhaps, that of John Dishington. Patrick was interested in them only as they increased the revenue to fund his own particular preoccupations, which now become evident. On 6 August 1602 the court of Shetland, under Dishington, finished its business at Sumburgh. Then it moved north and, six days later, on 12 August, it convened in Scalloway. Soon after, Patrick himself took over and the court moved into the new castle, the first of Patrick's major building works to be completed.[81] Commenced about 1600, it was a more obviously military building than his palace in Kirkwall was to be, though it had the same architect, and one showing less of its vaunting ambition; but the impression it created must have been striking enough. The military appearance is deceptive. True, it was an L-Plan design with the door in the re-entrant angle of the L to make attack difficult, but its approach and entrance were quite unwarlike. It was probably approached, not from the present road into the town of Scalloway, which passes to the rear of the building, but along the shore of the East Voe, through what a century ago was still called the castle bullet (bowling) green. Making his way from there through

---

78 Exchequer Records: Orkney [and Shetland] Rentals and Accs, NRS E41/7.
79 Reg. Deeds, NRS RD1/107, ff. 151r–2r; Exchequer Records: Orkney [and Shetland] Rentals and Accs, NRS E41/7.
80 Shetland Documents 1580–1611, 177, no. 385.
81 Both RCAHMS Inv., O & S, iii, 20 and W. D. Simpson ('The Castles of Shetland', Viking Congress, Lerwick, 1950, 182) state that Patrick built the house at Sumburgh in 1604, but there are two arguments against this. Firstly there is the very plain nature of the building, which seems more likely to have preceded than followed Scalloway and Kirkwall. Secondly there is the tenor of Patrick's 1592 charter to William Bruce of Symbister regarding the lands of Sumburgh, which specially reserves to Patrick's use the 'house and fortalice lately foundit upoune the ground of the saidis landis . . . on the south syde of the New Hall' [probably built by Earl Robert] (Reg. Deeds, NRS RD1/38, ff. 412v–14v).

Kirkwall in the time of the Stewart Earls: an impression

gardens,[82] the suitor of court was led to a grandly decorated doorway and up an ample staircase, no turnpike, into the great hall which took up the entire first storey, lit by nine windows and decorated with painted work.[83] It was here that the courts were held. Above were bedrooms and private apartments, including the earl's own chamber, hung with tapestries, the walls finished with plaster, the windows part-glazed, part shuttered, and guarded with iron bars; below were the kitchen and a store-room that doubled on occasion as a prison.[84]

But the acquisition of land on which to build his castle and surrounding estate was small beer in Patrick's scheme of things. He also targeted the wealth of the Bruce and Sinclair families. He attempted to redraw a contract that he had concluded in 1592 with William Bruce of Symbister, feuar of Sumburgh; this was to be the subject of a continuing significant dispute. Regarding the Sinclairs, Laurence Sinclair pledged his lands of Gott to the earl, and William Sinclair lost his lands in Ustaness. Robert Sinclair of Ramnageo disponed his inheritance, and Francis, his brother, entered into an exchange of lands.[85] Then Patrick turned to buying up debts among the family. Within three months – June, July and August 1604 – he acquired Francis Sinclair's liability, as well as James Sinclair of Brow's debt to William Sinclair of Ustaness, Sir Andrew Balfour of Strathure's to Malcolm Sinclair of Quendale, and that of Sinclair of Ustaness to James Pitcairn, vicar of Northmavine.[86] These deeds created earldom clients of debtor and creditor alike, and they reveal a rather different picture from that drawn by the Orkney rental. In both island groups, Patrick appears to have been willing to pick up udal land whenever it became available. Some of the land was used to enlarge the existing earldom centres, some of it was presumably bought simply for the small additional income it provided. But in Orkney the *rooms* came exclusively from humble folk; in Shetland much of it came from udal families who were among the most powerful in those islands, and Patrick's dealings with them hide a much more determined and grasping strategy. It is understandable that any sources controlled by the earl – the rental, the court book, the 'uthell buik' – should contain little that suggests the tyrant of legend. When we look outside them, we find a confrontation with the feudal landowners of Orkney and the great udallers of Shetland, a confrontation aimed at a much larger-scale grabbing of land and property, intended to keep afloat some extremely grandiose ideas.

Now that any doubt as to his title to the earldom of Orkney had been resolved in 1596, Patrick spent the next decade or so seeking to symbolise his power in sumptuous stone. By far the greatest of his schemes was in Orkney – his magnificent palace in

---

82 Lerwick Sh. Ct Recs, SA SC.12/6/6721; Smyth of Methven Papers, NRS GD190, box 21.

83 Brand, *Description*, 31; RCAHMS *Inv.*, O & S, iii. 119–20.

84 It was probably the '*lach volt*' in which Henry Wardlaw was held (Court of Session Recs: Acts and Decreets, NRS CS7/228, f. 81r and *v*).

85 Exchequer Records: Orkney [and Shetland] Rentals and Accs, NRS E41/7.

86 Reg. Deeds, NRS RD1/107, ff. 145*v*–50*v*.

Kirkwall. The buildings in the centre of that small city were already very impressive. Towering over all was the cathedral of St Magnus, which was in its externals essentially the building visible today. In 1593, after his father's death and burial in his own Stewart Aisle,[87] Patrick erected a gallery for his family and a seat for himself. It bore the legend that so irritated Brand when he found it in Robert's palace in Birsay – *Sic fuit, est et erit* ('So it was, is and shall be').[88]

To the north-east of St Magnus lay the castle, of which no trace now remains but which, as we shall see, was massive indeed. On the south stood the bishop's palace, the 'Palace of the Yards'. The name indicates that it had courtyards, making it a larger and more elaborate structure than the single range and corner tower that survive today. Patrick may have demolished the eastern range of the old palace to make way for his own, built in the years to 1606. The present terms used to describe the buildings – 'earl's palace' and 'bishop's palace' – are modern labels. Little distinction was made in the seventeenth century between the two; Patrick's structure is referred to as the 'New wark of the Yairdis', implying that the two buildings originally formed a single complex. At the south end of the older building lies an extension confidently attributed to Patrick, with arcading on the ground floor, and oriels above, whose elaborate corbelling corresponds strikingly with those on the new work.[89] At the west end of the south wing of the latter are the stumps of the walls and roof of a structure extending towards the other building.[90] There are other such signs from the north end of the 'Earl's Palace' towards the cathedral.[91] A square was thus formed by the old and new buildings to east and west, a linking range to the south (and possibly also to the north) and a cluster of older buildings at the north-west corner, principally the large and apparently ancient *mense* (manse, mass) tower, which formed a triangle with a smaller square tower and the round tower of the 'bishop's palace', both the work of Bishop Reid.[92] The complex is mysterious, as is even the name given to the mense tower. According to Douglas Simpson, Patrick meant to relegate the older building to the status of a retainers' forecourt.[93] Whether he intended this, or to demolish the old palace entirely and build his own in its place, there is no doubt that the final result would have been even grander than what exists.

87 *Rentals*, ed. Peterkin, app. 53.

88 R. Pococke, *Tours in Scotland* (SHS), Edinburgh, 1887, 148; Brand, *Description*, 31.

89 Douglas Simpson, successive editions of guidebook *Bishop's Palace and Earl's Palace*. 1965–1998, Edinburgh (though no specific note in RCAHMS, Inv.), also endorsed by Denys Pringle, 1991 and current edition, C. Tabraham, 2006.

90 According to D. McGibbon and T. Ross, the two palaces were connected with walls (*The Domestic and Castellated Architecture of Scotland*, vols I–II, Edinburgh, 1996, ii, 338).

91 Simpson, *Bishop's Palace and Earl's Palace*, 21.

92 For a sketch of the layout, see G. Low, *A Tour through the Islands of Orkney and Schetland*, Kirkwall, 1879, facing p. xlv.

93 D. Simpson, *The Castle of Bergen and Bishop's Palace at Kirkwall: A Study of Early Norse Architecture*, Edinburgh, 1961, 74–5.

The New Wark of the Yairdis

Patrick's works, as well as Bruce of Cultmalindie's castle of Muness, built three years before Scalloway in 1597, are all thought to have had the same intelligence behind them, probably Andrew Crawford, the earl's master of works, assisted by the mason John Ross.[94] In Douglas Simpson's words, 'What astonishes us about Earl Patrick's castle works is the extraordinary beauty and refinement of their architecture. At all of them it is obvious that he employed the same architect . . . an artist of the first rank, with a scholarly and sensitive acquaintance and understanding of contemporary design.'[95] The corbelled oriels on the west side, the bay-windows on their piers to the east, the great window and fireplace in the great hall, and the corbelled corner turrets, all combine to produce a building of great distinction. The links with the other projects, different as they are, are not too difficult to spot. The noble doorways of Scalloway and Kirkwall, both set in the angle between two wings and surmounted by elaborate mottoed panels and coats of arms (now unfortunately much worn away) are clearly related. Muness and Kirkwall, at first sight unlikely relatives, share 'a decorative device special to the Northern Isles at this period', in the form of corbels interspersed with imitation shot-holes supporting their corner turrets. This is also found at Scalloway.

Such beauty was costly. William Sinclair of Eday complained that from May 1601 to April 1603 the earl had broken up and worked the quarry at Towback on Eday without leave. The quantity of stone he was accused of removing, and the form it took, indicates a major source of material. Ten thousand 'rebattis' (*rabbets* or rabbetted joints), were cut and dressed, 10,000 *newels*, 10,000 lintels, 5,000 *quoins* and 5,000 'peitstanes' or coping stones. The total cost, according to Sinclair, was the astonishing sum of nearly £200,000.[96] Although there is probably a measure of exaggeration both in the amount of stone involved and its estimated value, it is the magnificence suggested by this and displayed in the final product that inclines one to take seriously the descriptions of Patrick's vainglorious and ostentatious extravagance.

His pomp, it is said, was so great that he went nowhere, not even the few yards from the castle to the kirk, without his retinue of servants and musketeers. For his progresses in Shetland he had a litter.[97] At both dinner and supper, three trumpeters sounded before each course.[98] We may be sure that the meals were correspondingly sumptuous, as Patrick did not stint himself at table. In March 1606, he was accused before the privy council of contravening an act against eating meat in Lent; he freely admitted doing so, though he incurred a fine of £100.[99] In fitting out his

---

94 RCAHMS, *Inv.*, O & S, iii, 117; Simpson, *Bishop's Palace and Earl's Palace*, 31; this view is upheld by Denys Pringle, who conducted a detailed study of all three buildings.

95 Simpson, *Bishop's Palace and Earl's Palace*, 17–18.

96 Court of Session Recs: Acts and Decreets, NRS CS7/232, ff. 192v–5v; Denys Pringle feels that the amount of stone involved far exceeds what would genuinely be required for the building.

97 Smyth of Methven Papers, NRS GD190, box 21.

98 *The Historie and Life of King James the Sext*, 386.

99 Privy council register of fines, NRS PC8/9.

great houses, Patrick took a particular interest in artillery weapons. He acquired by confiscation from pirates and 'uncouth fishers . . . sik collectioun of gret gunnis and uther weapons for weare, as no hous, palice, or castell, yea all in Scotland wer not furneist with the lyke'.[100] He employed William Irving of Sebay to retrieve the artillery from the Spanish Armada ship *El Gran Grifón*, which had foundered in Fair Isle. Believing there to be more than 36 pieces of artillery on board the ship, Patrick became impatient when, after two years Irving had raised only six.[101] In 1595 he received a brass cannon from Sir Duncan Campbell of Glenorchy, delivered to him by Francis, earl of Bothwell, during his flight from Scotland, perhaps in a vain attempt to enlist support.[102] These guns were also used to equip his ships, of which he had several. In April 1598 he concluded a contract with Alan Cunninghame and Captain Thomas Davidson of Crail to purchase a new ship the *Randbow* (Rainbow), which they had brought up to Orkney to show him, fitted up with 'lang wappinis' he had delivered to them the previous year.[103] In December 1601 Andrew Allan from Kirkwall is found as master of Patrick's ship the *Thomas*;[104] five years later he was operating out of Scalloway with the *Dunkirk*, his place being taken shortly afterwards by Captain Alan Lentroun.[105]

The maintenance of such an establishment could not be achieved by the simple purchases, rearrangement and increases revealed in the administrative records. What was required was a much more determined policy of confrontation with the magnates of the Northern Isles, aimed at commandeering their wealth and power for his own purposes. The result was to be fierce, occasionally murderous and, for Patrick, ultimately disastrous conflict.

Before looking at Patrick's struggles in this arena, however, it is necessary to take a step backwards, to look at other aspects of his life up to this point, with difficulties he had been experiencing elsewhere – at court and within his own family circle.

100 *The Historie and Life of King James the Sext*, 386.
101 Misc. Papers, OA D8/l/3; Craven Beq., NRS GD106/135.
102 Breadalbane Mun., NRS GD112/1/334–6.
103 Reg. Deeds NRS RD1/68, ff. 367v–8r.
104 Reg. Deeds NRS RD1/86, f. 174v–5r.
105 W. Morison, *The Decisions of the Court of Session*, Edinburgh, 1804, xxxvii, 16653.

10

Our Native Lord and Maistir

In the 1590s, the earl of Orkney was not universally popular among his fellow nobles. In June 1596 Robert, Lord Sanquhar, challenged him to single combat and the king had twice to intervene to prevent Sanquhar pressing the point.[1] The cause of their differences was said to be 'the wrong done by Orkney in taking . . . [Sanquhar's] chamber appointed in court with such other trifles of offence. But it is whispered that this coal was blown by persons of greater quality grieved against Orkney.' Sanquhar was an unpleasant individual whose vindictiveness and overweening pride in his skill as a swordsman were ultimately to bring him to the block,[2] and he could easily have picked a quarrel with Patrick without assistance; but there were indeed persons of quality with reason to egg him on.

A year later Patrick was called out again by an exceedingly dangerous opponent. On 5 September 1597 it was reported that 'a great debate is fallen out betuixt the two great Earls of the North, to wit Caithness and Orkney, either accusing the other of homicide and perjury.' Caithness had had swords and daggers made and sent to Patrick, offering him the choice of them: 'If this matter hold place either by law or arms it will divide the whole realm in discord for either of them have great friends . . .'.[3] Lord Livingston went to the king to intercede for his brother-in-law, the privy council having refused to interfere. In their quarrel, Caithness used the doubts over Patrick's titles as a deliberate annoyance, suggesting that he, Caithness, be made chamberlain of the earldom. In February 1599 both parties were charged to find surety under pain of 20,000 merks to suspend their quarrel until the end of the year.[4]

This was only the final eruption of a general uneasiness and antipathy that had existed before Patrick ever became earl. In January 1593 he had prevailed upon his brother-in-law, James Sinclair of Murkle, to try to 'agree all matters debatable' between himself, Caithness and another difficult nobleman, the earl of Bothwell,[5] Patrick's cousin, Caithness's half-brother. In the 1580s Bothwell had supported Robert Stewart, but relations had later deteriorated and in February 1590 it was

---

1 *CSP Scot.*, xii, 248–9.
2 *Scots Peerage*, iii, 230–1.
3 *CSP Scot.*, xiii, 78.
4 *RPC*, v, 523.
5 Reg. Deeds, NRS RD1/75, f. 20r and v.

rumoured that he intended to invade the islands to provide safe harbours for the
Spaniards, of whom he was one of the chief champions in Scotland.[6] In 1595, after an
extraordinary career in which he tried the king's patience to the limit, he was at last
forfeited.[7] In a manner curiously reminiscent of the previous earl of Bothwell after
Carberry, he fled to Orkney, then to Shetland, dropping anchor near where Henry
Colville, Patrick's representative, was staying at the time. Colville did not receive
him as Sinclair of Havera had done his predecessor, however, and he was soon on
the move again.[8] He made for France and, despite further rumours of an invasion of
Orkney in 1599, he was henceforth absent from the scene.[9]

Besides his father's enemies, Patrick inherited his father's debts. The longstanding
dispute with the Bellendens continued, but Patrick's marriage to Sir Lewis's widow
was doubtless intended to provide respite. He also had problems with his mother,
Jean Kennedy. During his father's last months, she had been suing Robert before
the session for maintenance arrears and, as we have seen, before the commissaries
of Edinburgh for divorce on grounds of adultery. When he died she was quick to
seek her just due from his estate. Her interests were threefold: firstly a liferent right
to the lands in Deerness, Stronsay and elsewhere, which Robert had granted her
in exchange for Birsay but feued off during his troubles; secondly a general liferent
right to the whole royal and bishopric lands; and thirdly her widow's right to one
third of the value of her husband's movables at death. In May 1594 she obtained
letters ordering the commendator of Lindores to vacate his bishopric lands in
Deerness, Margaret Bonar to leave the lands of Musbister, and the Scollays of
Strynie, James Fea of Clestrain and Malcolm Groat of Tankerness to quit their
estates.[10] All had been beneficiaries of the feuing of 1588–90, but Jean Kennedy,
her case upheld by the session, was able to reassert her title.[11] In November 1594
Patrick and his mother submitted their dispute to arbiters, Patrick represented
by Waus of Barnbarroch, the countess by Alexander King.[12] The agreement was
largely in Jean Kennedy's favour. She was held to have undoubted liferent rights to
all the king's and bishop's lands in the islands since the death of her husband. They
recommended that she empower her son to collect her mails and duties, pay her
8,000 merks of arrears by instalments and 3,600 merks annually; if he failed to do
so, she should 'have free regress into the whole living'. In return she should waive
her right to the customary widow's third or *terce*.

For the moment Lady Orkney was satisfied, and her son was free to try to sort
out the mess left by his father. Robert's will had appointed as executors his two sons-
in-law, the commendator of Lindores and James Sinclair of Murkle; his illegitimate

6   *CSP Scot.*, x, 842.
7   Willson, *King James VI and I*, 103–15.
8   *CSP Scot.*, xi, 574–6, 580.
9   *Salisbury Papers*, ix, 33–4; *CSP Scot.*, xii, 389–90.
10 Anderson, *Robert Stewart*, 127; Court of Session Recs: Acts and Decreets, NRS CS7/146, f. 302r and *v.*
11 *RSS*, NRS PS1/62, f. 79v.
12 *RSS*, NRS PS1/62, ff. 325v–7r

son James Stewart of Graemsay; and John Dishington. This document was set aside, probably because of the disarray of his affairs, and it was as sole executor that Patrick registered his father's testament, on 26 May 1597.[13] This disclosed movable assets of £8,685 9s 10d and liabilities of £4,800. The sum of £3,885 9s 10d was therefore left for division into three – among the children; to Jean Kennedy; and at Patrick's discretion. The dowager countess, who had had her own valuers at work, disagreed strongly with these figures. There should have been 30 work horses included, from each of his farms of Corse and Folsetter; a lot of silverware – basins, lavers, trenchers, spoons, etc.; as well as 60 stones of wool and 120 tons of cheese. But much the most important addition was a list of Shetland income and movables entirely absent from Patrick's enumeration of his father's possessions. The duties of Shetland for the year 1592 came to 11,000 merks, and there were *umboth* duties, dues from fishing boats, and more; around Feal on Ronasvoe and on the island of Vementry were 7,000 sheep.[14]

The matter was referred to the session, whose judgment largely supported Patrick.[15] The lords accepted that he had derived far more from the movables in Orkney than he had declared – a total of more than £13,000. Of this sum Jean Kennedy was to be paid one third. But they also approved Patrick's exclusion of Shetland from his father's testament. His tack of the estates was said to date from 'lang befoir' his father's death and escheat, and he had paid regular duties for it during his father's lifetime. He was further absolved from any payment to his mother of one third of the money noted in the testament, because all of it had been used up in paying off his father's debts. Besides the liabilities noted in the testament, which consisted chiefly of servants' back pay, there were larger bills elsewhere for various commodities: £770 to Stephen Paplay for wine, timber, iron, pitch and other wares; £570 to Mr Gilbert Bodie for wine and cloth; and the sum of £4,311 to William Morrison for wine, spices, expensive materials and tailor work.

This was much less than Jean Kennedy had sought from her son, and she did not live long to enjoy it. Early in October 1598, little more than three months after the conclusion of the case, she died following a short illness. Patrick wrote from Birsay to his kinsman, the master of Elphinstone, his words bearing witness to bitter feelings and lovelessness '. . . now I am advertisit that my mother is departit this lyiff: and hir executouris ar als busie as ever scho wes in hir tyme to put me to trubill'.[16] Elphinstone was himself pursuing Jean Kennedy's executors 'to quhome I hoip ye will schaw na mair courtessie nor favour ... nor ye did to my mother in her tyme ...'[17] These executors included Patrick's own brothers James[18] and John, who forced

13 Edin. Comm. Ct Recs: Reg. Tests, NRS CC8/8/30.
14 Court of Session Recs: Acts and Decreets, NRS CS7/170, ff. 166r–8r.
15 Court of Session Recs: Acts and Decreets, NRS CS7/175, ff. 242v–8v.
16 Fraser, *The Elphinstone Family Book*, i, 24.
17 Reg. Deeds, NRS RD1/67, ff. 389v–90r.
18 Warrants of Decreets, NRS CS15/77.

Patrick to pay up the money he owed to his mother's estate.[19] There also followed a series of unseemly carryings-on regarding the furnishings of the old countess's lodging in the Canongate. Her attendant Elizabeth Gib, daughter of the small local laird James Gib of Caribber, complained that John Stewart had immediately cleared the house of the movables that she insisted had been left to her by her mistress. John justified his actions by saying that he had not wanted his mother's modest effects to incur further rent by remaining in an empty dwelling that would also be 'ane reddie pray to thevis and malefactouris'. He attempted unsuccessfully to divert the case from the *commissary court* into the session, and in the summer of 1600 the commissaries of Edinburgh found in Elizabeth Gib's favour.[20]

Jean Kennedy's worldly effects were wound up amid the same ill feeling amongst her family that had characterised all the important junctures of her life. But it was not merely on her account that John and James Stewart were pursuing their brother; they had quarrels of their own, over land granted to them, under reversion, by their father. John had received estates in Hoy, Walls, Flotta and Rysa,[21] James and their younger brother Robert property in Sanday and Stronsay respectively. The precise terms of these grants are something of a mystery, and the lands in Sanday and Stronsay are not specified, but the property of both John and James were redeemable on payment of 10,000 merks, and Robert's was probably of similar value – a value which suggests that what was meant was all the kingsland in these two wealthy North Isles and in the richest part of Hoy.

There was particular ill feeling between Patrick and John, going back a number of years. In 1590, the two had concluded a contract setting out the terms for Patrick's redemption of the lands of Hoy, and in the same year there had been related dealings with John's ally, their illegitimate brother James Stewart of Graemsay, himself a landowner in Orkney. These contracts, concluded at a time when Patrick was in urgent need of cash elsewhere, gave rise to continuing disputes that culminated in Patrick imprisoning both of his brothers, pulling down James Stewart's house and extorting various written undertakings from him. In January 1595, matters were put in the hands of arbiters, including Waus of Barnbarroch. These set a date for Patrick's redemption of John Stewart's lands for 15,600 merks, and ordered the earl to hand back the documents he had forced his brothers to sign. John Stewart was to abandon all pretensions to lands in Orkney, and James Stewart, who had submitted to his brother, 'upoun his kneis asking the said earleis favour and pardoun for quhatsumever caus of miscontentioun he hes gevin his lordschip', was to forgive all the oppressions done to him, in return for being left in peace.[22]

At the end of May 1596 Patrick paid John what he owed;[23] less than a month

19 Court of Session processes, NRS CS15/77; Edin. Comm. Ct Recs: Acts and Decreets, NRS CC8/2/31; Court of Session Recs: Acts and Decreets, NRS CS7/178, ff.468r–9r.
20 Reg. Deeds, NRS RD1/147, ff. 330r–3r.
21 Reg. Deeds, NRS RD1/67, ff. 387r–9r.
22 Reg. Deeds, NRS RD1/147, ff. 330r–3r.
23 Reg. Deeds, NRS RD1/52, ff. 292v–3v.

later, on 24 June, the master of Orkney was brought before the justiciary court
charged with attempting, or at any rate planning, to murder his brother – and on
several occasions. Since the old earl's death in February 1593, he was alleged to have
contemplated various methods of doing away with Patrick, including murdering
him in his bed in the Palace of Birsay, or catching him unawares at a banquet in
Kirkwall. James Stewart and his other natural brother William had plotted poison
with him at William Moodie's house in Walls. Two people had already been
executed for their part in the plots. One was Thomas Paplay, who had reportedly
been hired to do the poisoning; the other was Alison Balfour, allegedly a notorious
witch, whom John Stewart was said to have consulted at her home in the Ireland
district of Stenness. Both died protesting their innocence. Balfour, put to death at
the heading-hill of Kirkwall on 16 December 1594, asserted on the scaffold that her
confession had been wrung from her in the cellars of Kirkwall Castle by torture in
the *caschielawis*, as well as of her aged husband in the weights, her son in the boots
and even her seven-year-old daughter in the *pilliewinkis*. She had been promised
mercy, falsely, by Henry Colville, parson of Orphir, who had apparently supervised
her torment. In her last moments she was asked what she knew of the 'auld Laird of
Stenhouse', in an attempt to implicate Patrick Bellenden in witchcraft and murder.
Why had he given her the wax that had been found in her purse? She averred that
this substance – said to be used in the fashioning of 'pictours' or images of a witch's
proposed victim – had been given to her purely to make an 'implaister' to cure Lady
Bellenden's persistent colic.[24]

John Stewart, master of Orkney, was tried for conspiracy on 24 June 1596. The
jury, as was common at the time, included persons with particular interests in the
matter in hand.[25] Sinclair of Brough and Bruce of Cultmalindie were there, as were
John Dick, the former servant of Earl Robert, and Patrick Cheyne of Esslemont; the
chancellor of the assize was Lord Sanquhar, whose aggressive challenge to Patrick
had been reported three days before. John Stewart was cleared of all charges; his
accusers were unable to substantiate their allegations with any sort of corroborative
detail apart from dubious confessions wrung from humble and expendable people
by hideous methods. Whether or not John Stewart or anyone else was guilty of
plotting Patrick's assassination, these proceedings led directly to a real murder.
Less than three weeks after Stewart's trial, Henry Colville, parson of Orphir, was
slain in Shetland.[26] Colville, who had been in the north for 25 years or so,[27] was
the third of a series of deputes whom Patrick had employed since becoming earl,

24 *Criminal Trials*, ed. Pitcairn, i, 373–7; for reference to the use of 'pictours', and indeed the whole
    background to the anxiety about witches in Scotland in the decade after the affair of the North Berwick
    witches, see E. J. Cowan, 'The Darker Vision of the Scottish Renaissance: the Devil and Francis Stewart',
    The Renaissance and Reformation in Scotland, Edinburgh, 1893, 124–40; also P. D. Anderson, 'Alison
    Balfour', *Biographical Dictionary of Scottish Women*, ed. R. Pipes and E. Innes, Edinburgh, 2006, 23–4.
25 *Criminal Trials*, iii, 280n.
26 *Criminal Trials*, i, 386–8, 392–7.
27 Watt and Murray, *Fasti*, 256; *REO*, 356, no. ccxxxiii.

having taken over from William Bannatyne of Gairsay less than a year before. Colville and Bannatyne had been involved in Patrick's dispute with his brothers, and in September 1594 Stewart of Graemsay and three of John Stewart's servants were required to find surety for their safety.[28] Colville is referred to only briefly in the account of Alison Balfour's sufferings, but the confession he extracted from her and his worthless promise of mercy that had induced her to make it, suggest that he was particularly interested in the sort of story she could be induced to tell. If therefore he was plotting to have John Stewart accused of capital charges then it helps to explain the chilling speed with which retribution fell upon him, putting the master of Orkney on trial for his life for the second time in six months.

There is a story that Colville's killers were two Orkney Sinclairs, said to be those noted in the 1595 rental as having lost their lands in Orphir by confiscation for theft.[29] According to this account Colville had sought sanctuary in Shetland from the wrath of his pursuers, which was so unmastered that after killing him, they tore his heart from his body and drank the blood from it.[30] This is pure fantasy. The immediate circumstances of Colville's death remain obscure, but the background is better known and rather more complicated. Like the first charge against John Stewart, it was preceded by execution of two individuals regarded as directly responsible – Gilbert Peacock, a servant of the master, and one William Stewart. Peacock's trial in Edinburgh, the only one for which proceedings survive, reveals little of the facts of the case. On 14 October 1596 John Stewart himself was charged with complicity in the murder at the instance of John Mercer, the late parson's half-brother. The actual killer was said to be Adam Gordon, brother of the laird of Avachie. Twelve days later Mercer instituted further proceedings, naming Sir Patrick Bellenden of Stenness, William Bannatyne of Gairsay and James Lockie, writer in Edinburgh.

All four of these individuals had reason to oppose Patrick. Sir Patrick Bellenden, the most prominent, is only briefly noted. It was the other three, led by Bannatyne of Gairsay, who were regarded by John's accusers as chief executors of the plot, assisted by Alexander Dunbar and Thomas Twaddell. Gordon, Dunbar and Twaddell sailed to Orkney from Montrose, took on supplies at Bannatyne's house (presumably Langskaill in Gairsay), then went to Shetland, to Burwick in Tingwall. They travelled overland to Neap in Nesting where Colville was staying on the earl's business (probably with William Magnusson, the underfoud), and there they killed him. In support of this story Colville's friends produced depositions by the executed Peacock and Stewart, together with a bond signed by John Stewart, Adam Gordon, Bannatyne, Twaddell and Lockie. A major issue at John Stewart's trial was to determine how far blame for the murder extended. Was Colville's death the sole responsibility of Peacock and Stewart, whom Patrick had put to death? Or of Bannatyne and his companions, as charged by Colville's relatives? Or a combination of the

28 *RPC*, v, 636.
29 *Rentals*, ii, 27.
30 S. Hibbert, *Description of the Shetland Islands*, Edinburgh, 1822, 291–3.

two? Whoever they were, they could still have taken their orders from the master. In any event it was not possible to prove any such link, and John Stewart was again pronounced not guilty.

So strong was his position that during the trial the defence aimed not at defending Stewart himself, but at exculpating William Bannatyne from the activities of those named with him. The depositions implicating Bannatyne and company, it was said, had been extorted from Peacock and Stewart by Colville's supporters in the presence of the earl. In fact the two were genuinely and solely guilty. Even if members of the second group were implicated, Bannatyne had played no part. Particularly important was the link between Bannatyne and Thomas Twaddell. Twaddell, said to be Bannatyne's servant, was in reality an officer of arms, 'with his own hous, wyff and famelie'. The bond mentioned in the charges as evidence of conspiracy had in fact a quite different purpose. It was intended to reconcile a longstanding feud between Bannatyne and John Stewart, one that had resulted in bloodshed on both sides 'as is notour to the haill toune of Edinburgh'. Faced with 'sa potent ane adversar', Bannatyne 'had maist just caus to bind up the stratest band of friendschip' with Stewart, even to the extent of sealing it with his own blood. In the circumstances, he could hardly be convicted even if the other parties to the bond had actually committed the crime.

Bannatyne who, like Colville, had been many years in the Northern Isles, is first encountered in Patrick's service in late 1594, joining Colville in his efforts to settle their master's financial affairs.[31] Shortly afterwards he became chamberlain and sheriff depute of Shetland, a move that he must quickly have regretted. He inherited the position from Patrick Monteith of the Fair Isle, who had got into great difficulties at the earl's hands. In order to pay off Patrick's debts to the merchants of Edinburgh (and no doubt those of his father), Bannatyne was required, as Monteith had been, to raise the enormous sum of 24,000 merks in a very short time. It was his attempts to do this that brought him into conflict with the master of Orkney. In the face of the latter's physical threats, Patrick himself encouraged Bannatyne to employ bodyguards, to 'gaird himselff weill with guid fellowis . . . nocht to spair for expenssis quhilk suld be weill allowit and payit to him . . . thair wes mair win nor spendit and . . . it wald tend gretumly to the . . . erle of Orknayes dishonour gif [Bannatyne] for feir of boisting (threatening), laik of gaird or expenssis suld relent ony pairt of his faithful service'.[32] Bannatyne still found it impossible to collect revenue in time to meet the earl's obligations and Patrick forced him to raise money on his own estates. He received no thanks for this; in March 1596 when he had served his purpose, Patrick 'chaissit and ejectit' him from Orkney.[33] A messenger sent to charge Patrick to answer letters of *lawburrows* was said to have

---

31 Reg. Deeds, NRS RD1/36, ff.67v-8v; Reg. House Chrs (Supplementary), NRS RH6, 1591–1600 (15 Dec. 1594/6 July 1595).

32 Court of Session Recs: Acts and Decreets, NRS CS7/159, f. 299r and v.

33 Court of Session Recs: Acts and Decreets, NRS CS7/253, ff. 120v–7r.

been imprisoned and put to the caschielawis.[34] Bannatyne was forced to make his peace with John Stewart; but the question remains open whether he was driven still further, to seek the life of Colville, or whether in befriending Stewart he was merely trying to avoid the same fate.

It is difficult to quarrel with the simplest analysis. Henry Colville, supporting Patrick in his dispute with his brother over money from the earldom estates, concocted a scheme to have the latter convicted of attempted murder. The most damning allegation against the master was that of witchcraft, the details being extorted by Colville from the wretched Alison Balfour and her family. The plot failed, and in retaliation Colville was murdered on John Stewart's orders. It may well have been Peacock and Stewart who carried these out, but to what extent were they countenanced by Bannatyne and his followers? There may have been cause for conflict between Bannatyne and Colville; the latter disputed a claim by Bannatyne to the subdeanery of Orkney, and he took over as chamberlain when Bannatyne was expelled.[35] There are also weaknesses in Bannatyne's defence against the charge of aiding the murderers. Thomas Twaddell, far from being an independent agent as was alleged, was named as one of his servants by Bannatyne in one of his own enactments as sheriff (Lockie was also present).[36]

If Bannatyne was involved in the murder of Henry Colville, parson of Orphir, it seems likely that this meant no more than provisioning the killers on their journey to Shetland, as much to placate the master of Orkney as to secure Colville's death. Bannatyne's significance in the story of Patrick is that his is the first of the many detailed complaints that the Scottish civil courts were to hear about Patrick Stewart. Since becoming earl, Patrick had had three chief servants in as many years. One had been murdered; the other two had had their fortunes gravely damaged. Bannatyne was one; the other his predecessor Patrick Monteith of the Fair Isle, whose son Robert was soon to be one of Patrick's most prominent Orkney opponents.

The courts had found nothing to link John Stewart with the actions of his servants. Patrick's part in these affairs is similarly mysterious. It may be that he did play no direct role, leaving the actual operations to his followers. Nevertheless the latter were not acting in isolation; behind their measures was an overall strategy that applied to Patrick's landed clients as much as to his family. His relations with his siblings had led to imprisonment, torture, execution and murder. Those with his clients in the 1590s were difficult, though hardly as horrific, and they did not at that time involve the many-sided oppression of individuals to be found after the turn of the century. They resembled those with his family in that they sprang from Patrick's desire, from the moment he took over from his ageing father, to reclaim all the land and income that, for various reasons, had passed out of the old man's control.

The first evidence of confrontation with local proprietors was the plea to

---

34 *APS*, iv, 396.
35 Court of Session Recs: Acts and Decreets, NRS CS7/186, ff. 390v–2r.
36 Bruce of Sumburgh Papers, SA D.8/2/1.

parliament in 1592 by a group of udallers from both Orkney and Shetland against Patrick's alleged attempt to have himself made their superior. The udallers were represented by the three prominent Shetland magnates, Thomas Cheyne of Vaila, William Bruce of Symbister and, much the most important and persistent of Patrick's opponents, Laurence Bruce of Cultmalindie, supported by the Orcadian Sinclairs of Tuquoy, Campston and Toab, Irving of Sebay and Cromarty of Cara.[37] Bruce of Cultmalindie and Henry Sinclair of Brough both had separate disputes with Patrick over their rival claims to a tack of the wadmel of Shetland against Patrick's own claims. Bruce alleged that Patrick, with 600 men, had fallen upon him when he had been collecting wadmel at the harbour at Laxfirth, and forced him to flee to the Out Skerries. Patrick did not pursue him there, but forced him on pain of banishment to renounce his tack. In July 1592 Sinclair complained to the session that Patrick's father had kept him for a long time in captivity, both on land and for 20 days at sea. Then he had been hauled before a court packed with the Robert's servants 'quha durst... do na thing bot as thai were commandit by him ... for feir of his extreme rigor'.[38]

In April 1591 Bruce forced Patrick to find surety of £2,000 for his safety, and in January the following year obtained an execution of homing against him before the privy council.[39] In October 1592, as a result of the udallers' representations, Patrick was summoned before the council to be relieved of his commission as royal lieutenant. Despite this, Bruce enjoyed no great success in his efforts to discomfit the earl. It may be that the implausibility in his story was noted; the 600 men he alleged Patrick had led against him would have amounted to approximately one eighth of the entire male population of Shetland.[40] Either support for the earl was much stronger in Shetland than Bruce was prepared to admit, or he was guilty of exaggeration bordering on absurdity. In any event, it was probably in settlement of the dispute regarding wadmel that he and Sinclair were compelled to grant a bond in August 1592 agreeing to pay £1,000 to James Stewart of Burray, one of Patrick's creditors;[41] and the attempt to mobilise other landowners to make a general complaint came to nothing. In October 1592 a large number of the 'undirfoldis and baillies of Orkney and Yetland' (in fact all Orcadians), undertook to offer dutiful obedience to the king and his choice of lieutenant, 'speciale the said Patrick, Master of Orkney, our native lord and maistir under your majestie, quhomeupone as yit we can nocht justlie complaine for ony occasioun bygane'. Besides such major landed figures as Bellenden of Evie and Balfour of Montquhany there were among the signatories Magnus Cromarty of Cara, William Irving of Sebay and Henry Sinclair

---

37 Shetland Documents, 1580–1611, 86, no. 198.
38 Court of Session Recs: Acts and Decreets, NRS CS7/203, ff. 157v–9v.
39 RPC, vi, 605.
40 Professor Donaldson estimates the population of Shetland in Patrick's time to have been between 10,000 and 15,000 (Shetland Life under Earl Patrick, 135).
41 Ct Bk of Shetland, 142–4.

of Tuquoy, all of whom had previously supported Bruce. The legitimacy of Patrick's commission was upheld.[42]

The defection of the Orcadians from Bruce's cause illustrates the contrast in standing between the independent landholders of Orkney and those of Shetland. Bruce's Orcadian allies were much less prominent in their islands, and much more easily persuaded to change sides, particularly when no more was heard of attempts by Patrick to assume possession of the udal lands. Whereas Bruce was to remain the focus of dissent in Shetland, opposition in Orkney was to come in future from the feudal proprietors created in the early 1560s and late 1580s; none of the Orkney udallers was of great significance again in this way. Within a very short time, Irving of Sebay was to be found in Patrick's service in Fair Isle and Sanday.[43]

It was to be several years before Bruce was able to mount further effective opposition to Patrick. When he did, his approach was different. In the 1590s a general appeal, with others, to parliament or the council clearly would not work, because of Patrick's prominence as a courtier, and because it was impossible to rely on potential allies. When Bruce and others renewed their opposition, it was as individuals, seeking to sidestep Patrick's jurisdiction in the north and pursue him in the central courts; in the end they were successful, but not without long and frustrating litigation, and it was not until Patrick's affairs were already in deep crisis that evidence can be found of direct co-operation between them. For the time being the dissension within the islands took a quite different form.

On 30 June 1597, the privy council imposed a *general band* on the landholders of Orkney and Shetland.[44] This peace-keeping device, favoured by King James at the time, charged all persons of note in the north to find caution to keep the peace.[45] The document provides an interesting picture of the principal men of the time and their relative importance. Patrick and his brother John were required, naturally enough, to find the largest securities, at £20,000 and 10,000 merks respectively. Next came five prominent magnates who were deemed worth 5,000 merks each. Representing Shetland were Bruce of Cultmalindie and Sinclair of Brough; the equivalent Orcadians were Balfour of Montquhany, Bellenden of Evie and Groat of Tankerness. The Bellenden, Bruce and Sinclair families also had junior members in the list. Bellenden's son Thomas was worth 2,000 merks, and William Bruce of Symbister/Sumburgh was among those required to find 1,000. Not unexpectedly, it was the Sinclair family who had much the most numerous representation. From Shetland came Arthur Sinclair of Houss and William Sinclair of Ustaness at 2,000 merks each; Adam Sinclair of Brow and Malcolm Sinclair of Quendale, both at £1,000; and Francis Sinclair of Uyea at 500 merks. Their Orkney cousins were Edward Sinclair of Eday (2,000 merks) and his son William (£1,000); Henry

42 *RPC*, xiv, 375–6.
43 Craven Beq., NRS GD106/135.
44 *RPC*, v, 744.
45 J. Wormald, *Lords and Men in Scotland: Bonds of Manrent, 1442–1603*, Edinburgh 1985, 65.

Sinclair of Tuquoy and Oliver Sinclair of Essinquoy (£1,000); and Edmund Sinclair of Flotta (1,000 merks).

Among the old clients of Robert or their descendants were Thomas Knightson, now designated 'of Bressay' and Robert Henderson of Holland, both obviously prosperous at 2,000 merks; Robert Monteith of Egilsay (£1,000); Edward Scollay of Strynie and William Gordon of Cairston (1,000 merks); James Scollay of Tofts (£500); and Hugh and Robert Halcro, heirs of William Halcro of Aikers (500 merks). Robert Stewart's illegitimate son James Stewart of Graemsay was required to find £1,000. There were also a number of representatives of the older families: Halcro of Halcro (2,000 merks); Umphray of Berrie, Flett of Hobbister (£1,000); Strang of Voesgarth, Cromarty of Cara (1,000 merks); and Sclater of Burness (500 merks). The remainder were a mixed bag. A number of them were clergymen – James Pitcairn, Thomas Swinton of Rennibister (both 2,000 merks) – and some were descendants of clergymen and administrators who had acquired land in the islands, such as Adam Moodie of Breckness (£1,000) and Andrew Gifford of Wethersta (1,000 merks). Others were comparatively recent arrivals from Scotland, such as Bannatyne of Gairsay (£1,000); Andrew Edmondston of Whiteness, James Murray of Garth and his grandson and heir Thomas (1,000 merks); and James Stewart of Burray (500 merks).

The document was a general enactment by the crown in response to widespread unrest, arising partly, though by no means entirely, out of the feud between Patrick and John Stewart. The latter, significantly, was the only one of Patrick's legitimate brothers to be required to find surety, just as James of Graemsay was the only illegitimate one. There were, however, other complaints by individuals that had led to similar general demands for surety, privately raised. In late 1597 there were bitter counter-complaints to the council about an action by Balfour of Montquhany, his son Sir Andrew Balfour of Strathure and Michael Balfour of Garth, naming Patrick, 20 of his servants and over 40 of the landowners of Orkney and Shetland.[46] The Balfours were not the only family to do so; Patrick himself was to complain to the council about similar actions by Sir Patrick Bellenden.[47] The council's general charge may have been intended to draw the private ones together; if so, it failed to prevent continuing litigation by the Balfours.

There was united opposition to this and others like it as a legal device. To Patrick and the other landowners, the Balfours' actions were based 'onlie upoun malice and invy', intended to cause trouble by drawing those charged out of their lands in time of harvest 'or uthirwayes to gett thame to the horn, that thairupoun thay may seik sum advantage'. The sums demanded as surety were so great that they could not find anyone who could meet them. Patrick's view was that letters had been obtained against. him by 'divers and sindrie malicious and invyfull personis ... be thair prevey moyen, upoun sinister narration'. Such general letters, requiring him and

46 Wormald, *Lords and Men in Scotland*, 428–30.
47 Wormald, *Lords and Men in Scotland* 436–7.

all his servants and vassals to find caution, were inappropriate, being intended for 'chevis of clannis, nobilmen and men of grit landis and rentis' lying in the Borders or the Highlands 'and quhais tennentis, vassallis and servandis ar daylie subject to commoun reiffis, spuilyeis, heirschippis, slauchteris, and depredationis'. It was not for 'nobilmen, gentilmen, inhabitantis of the *incuntreyis*, nor to particular personis duelland upoun thair proper landis and heretage, leving quyetlie undir the obedience of his Majesteis lawis, abhorring and detesting all stouth, reiff and oppressioun'. In a civil and obedient country such as Orkney and Shetland, anyone fearing harm from the earl should find remedy in the normal procedure of lawburrows, whereby surety was found for the complainer's safety by the individual complained of. This was a clear reference to the act of parliament of 1587 'for the quieting of the bordoris hielandis and Iles' which, he felt, had never been intended to apply to the Northern Isles.[48]

Patrick's particular cause of dispute with the Balfours concerned arrears of 12,000 merks from the lands of Westray, due to him from Sir Andrew Balfour, and money still unpaid by Balfour's father from the lands feued in Shetland. The Balfours' complaints suggest that he was using this as a means of wresting their lands from them. He had seemed to recognise the independence of Westray from his sway in September 1594 when the island was specifically exempted from his fishing contract with the Fife coast burghs. In 1597, however, after 'dyvers iniuries and oppressions' by the earl, the Balfours sought letters of horning against him. The messenger who sought to execute these, James Neven, was faced with a complete refusal by the populace at large to supply him with food, lodging or the use of their boats. He was forced to buy a *scaff boit* and row first from Kirkwall to Westray and thence all the way to Duncansby Head. The reason the islanders gave for refusing to help was fear of Patrick's 'wraith and indignatioun' though, as we shall see, a general suspicion of royal officials was to survive Patrick's fall.

The Balfours had obtained from the lords an exemption from the earl's jurisdiction, but in December 1597, using their arrears as a pretext, Patrick went to Westray and sought to impose his own will, forbidding Michael Balfour to hold courts on pain of death. He removed much of the produce of the farm of Noltland, confiscated 29 beached whales, and returned in September 1598 and again at the beginning of 1599 to strip Noltland so thoroughly that the lands were unworked for some time thereafter.[49] He was said to have 'consultit upoun divers secret and indirect practizeis and meanes' – a common way of describing witchcraft – to kill Balfour and his father, and had directed the commons to report any evil spoken of him, particularly by the Balfours, within 24 hours under pain of death and forfeiture. In November 1598, Balfour, like Neven, was forced to flee from the islands in a 'litle *yoill*', the earl having confiscated his ship. In his absence his kinsman George Balfour, former prior of the Charterhouse of Perth, who had come north in the

48 *APS*, iii, 461–7; *RPC*, iv, 787–9; Wormald, *Lords and Men in Scotland*, 130 and n, 76.
49 *RPC*, v, 535–7.

hope of settling matters, was compelled to surrender Noltland Castle to Patrick's illegitimate brother William.

In March 1598 Balfour secured execution of letters against Patrick for this exploit,[50] but in Orkney and Shetland, in a manner reminiscent of Bruce's experience, he received almost no support at all. The list of complainers against him included not only servants of the earl such as Thomas Barclay, Andrew Martin and John Dishington, but also many such as Bellenden and Bruce of Cultmalindie himself whom one might have expected to support a general complaint against Patrick. The response of Balfour's fellow lairds suggested that he had chosen the wrong means of fighting the earl. The final agreement between the two sides, drawn up in June 1599, suggested that he had also chosen the wrong issue. Patrick received the 12,000 merks he had sought, as well as sums still due out of feued lands in Shetland from Balfour's days as earl Robert's commissioner.[51]

Nevertheless, there were some points about the negotiation and conclusion of agreement that were ominous for any supporter of Patrick. Although the Balfour dispute lasted only about 18 months, it had dragged on more than it need have, given the apparent strength of Patrick's case, through his own wilfully obstructive behaviour. An attempt had been made by Patrick's lawyer, James King, to have the Balfours' letters suspended,[52] but when these suspensions were challenged, the earl had not turned up in court, so the letters were allowed to stand. A year later, when the case was heard in its entirety, Patrick again did not appear, and was pronounced rebel. When he finally agreed to settle, it was with the advice of Lord Ochiltree, the master of Elphinstone, and Sir William Livingston of Kilsyth. There is a strong impression that he simply ignored the courts, or at best prevaricated, until at length wiser heads prevailed. This was the first example of such behaviour by Patrick; it was not to be the last.

Further evidence of Patrick's contemptuous attitude towards the courts is seen in the session case brought by Bannatyne of Gairsay, in vain pursuit of all the money he had paid out on Patrick's business. At one stage the lords felt compelled to state roundly that 'in na tyme cuming they will heir ony excuis to be proponit be the . . . erll of Orknay to delay the saidis persewaris in the said mater (deith onlie exceptit)'. Bannatyne was also allowed to summon Patrick through his lawyer, Alexander King, instead of in person;[53] after James Neven's experience, this was understandable. Another case where Patrick may have had right on his side, but which had been allowed to escalate beyond all reason, was that of Magnus Paplay. Paplay, a former commissary clerk of Orkney, was in possession of the lands of Weyland and claimed to have been awarded a pension by Earl Robert. Patrick had disputed his right to these, sacking Weyland and imprisoning and banishing Paplay. Paplay's son Thomas was the same Thomas Paplay executed for plotting against Patrick, and his

50 *RPC*, v, 447–8.
51 Reg. Deeds, NRS RD1/71, ff. 14v–18r.
52 *RPC*, v, 447–8.
53 Acts and Decreets, CS7/184, ff. 152v–3r.

father accused the earl of his murder.[54] The problem was resolved by the master of Orkney and Sir John Livingston of Dunipace as arbiters. Patrick got his way so far as the pension was concerned, but he had to make numerous concessions in restoring Paplay's position,[55] and his followers had to guarantee the latter's safety.[56] This last point – the finding of surety on Patrick's side – indicated that the complaints of the earl and landowners of Orkney had been heard. The days of large-scale sureties were over, and the use of lawburrows – legal security demanded by one person of another for their physical safety – put in its place.

Patrick's arrogance was doubtless encouraged by the impotence of his opponents. The moves against him had come to nothing, the complainers being unable to co-ordinate or command support. But he was running out of room for manoeuvre. In 1599 he was 'deeply charged with great oppression'. In part, the opposition continued to come from the Balfours, but George Nicolson, the English observer, saw also 'some of his brethren against him'. Indeed it may have been James and Robert Stewart, rather than John – and more than any Orkney and Shetland individuals – who forced Patrick for the time being to compromise. Characteristically, however, his first response to a summons south to answer charges was evasive, and he remained on his estates 'upon pretence to keep the countries of Orkney and Shetland',[57] sending his wife in his place, as his father had sent his mother in his time. The ploy did not satisfy king or council, and he was further charged to come south 'as the device of my Lady's coming frees him not'.[58] He was forced to yield, and spent the next few months negotiating over his affairs with the secretary, the Octavian Elphinstone of Barnton.[59]

By early June the 'storm had passed over his head', but this did not mean he got off scot-free. It was at this time that he appears to have taken the precaution of granting a charter to his brother Master James, under reversion, of the earldom lands of Orkney.[60] The measures forced on him by the secretary indicate that the source of the trouble was not the violence complained of by the Balfours, but his refusal to acknowledge his obligations. The agreement with the Balfours was the only one settled in his favour. He had to pay off his brothers – James for 10,000 and Robert for 11,500 merks;[61] John Jackson, elder, burgess of Edinburgh for £7,616 10s;[62] and Gilbert Primrose, the royal surgeon, for 11,000 merks.[63] He owed smaller

54 Diligence Recs: GR Hornings Edin., NRS DI47/14, ff. 205r–7r.
55 Reg. Deeds, NRS RD1/75, ff. 127v–9r.
56 Court of Session Recs: Reg. Cauts in Susps, NRS CS290/21.
57 CSP Scot., xiii, 447.
58 CSP Scot., xiii, 452.
59 CSP Scot., xiii, 497.
60 Reg. Deeds, NRS RD1/70, f. 390r and v; RD1/71, ff. 23v–5r; a note survives in the Kinross House papers (NRS GD29/161) suggesting that Patrick actually granted a charter of the earldom, under reversion, for the money.
61 Reg. Deeds, NRS RD1/67, ff. 387r–9r; RD1/77, f. 65r and v. 70; RD1/77, ff. 395r–6r.
62 Reg. Deeds, RD1/77, ff. 395r–6r.
63 Reg. Deeds, RD1/75, ff. 139v–40v.

amounts too, having been escheated by his tailor, Alexander Ostean, for debts totalling nearly £1,300. On paying these off, he was permitted to go home; he was to
return by 20 November, but this was to act as gentleman of the bedchamber when
the king returned from his summer progresses, rather than because of his financial
affairs. Until his return all actions were suspended. In fact there is no evidence that
he did return to the north, but for the moment the murmurs of discontent, and the
representations that had brought him south against his will, were silenced.[64]

This settlement of Patrick's affairs paved the way for his receipt of the charters
of the earldom and bishopric lands, and helps to mark the end of the first half of
his period as earl. For the time being he was in a seemingly strong position: his
financial concessions had satisfied the secretary; the opposition in the north had
faded away; and he was about to come into his own. Yet the elements that were to
combine to bring him down were all plainly visible. There was the extravagance and
lack of respect for law and advice that had allowed his affairs to get into such a mess.
There were the enemies he had made, not all of whom had been dealt with by his
arrangements – Bannatyne and Magnus Paplay were still acting against him and,
more importantly, the earl of Caithness and the Monteith family. Moreover, the
change from the unpopular policy of demanding general sureties meant that future
pursuers of the earl would invoke the power of the session against him. The 10,000
merks of caution that he had had to find at the hands of Michael Balfour were to
set a crucial precedent. This particular obligation was soon suspended, but in May
1599 Patrick had to do the same in £5,000 for Robert Monteith of Egilsay and in
March the following year for his own illegitimate half-brother William Stewart of
Lyking;[65] three years later he had to do likewise for Bruce of Cultmalindie.[66] These
sureties were not suspended, and they were to carry great weight in the future.

64 CSP Scot., xiii, 497, 516.
65 Court of Session Recs: Reg. Cauts in Susps, NRS CS290/20, 21.
66 Court of Session Recs: Reg. Cauts in Susps, NRS CS290/24.

11

Craftie, Malicious and Invyous Personis

A fter 1600 Patrick lost little time in embarking on the courses that were to bring him to disaster. Even as his affairs were being temporarily settled, his great building campaigns were beginning and it was these perhaps more than anything else that prompted a desperate search for cash, which spread its net ever wider, drawing in more families, more antagonists. In Orkney, the Sinclair of Eday family were notable victims of this campaign, and ones who sought unusual means of combating it. In the 1590s there had been no more than the briefest of disputes between the earl and the Sinclairs – the temporary forfeiture of Edward Sinclair in June 1597 for non-payment of duties[1] – but in September 1604 William Sinclair, Edward's son, complained to the privy council. He said that the earl and his servants under Henry Black, captain of Kirkwall Castle, had twice invaded his lands in Eday, ejected him from his house at Holland and removed the whole of the plenishings. They had imprisoned a Sinclair messenger, prevented James Sinclair from joining his brother William on the island, and worked the quarry at Towback there on a vast scale.[2]

The earl's response was colourful, painting a picture of vicious dispute within the Sinclair family, which he as sheriff, justice and lord of *regality*, was seeking to regulate. William Sinclair had tried to kill his father Edward, said to be about 100 years old, both by shooting and by 'nipin him in the craig as he had bene ane dog, thinking to half *wirreit* (strangled) him'. William and his brother James had enlisted the aid of six or seven boatloads of 'vagabondis, broken highland men of Caithnes'. The 'auld, decrepit man' had sought Patrick's protection and appealed to the men of Orkney for help, 'for of the cuntrie men of Caithness thair barbarous interpryissis lang of befoir aganis the cuntrey of Orknay thair remaneis yit experience.'[3] Henry Black wrote to John Dishington, telling of a 'Caithnes bott' that had arrived there in secret, bearing with it William Sinclair's wife and her supporters. They had broken into the Sinclair house and taken away all the household effects, the livestock and butter set aside for the earl. While they were doing so, Sinclair's wife had 'malisiouslie . . . detrakit and spoikine in blasflemasiounis of my lord that giff his lordschip had

1 *RSS*, NRS PS1/69, f. 160v.
2 Court of Session Recs: Acts and Decreets, NRS CS7/232, ff. 192v–5r.
3 *RPC*, vii, 737–8.

twa heidis scho suld gar hime want the ane of them and giff his lordschipis hail forss war in Ethay scho suld haiff hir awine of his lordschipis hairt'.[4] This she would do with her husband's own forces, which were 'to cume owt of Caithnes schoirtlie'.

William Sinclair was indeed an aggressive and dangerous man,[5] but Patrick's feud with him had much deeper causes than his ill-treatment of his own father. The presence in Eday of forces from across the Pentland Firth resulted directly from the dispute between Patrick and the earl of Caithness. In February 1599 both earls had had to find surety for their good behaviour[6] but in September 1601 George Nicolson wrote to his master Sir Robert Cecil that the two lords were 'very like ... for to go to the worst. Caithness is ... buying an isle in Orkney, which if he do will put them by the ears together'.[7] The isle Caithness was buying was Eday. By a contract of 25 May 1601 the Sinclairs, Edward and William, became clients of the earl, 'thair chief'. They had been in debt for many years, ever since 1576 when Edward Sinclair had granted a bond to the Edinburgh merchants James Hathoway and his wife Janet Fockhart. Both of these were now dead, but Caithness had bought up the bond for 3,000 merks, and assigned it back to his Eday cousins, with a loan of a further 1,000 merks, 'haifing compassioun of the lange ley land lyand unoccupyit' and relieving the Sinclairs 'fra the grit danger and perellous estait wherein thay and the isle of Eday stood'. For this the Eday Sinclairs were to pay 400 merks annually, sign a bond of maintenance and accept the earl's choice of husband for William Sinclair's daughters.[8]

The contract had been concluded by William Sinclair, supposedly with the consent of his father, yet the tenor of a separate agreement between them, concluded the same day, suggests an uneasy relationship.[9] Patrick took the part of the 'auld gudman', though his solicitude was a transparent excuse for seizing control of William's lands; in December 1602 he had already tried unsuccessfully to have Sinclair's original title to the lands reduced by the session.[10] In April 1604, shortly after his first invasion of the Eday lands, he concluded a contract with the old man alleging that William Sinclair had 'sa ungratiouslie and unnaturally behavit him self in sa mony wayes towardis his ... father and gevin evident taikenis of ane intentit paraceid concludit in his hart'.[11] In return for protection, Edward sold Patrick all his lands, both in Orkney and in Roslin.[12]

---

4   O & S Papers, NRS RH9/15/180.
5   Court of Session Recs: Acts and Decreets, NRS CS7/396, ff. 427r–9r.
6   RPC, v, 523.
7   CSP Scot., xiii, 875.
8   Reg. Deeds, NRS RD1/239, ff. 310v–14r; James Hathoway (Hathewie, Hathrew), Janet Fockhart's second husband (M. H. B. Sanderson, Mary Stewart's People: Life in Mary Stewart's Scotland, Edinburgh, 1987, 91–102), was in Shetland in 1576, where he had a confrontation with Laurence Bruce's followers (Shetland Documents, 1195–1579, 219; Anderson, Robert Stewart, 167).
9   Reg. Deeds, NRS RD1/107, ff. 26v–7r.
10 Court of Session Recs: Acts and Decreets, NRS CS7/205, ff. 55v–6r.
11 Reg. Deeds, NRS RD1/114, ff. 450v–1r.
12 Session Processes, NRS CS15, box 123, no. 10.

In the first half of August 1602, Patrick invited Caithness's enemies the earl of Sutherland and his brother Sir Robert Gordon to Orkney, sending his 'warre-ship' the *Dunkirk* to convey them from Cromarty to Kirkwall. After eight days of hearty entertainment at Birsay and the same in Kirkwall, the two parties signed a bond of friendship.[13] Two years later Patrick paid a reciprocal visit to Dornoch. There he was 'honorabilie interteyned with comedies and all other sports and recreations that Earle John culd mak him'. He was made godfather to Sutherland's short-lived eldest son, who was called Patrick.[14]

In April 1603 the privy council again ordered Orkney and Caithness to deliver sureties to each other,[15] and for the next five years a running battle continued. In 1605, the year after his complaint to the privy council, William Sinclair began to pursue Patrick for spuilyie before the session.[16] During four years of legal action he borrowed further sums from Caithness, and the earl made writs available to support his case.[17] According to Robert Gordon, Caithness's next direct intervention took place in 1608, when some of Patrick's servants were forced by bad weather to land in Caithness. He received them, but deliberately made them drunk, shaved off half their beards and half their hair, then forced them out on the Pentland Firth in the same weather that had compelled them to seek shelter in the first place.[18] Patrick complained to the king as well as taking measures of his own. Henry Black and his men were said to have gone to Duncansby and killed Donald Groat of Warse, Walter Groat his brother and James Steven, all Caithness servants.[19] The council and justiciary were to investigate both actions the following year.

By 1608 Edward Sinclair's long life had come to an end, and Patrick was deep in dispute with Edward's son over their respective rights to the lands, mill, fishings and quarry of Eday. In May of that year Henry Black wrote to Patrick from Greentoft, where he had been searching unsuccessfully for the 'ald guid maneis sesing' – Edward Sinclair's original title, granted forty years or so before, either by Adam Bothwell or Oliver Sinclair of Pitcairns.[20] This was crucial to Patrick's case, since it justified the old man's right to make the concessions the earl had wrung from him, including the contract of April 1604, a licence of February the same year to work the quarry, and a commission to pursue William Sinclair for writs he was said to have taken from his father. William's case was based on an infeftment dated 3 November

13 R. Gordon, *Genealogical History of the Earldom of Sutherland*, Edinburgh, 1813, 248; quoted in E. Tyrell, 'Birsay Palace, Orkney', *The Antiquary*, xlvii (1911), 183.

14 Gordon, *Genealogical History of the Earldom of Sutherland*, 352; quoted in Tyrell, 'Birsay Palace, Orkney', 183.

15 *RPC*, xiv, 402–3.

16 Court of Session Recs: Acts and Decreets, NRS CS7/215, ff. 114v–15r.

17 Reg. Deeds, NRS RD1/107, ff. 202v–3v; Deeds Warrants, NRS RD11/52, nos 330–1.

18 Gordon, *Genealogical History of the Earldom of Sutherland*, 258; quoted in Tyrell, 'Birsay Palace, Orkney', 183.

19 *Criminal Trials*, iii, 53–4.

20 O & S Papers, RH9/15/115.

1591, following on a crown charter. There is every reason to suppose that Edward Sinclair had received a grant of the Eday lands, but Patrick found this impossible to substantiate, and on 14 February 1609 the session found in William's favour.[21]

The Eday family were not the only Sinclairs who suffered at Patrick's hands. In 1608 Robert Sinclair of Campston and Edmund Sinclair of Flotta were arrested by Patrick's men and taken to Kirkwall Castle. Campston obtained letters from the privy council exempting him from Patrick's jurisdiction, but was still there in March 1609 when he got word to Edinburgh of his plight.[22] Flotta was imprisoned for six weeks in a 'vyld and miserabill hoill not sax fute braid', the earl 'thinking to hae devourit him with rottynis and vermin'.[23] Eventually he was brought before an assize, accused of trumped-up charges. The assize bravely found him not guilty, 'for the quhilk thay are like to undergo great truble', and he escaped from Orkney to add his own voice to the clamour of litigation. Neither Campston nor Flotta stated why they had been treated in this way, though the former had been involved in a serious dispute with the Shetland Sinclairs over the murder of his brother Matthew, a dispute in which the earl had taken a hand.

Other families complained too. In February 1601 Sir Patrick Bellenden accused the earl's illegitimate brother William Stewart of Lyking of breaking into his house in Stenness and removing the contents.[24] The case came to nothing at the time, but was considered by the privy council four years later.[25] The complaint, coupled with one by Robert Henderson of Holland, failed for lack of evidence, but both alleged that the earl had sought to extort their lands from them. He was said to have tortured Bellenden's eldest son Thomas in the *boots*, imprisoned his brother Adam, and finally removed the aged and bedridden Sir Patrick himself, wicker bed and all, from his house in Stenness, and placed his own servants there.[26] In his old age, Sir Patrick had no capacity for a confrontation with the earl, and little further happened until the Bellenden case joined others in Patrick's first trial in 1610.

Robert Henderson of Holland's complaint, and that of his mother, Margaret Bonar, widow of Earl Robert's old servant William Henderson, was less specific. It spoke of 'many horrible acts of oppression, imprisonment, causing thaim grant severall bandis for soumes of money, imposing taxationes etc.'.[27] These centred round a contract that the earl had forced from Henderson's mother in February 1605 after several months' imprisonment in Kirkwall.[28] He exacted a lump sum of £1,000 and a pension in kind in return for agreeing not to challenge her rights in

21 Court of Session Recs: Acts and Decreets, NRS CS7/240, ff. 122r–7v.
22 *RPC*, viii, 256.
23 Diligence Recs: GR Hornings, NRS DI3/38, ff. 2r-3v.
24 Court of Session Recs: Acts and Decreets, NRS CS7/194, ff. 98r and v.
25 *RPC*, vi, 601.
26 *RPC*, vi, 133, 156.
27 *RPC*, vii, 156.
28 The contract was revoked on 20 July 1605 (Edin. Comm. Ct Reg. Deeds, NRS CC8/17/4).

North Ronaldsay.[29] In January 1607 a further complaint was brought before the council by James, Robert Henderson's younger brother. Edward Scollay, Patrick's deputy, had unjustly imprisoned him 'ane lang space' in Kirkwall Castle. He was freed on council orders, but had to rely on friends who 'convoyit him saulf away' from Scollay and his men, who had orders to kill him. Scollay followed him to Sanday and attacked him and his brother near the kirk there, breaking their swords and beating them about the head. The Scollays refused to appear before the council to answer these charges and were accordingly declared guilty.[30]

Kirkwall Castle therefore saw a succession of Orkney notables in its cellars – Sinclair of Campston, Sinclair of Flotta, Thomas Bellenden, Margaret Bonar, James Henderson and others. Their treatment is best described by one of their number who occupied a special and rather curious position in Orkney affairs. William Stewart of Lyking, Patrick's natural brother, had been one of those whom Patrick Bellenden had accused of ill-treatment on the earl's orders. He appears to have been something of an adventurer; he had been employed by his father as pilot of the 'Spanish Barque' and Patrick was later to recommend him to the king of Sweden as a mercenary.[31] Yet, like his illegitimate sibling James Stewart, he was treated no better than Patrick's other vassals. In March 1600 he compelled Patrick to guarantee his safety under pain of £5,000, but one December night the following year the earl's followers came to his house at Dale in Orphir and took him off to Kirkwall. There he was kept in a tiny cell – perhaps Flotta's 'vyld and miserabill hoill' – on short rations, watched day and night by a servant with a loaded hagbut. The captain of the castle, William Martin, told him several times to 'provid himself for deith' and in Patrick's presence he had 'presentit to him the buittis'. He was told he was to 'suffer the torment thairof sua lang as his legis mycht lest or than confes'. Patrick forced from him his Sandwick estates of Lyking, Voy and Clumlie, burned his titles and compelled him to say that they were forgeries in any case. He had to grant two bonds for 600 merks to Bernard Stewart, the earl's master stabler, and two others renouncing other actions against his brother. Understandably, William Stewart signed everything that was put in front of him. As security Patrick made him arrange for his friends to deliver these documents to him with £1,000 of borrowed money.[32]

When Stewart sued his brother in February 1603 Patrick was, typically, ready with an answer. His actions were legitimate, he said, because William was guilty of the murder of his first wife Katherine, sister of Thomas Bellenden, who had indeed died mysteriously. All Patrick had done was to apprehend him under his regality jurisdiction and make him undertake to answer for the crime. The response of Stewart's counsel was that Patrick's powers extended only to fugitives or those

29 Reg. Deeds, NRS RD1/107, ff, 148v–9v.
30 *RPC*, vii, 156, 307–8.
31 T. A. Fischer, *The Scots in Sweden*, Edinburgh, 1907, 72; Anderson, *Robert Stewart*, 125.
32 Court of Session Recs: Acts and Decreets, NRS CS7/207; ff. 13v–14r, 110r and v, 113r–14r, 294v–5r, 321r–3r.

caught red-handed; the death of Katherine Bellenden, whatever the circumstances, had taken place six years before.[33] Patrick was found liable to pay £5,000 on each of three counts of oppression – the imprisonment of Stewart, and the plundering of his estates and those in Hundland of his second wife. A very important feature of these hearings was the presence of the king's advocate, Thomas Hamilton. Variously known as of Monklands and of Byres, later Lord Binning and ultimately earl of Haddington, Hamilton was one of the ablest men of his time. He had probably encountered Patrick before during his work as an Octavian, but this was the first evidence of the interest in Patrick's activities of a man who was in the end, more than anyone else, to be Patrick's nemesis.

Another family described as a major opponent of Patrick is that of Moodie of Breckness, in particular Francis Moodie – 'Wanton Francis', according to one of the family's historians – who 'carried the family feud with the Earl of Orkney to extremes of lawlessness and ruffianism . . . for ten years Orkney was in an uproar, and murder would almost certainly have been done by one or other party, had Patrick not been beheaded for high treason . . .'[34] This view takes Francis's own account of events at face value; it was not until after Patrick's final departure from Orkney that his followers came into conflict with the Moodies. Among the charges against Patrick at his indictment in 1610 was that of pursuing Adam Moodie, Francis's father, in his courts and imprisoning Francis's servants for transporting Francis against the earl's orders. The unrest was apparently of recent origin. In July 1609 David King, bailie of Hoy and Walls, had attacked Robert Moodie, Francis's younger brother, at Osmondwall, cut the tails of his horses, driven them into his corn and set dogs on his sheep[35]. In the months that followed, Francis Moodie was said to have swaggered about Kirkwall, armed with two pistols and 'saying that he helpit to put that mansworne tratour . . . in waird, and that he sould help to forfalt the said Erll, and hoipit to sie his armes riven at the Croce, that he micht dicht his ers thairwith'.[36] For such 'uncomelie speitcheis', Patrick brought actions against him. Moodie assaulted his messenger, and he and his supporters, including James Stewart of Graemsay's sons, attacked and stabbed the earl's servant Alexander Leggat. At length he was taken by the earl's men, assisted (he said) by 'most of the inhabitants' of Kirkwall and placed in the castle 'as if he had been a notable malefactor'. Moodie was no doubt a turbulent individual, who had been accused of assaulting a messenger before,[37] but the brief squabbles of 1609–10 are all that can

33 Katherine Bellenden's death, or killing, which apparently occurred while she was pregnant, is a mystery. Stewart was charged in March 1600 to find caution that he would appear before a justice-ayre (*RPC*, vi, 93), but nothing more is known of the circumstances; it may help, however, to explain why there was no love lost between Stewart and the Bellendens. William's second wife was Katherine Douglas, relict of Henry Colville, parson of Orphir (Court of Session Recs: Acts and Decreets, NRS CS7/254, ff. 279r–80v; 255, ff. 188r–9r).
34 E. H. Burrows, *The Moodies of Melsetter*, Cape Town, 1954, 12.
35 *RPC*, viii, 451.
36 *RPC*, ix, 209.
37 *RPC*, viii, 329; Craven Beq., NRS GD106/178; Burrows, *The Moodies of Melsetter*, 12; Ruvigny, *The Moodie Book*, privately printed, 1906, 16–17.

be credited to the Moodies before their claims against the earl are submerged in the tide of protest which at last engulfed Patrick.

Much more important in the Orcadian opposition to Patrick were the Monteith family, led by Robert Monteith of Egilsay. Their dispute began in November 1591, when Patrick borrowed 12,000 merks from Patrick Leslie, commendator of Lindores, his brother-in-law, and a similar sum from William Monteith, a Leith merchant and long-term financier of the old earl.[38] The money was to be employed by Patrick upon 'wechtie effairis' – his financial difficulties at the time. Two thousand merks of the money were assigned by Patrick to William Monteith's kinsman, Patrick Monteith of the Fair Isle, sheriff depute and chamberlain of Shetland, possibly as an advance on his expenses in gathering in the earl's rents.[39] William Monteith died shortly afterwards, and in the next two years about half the debt was paid off to his widow.[40] The money due Patrick from Patrick Monteith and the earl's own debt to Lindores were another matter.

In 1594 Patrick pursued Monteith of the Fair Isle for the dues he had been engaged to gather from Shetland.[41] Monteith claimed successfully that he had already paid up, partly in money and partly in furnishing for the earl's house, but by then he had been forced into banishment to escape Patrick's 'wraith and furie . . . consavit aganes him without onie just caus or occasioun, but onlie sterit up thairto be the malice of certane evill affectionat persounes about him'.[42] Patrick Monteith died in 1597. His lands passed first to his nephew James Monteith and then to James's younger brother Robert.[43] The family's Orkney interests were several. Besides a claim to the island of Wyre, there were lands in Westray, Yairsay in St Ola and a tenement in Kirkwall.[44] In Shetland there were the king's and bishop's lands in Fair Isle, from which Patrick Monteith had taken his designation.[45] But the estates that suffered most in a fierce and interminable dispute between Robert Monteith and the earl were those of Kirbest and Meaness in Egilsay, and of Work in St Ola.

---

38 Diligence Recs: GR Hornings Edin., NRS DI47/21, f. 82v; Reg. Deeds, RD1/38, ff. 298r–302r, RD1/47, ff. 424v–5v.

39 Gardie House Papers; Court of Session Recs: Reg. Cauts in Susps, NRS CS290/14.

40 Edin. Comm. Ct Recs: Reg. Tests, NRS CC8/8/26, ff. 134v–6r; Reg. Deeds, NRS RD1/44, ff. 161v–2v.

41 Reg. Deeds, NRS RD1/47, ff. 424v–5v.

42 Court of Session Recs: Acts and Decreets, NRS CS7/160, ff. 30v–1v.

43 RCAHMS *Inv.*, O & S, ii, 131; James Monteith of Saltcoats was served heir to Patrick Monteith of the Fair Isle on 17 March 1600 (*Inquisitiones Generales*, ii, 34) and granted Robert Monteith the latter's lands in Fair Isle, Egilsay and St Ola (Baikie of Tankerness Mss, OA D.24, box 3, no. 52). There were some differences in the holding; Robert is referred to only as tacksman of Fair Isle (Court of Session Recs: Acts and Decreets, NRS CS7/190, ff. 118r–19r) and took 'of Egilsay' as his designation instead.

44 Court of Session Recs: Acts and Decreets, NRS CS7/132, f. 132r and v; 135, ff. 56v–7r; 161, f. 256r and v; 165, ff. 275r and v; 169, ff. 367v–9v; 172, ff. 247r–8r; Reg. Deeds, NRS RD1/68, ff. 120r–1v; RD1/71, ff. 396v–7v; Court of Session Recs: Reg. Cauts in Susps, NRS CS290/17; *RMS*, vi, no. 546; Baikie of Tankerness Mss, OA D24/3/53.

45 *REO*, 157, no. lxxi; Baikie of Tankerness Mss, OA D24/3/55.

About the time of Patrick Monteith's death, John Arnot, now knighted as Sir John, drew to the earl of Orkney's attention 'thir Menteithis, to quhome youre Lordschip wer . . . oblist in gude will . . . and thairfoir foryet nane nor be nocht ingrait to nane nor yit to thir friendis that evir hes done your Lordschip pleasour'.[46] The earl paid little attention. He clearly held Robert Monteith responsible for his uncle's debts as chamberlain. In May 1599 Robert complained that he had been warded in 'ane fould vyld presoun hous quhair he wes maist barbaruslie and inhumanelie usit'. On his release the Orkney sheriff court declared him an outlaw, and he was forced to flee from the islands like his uncle, the earl in murderous pursuit.[47] His lands were plundered to the tune of £20,000, a sum of the same order as that which the earl had extorted from Bannatyne of Gairsay and as that of the extraordinary taxes that he was later to be accused of levying in the years 1594-6.[48]

In May 1599 Robert Monteith compelled Patrick to find surety for his safety in the sum of £5,000, after which the two men agreed to renounce all actions against each other.[49] There followed measures of retrenchment and rationalisation among the Monteiths that confirmed Robert's succession to lands in St Ola, Egilsay and Fair Isle.[50] Patrick attacked Monteith's possession of all three. He invaded the lands in Egilsay and St Ola, dragged Monteith's men from the houses and from behind his ox-ploughs and stripped the properties of everything of value, amounting in cash to just short of £10,000.[51] Pursued by Monteith before the session from July 1602, Patrick justified himself by alleging that Monteith had obstructed his officer, John Sinclair, who was poinding the Fair Isle lands for arrears in the form of 12 gudlings of fish.[52] For this he had confiscated Monteith's whole goods.[53] The session rejected Patrick's defence and reduced his claims on Monteith to £500, though this sum was itself much greater than the value of the fish at the centre of the dispute.[54]

There followed eight years of legal tussling between Patrick and Monteith. In 1603 and 1604 there was horning and counter-horning; Patrick pursued Monteith in the Orkney courts for debt and alleged assault on one of the bailies of Kirkwall,[55] while Monteith sought from Patrick a copy of the court proceedings recording his fine for non-payment of the Fair Isle fish.[56] In June 1605, Monteith was still seeking

---

46 O & S Papers, NRS RH9/15/107/1.
47 Reg. Deeds, NRS RD1/72, ff. 409r–10r; Diligence Recs: GR Hornings Edin., NRS DI47/14, ff. 271v–5r.
48 *APS*, iv, 396.
49 Court of Session Recs: Reg. Cauts in Susps, NRS CS290/20.
50 Diligence Recs: GR Hornings Edin., NRS DI47/15, ff. 68v–70r; Reg. Deeds, NRS RD1/71, ff. 396v–7r; RD1/88, ff. 333v–5r, RD1/102, ff. 44r–5r; Court of Session Recs: Acts and Decreets, NRS CS7/185, 20r, CS7/186, ff. 337v–8r; *Inquisitiones Generales*, ii, 34; Baikie of Tankerness Mss, OA D24/3/52.
51 Court of Session Recs: Acts and Decreets, NRS CS7/202, f. 160r and v; CS7/207, ff. 356r–60v.
52 Diligence Recs: GR Hornings, NRS DI3/6, ff.238v–40v; DI3/7, ff. 84v–6v.
53 Reg. Deeds, NRS RD1/91, f. 430r and v; Court of Session Recs: Acts and Decreets, NRS CS7/203, ff.94r–5r.
54 Court of Session Recs: Acts and Decreets, NRS CS7/207, ff. 356r–60v.
55 *RPC*, xiv, 408.
56 Diligence Recs: GR Hornings, NRS DI3/6, ff.238v–40v; DI3/7, ff. 84v–6v.

redress for the despoiling of his lands,[57] but Patrick was proving wilfully obstructive. He had absented himself from the courts and refused to confront the king's
officers in their attempts to execute letters against him. He declined to answer the
door of his house at Holyrood or that of Lord Elphinstone there.[58] He refused to
allow Monteith the documents he needed to pursue his case, and on one occasion
did not even bother to appear in court for Monteith to produce the decreet against
him, although he had demanded to see it himself.[59] Above all, he did absolutely
nothing to reinstate Monteith in his lands. Instead, he was accused of several infrac-
tions of the lawburrows obtained by Monteith in 1603. Each contravention proved
would bring a fine of £5,000.[60]

From July 1605, the king's advocate began to keep an eye on what was happening,[61]
just as he had done two years before in the case of Stewart of Lyking. In February
1606 he noted a judgment by the lords that Patrick had extorted 2,000 merks from
Andrew Umphray of Berrie by threats, a finding incidentally which has remained a
famous case in Scots Law, 'Stewart contra Vinfra' (sic), which has been held to define
the concept of 'just feir and dredour'. Umphray, who had become caught up in the
earl's persecution of Monteith, alleged that he had been forced to sign a contract at
sword's point to hand over the money in respect of Monteith's former lands of Fair
Isle. Umphray contended that the fear involved rendered the contract null, and this
argument has been used since, though more modern research has indicated that
the dispute was less one-sided than the canny and surprisingly resolute Umphray
suggested.[62]

The king's advocate was also monitoring the litigation against Patrick of Bruce of
Cultmalindie, which paralleled that of Monteith. During that summer the two cases
ran side by side, the hearings sometimes happening within days of each other.[63]
Monteith was not now representing only himself. He had become assignee of some
of Patrick's other creditors – William Fairnie of that Ilk, to whom the earl owed
7,300 merks[64] and Patrick, commendator of Lindores, who was still seeking the
12,000 merks he had lent in November 1591, as well as arrears of interest, which
now exceeded the principal.[65] Monteith began successful proceedings to reduce not
merely his forfeiture, but also the original poinding.[66] In January 1607, the earl's

57 Court of Session Recs: Acts and Decreets, NRS CS7/215, f. 241v.
58 Diligence Recs: GR Hornings Edin., NRS DI47/20, ff. 94r–101v (esp. 101r and v).
59 Court of Session Recs: Acts and Decreets, NRS CS7/212/, f. 381v.
60 Court of Session Recs: Reg. Cauts in Lawbs, NRS CS295/1.
61 Court of Session Recs: Acts and Decreets, NRS CS7/216, ff. 119v–20r.
62 A. D. M. Forte, 'Black Patie and Andro Umfra', Stair Society Misc., v (2006), 89–191 explores this whole
    matter in detail. See also Morison, Dictionary of Decisions, xxxvii, 16481, and Court of Session Recs: Acts
    and Decreets, NRS CS7/215, f. 6r and v.
63 e.g. Acts and Decreets, CS7/216, f. 110r (26 July) and f. 119v–20r (30 July).
64 Reg. Deeds, NRS RD1/127, f. 237v–8r.
65 Reg. Deeds, RD1/116, f. 97v–9r.
66 Court of Session Recs: Acts and Decreets, NRS CS7/217, ff. 229v–31v.

decreet against him was annulled.[67]

During 1606 and 1607 there were concerted efforts, reminiscent of those in the late 1590s, to induce Patrick to face his responsibilities and put his affairs in order. Hamilton of Monklands assembled the most serious complaints against him into an indictment for treason, which was laid before parliament on 1 January 1606. This threat not even Patrick could ignore, and he was present with his counsel at each hearing – on 20 January, then on 17 June and again on 1 and 3 July. The indictment was detailed, and reminiscent of that against Patrick's father in 1575, containing charges going back ten years or more.[68] Behind its allegations lay Patrick's commission of lieutenantry, which was said to be a forgery made up by Andrew Martin, complete with signet and royal signature. Using it, the earl had usurped the royal prerogative with a number of decrees: against the carrying of arms without licence; prohibiting appeal to courts outside the islands; compelling report of murmurings against him; prescribing the death penalty for conspiracy and imposing it on two occasions; levying additional taxation and pressing the islanders into labour service. He had compounded the treason by sending large sums of money to the forfeited earl of Bothwell through Henry Colville, and had 'often convened with' Colville's brother John, a condemned rebel. He had laid siege to Kirkwall Castle in 1592 and Noltland three years later. He had ignored all attempts to bring him to book, threatened crown representatives and even defied the king himself.[69] It was perhaps this that forced him into arbitration in March 1607, five years after his original invasion of Monteith's lands and four after the first decreet against him.[70] He was represented by Sir Robert Crichton of Cluny and Lord Blantyre, an Octavian, a former schoolfellow of the king, and a favoured royal servant of long standing. An agreement was drawn up, but it simply provided one more cause of dispute. Patrick used it as justification for not honouring the original session decreet against him, while Robert Monteith claimed that it was null because it was not signed by one of his representatives. The case continued during the summer of 1608,[71] but by then interest in what was happening had spread beyond the antagonists, beyond the king's advocate, beyond parliament. The king had been aware of Patrick's activities for some time; the presence of Lord Blantyre, like that of Hamilton of Monklands, indicated a strong royal concern. James's patience was now wearing dangerously thin. In September the privy council was writing in response to a stern warning from London,[72] and the long-postponed disaster was at hand.

* * *

---

67 Acts and Decreets, CS7/224, ff. 259r–61r.
68 APS, iv, 396.
69 APS, iv, 396.
70 Acts and Decreets, CS7/235, ff. 35r–8r.
71 Diligence Recs: GR Hornings Edin., NRS DI47/21, ff. 31r–8r.
72 RPC, viii, 529; State Papers and Miscellaneous Correspondence of Thomas, Earl of Melros, vols I–II (Abbotsford Club), Edinburgh, 1837, i, 55.

Laurence Bruce of Cultmalindie was the most determined opponent of Patrick in either Orkney or Shetland. After the early dissension between the two men in the 1590s there had been little sign of ill-will, and Bruce had consolidated his holdings in the north of Shetland – Yell, Fetlar, Unst and Northmavine – crowning them in 1598 with the erection of Muness Castle.[73] Within months of Patrick's receipt of his charters, a bitter struggle began. Some of the bones of contention were of long standing. In May 1601 Patrick again pursued Bruce over the payment of £1,000 that he and Sinclair of Brough were to have made to Stewart of Burray during their dispute over wadmel.[74] Bruce, with Andrew Bruce of Scatsta his son, brought a counter-claim before the session in December 1602. In part, it concerned the loss of rights to wadmel; but there were other more recent, and more notorious, allegations. Bruce asserted that from Whitsunday 1599 his servants and tenants from Aith, Hillswick, Tresta, Muness and Scatsta had been compelled to make their way to Scalloway and work on the building of the new castle. They had to carry stones, timber and mortar for as much as eight days at a stretch, at their own expense and without food or drink. This had destituted many of them, and laid Bruce's lands waste for lack of their labour.[75]

This famous charge forms the chief basis of the grim reputation of both Patrick and his castle and, as in the case of his alleged appropriations of udal lands, it is ironic that Bruce of all people, the tyrant of the 1577 Complaints, should be its main source. Patrick had raised and rigorously enforced new taxes on Bruce's lands, particularly in 1599 and 1600, at the rate of one angel noble per last of land. In April 1602, while Bruce was away from Orkney on business, Patrick imprisoned Bruce's servant Henry Wardlaw in Scalloway Castle. He was released after a short time on finding surety, but was rearrested the same August. Wardlaw was accused of the murder of Nicol Magnusson, youngest son of Magnus Jacobson, shepherd of the earl's flocks on the island of Vementry. On a December night in 1601 Wardlaw and his accomplices were said to have attacked Magnusson near his home and thrown his body into the sea, to drown if he was not already dead.[76] Wardlaw was tried and acquitted on 19 August 1602 by an assize led by Arthur Sinclair as chancellor. Not satisfied, the earl tried him again the following day before a second assize, described by Bruce as consisting of 'the ignorant common people of the country', personally chosen by the earl. In fact the assize was led by Mouat of Heogaland, an important figure, who was neither ignorant nor common, and it too acquitted Wardlaw.[77] Patrick continued to detain him in the 'lach volt' of the castle, despite a session order for his release, and later confiscated his lands of Clousta in Aithsting.[78] He was set free on 31 August at six

73 RCAHMS *Inv.*, O & S, 129–31; W. D. Simpson, 'The Northernmost Castle of Britain', *SHR*, xxxviii, no. 25 (1959), 3.

74 *Ct Bk of Shetland*, 142–4.

75 Court of Session Recs: Acts and Decreets, NRS CS7/203, f. 157v–9v.

76 Justiciary Ct Small Papers, Main Series, NRS JC26, box 4, bundle 6.

77 Court of Session Recs: Acts and Decreets, NRS CS7/228, f. 81r and v.

78 Acts and Decreets, CS7/229, ff. 43r–7r.

Muness Castle

o'clock in the evening, an hour when, as Bruce said, any of his likely supporters had gone home. Three of Patrick's servants, James Crawford, William Robertson and Bernard Stewart, awaited him as he came out of the building. The earl himself stood at the castle head to watch. Wardlaw ran for his life to the house of John Buchanan, a well-known Scalloway merchant, but was forced to surrender when the earl's men threatened to burn the house down. By his account, he was then severely beaten up, a 'double musket staff' being broken over his head.

Bruce's complaint to the session did not give any reason why Patrick should detain or ill-treat his servant, nor did he mention that he himself had had to stand surety that Wardlaw would appear before the king's justices; but the fact that the central courts were taking an interest in the case was significant. The dispute over Wardlaw assisted Bruce in an aim that he had been pursuing for some time – that of securing exemption from Patrick's court in favour of hearings before the session. In July 1602 he had appealed to the lords of council in a dispute with Ola Sutherland, the underfoud of Fetlar, accusing Sutherland of allowing his swine to run wild on Helliersness, killing his lambs, and of deliberately driving some of his horses over a cliff – normally the sort of case that would have been heard in Shetland's own courts.[79] Now, in his representations to the lords regarding Patrick's ill-treatment of his tenants and Henry Wardlaw, he asked specifically that he be excluded from Patrick's jurisdiction.

He was not the only, nor the first, to do so. Hugh Sinclair had managed it, on paper at least, as early as 1592. So too had the Balfours and Sinclair of Campston,[80] and Malcolm Sinclair of Quendale tried to do the same.[81] But Bruce's case was much more significant, and the exemption from Patrick's justice of himself, his son Andrew and their followers was the only one to be remarked on in the Shetland court book. Patrick had not bothered to defend himself in open forum and his absence, depriving him of any opportunity to object, was noted in the judgment.[82] In June the following year, Andrew Bruce stated before the earl's court, held by John Dishington in Unst, that Nicol Jacobson, as his father's tenant, should not be tried there for theft 'in respect of the alledgit proces of exemptioun standand betwix my lord and his father befoir the lordis of the sessioun'. Dishington took the view that Jacobson was 'nocht altogidder' Bruce's tenant, since he paid skat to the earl, and found Bruce guilty of 'usurpatioun of the kingis auctoritie and hie contempt in the taking away the said Nicole out of jugment'.[83]

This episode has been described as looking like 'an attempt to secure recognition for a baronial jurisdiction',[84] and it may be that Laurence Bruce was seeking

<hr />

79 Court of Session Recs: Acts and Decreets, NRS CS7/195, f. 448r and v; cf. Ct Bk of Shetland, 78; Donaldson, Shetland Life under Earl Patrick, 29.
80 PR Horning Edin., NRS DI.47/14, ff. 80r–4r; RPC, viii, 256.
81 Reg. Deeds, NRS RD1/190, ff. 13v–14v.
82 Court of Session Recs: Acts and Decreets, NRS CS7/203, fl 157v–9v.
83 Ct Bk of Shetland, 70, 98–9.
84 Ct Bk of Shetland, vin.

some kind of independent legal status, exempt from the earl's control. Patrick's reaction, however, suggests a general attempt to prevent litigants, of whom Bruce was the most important, from going over his head. On 24 August 1602 the court of Shetland, under the earl himself, passed two general acts. The first said that no-one from Shetland should raise actions in the session or any other court outside the islands 'unles it be tryit that they ar refusit of justice within the coyntrie itselfe'. It was couched in general terms, stating that many of the gentry and commons of Shetland had complained of being 'hevelie hurt and prejugit be dyverse and sindrie craftie, malicious and invyous personis within the contrie' raising actions outside Shetland. The second enactment, also said to be in response to complaint, stated that the fouds had given licence to 'a greit number of servandis and . . . indwellairis within the land' to leave Shetland; as a result 'a greit part of the landis of the contrie ar liklie to ly ley without tymous and speidfull remeid be butt [sic] thairto'.

Bruce was in a very strong legal position, and not simply because of his exemption from Patrick's courts. Like Monteith of Egilsay, he had compelled Patrick at an early stage in his troubles to find surety for the safety of himself, his family and servants, under the penalty of £5,000.[85] His complaint of December 1602 made no reference to this, but after about two years he revived Wardlaw's case, citing it as a contravention of the lawburrows. Patrick did not trouble to respond,[86] even on 27 July 1605 when the session found in Bruce's favour, rendering him liable to a fine of £5,000, divided equally between Bruce and the authorities, with expenses of £25.[87] At the beginning of the following year, however, under the same pressure that caused him to try to settle with Monteith, he sought to reverse the original session decision in Bruce's favour. He brought witnesses south to testify against Wardlaw[88] and justified his treatment of Bruce's man by describing his contemptuous attitude towards the Shetland court. Wardlaw had publicly shown his derision by putting his thumb and forefinger in his mouth and whistling – blowing a raspberry in modern parlance. He had then stated his defiance of the earl and simply run out of the courtroom. Pursued by officials, he 'offerit thame straikis', and could only be subdued by rough treatment. [89]

It is quite possible that Wardlaw overstepped the mark in suggesting publicly that, as Bruce's servant, the earl had no power over him; but inevitably it was Bruce's

85 Court of Session Recs: Reg. Cauts in Susps, NRS CS290/24.
86 He was not represented at any of the diets from 2 March (Court of Session Recs: Acts and Decreets, NRS CS7/215, f.6r and v) till 27 July (CS7/219, ff. 131r–4r).
87 Court of Session Recs: Acts and Decreets, NRS CS7/219, ff. 131r–4r.
88 Smyth of Methven Papers, NRS GD190, box 21.
89 Court of Session Recs: Acts and Decreets, NRS CS7/219, ff. 316r–17v. The Shetland court book makes no mention of either trial, although reference is made to Wardlaw's incarceration (pp. 21, 36). The diet of 13 August was not held by Patrick, but by John Dishington; that of 20 August was held by Patrick, but makes no mention of Henry Wardlaw. The assize of 16 August was indeed headed by Arthur Sinclair of Aith (there is some discrepancy between the dates given in the court book and the account of Wardlaw's trial given elsewhere. No satisfactory arrangement has been arrived at regarding this), and that of 21 August by Andrew Mouat of Heogaland.

version that the lords accepted.[90] As in the case of Monteith, Patrick's attempts to settle matters solved nothing. He continued to withhold payment of his fine.[91] Unlike the case of Monteith, however, the next stage of Bruce's pursuit of the earl involved the marshalling of a wholly new set of charges. On 7 July 1604, he said, his servants had sailed for Uyeasound to transport him and a cargo of butter and fish to Sumburgh. On the way they were intercepted by the earl's vessel the *Dunkirk* under the command of Capt. Allan Lentroun, who confiscated their boat and took them prisoner. Bruce was forced to make his own way to Sumburgh, where he was to board the ship of Andrew Addison, a St Andrews merchant and regular visitor to Shetland,[92] whom he had engaged to transport him south with his goods. Addison, however, learned of an order by Patrick forbidding anyone to convey Bruce out of Shetland on pain of death, and when the laird came on board, the merchant told him that he could no longer honour their agreement. When Bruce insisted, Addison and his company rowed ashore, leaving Bruce standing impotently on the deck of a crewless vessel. At length he had to shout for a boat to ferry him back to land, where he met a reception committee, led by the foud of Dunrossness, William Farmer, and a number of the earl's men, including James Crawford, one of Wardlaw's attackers, and Alexander Leggat, a servant of the earl.

Although these men had already been calling to Bruce across the water, summoning him to meet Lady Orkney who was in Shetland acting for Patrick at the time, they did nothing, but sought merely to ensure that he did not leave Shetland, and he was permitted to remain at the house of John Scott at Exnaboe. Soon, however, they came to him with a demand that he find surety for the safety of Osie Scott in Reafirth. Scott had brought a case against Bruce before Patrick, stating that Bruce had 'maid ane pretendit quenquis [conquest] of mony landis and be his authoritie and power settillit himself in possessioun of the same, [and] ejectit the rycht possessouris thairfra', including Scott himself.[93] Because Scott refused to yield his lands, Bruce 'forgis all the quarrellis that he can againes me', and had raised actions against him before the council 'evin as thar wer na justice to be had within your Lordships jurisdictioun'. Bruce refused to comply, so Patrick's men decided to take him to their master. They provided him with a 'lytill neg' – possibly a Shetland pony – on which he had to ride to Maywick, a distance of about nine miles as the crow flies. From there they forced him to march on foot, booted and spurred, the whole way to Scalloway.[94] When he arrived he was closeted with Patrick's wife for only half an hour, after which – presumably tired out – he was allowed to make his way to Lilias Boynd's tavern close by. The following day he dined with Patrick and remained in the area for three or four days until the earl let him go. He sailed back

90 Justiciary Ct Bks of Adjournal, NRS JC2/4, ff. 162–3, 167, 182, 184; Small Papers, Main Series, NRS JC26, box 4, bundle 6; box 5, bundle 2.
91 Diligence Recs: GR Hornings, NRS DI31l5, ff. 143r–6r.
92 Reg. Deeds NRS RD1/180, ff. 315–16.
93 Session Processes, NRS CS15/103.
94 Court of Session Recs: Acts and Decreets, NRS CS7/239, ff. 152r–3r.

to Sumburgh on a herring boat, and thence to Scotland.

When the case was heard in February 1606, Patrick's defences were legalistic in nature. His lawyers did not deny the expropriation of Bruce's boat, but sought rather to distance the earl from the actions of his servants, implying that Skipper Lentroun was 'fugitive, and never reset by his master'. They attempted to disqualify Bruce's servants as witnesses, saying that Bruce had 'craftily' omitted their names from his complaint so that they might be witnesses for him rather than pursuers themselves. Neither of these points was entertained by the lords.[95] On the second charge, the marching of Bruce to Scalloway, Patrick was unable to provide any defence, even though there were some discrepancies between Bruce's version of events and that of eyewitnesses. Bruce stated that he was marched immediately from the Sumburgh shore all the way to Patrick's capital, a distance he described as about 26 miles, but it is clear from one account that Bruce remained for some time in Sumburgh, and did not begin his walk from there.[96] The journey from Maywick to Scalloway was extraordinary enough – northwards along the shores of Clift Sound, over the Clift Hills and the Hills of Easterhoull and round the head of the East Voe of Scalloway. It was a journey (in Bruce's words) through 'moss and myre and wilderness', where the only sign of human habitation for much of the journey would be the settlements at Wester Quarff and Sundibanks. It was undertaken on foot by Bruce and his captors alike because 'na man mycht ryd that gait', and Bruce was not a young man.

Why it happened at all remains mysterious. Bruce obviously intended it to be regarded by the lords of session as a deliberate humiliation and as such a contravention of Patrick's surety, but it is hard to imagine that such a course was actually thought out beforehand. It was not necessarily an odd way to go from Maywick to Scalloway; there is evidence that the west coast route overland was in habitual use by the men of Bigton and the Ness, at least in later times.[97] It is more likely that the journey to Maywick was made in order to find a boat to convey the party up the coast to Scalloway. If no boats were to be had, those of the district being out at the fishing,[98] then the only alternative would be a long detour to reach the more hospitable country up the east coast of Dunrossness. It is possible that Patrick's men chose rather to push on northwards with their unwilling charge, fearful of the earl's reaction at any further delay.

During 1607 and 1608, Bruce and Hamilton of Monklands assembled their case against Patrick, taking statements from the Dysart seamen and merchants who had witnessed what had happened.[99] Meanwhile, even before the murder case

95 Morison, *Dictionary of Decisions*, xxxvii, 16653.

96 Of Andrew Brown in Myreside, a servant of the duke of Lennox (Session Processes, NRS CS15/103).

97 I. J. D. Anderson, 'Anderson's Ambles: the West Coast Walk', *Shetland Life*, xvii (March 1982), 26–8.

98 I am grateful to Brian Smith for relaying to me these thoughts of Mr Robert Leask, a native of Bigton and authority on all matters Shetlandic.

99 Session Processes, NRS CS15/103.

against him was dropped, Henry Wardlaw was pursuing Patrick and his servants for eviction and spuilyie,[100] and Patrick's men undertook that he would produce the court rolls covering the case. The high court proceedings against Wardlaw were deserted and on 11 February 1608 Patrick undertook to restore Wardlaw's lands.[101] By the autumn of 1608 Patrick's opponents had put him in an extremely difficult position. On 4 August Andrew Bruce obtained relaxation of a horning that Patrick had imposed on him for not finding surety – he had been unable to do so since the earl had forbidden anyone to ferry him out of Shetland.[102] On 1 November, in a clear indication that the Orkney and Shetland opposition to Patrick was coming together, Andrew Bruce and Robert Monteith were granted a commission by the privy council to apprehend the earl and keep him 'in sure ward' until he gave satisfaction for all the hornings and complaints against him.[103] On 17 December, in the climax to Bruce's second case against Patrick, he obtained a decreet for further contravention of lawburrows and the earl was ordered to pay over another £5,000.

Patrick's characteristic response was to do nothing. The terms of Bruce's award – standard practice in the circumstances – were that payment had to be made within 40 days, failing which various formal stages would be gone through leading to an outright declaration of outlawry. The actual procedures were familiar – open proclamation at the mercat cross of Edinburgh and the pier and shore of Leith, the posting up of notices there, the personal warning of the earl's lawyer and agent – but there was no requirement that any of the rituals be gone through in the north 'becaus na officiar of our armis dar resort or repair to the countrey of Orknay . . . for feir of thair lyffis be reassoun of the crueltie notourlie . . . usit be [Patrick] aganes . . . our messingeris executouris of our utheris lettres . . . aganes him in tyme bygane'.[104] Despite the repeated warnings, both public and by representations to

100 Court of Session Recs: Acts and Decreets, NRS CS7/229, ff. 43r–7r; Court of Session Recs: Reg. Cauts in Susps, NRS CS290/29.

101 Reg. Deeds, NRS RD1/145, ff. 103r–4r.

102 Diligence Recs: GR Hornings, NRS DI3/32, ff. 14v–15v.

103 RPC, viii, 775.

104 Court of Session Recs: Acts and Decreets, NRS CS7/239, ff. 152r–3r; the ill-treatment of crown representatives did not merely extend to messengers on specific errands; it affected one official who appears to have been appointed to Orkney and Shetland on a permanent basis. Thomas Black of Strom's actual function is unknown, though it is possible he was trying to find out exactly what was going on in the north. Further conflict may have arisen through Black's relationship with Bruce of Cultmalindie. He married Jean Bruce, widow of Hugh Sinclair of Brough, from whom he derived his designation 'of Strom'. He was involved in constant litigation with Patrick (Diligence Recs: GR Hornings, NRS DI3/33, ff. 429r–30r, DI3/38, ff. 352v–4v, 400v–1r; RPC, viii, 801, ix, 60; Court of Session Recs: Reg. Cauts in Lawbs, NRS CS295/6), and was to complain of continual persecution. He also built a small castle in the Loch of Strom, it is said to barricade himself against the attentions of Patrick (Smith, 'Black's Castle', Unkans, ii, 4.) In November 1601, he was taken by William Martin, captain of Kirkwall Castle, and forced to put to sea in a storm. He was driven ashore on the island of Burray, but survived. Seven years later he was pursued to his house on Whalsay by the earl's followers (RPC, viii, 254–5). In 1612 Bruce assigned him £2,500 which he was due from Patrick for contravention of lawburrows (Court of Session Recs: Acts and Decreets, NRS CS7/268, f. 191r and v).

Alexander King, Patrick's lawyer, and John Home, his agent, nothing happened, and on 4 March 1609, Patrick was declared an outlaw, being formally required to surrender himself for incarceration in the castle of Dumbarton.[105] There was now virtually nowhere he could turn and the end of the road was firmly in sight.

In analysing Patrick's disputes with his enemies, it is necessary to distinguish between several different elements. There is the complaint against the earl, alleging invasion or imprisonment. There are self-justifying counter-claims. Beneath both may lie a definite cause of dispute, perhaps legitimate but not necessarily the same as the offence alleged by the earl. Balfour, Sinclair of Eday, Monteith, Bruce, Umphray of Berrie and Wardlaw provide the primary complaints. Patrick counters with allegations that both Wardlaw and Monteith showed active contempt for his courts; that William Sinclair ill-treated his father; and that Bruce had behaved oppressively towards Osie Scott. Beneath both there lies Patrick's constant desire for money, which inspired repeated acts of oppression, even when he was a legitimate creditor.

Occasionally, there were weightier reasons for his campaign against an individual. The Wardlaw case is one example. Another where a killing enabled Patrick to amplify a relatively minor cause for action was that of Adam Sinclair of Brow; this was in addition a complex affair, involving other prominent Shetland landowners, and is perhaps a suitable starting point for an examination of Patrick's dealings with the Sinclairs of Shetland. In 1602, three days after midsummer, Matthew Sinclair of Ness, son of one Robert Sinclair of Campston, brother of another and a descendant of the last Sinclair earl, was murdered in Dunrossness.[106] Those directly involved were Francis Sinclair of Uyea and Robert Sinclair of Ramnageo, but the individual pursued most strongly by the Shetland authorities was their cousin Sinclair of Brow; all three traced their ancestry through another branch of the Sinclairs, back to Ola and Henry Sinclair of Havera. According to the younger Robert Sinclair of Campston, Brow 'gave up freindschipe' with his brother the night before his death, and had provided Francis Sinclair with a horse for his getaway 'immediatlie eftir the heit bluid in the feildis'. Brow's servant John Bruce was also among those charged with complicity.[107]

Sinclair of Brow's trial in 1602 was the most notable heard by the old Shetland court during the three years of its extant proceedings. The origins of the Havera line are now lost to view, but Sinclair of Brow thought well enough of his ancestry to demand 'ane conding [condign] essyse agreabill to his bluide and rank'. There was discussion about whether this should be permitted in preference to an 'essyse of the contriemen of Yeitland . . . without ony respect of degreis, in consideratioun of

105 Diligence Recs: GR Hornings, NRS DI3/33, ff. 408r–10v.
106 Ct Bk of Shetland, 38; Sinclair of Ness's testament gives 22 July 1602 as the date (Edin. Comm. Ct Recs: Reg. Tests, NRS CC8/8/37) but is alone in this.
107 Ct Bk of Shetland, 31 and n.

The House of Sumburgh. 'Plain but stout', this was the most important Shetland administrative centre before the move to the more elaborate and pretentious, but more centrally situated, Scalloway Castle. Its builder, and patron, are unknown – perhaps Robert Stewart in his early years in the islands, but possibly Sir David Sinclair of Sumburgh at the beginning of the sixteenth century.

The Bishop's Palace. 'The Palace of the Yards' – or what remains of the ancient core of it – dating originally from the construction of St Magnus Cathedral itself in the early twelfth century, as a house for its bishop, William the Old, though remodelled several times thereafter. Under Bishop Robert Reid it was substantially reconstructed, before Patrick's attempts at a magnificent 'New Wark'. In this view from the cathedral, Bishop Reid's 1540s tower dominates.

Above. **Kirkwall Castle.** 'One of the strongest houssis in Breitane . . . nevir . . . biggit . . . without . . . the consent of the divile': a fourteenth-century tower house, with massive curtain walls and block-houses added a century or so later, it was a strong and grim structure, but is now entirely vanished, apart from a commem-orative plaque and a capped well beneath the roadway.

Right. **St Magnus Cathedral, Kirkwall.** This view from the Castle shows how the Cathedral towers over the surrounding buildings, but also how close the two buildings were, with the intervening space a scene of artillery and musketry in 1614. Pockmarks are still to be seen on the sacred walls.

Earl's Palace, Birsay. Robert Stewart had this imposing two-storey residence built in two stages, in the fifteen years or so from 1569, on the shore of Birsay Bay. Even in ruins, it still dominates the village of Birsay and surrounding area, as was Robert's intention. This is the west range, originally with a gallery lit from the west, with 'lach sellars' below for storage, now much dilapidated.

Earl's Palace, Birsay. The east range, looking north towards the remains of the corner tower and the later north range.

Above. **Muness Castle**. The first of Andrew Crawford's great works in the Northern Isles, assisted by the mason John Ross. Though built for Patrick's sworn enemy, Laurence Bruce, it forms an architectural trio with Patrick's own commissions, Scalloway Castle, built three years later in 1597, and the masterpiece, the 'New Wark', in Kirkwall.

Right. **Cathedral and the 'New Wark of the Yards'**. Another aspect of the constellation of strong defensible buildings in the centre of Kirkwall; the cathedral tower's view into the palace made life difficult for those defending it, and it is easy to see why.

Patrick's 'New Wark'. 'Possibly the most mature and accomplished piece of Renaissance architecture left in Scotland.' General views are difficult to come by, but this shows a fair variety of examples of architectural and masonic virtuosity. The turrets on the left had second storeys and conical roofs, giving a most imposing effect in the French style.

Patrick's 'New Wark' – the Great Hall. One of the finest of its kind in the country, with a fireplace 'unusually large' but 'quite in scale with the apartment'.

Above. **The Great Hall – south window.** A fine three-light window, originally transomed.

Right. **The Great Hall – south window.** Seen from within the hall, casting its light.

The Great Hall – oriel windows. During the attacks by the earl of Caithness in 1614 the cannon *Thrawn Mouth* was positioned to fire on the massive oriel windows of the Great Hall but, before she could go into action, young Robert Stewart surrendered the house.

Patrick's 'New Wark' – corbelled turrets. This is an example of a decorative device special to the Northern Isles at this period, corbels interspersed with imitation shot-holes supporting their corner turrets. Characteristic of Andrew Crawford's practice, such corbels are also found at the castles of Muness and Scalloway.

Muness Castle: one of the turrets.

Scalloway Castle: one of the turrets.

Patrick's 'New Wark' – doorway. An elaborate structure, lending emphasis to Earl Patrick's lineage and pretensions.

Scalloway Castle – entrance. Only slightly less grand than Kirkwall, the only overtly practical element in both being the positioning of an impressively decorated doorway in a traditionally defensive position in the building.

Above left. **Scalloway Castle – stairway.** Having approached the castle from the seaward side on the East Voe of Scalloway, the suitor of court was led through the grand doorway and up an ample staircase, not a turnpike, into the Great Hall. Defensive capabilities are sacrificed in favour of intimidating grandeur.

Above right. **Scalloway Castle.** Looking down into the Great Hall. The floors have gone, but the outer walls are intact to the heads, and give some clue to the scale of the building as it was.

Left. **Scalloway Castle.** View from the south-west, not far from the modern approach from Castle Road, which passes to the rear of the building as originally planned.

Right. **Tombstone of Andrew Crawford:** 'an artist of the first rank, with a scholarly and sensitive acquaintance and understanding of contemporary design'. The stone has now parted company with the original grave, but Crawford's memory is still preserved here, in the grounds of the kirk of Tingwall.

Below. **Bu of Corse.** View from St Magnus Cathedral. Corse can be seen in the distance, just below and to the left of Braehead, the farm on the crest of the hill.

St Magnus Cathedral from the Bu of Corse. This shows why this earldom farm was such a good starting position for a campaign to take the town.

Bu of Corse. The farm of Corse today – close-up view.

The road from Carness to Kirkwall. 'At ten o'clock in the morning they brought ashore the smaller of the two guns, and laboriously dragged it through deep soil the two miles to Weyland, about three quarters of a mile north-east of Kirkwall Castle.'

St Magnus Cathedral from Weyland. The first positioning point for the earl of Caithness's artillery to fire on cathedral and castle. Early successful hits were not repeated, and eventually the guns were moved into the town.

the prectikis usit in the lyk causses of befoir'. This debate paralleled that concerning Bruce's right to seek justice in the south, as well as his earlier criticism of Wardlaw's assizemen as bumpkins. In the end Sinclair of Brow faced a local trial on 23 August 1602 before John Dishington and an assize of 34 men of Shetland, including Mouat of Heogaland (chancellor of Henry Wardlaw's second assize) and Cheyne of Vaila. This assembly, after 'lang and mature deliberatioun, be the inspectioun of the chepturis of the law buik and *parteikis* [legal precedent] of the contrie in sic caices', found the charges proved. Sinclair of Campston, supported by Edward Scollay of Strynie, demanded the death penalty, but Brow was sentenced only to escheat and banishment under pain of death. In a sardonic response to his claims to rank, execution in the case of his return was to be by beheading rather than the hanging employed or threatened with humbler persons.[108]

In exile, Brow was not slow to complain. In February 1603 he told the session that the whole case against him had been concocted by the earl as justification for confiscating his estates. Patrick had attempted several times before to use the law against him in this way, but his confident willingness to stand trial had meant that 'the . . . erle wes frustrat of wrangous and evill intentioun'.[109] The lords suspended the sentence against him, and he returned to the north. Patrick continued to bring pressure to bear,[110] and in September 1605 Brow granted him an obligation for £1,000, using his estates as security.[111] Patrick nevertheless confiscated them. In January 1607 Sinclair complained to the privy council,[112] and soon after the earl was forced into arbitration. Lord Ochiltree, Lord Blantyre, the bishop of Ross and George Sinclair of Mey decided between them that in return for payment of the £1,000, Sinclair of Brow's lands should be returned to him.[113] It is clear that behind all these goings-on was the fact that Sinclair of Brow genuinely owed Patrick money, but that this was used as justification for extorting greater penalties.

Behind this too were other affairs, the political ramifications of which are complicated and obscure, in particular the squabbles between Bruce and Sinclair. There is one major contemporary account of these. This states that on the death of William Sinclair of Underhoull, father of Francis and Robert Sinclair, their stepfather William Bruce of Symbister 'sat downe' in his lands, 'and pat all the bairnes to the doore and would acknowledge none of them'. The young men therefore 'fell in evill companie and became airt and pairt of slaughter, and sua unlegall, which was a thing . . . William Bruce most desyred'.[114] Bruce of Cultmalindie as sheriff depute then confiscated such lands of Francis and Robert as were not controlled by William Bruce and gave them to his own son Andrew. Francis and Robert complained to

108 *Ct Bk of Shetland*, 42–3.
109 Court of Session Recs: Acts and Decreets, NRS CS7/207, ff. 99v–100r.
110 Court of Session Recs: Reg. Cauts in Susps, NRS CS290/29.
111 Reg. Deeds, NRS RD1/118, ff. 211r–12r.
112 *RPC*, xiv, 599.
113 Reg. Deeds, NRS RD1/131, ff. 61v–5r.
114 Shetland Sh. Ct Recs, SA SC12/65/3.

Patrick. This is very much a Sinclair account of events; it takes the form of a legal memorandum, written quarter of a century later for James Sinclair of Scalloway who was still pursuing the matter with Andrew Bruce. It is significant that it makes no reference to Sinclair of Brow, and more or less admits that Francis and Robert Sinclair were the killers of cousin Matthew, even though it is unspecific about the 'slaughter', and mentions the actions of the 'young men' in a spirit of exculpation. The central role assigned to Bruce of Cultmalindie is also important. Although by the time of the murder Bruce had long ceased to be sheriff depute, he did have interests in the Uyea Sinclairs' lands.[115]

Francis Sinclair of Uyea and Robert Sinclair of Ramnageo did become dependers of Patrick, though this was not simply due to a desire for support against Bruce of Symbister. In October 1603 they actually concluded a contract with Bruce,[116] and Francis Sinclair granted him a charter of his lands in Uyea.[117] It seems that Bruce received these lands, not by 'sitting down' in them, nor through legal penalties against Francis Sinclair as a murderer, but through the financial difficulties of Francis himself, a notorious wastrel, who was 3,000 merks in debt as a result of earlier indiscretions in Edinburgh.[118] Patrick sought the support of the Uyea Sinclairs as part of his own struggle with the Bruces for power over the whole Sinclair family in Shetland, following the death of the last's most important representative, Hugh Sinclair of Brough, in December 1602. It must have been clear for many months before he died that Hugh Sinclair's days were numbered. Between January 1601 and the end of the following year, within days of his passing, he acquired no fewer than 15 grants of udal lands, representing 25 or so separate lots.[119] These were divided among his two families of sons, to whom both Patrick and the Bruces were quick to offer support. The earl prevailed upon Robert Sinclair of Brough, son of his father's first marriage to Patrick's own illegitimate half-sister Grizel and newly come of age, to accept his counsel and that of Edward Sinclair of Marrister, as his uncles.[120] On the other side Andrew Bruce became tutor to Robert Sinclair's half-brothers, acting in concert with their mother, his sister Jean.

Patrick's new relationship with Robert Sinclair of Brough enabled him to further his policy of creating dependants among members of the family. Young Brough's affairs, it was said, had suffered during his minority by the assigning to his half-brothers of debts to his father that he would otherwise have inherited, among them the 3,000 merks owed by Francis Sinclair. Patrick acquired this liability, among a

115 Reg. Deeds, NRS RD1/107, ff. 143r–4v.

116 Reg. Deeds (Min. Bk ref. only – NRS RD.6/l/1).

117 *Shetland News*, 27 Jan. 1894 ('Notes and Queries', no. 67); Reg. Deeds, NRS RD1/1 13, ff. 84r–7r.

118 Reg. Hornings Edin., NRS DI47/14, ff. 313v–17r; DI47/17, ff. 11r–12v; Reg. Deeds, NRS RD1/99, f. 172r and v; RD1/lo4, f. 443v–4r; RD.1/108, ff. 187r–8r; RD.1/113, f. 84r–7r; RD1/166, f. 257r and v; RD1/271, ff. 73r–5v; *RSS*, NRS PS1/74, f. 8v.

119 *Shetland Documents 1580–1611*, 136, nos 305, 307, etc.

120 *Ct Bk of Shetland*, 154–5; Reg. Deeds, NRS RD1/94, ff. 149r–51v; *RSS*, NRS PS1/71, f. 163r and v.

number of other debts among members of the family.[121] On 22 August 1604 young Sinclair of Brough, represented in Patrick's court by Andrew Martin, complained about the actions of his stepmother, Jean Bruce. She, backed by her brother Andrew, who had been appointed tutor to her children, had set herself up as their representative. This enabled her to lay hands upon the interest on the debts assigned to them. She and Andrew had been forced into desperate measures in drawing up the bond that gave her authority. Its witnesses, who included Sinclair of Aith and Hugh Sinclair's brothers Oliver and Edward, were said never to have seen the document actually sealed. In court it was found that the signature of William Bruce as a witness was a forgery, executed by Jean and Andrew's illegitimate brother, Scipio.[122]

Bruce of Symbister denied all knowledge of the bond. He was unwilling to assist his Cultmalindie cousins in their activities, either at the concocting of the bond in January 1603 or at its exposure in court late the following year. This was because he had his own battles to fight with my lord. In March 1592 Patrick had granted him a charter of 20 merks of kingsland in Sumburgh.[123] The earl retained the house he had built there and its adjacent parks, which were to be maintained by Bruce in his absence. This arrangement lasted for 12 years, until 5 August 1604, when he and the earl concluded a contract whereby Bruce returned the Sumburgh lands, and others in Underhoull in Unst (originally belonging to Francis and Robert Sinclair's father) in exchange for estates in Sandwick.[124] The agreement was forced on Bruce, Patrick's probable intention being to redevelop the site at Sumburgh as another focus of his power in Shetland.

Less than a year later, in November 1605, the arrangement was rescinded. The reasons given were the 'little profit' that Patrick had gained by the transaction and the 'spetiall requist desyre and mediatioun' of Sir John Arnot of Barswick.[125] In fact it coincided with the efforts of Arnot and others to persuade Patrick to behave in a more reasonable manner. These efforts had no greater success in respect of Bruce than in other areas of the earl's activities. Two and a half years later, in June and July 1608 Patrick and his followers invaded Sumburgh. They stripped the lands of their livestock and crop, removed the entire contents of Bruce's house and built a high wall round the lands close to that of the earl.[126] According to Bruce, those responsible were Francis Sinclair of Uyea, Robert Sinclair of Ramnageo, Adam Sinclair of Brow, James Sinclair of Gott, Laurence Sinclair of Houss and Laurence Sinclair of Ustaness. This list is identical to that of the alleged murderers and accomplices in the death of Matthew Sinclair, even to being in the same order as they were named

121 Reg. Deeds, NRS RD1/107, ff. 144v–52r.
122 Ct Bk of Shetland, 147–51.
123 Reg. Deeds, NRS RD1/38, ff. 412v–14v.
124 Reg. Deeds, NRS RD1/107, ff. 143r–4v; O & S Papers, NRS RH9/15/79.
125 Reg. Deeds, NRS RD1/113, ff. 132r–8r; RMS, vi, no. 1679; see also Diary of the Rev. John Mill, Minister in Shetland 1740–1803, ed. G. Goudie (SHS), Edinburgh, 1889, 190–4.
126 Court of Session Recs: Acts and Decreets, NRS CS7/238, ff. 307r–11r.

in the court book.[127] Later the list was cut to three – Uyea, Ramnageo and Brow[128] – the three centrally involved in the murder.

The death of Matthew Sinclair seems to have been a family matter, perhaps a quarrel between the Orkney and Shetland branches; the darkness surrounding it suggests personal rather than wider political differences. Its significance lies in how Patrick used it to make clients of Francis and Robert Sinclair (who were never prosecuted for the crime), and enlist their animosity against Bruce of Symbister in pursuing his own ends; and in how he cited the murder as cause for discomfiting Sinclair of Brow, with whom he had a quite separate dispute. Bruce of Symbister's complaint against Patrick joined the others before the session until July 1609 when, with Sir John Arnot and Lord Gray as his cautioners, the earl came to an agreement.[129] By that time, however, Patrick's affairs were deep in crisis.

That crisis, seemingly so long in coming, was not, though, the result of a sudden crackdown by the government. Long before Patrick's fall, there had been evidence of increasing impatience with him. It is now necessary to examine this, forming as it does the wider background to his interminable squabbles in the islands.

127 *Ct Bk of Shetland*, 38; in fact Sinclair of Brow does not appear personally in the original indictment, but the servant who represents him appears in the same place in the order of accused as Sinclair himself does in Bruce's complaint.
128 Court of Session Recs: Acts and Decreets, NRS CS7/238, ff. 307r–11r.
129 Reg. Deeds, NRS RD1/176, ff. 10v–12r.

12

Proud and Heich Dissobedience

On 26 March 1603, two days after the death of Elizabeth of England, King James was informed of his succession to her throne;[1] one week later he was on the road to his new kingdom. With him on his triumphal procession went John Stewart, master of Orkney.[2] Queen Anne was left behind. The original timetable for her progress to England would have seen her leave Scotland on 1 May. This was interrupted, ostensibly so that her children could be made ready for the journey, but in fact because she had taken the opportunity of the king's absence to agitate once more over the custody of Prince Henry, who was to go south separately. Again Patrick was involved. On 7 May Anne set off for Stirling. She visited her daughter in Linlithgow, then was escorted by Thomas Hamilton the king's advocate and Lord Fyvie the lord president as far as Avon Brig.[3] There she was committed to the protection of Lord Orkney and a few servants.

In the council four days later, the earl of Mar complained that the queen's party had conferred together at Patrick's house in Edinburgh and concocted a letter to the king in which they had 'dealt for delivery of the prince'.[4] While Patrick was with the pregnant queen at Stirling, her fury at the continual thwarting of her wishes probably led to her having a miscarriage. The day after the council meeting at which Mar raised the issue, 12 May, she requested Patrick to go and put her case to the king. Within a few days he was on the road to England, leaving behind him his many disputes. He arrived in London in early June, accompanied by his brother Robert, other advisers including John Arnot, and four footmen, two pages and a trumpeter, splendidly arrayed in yellow worsted and red satin.[5] Unfortunately, he was preceded into the king's presence by the earl of Mar's son who gave his father's account of events and was greatly praised for having attended to the royal wishes. When Patrick entered to give the queen's version, he was received with undisguised distaste. The Venetian ambassador, who spoke of the meeting, believed that the queen, though

1 Willson, *James VI and I*, 159.
2 *Salisbury Papers*, xv, 41.
3 *Sic* – geography suggests that this is not the modern village of Avonbridge, but that of Linlithgow Bridge, to the west of Linlithgow.
4 W. Fraser, *Memorials of the Earls of Haddington*, vols I–II, privately printed, Edinburgh, 1889, ii, 209–13.
5 O & S Papers, NRS RH9/15/108.

indeed very ill, was exaggerating in order to win the king's sympathy.[6] In the end she did succeed in this, and James allowed her to take Prince Henry with her when she came south,[7] but Patrick did not profit from the episode as he might have wished. The earl of Orkney's stay in England was short and unsuccessful. Though he spent most of his time at the court, there was no sign of royal interest in his activities beyond the one frosty meeting. The only seeming mark of favour, a grant of land in the Isle of Man to John Sorlett, described as one of Patrick's servants, seems more than a reward for a royal retainer deputed to attend the earl of Orkney during his stay at court.[8] The king no longer showed any personal regard for Patrick; from now on any concessions by James to the earl were prompted only by embarrassment at his increasingly humiliating predicament. Moreover the king's departure for England had changed the situation irretrievably. Far from Edinburgh, he was acquiring a wholly different perspective on Scottish affairs, and Patrick's personal influence, already in decline, was even less of an asset. In future he had to rely on the influence of his brother John and other sympathetic relatives.

The clouds were beginning to gather ominously over him. His journey to England had been preceded by the first united complaint against him for many years, and even in the course of the trip his problems pursued him. Robert Monteith's letters of horning were executed against him twice – at Windsor on 11 July and at Hampton Court eight days later.[9] On his return, he went straight to Birsay, avoiding his pursuers in Edinburgh. On 19 September, he wrote to his brother-in-law, Lord Elphinstone, seeking assistance 'Giff . . . my *fasheous* [troublesome] effairis sall happin to inoportune your lordschip . . . I pray your lordschip to have patience, and sie thame advanced . . . as I sal be willing to tak the lyk or grittar panes for your lordschip, quhen it sall pleis your lordschip imploye me.'[10] During the next year, he made strenuous attempts to raise cash, particularly in Shetland. They brought little return; in December John Arnot wrote to him about the lack of money gathered due, it was said, to the fact that the 'Duchemen ['Dutchmen', i.e. merchants from northern Europe, modern Germany, the Netherlands and Belgium] come nocht weill provydit'. Alexander Bruce the chamberlain had been sent back with them to ensure provision of the money that they had promised. He was very anxious that this promise be kept because Patrick's legal struggles ('wairris') were 'lyk to be wers and wers in this cuntrie'.[11]

During 1605, as the session cases of Monteith and Bruce moved into a critical stage, the co-ordination of their opposition to Patrick, first noted in 1603, became more marked. Moreover Patrick was being pursued, not only by most of the individuals of any consequence in the Northern Isles, but by others known and well regarded

6   *CSP Venetian* (1603–7), 43, no. 69.
7   Willson, *James VI and I*, 165.
8   *Salisbury Papers*, xvi, 110.
9   Diligence Recs: GR Hornings Edin., NRS DI47/20/94.
10 Fraser, *Elphinstone Family Book*, ii, 168.
11 O & S Papers, NRS RH9/15/107/4.

by the king. From March 1605 until his death in 1608, Thomas Craig, author of the 'Treatise on the Union of the Kingdoms of Britain' (*De Unione Regnorum Britanniae Tractatus*) and a Bellenden connection, sued Patrick for his pension from the thirds of the Orkney bishopric, awarded for his work as counsel to the kirk.[12] In 1606 Craig was joined by Thomas Henryson, for the same reason.[13] Patrick was in dispute with the son of David McGill of Cranstounriddell, a former lord of session, over the ownership of a silver basin and *laver* worth £420.[14] His own servants too were owed large amounts of arrears. In January 1605 James Annand took out a personal loan of 400 merks from Arnot to pay his expenses in Patrick's service;[15] later he was to pursue the earl for £5,800-worth of such sums, to say nothing of £1,300 of unpaid wages.[16] Even Annand was relatively lucky; John Livingston of Baldorran, who had accompanied Annand and his master to England, was to sue for 11,000 merks, with 10 per cent interest.[17]

But Patrick's greatest creditor was undoubtedly Sir John Arnot. The king had almost certainly placed Arnot at Patrick's side as a financial adviser. A prominent merchant, twice lord provost of Edinburgh (the second time as the king's personal choice), member of a number of royal commissions, a collector of taxes and an energetic depute to Treasurer Dunbar, he was in an ideal position to take his strong and at times almost avuncular interest in the earl's affairs.[18] It is the forbidding complexity of these, and the unremitting effort of coping with them, evident from his letters, that earns Arnot some measure of our sympathy. Although he ultimately gained complete financial control of the Orkney and Shetland estates, he does not appear to have been a grasping financier seeking to draw Patrick into his clutches. About 1597 he was counselling the earl on foreign currency investment, when he had abruptly to withdraw the advice in view of legislation that all foreign currency be 'cryit doun' and brought into the mint.[19] He himself was among those appointed to draw up the tables of exchange.[20]

He had begun to acquire interests in Patrick's estates in the late 1590s, about the time of the first attempt to force Patrick to put his affairs in order. In October 1599 he is found acting for the widow of John Dick, an Edinburgh merchant who had long served the interests of both Stewart earls, and who had died in 1596 in possession of

12 Court of Session Recs: Acts and Decreets, NRS CS7/211, ff. 287v–8r.
13 Court of Session Recs: Acts and Decreets, NRS CS7/243, ff. 296r–7r.
14 Court of Session Recs: Acts and Decreets, NRS CS7/217, ff. 217v–18r, 296v–7r.
15 O & S Papers, NRS RH9/15/112.
16 Court of Session Recs: Acts and Decreets, NRS CS7/275, f. 253r and v; CS7/290, ff. 42r–3r.
17 Court of Session Recs: Acts and Decreets, NRS CS7/232, f. 256v.
18 *Extr. Recs Edin., 1589–1603*, 6–47; *1604–1626*, 47–13; J. B. Craven, *Sir John Arnot of Barswick and the Family of Arnot in South Ronaldsay*, Kirkwall, 1913; *Church Life in South Ronaldshay and Burray in the Seventeenth Century*, Kirkwall, 1911, 12; a chapter on the life of Sir John Arnot is to be found in J. Arnott, *The House of Arnot, and some of its Branches: a Family History*, Edinburgh, 1918, 62–87.
19 O & S Papers, NRS RH9/15/107/3.
20 *RPC*, v, 483.

Patrick's bond for 39,000 merks.[21] It is likely that he had acquired the lady's interest for himself, perhaps as a means of consolidating the earl's debts. Arnot also acted on Patrick's behalf in his dealings with his mother, settled his debts with the merchants Andrew Bauchop, William Fowler and John Jackson, and tackled those of Janet Fockhart's heirs and of Gilbert Primrose, the royal surgeon to whom Patrick owed 11,000 merks.[22] In payment, he acquired rights to the duties of the vicarage of Yell and Fetlar, contested Patrick Bellenden's longstanding claims to the subdeanery of Orkney on his own account, and acquired a feu from Bannatyne of Gairsay of lands in Evie, Rousay and Fair Isle.[23] He also sought, for 1,000 merks, to secure for Andrew Umphray of Berrie infeftment in the kingsland in Fair Isle against the competing claims of Robert Monteith.[24] About mid-1606 he began to be known as 'of Barswick', from the 6d land of that name in South Ronaldsay, chief property of the provostry of Orkney, which he acquired from Bannatyne of Gairsay as security for a loan of 3,000 merks. He took the provostry lands over permanently two years later, in September 1608.[25]

Arnot's control over Patrick himself was limited, and despite his attempts at financial management, the earl's liabilities had risen by July 1601 – during his major period of building – to just short of 80,000 merks. Two years later, in July 1603 during his visit to England, he granted Arnot a further bond for no less than 73,700 merks.[26] Patrick would have been hard put to it simply to pay the interest on such sums. In July 1606 he granted Arnot virtually his whole estates in Orkney – the 'lands and isles' of Birsay, Sandwick, Hoy, Walls, South Ronaldsay, Shapinsay, Deerness, Sanday, Stronsay, Egilsay, Rousay and North Ronaldsay, all under the colossal reversion of 200,000 merks.[27] This was followed in November 1607 by another bond for more than 77,000 merks. Of this 21,000 merks was for Arnot's buying out of Balfour of Montquhany's interest in Westray and Papa Westray, the whole to be paid for by a grant to Arnot of the oil and butter dues of Shetland.[28] In July 1608 he received Patrick's escheat at the instance of Monteith of Egilsay. This was queried unsuccessfully before the session by Patrick and his counsel in January 1609,[29] but one year later Patrick granted Arnot yet another bond for 40,000 merks. There was no possibility of Patrick repaying such a sum, yet the penalty for non-payment was heavy indeed – £4,000 annually together with 10 per cent of the principal, a further 4,000 merks. Patrick also owed interest on other loans and had to grant Arnot a further bond in September 1610 for over 20,000 merks and another a year later for

21 Edin. Comm. Ct Recs: Reg. Tests, NRS CC8/8/31, ff. 61v–3r; Session Processes, NRS CS15/102.
22 O & S Papers, NRS RH9/15/107/3.
23 Court of Session Recs: Acts and Decreets, NRS CS7/195, f. 357r.
24 Reg. Deeds, NRS RD1/107, f. 150r–1r.
25 Deeds Warrants, NRS RD1/162, no. 509.
26 O & S Papers, NRS RH9/15/108.
27 APS, iv, 320.
28 Reg. Deeds, NRS RD1/139, ff. 441r–2v.
29 RSS, NRS PS1/77, f. 67v; Court of Session Recs: Acts and Decreets, NRS CS7/240, ff. 69v–71r.

more than £23,000.[30]

It will never be possible to work out finally the total sum of Patrick's liabilities. We cannot always be sure that the records of his debts are comprehensive,
or whether the sum contained in any given obligation includes others previously
owed or is in addition to them. On the other hand, it seems unlikely that there are
any other major creditors of which we have no record, and several of the obligations to Arnot specify that the sum owed is in addition to previous ones. There is
doubt as to just how much was owed to some creditors; Monteith pursued Patrick
during his lifetime for 7,300 merks, but in 1621, six years after Patrick's death, he
was alleging a total liability of £40,000.[31] On the whole, it is clear that by the end,
Patrick owed in excess of a quarter of a million merks. He was indeed, in the words
of the author of *The Historie of King James the Sext*, 'drownit in debt'. Where had all
the money gone? Besides the loss of a large chunk of his fortune at the hands of
Capt. Gwynn, there were meeting inherited liabilities; building a strong castle and
a palace, sumptuous at least by Scottish standards; refurbishing the cathedral and
building a new house at Sumburgh; trying to mop up by purchase estates in the
Northern Isles outwith his control; maintaining a splendid suite, at home in the
north as well as in Edinburgh and London; adventures such as the pursuit of the
hand of the princess of the Netherlands; incurring numerous fines at the hands of
the crown for ill-treatment of individuals, compounded by penalties for ignoring
the decisions against him; and soaring interest on the lot.

As his fortunes spiralled inexorably downwards Patrick, though clearly conscious
of the danger of his position, showed little grasp of reality. In 1608, during his last
long stay in the Northern Isles, there was another determined pursuit of udal lands.
This may have added to his reputation for rapacious land-grabbing but, set beside
his monumental liabilities, it can only be seen as panic-stricken and pathetic. What
possible use to him were the pennyland in Deerness belonging to the sisters of
Alexander Peterson;[32] the quoy in Sanday of Iweir Turbesoun;[33] James Burgar's
farthing lands in Sanday?[34] In Shetland his gains were no greater: five merks in
Whalsay from Ola Uriounsone in Bergen, and in North Yell from Marion Fraser,
and a tiny half-merk in the hands of Marion Erasmusdochter, also in Whalsay – all
bought up on the same day and formally received two days later.[35]

At that time he also sought to curry favour in London, not with the king, whose
sympathy he had long since squandered, but with his son, the gilded youth Prince
Henry. On 20 August he wrote from Kirkwall seeking 'tua lynis of your heines
hand quhilk wad be verie confortabill to me in respect of my far distance from your

30 Reg. Deeds, NRS RD1/170, f. 208r and v; RD1/177, f. 302r and v; RD1/203, f. 21r and v.
31 *State Papers of Melros*, ii, 439–40.
32 O & S Papers, NRS RH9/15/10.
33 O & S Papers, NRS RH9/15/43.
34 O & S Papers, NRS RH9/15/32.
35 *Shetland Documents 1580–1611*, 215, 451, 453–5.

heines, bot sall nocht be far distant quhen it sall pleis your heines to command my humbill and obedient service . . .'[36] In October the following year, 1609, by then in ward, he wrote again, saying that he had intended to send the prince two Shetland ponies, but they had become 'lame and crookit' in the passage to Edinburgh. He would, however, provide two more the following year. He asked Henry to inter-cede on his behalf with the treasurer, the earl of Dunbar, who he felt was 'the man that may do me maist plesour', pleading 'your heines to be eirnist with him quhat wrangis I sustein.'[37] None of this was of any avail whatever.

It was not Patrick's debts alone that were disturbing the council and angering the king. Much graver was his refusal to obey the courts. In April 1605 Arnot wrote, 'It grieves me very meikle and piercis my Hairt to hear your Lordships name bladit out at the market croice as it is'; even as he was writing Patrick was being charged at the instance of William Sinclair of Eday. 'I am feirit that it sall move his Majestie to extreme anger against your Lordship for his Highness is of another kind of Disposition nor he had been in Scotland quhen he was heir.'[38] All Patrick's friends were by then extremely worried. John Stewart in particular was active on his broth-er's part as an intermediary with the council. His behaviour contrasts strongly with the dark doings of ten years before, but he had a motive. Patrick had now been married for nearly a decade with no sign of an heir. John, already heir presumptive and since 1607 ennobled as Lord Kinclaven,[39] looked increasingly likely to succeed to the earldom.

With the master of Gray, he managed to stave off the grant of a council commis-sion to Patrick's adversaries to apprehend him as a rebel. The last had acquired a Flemish ship of 120 tons, and the two men planned to outfit a vessel of their own, declaring that they would suffer death rather than Patrick's dishonour. Stewart's next aim was to prevent his brother's opponents bypassing an indecisive council and approaching the king. He wrote from Scotland to Lord Salisbury in July 1605 in an attempt to head them off.[40] His letter has about it an unconscious irony; direct approaches to the king were 'a matter for the precedent to be eschewed. For if every man shall have recourse to his Majesty, not being contented with the censure of Council, seldom shall his Majesty have ease'. It was Patrick who was to miss most the ear of the king. Stewart also engaged Lady Elizabeth Stewart to forward a letter

36 Shand of Broughty Ferry Scrapbooks, SA ref. D.1/135/2, 178; newspaper containing transcription of BL Harleian Mss 7007, f. 308.

37 BL Harleian Mss. 7007, f. 204.

38 J. Wallace, *A Description of the Isles of Orkney*, Edinburgh, 1883, 237; *Notes on Orkney and Zetland*, ed. A. Peterkin, Edinburgh, 1822, app. 58–9. Arnot actually lived within sight of the mercat cross (he had entertained various dignitaries to the viewing of an execution there (*RPC*, viii, 476) and what he was saying may have been literally true, the denunciation ringing in his ears as he wrote. The Grassmarket, more usually associated with executions in Edinburgh, did not become the normal venue until later in the seventeenth century (*Old and New Edinburgh*, ii, 231).

39 *Scots Peerage*, ii, 441.

40 *Salisbury Papers*, xvii, 338.

to Salisbury, hoping that he would 'pacify the King in his anger' till Stewart himself returned south.[41] Salisbury replied to a similar approach from an unnamed Scottish lord, probably the master of Gray, with some suave pieties about the impropriety of interfering in essentially Scottish matters.[42]

On 2 August 1605 the council wrote to the king complaining that Patrick, 'continewis dissobedyent, without ony intentioun, as appeiris to us, to conform him selff to law and reasoun'.[43] Justifying their refusal of personal authority to pursue him, they made no reference to Gray and Kinclaven, but said that it was felt a bad precedent to allow one party to a dispute to take the law into his own hands. Perhaps the king's personal intervention might move him to obedience. Patrick himself was not unaware of the grave trouble he was in, but the solution that he proposed to Arnot – that of going south to meet directly with the king – was not the answer. Arnot's opinion was 'that your lordschip be nocht haistie to that jornay'.[44] Instead he prevailed upon the earl to make concessions. In October 1605 Patrick came south, secured relaxations of the hornings at the hands of Bruce, Monteith and others,[45] and offered fresh sureties, not only to Bruce and Monteith, but to a host of others such as Andrew Bruce, Umphray of Berrie, Balfour of Montquhany, Lord Lindores and Margaret Bonar and her son.[46] He undertook to pay Monteith the money owed him in respect of Fairnie of that Ilk, and agreed to rescind the contract of August 1604 complained of by Bruce of Symbister.[47] Lord Linlithgow, Lord Ochiltree and Sir James Scrimgeour of Dudhope guaranteed that he would remain in southern Scotland, and Arnot that he would appear before the council. In return he received a protection of his person against his creditors[48] and, still a councillor himself, was able to add his subscription to a letter of 14 November from the council to the king.[49]

The summons of treason, however, referred to earlier, hung over his head. The charges it contained add further detail to what has been encountered elsewhere. Among those who suffered at Patrick's hands had been John Stewart, his brother, arrested for carrying a weapon; his illegitimate half-brother James, whose house was destroyed; and Bannatyne of Gairsay, who was banished. A messenger executing letters for Bannatyne was tortured in the caschielaws, this time described as Patrick's own invention. Thomas Paplay and William Stewart were those executed under the

41 *Salisbury Papers*, xvii, 643.

42 *Salisbury Papers*, xvii, xviii, 441.

43 Fraser, *Elphinstone Family Book*, ii, 151.

44 *RPC*, xiv, 420; the writer is given as Sir John Bruce, but verification of the original indicates clearly that this is a misreading of Arnot (Privy Council Papers, NRS PC10/14b, no. 200).

45 Diligence Recs: GR Hornings, NRS DI3/14, ff. 55r–64r.

46 Reg. Deeds, NRS RD1/112, ff. 350v–1r; Court of Session Recs: Reg. Cauts in Susps, NRS CS290/27; Court of Session Recs: Reg. Cauts in Lawbs, NRS CS295/2 (*bis*); *RPC*, vii, 617.

47 Diligence Recs: GR Hornings Edin., NRS DI47/14, ff. 271v–5r.

48 *RPC*, vii, 140, 616.

49 *Salisbury Papers*, xvii, 486.

law against plotting. The prohibition on appealing beyond Patrick's courts, noted in the Shetland court book, had been proclaimed in Orkney no fewer than three times – in 1595, 1598 and 1600. Patrick was said to have levied additional taxes to what was customary of 20,000 merks in 1594 and 1595, and of £20,000 in 1595 and 1596; these recall the sum of £24,000 that Bannatyne said he had been required to raise as chamberlain, and the dispute between the earl and Patrick Monteith, whom Bannatyne had succeeded at the end of 1594. The sum for 1596 was aimed specifically at building a great ship, presumably that named later as the *Rainbow* (*Randbow*), contracted for in April 1598.[50] The siege of Kirkwall Castle, mentioned nowhere else, suggests the confrontation between Patrick Bellenden's servants and those of his father in the last weeks of the latter's life, over control of the strong points of the earldom. The references to the caschielawis suggest that Patrick intro-duced it to the islands (he is hardly likely to have invented it) and that it was among the cruelties practised on opponents' representatives.

In the end the indictment came to nothing. On 9 August Patrick was relieved of his undertaking to remain in the south,[51] and on 19 November a warrant was obtained from the king to dismiss the summons of treason 'as the reasons contenit thairintill are altogidder false and frivolous'. This was ratified by parliament on 11 August the following year.[52] There had perhaps been some measure of exaggera-tion and inaccuracy in the charges. Patrick's commission, though uncommonly wide-ranging, was never challenged elsewhere in point of authenticity. If Patrick did earmark the £20,000 of 1596 for construction of the *Rainbow*, he paid only 8,800 merks for the ship itself. And the peculiar position of the earl under the Norse laws of the islands meant that the legality of Patrick's enactments was difficult to deter-mine with certainty. But there were other more important reasons for the rehabili-tation of Patrick than the shortcomings of the complaints against him. The king had decided to incorporate settlement of the situation in the Northern Isles as part of something of much more general importance – his plans for church government, in particular the reintroduction of episcopacy.

In February 1605 James Law, minister of Kirkliston, was provided to the bishopric of Orkney.[53] Law was one of the three most important figures of the Scottish pro-episcopal party, the others being Archbishops Spottiswoode of Glasgow and Gledstanes of St Andrews. He was a man of outstanding ability; even Wodrow, the ecclesiastical historian, no admirer of his politics, acknowledged as much, believing him to be second only to Spottiswoode in managing 'the turn of affairs'.[54] Spottis-woode was a longstanding friend with whom, in their early ministry, Law had been rebuked by the synod of Lothian for playing football on the Sabbath. This was

50 Reg. Deeds, NRS RD1/68, ff. 367v–8r.
51 *RPC*, vii, 617.
52 *APS*, iv, 396.
53 Church Recs: Reg. Pres., NRS CH4/1/3, f. 98r.
54 Robert Wodrow's ms life of James Law, GUL Mss Gen. 1198, 1207.

perhaps a reflection of both men's unpuritanical attitude to church matters that also found expression in their views on church government. The king had made Spottiswoode his first archepiscopal appointment, even as he was journeying south to the English throne, on hearing of the death of the aged Catholic incumbent of Glasgow, James Beaton.[55] The choice of Orkney for Law's advancement was of particular significance. Although Adam Bothwell had styled himself bishop to the end of his life in 1593, the bishopric of Orkney had been spiritually a dead letter since the late 1560s. Since 1600 Patrick had been superior of the bishopric estates. The resurrection of the see as an independent entity promoted the king's ecclesiastical policy and introduced a strong presence into a turbulent area, as well as furthering the career of an able and favoured man. Promotion to Orkney was not exile; Law remained in constant touch with his royal master.

The king did what he could to smooth Law's path. Queen Anne resigned her long-standing claims upon the estates of the see.[56] Patrick was ordered to pay Law the teinds for 1605.[57] The bishop had to pursue Patrick before the session for his Shetland dues,[58] but in September 1606 the king summoned the earl to Hampton Court. At the conference there the king laid his proposal for the restoration of bishops before eight leading members of the Scottish clergy, among them the strongest opponents of his intentions.[59] Patrick witnessed the hot debate between the king and Andrew Melville, leader of the Presbyterians, and his companions, then remained in England during October and November while foundations were laid for the new arrangements. He had to pay a high price for the dropping of the treason charges. By his contract with Law, drawn up in January 1607 on the king's instructions, Patrick was obliged to pay the bishop 4,000 merks annually in maintenance, guaranteed by Sir John Arnot, and the stipends of the ministers of Orkney. Law became superior of all the bishopric property and income, excepting any previous grants by the earl or his predecessors. Perhaps the most symbolic of all the elements in this wing-clipping exercise concerned the bishop's residence; Patrick was to hand over to Law the 'New Wark with the Yeards' – in other words the whole Kirkwall palace complex, including his own magnificent creation.[60]

On 13 December 1606 Patrick was back in Scotland, attending the privy council.[61] Following the contract with Law, he faced less in the way of public opposition, but throughout 1607 Monteith and Bruce continued to gather evidence against him. The year 1608 was critical, in this as in other aspects of his affairs. As preparations were being made for the hearing of Bruce's case, that of Monteith reached a climax. Full and detailed decrees were pronounced against both Patrick himself and Sir

55 Willson, *King James VI and I*, 314.
56 *RMS*, vi, no. 1572; *Rentals*, app., 87–8.
57 Court of Session Recs: Acts and Decreets, NRS CS7/218, f. 152r–3r.
58 Session Processes, NRS CS15, box 92.
59 *Letters on the Ecclesiastical Affairs of Scotland*, vols I–II (Bannatyne Club), 1841, i, 60.
60 Reg. Deeds, NRS RD1/129, ff. 122r–5v; O & S Papers, NRS RH9/15/113.
61 *Letters on the Ecclesiastical Affairs of Scotland*, i, 71.

Robert Crichton of Cluny, his guarantor in the Lindores contract of 1591.[62] Patrick again paid no attention, but this time things were different. Monteith and his representatives, impatient at the lack of action on the part of the council, did what John Stewart had feared in 1605. They made their way in person to the king, seeking the commission to apprehend the earl that they had previously been denied. On 16 September 1608 King James wrote to his council in Scotland that Monteith and other Orcadians had been 'most cruelly oppressed' by the earl, having been 'driven from their lands and possessions without order of law or justice'. Despite decrees against him and many approaches to the council, the complainers were 'hithertillis postponit, differrit, having no redres at all maid unto thame, bot forceit to leve in banishement frome their awne houssis for feir of incurring hasard of thair lyveis', denied redress either by royal authority or by personal commission. For this the king could 'not bot justlie blayme' the council; if it could not offer its support, he saw no reason why the complainers should not be granted the power to help themselves.[63]

The council replied on 1 November, conceding that Monteith and his companions were 'verie havelie distressit', but denying that they had received anything but justice. The problem lay in enforcement. As the king was aware, they had no forces to send to Orkney to bring Patrick to heel but the king's own guards, who could not be spared from royal duties. They were reluctant to grant a personal commission since the device was normally used only in criminal matters;[64] everything Bruce and Monteith had done so far had been in the civil courts. The council passed the matter back to the king, enclosing for his authorisation a draft commission to Andrew Bruce of Sandwick and Robert Monteith of Egilsay.[65]

James Law also wrote to the king. His florid epistolatory style was calculated to appeal to the king's love of learned allusion – one of his more recent efforts had been garnished with quotations from Seneca and Plato – as well as the taste for elaborate flattery, which had been fostered in James by English courtly practice.[66] The bishop's letter of 17 November eschewed classical texts, but expressed his meaning in characteristic terms. He presented:

> upon my kneis . . . my most humble and serious Supplicatioune in favouris of those distressed and oppressed people, that it will please your Maiestie now at last to be so touched with princelie pitie towards thame, that by your Maiesties greate wisdome and Royall power and autoritie, some comfort and reliefe may be provyded and procured unto thame. Alace, deare and dreade soveraigne! Trewlie it is to be pitied, that so many your Maiesties subjects ar so manifoldlie and grevouslie oppressed;

62 Diligence Recs: GR Hornings, NRS DI3/31 (19 Aug. 1609); Diligence Recs: GR Hornings Edin., NRS DI47/21, ff. 31r–8r.
63 *RPC*, viii, 529.
64 *RPC*, viii, 531; *State Papers of Melros*, 55.
65 *RPC*, viii, 775; the commission was presented to the council by Monteith himself.
66 Willson, *King James VI and I*, 168–74.

some by ejectioune and banischment from thair houses and native soile; otheris by contorting the lawis and extorting thair goodis, the most parte being so impoverisched, that some of thame nather darre nor may complane, bot in silent and forced patience grones under thair grevances, as hoples of help; others ar compelled, with greate trouble, danger and damnage to thair poore persones and estates, to seeke remedie be ordinarie justice, which when they have obtened, they must nevertheles, through proud contempt and lack of executioune, ather thus molest your Maiestie, as the only strenth and stay of thair hopes under God, or els be uttirlie disapointed and lose all.

He therefore prostrated himself at the king's feet

not in humble ambitioune nor in covered covetousness, intending and aiming be the correctioune of that Nobleman, to seeke the erectioune of my base estate and poore fortune, bot ones to acquyte myself of that dewtie whiche, as I think, God, my conscience, my calling, your Majesties favouris towardis me, and the fidelitie of my bounden service dois requyre at my hand. . .[67]

The king's reply to the council accepted that it was unusual for a commission based only on civil hornings to contain provision for 'leveying of men, beseiging of houssis, rasing of fyre, and dispensatioun with slaughter in the useing of it'. Nevertheless the 'miserie of the poor distressit people whose hard famiseing estate is worse than deathe . . . [was] to the grite scandale of oure kingdome and counsell'. The earl of Orkney's 'contemptuus rebellion', his refusal either to satisfy complainers or relax himself from the horn, 'can haif no better construction of us then that it is become of the natour of a criminall'. However James had 'ever bene unwilling to condemne ony pairtie unhard, and thairwith loath to cutt af a member quhair thair is ony hoip of recoverie thairof'. He therefore instructed the council to summon Patrick before them to explain himself and grant satisfaction. Should he not do so, then not only would the commission be granted, but the commissioners would be 'assisted with oure pouer and authoritie bothe by sea and land'[68]

This was on 6 December 1608. The date set for Patrick's appearance before the council was 2 March, giving roughly the usual 90 days' notice customary when summoning inhabitants of the Northern Isles; in fact Patrick received a postponement until the end of May, when he duly attended.[69] The circumstances of his coming south are not known. There are legends that suggest that Monteith and Andrew Bruce received their commission, went north well accompanied, penetrated Patrick's Scalloway stronghold and laid their own hands upon his person.[70] The fact

67 *Letters on the Ecclesiastical Affairs of Scotland*, i, 167–9; D. A. Laing, 'Decreit of Spuilzie . . ., *Archaeologia Scotica*, 1847, iv, 387–8; J. B. Craven, *A History of the Church in Orkney 1558–1662*, Kirkwall, 1897, 92–3.
68 *RPC*, viii, 541–2.
69 *RPC*, viii, 587.
70 A full examination of the legends – for that is what they are – regarding Patrick's apprehension and convoying south to meet justice can be found in *Black Patie*, ch. 1. This is still readily accessible in libraries, but space does not admit of their inclusion here.

that the king was now prepared actually to contemplate such a move might have fuelled the rumour that it actually took place. What we do know of events suggests rather that Patrick, at last aware of the strength of the king's feelings, had made his own way to Edinburgh to try to mend matters. For one thing he was not imprisoned immediately on coming south. For another, the first question at issue before the council did not concern Monteith and Bruce.

Patrick was not alone, but was accompanied by the earl of Caithness. The latter had also been summoned to answer complaints against him, but to begin with each complained of the other – Patrick about the humiliation of his men, Caithness of the murder of his. Both were required to find caution in £20,000 that they would remain in Edinburgh[71] – and in their 'ludgeingis', such was the ill-feeling between them.[72] At the hearing, on 31 May, the councillors discovered that behind their backs the two earls had reached an agreement under the influence of 'some noblemen, thair freindis'. The councillors were sceptical, and asked if there remained 'ony scruple or miscontentment in thair hairtis, the one aganis the uther'. They said not, acknowledging that, 'upoun sinister informatioun, without good ground or warrand, thay had rased thir complaintis and gone too far thairin, and that now thay could not prove the same'. They then embraced heartily and shook hands.[73] A month later the murder charges against Patrick's men were dropped.[74] According to Robert Gordon, in his Sutherland history, the earls had settled out of court 'least they should reveile too much of either's doeings'.[75]

One of Patrick's enemies had thus been silenced for the time being, but it made little difference to his situation. The council, anxious lest he evade them, went beyond the king's order that he merely undertake to stay in the south. On 4 July 1609 he was confined to Edinburgh Castle, and was never to know complete freedom again.[76] On 10 October he had to find further surety in 4,000 merks for a comprehensive catalogue of those he had made his enemies, headed by Monteith, the Bruces and Henry Wardlaw, and James Stewart of Graemsay. There was Sinclair of Eday and the Sinclairs of Campston, Tuquoy and others of the Orkney family; there were the Shetland Sinclairs of Quendale, Malcolm and his son James, Laurence Sinclair of Brough and William Sinclair of Ustaness, also another with related interests, Thomas Black of Strom. Francis Moodie of Breckness was there, William Bannatyne of Gairsay, James Fea of Clestrain, James Tulloch of Rothiesholme and Robert Henderson of Holland. Malcolm Groat, a longstanding servant of Patrick, was unexpectedly named, with his son William. There were the Shetland magnates Andrew Umphray of Berrie and Thomas Cheyne of Vaila.[77]

71 *RPC*, viii, 292, 322–3.
72 *RPC*, viii, 299, 587, 756.
73 *RPC*, viii, 294, 587.
74 *Criminal Trials*, iii, 54.
75 Gordon, *Genealogical History of the Earldom of Sutherland*, 258.
76 *RPC*, viii, 312–13.
77 Court of Session Recs: Reg. Cauts in Lawbs, NRS CS295/5 (regd 18 Oct. 1609).

Patrick, imprisoned, hopelessly insolvent, faced with litigation at every turn, seemed to have little alternative but to assent to any undertaking put to him. Yet his allies and advisers were still at work. Lord Gray wrote to Lord Salisbury (and through him to the king) stating that Patrick's committal had been 'through malice of his servants' and hoping that 'his oversight may be attributed rather to simplicity than to malice'.[78] He and Lord Blantyre, who together had probably been responsible for the agreement with Caithness, stood surety for Patrick on 18 July, when his ward in the castle was relaxed from a single chamber to the bounds of the castle walls.[79] The earl could also rely, to an extraordinary degree, on his servants, and he was to continue to do so right up to the end. At this point his men were led by his brother Master James, and included Edward Scollay and David King, sheriffs depute; Henry Black, captain of Kirkwall Castle; Thomas Sinclair; and James Crawford. During the summer of 1609, he sent directives to Edward Scollay regarding lands granted by him many years before to William Halcro of Aikers.[80] These were innocent enough, but it became increasingly clear that the earl's followers were doing more than keeping the administrative wheels turning.

In April 1610 complainers brought specific charges against Patrick's servants, in particular David King, an uncle of his lawyers, James and Alexander King. Not all the charges were recent, though they painted a familiar enough picture. James Stewart of Graemsay appeared personally for himself and his son Henry. 'Almost every day' for the past ten years, he said, his tenants and servants had been compelled by King to place horses and boats at the earl's disposal; if they refused he 'batonit thame with grite batonis'. Once, in 1602, Stewart's men had transported Robert Monteith, his brother-in-law, over to Caithness. On their return, they were captured by King, tied up and thrown into a boat, then taken to Kirkwall where they were kept in 'stokis and irnis . . . untill the blood burst furth at thair schynnis'. More recently King had challenged Henry Stewart to single combat and attacked the Moodie farms at Osmondwall.

It was the continuation of such action, in the absence of Patrick and in defiance of the council, that particularly exercised the king. Monteith and his followers were able to keep up their representations to James, who in turn pressurised the council into unwontedly decisive action. In October 1609 they ordered Patrick back to close confinement.[81] They were to summon his men before them, including his brother James, and appoint commissioners of the peace for Orkney and Shetland to whom Patrick was to surrender his strongholds.[82] On 16 December they were ordered to take speedy action to improve 'the present hard and miserable estate of these poore ones – unto whome delay of redres is no better than deathe itselff . . .'[83] In January

78 Vaila Papers, SA D10/9/1.
79 *CSP Domestic* (1603–1610), 526.
80 *RPC*, viii, 323, 702.
81 *RPC*, viii, 371.
82 *RPC*, viii, 603.
83 *RPC*, viii, 611.

1610 the king ordered a commission to James Law to go north to 'tak ordour for a goode reule . . . thair', both for church and civil government.[84] The council drew this up a month later,[85] but James continued to hound the councillors over their dilatoriness. In March he charged them to compel Patrick to obey his orders, on pain of 'hard and rigorous proceiding against him'.[86] Three weeks later they finally ordered Patrick to hand over all his houses – the castles of Kirkwall and of Scalloway, the palaces of the Yards and of Birsay, as well as the house of Walls, seized from the Moodies.[87] In May 1610 the king wrote again, anxious that the council ascertain Patrick's part in the continuing 'insolent ryottis' in the north, because 'we cannot bot heichlie be incensit thairat, since griter contempt of our authoritie than it is can not be committit'. Should they find justification for criminal prosecution, they should give appropriate orders to the advocate.[88] On 29 May he directed that no ships make their way to Orkney until order had been restored.[89]

So far, Patrick had shown little sign of contrition or compromise. On 9 November 1609 he appeared before the council and produced what one witness described as 'the most ampill commissioun of lieutenandrie and justiciarie, granted to him in *anno* 1591 or thairby, that evir I saw'.[90] This was an appropriate beginning to the council's investigations into the complaints against him, since it indicated his refusal to accept that he had done anything wrong or outwith his powers. The list of complaints itself, however, though wide-ranging and embodying most of the general discontents, was disappointingly unspecific and, as Patrick and his counsel were quick to point out, hardly the stuff on which to base a criminal prosecution.[91]

He provided rebuttals in a confident and peremptory tone. For example, the charge of compelling people to swear to reveal anything that 'may mak ane unlaw to the erle' on pain of forfeiture was so 'generall and inept that no probatioun can be led or deducit thereupone'. Who made the people swear? Was it the earl, or not? What exactly had they been forced to swear? What punishments were imposed for not swearing? Other allegations were similarly general in approach – 'The pure ones of the countrey ar forbidding to succour or releife any schipis distressit with stormes or tempestis'; the islanders were 'extraordinarily compellit in service without either meat, drink or any alowance therefor'; they 'might not pass freely over the ferries without passport'. Patrick's defences were comprehensive; there was no proof that these measures had been enacted, or enacted by him, or were illegal, either under the laws of the islands or his justiciary powers.

The vagueness in the drafting of many of the charges played into Patrick's

84 *RPC*, viii, 615.
85 *RPC*, viii, 406.
86 *RPC*, viii, 619.
87 *RPC*, viii, 444.
88 *RPC*, viii, 624.
89 *RPC*, viii, 469.
90 *RPC*, xiv, 612.
91 O & S Papers, NRS RH9/15/149a; *Notes*, ed. Peterkin, app., 77–82.

hands, but only in three cases did he use this as his main defence. He had allegedly compelled the islanders to agree a contract that granted him their whole fishing catch; no such contract had been found, he said, but if one were 'it sall be found verie guid of the law and lauchfull and profitabill for the inhabitants'. The charge that he ejected ministers from their glebes and confiscated their wool and teinds cited no examples and was in any case, he said, a civil matter. So was his reported withholding of the lands of Balliasta from their inhabitants. Against the other charges he was more positive, citing right, custom and the peculiar viciousness of the people. His exaction of a fat ox and 12 sheep from every parish was an 'auld accustumat deutie' paid in his father's time as well as his own. He and his father had both received duties from willing foreign merchants, as did all noblemen with maritime estates. His forfeiting and restoring of men's heritage 'as if he were a sovereign prince' was in accord with ancient custom in both Orkney and Shetland, as well as with his justiciary powers.

Patrick's contempt for the islanders and their way of life was manifest in several of his defences. Their 'evill inclinatioun and unhappie natour' made necessary the strict 'auld Dens lawis', which could impose forfeiture for trivial offences. Confiscating goods that were unmarked or wrongly marked was accepted practice, 'for the people being so accustomat to thifte ... thair wickit inclinatiounis movit to mak the ordinance that they suld mark ther awin geir and pretend no ignorance in taking of ther neichbouris geir'. Heavy fines imposed for consulting a warlock or 'abusar' called Nerogar were lawful, not only because witchcraft was wicked in itself, but also because, without prompt discouragement, it 'would have owergaine the heall Iyll and ... they wald all have becommit witchis and warlockis, for the people ar naturally inclynit thairto'. This comment was no doubt intended to echo James's own views on witchcraft. This he said was 'thought to be most common in such wide partes of the world as Lap-land and Fin-land, or in our North Iles of *Orknay*', these being the kind of places where 'the Devil findes greatest ignorance and barbarities'.[92]

Far from Patrick preventing relief of the shipwrecked, the truth was that when ships were driven ashore 'the people so miserably and unmercifully invaiddit the distressit persounes ther guids and geir that no knawledge culd be gottin thaireftir of ther particular intromissioun'. Because those guilty were the 'maist pure miserable and debochtit people', no redress could be obtained, and the earl had therefore enacted that no-one should 'presume to invade sic persones as war distressit be sie under precept of ther succour' without the regulation of the local bailie. The same disdain was expressed at the charge of preventing the islanders from pleading in courts outside Orkney or Shetland. Patrick admitted that he had passed such an

92 'Daemonologie', *King James VI and I, Selected Writings*, 190. The figure of Nerogar is a curious one. The name bears a superficial resemblance to a place name (perhaps a -garth name, cf. Nistigar (Ork.), Nornagarth (Shet.)), but the first element is unknown, and the use of a place-name and the lack of a forename are unusual.

act. He defended himself, first on the ground of his justiciary powers and secondly that he 'knawing the malitious nature of the people and that the moist substantious and potent usit that forme of oppressioun towardis the mene inhabitantis of the country that they raisit malitious and fals summondis befoir the lordis of sessioun'. This meant litigation, which was expensive in itself, and in the need to travel repeatedly to Edinburgh; some were ruined by it. Patrick was no more specific about just who was involved than his accusers had been, and said that no-one was ever troubled for violation.[93] He admitted, however, that he had been compelled before parliament to rescind it in August 1607. The whole was an obvious allusion to the activities of Bruce of Cultmalindie. This was scarcely surprising, since the strong Shetland element in the allegations – the forced labour, the impositions on foreign merchants, the reference to Balliasta – suggests that Bruce himself had a strong hand in drafting the indictment.

Patrick denied outright that he had made extraordinary demands on the services or purses of the islanders, or restricted the ferries. No service had been demanded that was not either customary or voluntary. Food and drink were provided. Had he regulated movement by ferry, it would not have been a crime and might well have been beneficial – for example in excluding plague in the south. In any event 'passport was refused to no man having lawful and honest cause'. On the other hand some of the islanders had transported Patrick's enemies – in particular the followers of the earl of Caithness – 'and forder the malitious nature and inclinatioun of the people being so great that they being daylie subject to murder, slauchtaris, thiftis, witchcraftis and extraordinar crymes', it was necessary to intercept fugitives seeking to escape. A taxation of 4,000 angels (£16,000) which he was said to have taken up was either part of royal taxation or was given willingly. He was less positive on the allied charge that his exactions were ten times those of the king (this was a further reference to the heavy taxations of the 1590s, £20,000 being approximately ten times the £2073 6s 8d paid annually to exchequer). Here he took refuge again in the charge's vagueness and suggested that the complainers pursue the uptakers of the tax. (He would not admit to having taken up tax himself.)

As with previous complaints about Patrick and his father before him, it is necessary to read between the lines. On the one hand, there is no doubt that he had some legal justification for what he had been doing. The reference to levies on foreign merchants clearly means the cowp bill, an ancient and accepted charge. The earl's rights to labour, to levy fines in his courts, to collect wrack and waith, to regulate the marking of goods, were all time-honoured, and the complaints made no effort to substantiate the charge that they were being abused. When Patrick speaks disparagingly of the people of Orkney and Shetland he makes little distinction between the native population and incomers like Bruce. His action in forbidding referral to courts outside Shetland was, he said, purely intended to protect the 'indigent' (presumably the likes of Culben Ormeson and Osie Scott) from the 'potent'

93 APS, iv, 396.

(Cultmalindie). On the other hand there is clearly an element of sophistry in his defences; in particular he states that he had not regulated the ferries; that it was not illegal to regulate the ferries; and that he had regulated the ferries, but had had good reason. This strong legalistic element in Patrick's defences, coupled with his past lack of respect for the central courts and his well-known desperate need for cash, meant that for all their certainty and glibness, their hopeful appeal to the king's own preoccupations, his defences earned no respect from the council.

Patrick was indicted for treason on 4 June 1610.[94] The charges included only a few of the general complaints, but unlike these, they named names and cited instances. Ever since 1589 (about the time he had first taken *de facto* control in Orkney and Shetland) he had committed various acts of oppression against familiar figures – Bellenden of Evie, Balfour of Montquhany, Monteith of Egilsay, Bannatyne of Gairsay, Sinclair of Eday, Moodie of Breckness, Bruce of Cultmalindie and Henry Wardlaw. He had usurped royal authority in issuing decrees convicting them of treason and then, compounding the usurpation, had spared their lives and banished them instead. William Sinclair of Eday, with Henry Sinclair of Tuquoy, Robert Henderson of Holland, William Irving of Sebay, Adam Moodie and many others, had been compelled to subscribe a bond of manrent including the familiar obliga-tion to report sedition, on pain of punishment not merely of themselves but of their heirs after them. This condition was unjust and tyrannical, and should only have applied to the reporting of treason itself. Patrick on the other hand was said to have freely acknowledged the existence of the bond, and asserted its legality. Francis Moodie repeated his story of ill-treatment of his men for transporting him and similar stories were told of the men of Swona for transporting Bannatyne of Gairsay, and those of Flotta for conveying their master Edmund Sinclair. Finally there were the matters of excessive taxation and forced labour. No names were mentioned, but there were more details of the tasks involved – working in Patrick's quarries, loading his ships with stones and lime, building his park dykes, all without meat, drink or hire.

On 20 June Patrick was charged to find surety to appear before the justice clerk to answer the charges;[95] but, as in 1606, strong efforts were made to ensure that the case never came to trial. Instead, pressure was brought to bear on Patrick, and he was induced to make concessions to the most important complaints against him – not those of the Orcadians and Shetlanders, but those of the bishop and the king. Guided by Lord Gray, he had discussions with his 'honorabill friends', which led to a series of offers for the satisfaction of both. To Law, 'seing it is his majesteis plesor that a bischop in Orknay sall have the same absolut priviledg that any uther Bischopes have within this kingdome', Patrick offered 1,200 merks annually in addition to the 4,000 in their contract of 1607, the free use of the Palace of the Yards, and the right to the presentation of all the kirks within the diocese. He undertook

94 *Criminal Trials*, iii, 85.
95 *RPC*, viii, 845; Kinfauns Mun. (Lord Gray's Papers), v, nos 1–2; viii, no. 9.

to submit himself to the judgment of any four of the council, with Lords Blantyre and Fyvie to represent his interests. Regarding the 'insolencies' of his servants in the north, which had so annoyed the king, he had sent for James Sinclair of Murkle, who would stand caution that the miscreants would appear. Gray sought intercession with the king from an unknown lord (possibly Blantyre or Fyvie), pleading with him to 'have a caire of the earle of Orknayis present estait quhich . . . without his majesties mitigatioun can not bot leid to the ruine of the earle and extirpatioune of his hous'. Patrick had displayed 'so franck a willingness to satisfie his majestie in all poyntis', that he was amenable to all advice. His intentions would be conveyed to the king by his brother Lord Kinclaven, who would do anything else necessary for the king's satisfaction.[96]

The council waited for the king's response. On 22 July James indicated that he was still willing to countenance the rehabilitation of Patrick; however his cousin's offences were of 'so heich a natur as the usurping of our authoritie, his proud and heich dissobedience in contempt of us and our lawis, his monyfauld wrongis and pitiefull oppressionis of oure peiple and subjectis' that he wished to see the performance of his promises before trusting in them. The council were therefore ordered to ensure that the earl bring his brother James and servants before them, satisfy those who complained against him as well as the bishop, and give surety for peace and justice in his dominions in the future. To see these things done, he was content to continue the case at the council's discretion. [97]

Patrick made a number of formal appearances before the council in August, during which he took care not to admit to any wrongdoing.[98] Sureties were found for the appearance of James Stewart, Thomas Sinclair and David King before the council.[99] Finally on 24 August 1610 he concluded a lengthy agreement with James Law. The earlier arrangement was replaced with one in which he abandoned absolutely all claim to the bishopric, its lands, teinds, thirds, superiorities etc. He had also to pay the feu mails of the earldom to the bishop. At the beginning of September the earl's ward was relaxed again to give him the freedom of the castle, under Sir John Arnot's guarantee of £20,000.[100] The easing of the situation was short-lived. By early October, when the chancellor and treasurer made their way to England to discuss matters with the king, yet further allegations were made. On 16 September, Sinclair of Eday and the king's advocate had brought a complaint against Henry Black and Edward Stewart, for invasion of Sinclair's house of Greentoft and ill-treatment of his wife and daughter.[101] In October Eday featured again among a whole series of complaints against the earl's servants in Orkney. Patrick Halcro, a

96 *RPC*, ix, 566.
97 *RPC*, ix, 566.
98 *Criminal Trials*, iii, 86–7; O & S Papers, NRS RH9/15/149a.
99 *RPC*, ix, 49, 660.
100 *RPC*, ix, 659.
101 *RPC*, ix, 51.

particularly able and determined man, who was soon to play a crucial role in events – had taken the house of Eday 'with the same souldiouris that did keepe and tak it wrangouslie of befoir'. The Moodies' house of Snelsetter, vacated by David King on being summoned south, was now occupied on the same basis by one William Craigie. Thomas Ramsay had been appointed sheriff and keeper of the castle of Kirkwall and had put men back into the earl's strongholds. Bernard (master of Patrick's stables) and Simon Stewart had beaten up Robert Stewart, minister of Hoy and Graemsay, in the course of his duties.

The king was furious. These incidents, in high contempt of his authority, 'justlie merite the recalling to our rememberance of all his formair misdemanouris and ane exemplair punishement for all togidder'. Meeting his Scottish officials at Hampton Court, his orders were direct. Patrick was to be convoyed personally from the castle to the council chamber by the provost and bailies of Edinburgh. The council were to examine him 'most straitlie' on these matters, and convey their verdict to the king as swiftly as possible. They were to assure Patrick that the king had ordered the chancellor on his return to Scotland to proceed against him 'without ony forder favour'. In the meantime he was to be confined to his chamber.[102] Before the councillors, Patrick persisted in the same obdurate denials as before. Thomas Ramsay had not been appointed to any office; his strongholds contained only a few simple servants; the house of Eday was in the peaceful possession of William Sinclair of Eday; that of Snelsetter was occupied only by David King's wife and children. Any dispute between Bernard, Simon and Robert Stewart was a personal one of which he was ignorant.[103]

Patrick was returned to the castle. He was now in an even more hopeless position than before, if that were possible. Yet despite all that had happened, for all the broken promises, the fury of the king, the lawlessness in the north, and the obstinate refusal to bend to the will of the courts, it was only now, after 17 years of rule and perhaps a decade of growing serious complaint, that the scene was finally set for the downfall of Patrick Stewart.

102 *RPC*, ix, 584.
103 *RPC*, ix, 581–2.

13

Ane Unhappie Man

As 1610 became 1611, Patrick remained obstructive, making concessions only when he had no alternative, and even then seeking to worm his way out of them. He continued to ignore the threat of criminal prosecution hanging over his head and could not be compelled to fulfil his promise to Law of further bishopric income. In May 1611 Law wrote to the king describing Chancellor Dunfermline's attempts to persuade the earl to acknowledge his obligations. Dunfermline had left 'no means unasseyed'. On the one hand, he had threatened Patrick with imprisonment in the castle of Dumbarton, much grimmer and more isolated than Edinburgh; this 'did so affray' him that he agreed, much against his will, to sign the contract with the bishop.[1] On the other hand, council representatives sought to induce Patrick to abandon his interests in the north by promising him the keepership of one of the royal palaces – Holyrood, Linlithgow, Stirling or Falkland – with all its perquisites and a rent of £10,000 a year. This he 'playnelie and absolutlie refusit'.[2] On 8 March 1611, he offered himself for trial, 'disassenting simpliciter to all forder continuation'.[3]

When he had entered his confinement, Patrick brought with him the necessaries for a comfortable existence. His apartment was lit by his own iron and brass chandeliers. For the preparation of meals there was pestle and mortar, spit and frying pan, and a brass chafing-dish. There were plates and trenchers of pewter and wood, a tin pint and a quart stoup, on a table covered with Holland cloth and napkins of linen. He had a sweet tooth, leaving behind him an ounce of sugar candy, a loaf of sugar and a pound of raisins. He possessed three pairs of white boots, one pair of black, three of black leather shoes, a pair of white slippers, a red taffeta riding hood stitched with silk and two pairs of gilt spurs. He had a looking glass and a brush. He washed from a pewter basin and laver, using a sponge. He dried himself on linen or Holland cloth towels, and he slept between sheets of the same material. He relieved himself with his own 'stuill of eise'. If these stuffs seem mundane when set beside his former pretensions, there were reminders of happier times. His bible and prayer book both had gilt covers. He kept with him a collection of small treasures, many of them silver: two goblets; two salt cellars; the 'walkener' (alarm mechanism) of

1 *Letters on the Ecclesiastical Affairs of Scotland*, i, 267–8.
2 *The Historie of King James the Sext*, 384–7.
3 *Criminal Trials*, iii, 87.

a clock; a watchcase, gilded in the fashion of Paris, and a watch-chain; a small bell in a black purse contained in a kist covered with cloth of gold, enclosed within a black coffer; a small barrel-shaped bone box containing six pearls and 20 red coral beads; and another containing a compass with dial. For recreation, he possessed bowstrings and golfballs, and he retained the materials for conducting his increasingly difficult affairs – a quire and a half of paper, a lens, sealing wax and a sealskin wallet. Sealskin is perhaps the one material that indicates a source within Patrick's northern lands; it covered two of the four kists that held his effects at the end.[4]

But Patrick had no income. The valuables he still possessed represented his sole wealth, and he was clearly reluctant to part with them. Even within his prison, this was difficult. One of his own servants stole his watch and, though the thief was caught, the watch was never seen again.[5] By early 1611 even Patrick's astonishing pride and obduracy were unable to conceal the extreme difficulty of his position. He was pursued not merely by Arnot, Law, Caithness and the landowners of Orkney and Shetland, but by the tradesmen and merchants of the capital – the fleshers John Dobie and John Davidson, Alexander Park the fishmonger, James Simpson the baker and Peter Yibbs, a Flemish clothier in the Canongate, to whom he owed, both on his own behalf and that of his wife, a total of over £3,000.[6] In mid-November 1610 the council passed on to the king news from the castle that Patrick was 'reduceit to suche a poore estate and conditioun that he hes nouther the meanes, credite, nor possibillitie to interteyn himselff, he being so far ingageit for his bigane interteynment that his furnisseris, being dispairit of pament, doeth now refuse him', so that he had nothing by way of sustenance but 'breade and drink, and that very sparringlie'.

Patrick himself had said nothing to the council, preferring to conceal his humiliation, and 'making choise rather to undirly whatsomevir extremitie and want then to divulgat his necessitie, and being ashamed that ony man would know the same, he is silent'.[7] The council referred the matter to the king not, as they took care to emphasise, to extenuate his 'errouris and folyis in ony poynt', but in consideration of the earl's birth and the 'place and dignitie whiche formarlie by your majesteis favour he possest in this kingdome'. For the time being the king left Patrick as he was; not until early 1613 did the council at last allow him £4 daily for subsistence,[8] the smallness of the sum justified to the king and Patrick's remaining allies by his past obstinacy.[9] Even in this extremity, when his dignity of birth could do no more

---

4 *RSS*, NRS PS1/85, f. 96v–8r.

5 *RPC*, x, 110–11.

6 Court of Session Recs: Acts and Decreets, NRS CS7/245, ff. 222r–4r; CS7/246, f. 207r, CS7/247, ff.147v–8r, CS7/249, ff. 13r–14v; Diligence Recs: GR Hornings, NRS DI3/36, ff. 299v–302r.

7 *RPC*, ix, 586.

8 *RPC*, x, 90.

9 Letter from Sir Thomas Hamilton to the king (Balfour of Denmilne Papers, NLS Adv. Ms. 33.1.1 (v, 9); *State Papers of Melros*, 100). The letter is dated 28 January; the year is probably 1614, since the council meeting to which it refers took place on 29 June 1613.

than preserve him from public destitution, he still entertained extraordinary hopes. In Law's words to the king he remained 'in assured houp of your Majesties favour, and of his full libertie and returning to Orkney, and that upon this litill point of obedience to your Majestie and satisfaction to me'. Some money to the bishop, a promise of good behaviour to the king, and all would be well. But now he was truly in the abyss. His credit with the king was quite exhausted, and he had nothing left to bargain with, since everything was now in the hands of Sir John Arnot.

On the other hand, any major administrative decision regarding Orkney and Shetland still required his consent. Law, faced with a yearly struggle for his legitimate income, suggested to the king that the time had come to follow the only reasonable course of action left – the forcible parting of Patrick from his lands and offices and the installation of another administration.[10] This possibility had been in the minds of the king and his advisers for some time. It was mooted as early as March 1610,[11] and moves towards it had been used to threaten Patrick during that year. The reception accorded to the measures already taken made it clear that nothing short of it would have any effect. In September 1610, for example, the reading of council proclamations in Kirkwall had been disrupted by the earl's supporters, including some of the most prominent – Thomas Ramsay, Alexander Leggat, Patrick Halcro and John Guild. 'Out of thair foolische and distemperat humouris, with oppin schouting', they 'did mock and disdanefullie dereid the . . . proclamationis . . . saying thay wald not gif the pairing of thair naill for all the warrantis, papiris and proclamationis that his Majestie or his Counsaill . . . micht send thair'.[12]

On 6 November, among other commissioners of the peace for various parts of the country, Law and Arnot were appointed for Orkney and Shetland, together with the archbishop of St Andrews. They were to be assisted in Orkney by James Stewart of Graemsay, his namesake of Burray, William Irving of Sebay and Hugh Halcro of Halcro; and in Shetland by James Sinclair of Quendale, Arthur Sinclair of Aith, Andrew Gifford of Wethersta and Thomas Cheyne of Vaila.[13] Provision had already been made for the introduction of one feature of the Scottish legal system into the Northern Isles. Understandably in the circumstances, this was the *register of hornings*, which commenced on 2 November 1610.[14] Among its earliest subjects was David King, who had been outlawed for his treatment of James and Henry Stewart of Graemsay and was now incarcerated in Edinburgh beside his master.[15] The entries in the register for 1611 played their part in unravelling the tortuous affairs of the earl. Of the 25 deeds recorded, Patrick featured in all but five.

On 28 May 1611 James finally switched from his policy of persuasion and threat to more direct action. He wrote to his council, instructing that the criminal charges

10 *Letters on the Ecclesiastical Affairs of Scotland*, i, 267–8.
11 *RPC*, viii, 619.
12 *RPC*, ix, 163–4.
13 *RPC*, ix, 163.
14 *RPC*, 79–80.
15 Diligence Recs: GR Hornings, Orkney, NRS DI85/1, f. 4r and v.

against Patrick be abandoned;[16] the letter was accompanied by instructions aimed at dismantling the earldom – to dismiss Patrick's servants, end the islands' peculiar legal system, order surrender of the castles, and command obedience to Law when he came north to prepare a report.[17] These were enacted immediately, and Patrick's rule in the north was now, officially at least, at an end.

Of the three commissioners for Orkney and Shetland appointed in November 1610, only Law was active. The involvement of the archbishop of St Andrews was purely formal, and Sir John Arnot, though deeply involved financially, never participated in administrative matters. On 4 June 1611, a proclamation on behalf of Law and Arnot drew public attention to their instructions; they were to hold justice and sheriff courts, summon and sentence offenders, make ordinances for maintenance of the peace and examine the claims of poor people who had been 'violentlie . . . dispossesst and ejectit furthe of thair kyndlie rowmes and possessionis, and spoylled of thair goodis and geir and hes not moyen (means) to persew the same . . . befoir the Lords of Sessioun'.[18]

Law spent the summers of 1611 and 1612 in the Northern Isles. During the first visit the chief task, carried out by his deputy Henry Aitken, was the reform of the commissary court. In the past there had been commissaries in Orkney and Shetland,[19] but these appear to have confined themselves to pronouncing decreets on questions of succession and inheritance. They did not produce the customary register of testaments, but allowed native practice in testamentary matters to continue. One commissary, Robert Cheyne of Urie, had been charged before the Edinburgh commissary court in 1592 with making no account of 'cote [quot] money' – testamentary fees – for Orkney and Shetland. Cheyne had blamed Patrick who, he said, had prevented him from confirming testaments within his jurisdiction.[20] Patrick had been ordered to find surety that his interference would cease, but no more was heard of this and it seems more probable that quot money was wanting because the register that generated it simply did not exist. Aitken lost no time in remedying this.[21]

Testamentary arrangements in Orkney before Aitken are a mystery. The general council of the Scottish church had laid down as early as 1549 that Scottish practice should be introduced,[22] but there is no evidence of a functioning register. The lack of adequate provision is illustrated by Aitken's register, which included the testaments

16 RPC, ix, 611–12.
17 RPC, ix, 181–2.
18 RPC, ix, 186.
19 John Stewart (REO, 203, no. xcix); Robert Cheyne of Urie (RPC, iv, 546–7); John Dishington (REO, 309, no. cxc).
20 Court of Session Recs: Acts and Decreets, NRS CS7/135, ff. 73v–4v.
21 He was appointed on 28 May 1611; the first fragment of commissary court book is dated 19 July 1611 (O & S Tests, NRS CC17/2/1).
22 Statutes of the Scottish Church, 1225–1559 (SHS), trans. and ed. D. Patrick, Edinburgh, 1907, 115–16, quoted in Donaldson, Shetland Life under Earl Patrick, 13.

of numerous individuals who had been dead for many years – in one case since as far back as 1573. In 1612, his second year of operation, no fewer than 18 out of a total of 83 testaments concerned persons who had died before 1600. This figure declined over the next few years, though a person who had died before the introduction of Scots law had a testament registered as late as 1627.[23] Orkney must presumably have relied on informal family agreements to decide the destination of movable property or heritage, but in Shetland the *schound* still survived. The *schownd bill* – the document drawn up by the executors – performed much the same function as the Scots testament, though it included heritage as well as movables. The text of three such documents is known; the subjects of two of them, James Spence of Midbrake and Peter Nisbet of Kirkabister in Yell, also have testaments registered in their name.[24] It may have been the difficulties caused by the inclusion of heritable property in the schound that made Scots administrators reluctant to introduce their own practice, rather as udal provisions were to survive the abolition of Norse Law as a whole. On the other hand, the combination of commissary court and schound in Shetland does sound like the famous accusation of using both law codes according to convenience, though the surviving schounds give no evidence of the earl deriving income from them which would otherwise have gone to Edinburgh.

At the end of 1611 the privy council passed a measure that abrogated the 'unlawful acts or customs' of which Patrick had been accused – confiscation of land for concealment of offences, prohibition of assistance to wrecked ships and the rest.[25] The response to the new dispensation remained a mixed one. James Stewart of Graemsay, who had long suffered at Patrick's hands, was a known supporter of the crown's measures, but when in 1611 he was appointed a justice of the peace for Orkney, he found himself quite unable to act, being alternately threatened or ignored. He and his colleagues had imprisoned in the castle an unnamed 'violent and tumultuous person, quha had committit ane heiche contempt and ryote'. The individual was then liberated by 'my Lordis shireff depute withowt knowledge of us, so that, if we had found any fault thairwithe, we wer in no les hazard then owre lyves'.[26] The impotent justices were forced to make their excuses to the council.

In Shetland matters were no different. In 1611 Bishop Law himself faced scant regard for his dignity and that of the crown. He arrived in Scalloway in June and summoned Robert, son of William Bruce of Symbister, and Laurence of Ustaness, son of Arthur Sinclair of Houss, in an attempt to resolve the long-standing feud between the two families. The Bruces, father and son, duly arrived, but Sinclair assembled 40 followers and attacked them. They were left for dead close to the gate of the bishop's house. On being summoned to appear before the privy council, Sinclair sought an agreement with Bruce, who was prepared to accept this for the

23 *Orkney Testaments*, ed. Barclay, 10.
24 *Shetland Documents*, 1299–1579, app. 6 ; 1580–1611, 188, no. 188.
25 *RPC*, ix, 297.
26 *RPC*, xiv, 570–1.

sake of peace. Nevertheless some time after, in the house of Edinburgh burgess Thomas Fisher, Sinclair had drawn his sword and held it to Bruce's breast 'with mony horrible and execrable aiths' and threats of death. He was ordered by the council to enter the tolbooth.[27]

A much more significant act of defiance, very shortly after Bishop Law's return south in 1611, was Patrick's appointment of his natural son Robert as his deputy. With the changes in the islands, Patrick had briefly been regarded as less of a threat to peace there, and he was allowed to move back into the town of Edinburgh, though still confined to within four miles of the mercat cross.[28] Three weeks later the king, who was plainly well supplied with information, was writing to the privy council about Robert Stewart who, he understood, had already held court in Kirkwall.[29] The council were therefore to call Patrick before them, and if the reports were true, to return him to the castle and punish his son. On 1 October, Patrick admitted to the council that he had told Robert to go north, but only to gather in his arrears and debts. This was disputed by the bishop, who stated that Robert was acting as sheriff. Patrick was returned to his imprisonment in the castle.[30]

Young Robert Stewart was Patrick's only son, one of three illegitimate children by his obscure mistress, Marjorie Sinclair.[31] He was a tall, good-looking boy, but was never to prove himself an impressive or decisive figure, and when he first appears, aged about 19, he is merely a name among those jeering at the proclamation in Kirkwall. He was, however, a figurehead for what was still a strong force in the islands. Assisted, or manipulated, by Alexander Leggat, John Guild, Thomas Auchinleck and other long-standing adherents of his father, he was said to be committing 'all kynd of iniquitie and wickednes', ignoring the king's commissioners and establishing power over 'the poore inhabitantis . . . over quhome thay may be maisteris and commanderis'.[32] On 28 November Robert and his followers, as well as the Shetland Sinclair supporters of Patrick – Ustaness, Uyea and Brow – were denounced as rebels.[33] In February 1612 the king, believing that Patrick's presence in Edinburgh was 'prejudiciall to many of our good subiectis' in Orkney and Shetland, committed him to the fate he had feared so much before – imprisonment in the castle of Dumbarton.[34]

By the spring of 1612 there were rumours of a rising in Orkney and Shetland. It was said that certain individuals 'upoun foolische, ymaginarie consaits and apprehensions of thair awne', were raising forces to be sent to Orkney. The council deemed them worthy of the royal notice only because they might induce the simple

27 RPC, ix, 320.
28 RPC, ix, 24.
29 RPC, ix, 631.
30 RPC, ix, 257.
31 Scots Peerage, vi, 576–7.
32 RPC, ix, 290.
33 RPC, ix, 290, 347.
34 RPC, ix, 340.

folk of the islands to join them in their 'madness and headlong run to thair awne ruyne and perdition'. Robert's men took the strongholds of Kirkwall and prepared for siege, breaking open the girnel and seizing the grain inside. Two years later, in 1614, as we shall see, there was a much more determined and fateful rising, for which this disturbance was almost a dress-rehearsal. During the interrogations after the siege of 1614, these events are touched on only lightly, but there is no doubt that 1612 was seen as a year of rebellion, and in 1614 negotiated pardons were denied to those who had participated earlier.[35]

The council responded by re-enacting the restrictions on sailing to Orkney, and ordered Robert and Master James Stewart his uncle, to surrender the castles and palaces.[36] James Law, who had now been appointed chamberlain of the earldom for the coming year, made ready to go north. He consulted the earl of Caithness, the keeper of Dumbarton Castle and 'divers honest men' who travelled regularly to Orkney, concluding that Patrick was directly responsible for the troubles, through his instructions to his son, brother and servants. Before departing, the bishop wrote to the king seeking to confine Patrick to his room in Dumbarton Castle, with only permitted servants having access, and to compel him to order his son to surrender.[37]

When he arrived in Orkney and Shetland, the bishop was quickly successful in prevailing upon Robert Stewart to surrender his father's houses. We know nothing of the arguments and promises he put to the young man, though Patrick was afterwards to speak of treachery, and Robert Gordon believed the second rebellion took place because 'such conditions were not performed as the bishope had promised [Robert] when the . . . castle was rendered by him'.[38] When Robert's indecisiveness and naivety become apparent, it is not difficult to imagine the ease with which the urbane and able bishop would sway him. In all probability, Robert made his way south in the bishop's own train, and on 13 January 1613 Law stood caution that the young lad would behave himself and stay away from the Northern Isles.[39]

During his visit, Law held his first sheriff court in the islands in the cathedral of St Magnus. This heard no causes, but confined itself to restoring local government within the burgh – appointing bailies and councillors, ordering them to assist in the kirk's work, naming the mercat day, and ordering an act to discourage drunkenness. The equivalent sitting for Shetland took place at Scalloway Castle, where Law appointed his court officials; the clerk was to be Henry Aitken the commissary, also sheriff depute, and the procurator fiscal was Robert Coltart. The first measure was a series of 'country acts' – public order measures on the regulation of beggars and vagabonds, chapmen and forestallers; on slander, theft, 'ryding uther mens horssis

35 RPC, x, 262, 703–4.
36 RPC, ix, 362–3, 384.
37 Letters on the Ecclesiastical Affairs of Scotland, i, 289–91.
38 Gordon, Genealogical History of the Earldom of Sutherland, 301.
39 RPC, ix, 533.

and stowing of thair taillis', and on the old difficulty of allowing pigs to wander on neighbours' ground. Law sat in Scalloway until 26 August, after which he returned to Orkney to hold further courts until his departure in October, when his place on the bench was taken by Aitken.[40] The court record for this period shows little sign of the upheavals that had brought it into being. Henry Wardlaw appeared in Shetland regarding an agreement about his lands of Clousta, which Patrick had tried to wrest from him;[41] and Robert Monteith had a decreet pronounced against John Mowat of Heogaland over a debt.[42] Neither of these matters related directly to the events of the past, but nor were all the decisions of the former courts ignored: John Wilkie in Birsay was ordered to pay 27 meils of malt in compliance with a decreet obtained before Edward Scollay of Strynie in May the previous year.[43]

On Law's return to Edinburgh the king's plans for Orkney and Shetland were laid before parliament. Sir John Arnot and his sons William and John were bought out of their comprehensive interests in the islands – the earldom lands, their rights in the udal lands, the offices of justiciary, sheriffdom and foudry, the regality rights of the bishopric, the keeping of the castle of Kirkwall, etc. – for £300,000. The whole was now to be annexed permanently to the crown and erected into a stewartry. A number of prominent members of the privy council and the bench were appointed to negotiate on the respective interests in the bishopric lands of the bishop himself and the king. This was the first step in a massive reorganisation of the earldom and bishopric lands of Orkney. It was undertaken, according to the commission, because

sutche disorders as . . . have arisin when the cuntrie being devidit in landis haldin of the king and . . . of the kirk, the tennentis and possessouris . . . leaning to thair particular superiouris [crown or bishop] . . . have fallin in sutche oppositioun and stryff as hes procedit to slaughters, murthers, factiounes, seditiones and sutche heicht of confusioun as the lyves of the bischops hes many tymes bene in danger and the people liklie to have drawin strangers into the cuntrie who under pretext of assisting thair freindis mycht upoun occasioun preafit to have possest thame selffis of the whoill cuntrie . . .[44]

Alongside the bishop with his legal responsibilities, a principal tacksman was appointed to administer and reorganise the island estates, both earldom and bishopric. This was Sir James Stewart of Killeith, later Lord Ochiltree. The actual measures required for the accomplishment of this task were entrusted to his deputy John Finlayson, his brother-in-law, who was designated sheriff depute, though there is no evidence that he ever held courts. Finlayson set to work to bring in rents, both current and in arrears, and arrive at a final picture of the finances of the island estates

40 Ct Bk of O & S, 1612–13, 32.
41 Ct Bk of O & S, 1612–13, 26.
42 Ct Bk of O & S, 1612–13, 28.
43 Ct Bk of O & S, 1612–13, 31.
44 APS, iv, 480–3.

under the old regime. On 18 November 1612 Law handed Patrick's 1595 rental into exchequer so that work could begin,[45] and for a year Finlayson and his assistants pursued their task, culminating in the submission during November and December 1613 of accounts by the tackmen of Orkney and underfouds of Shetland.[46]

The massive campaign of revenue collection began with the formal 'denouncing' of every 'toun, holme and skerrie' within the earldom and bishopric, including the bishop's lands in Caithness – charging the inhabitants to pay their mails to the king's representative. This involved writing out 2,400 copies of the denunciation for public display, and an arduous tour of the lands, lasting from January till September 1613, making personal verbal pronouncement in each. The man in charge of this was Walter Ritchie, a public servant who is variously found in the employment of Arnot, Stewart of Killeith and the crown itself.[47] His accounts give a clear indication of his progress. He set off from Burntisland on horseback and travelled to Peterhead, where he hired a pinnace that set him on board a barque bound for Caithness. In Wick he proclaimed his letters at the mercat cross, then crossed to South Ronaldsay and thence to Kirkwall, his centre of operations. There he made preparations for receipt of the revenues; a wright was employed to repair the stair of the malt girnel, damaged by Robert Stewart's men, and a blacksmith to make iron bands for its doors. He arranged for the transport of horses from Cromarty to replace those on the Bu of Corse which had died of the scab. He also visited the castle of Kirkwall to examine an inventory of its contents prepared by James Tulloch of Rothisholm, its new captain.[48] From Kirkwall he began his official tour of the estates with a trip to Stembister in St Andrews en route for Copinsay. He went to Shapinsay to denounce the Bu of Sound. He hired horses for his visits to the Mainland parishes, then the North Isles, then the South Isles.

When this was done, he took a ship bound for Norway that set him down in Shetland, probably in Sumburgh. From there he followed in Bruce's footsteps to Maywick, where he was luckier in finding a ferry to Scalloway. He set off for Laxfirth and Neap, to Whalsay, to Linga and other holms, then to the North Isles, including Uyea, Bigga and Hascosay. On the larger isles, he hired horses. After this he started at Gluss in Northmavine and made his way by boat down the west coast, by Wethersta, Olnafirth, Gonfirth, Aith, Papa Stour, Papa Little, Vementry, Voe and back to Scalloway. He interrupted this tour by setting out from Walls for Foula, taking care to have a barrel of bere for himself, his witnesses and his oarsmen, in case they 'should be stayit thair with evill wether, in respect of the povertie of the peple in that ile'. He visited the Skerries, crossing 'fortie myles or thairby of

45 *Rentals*, ii, 2.
46 Exchequer Records: Orkney [and Shetland] Rentals and Accs, NRS E41/3.
47 Servant of Arnot, 27 Aug. 1606 (Bruce of Symbister Papers, SA GD144/6/27); royal messenger, 1610–12 (Diligence Recs: GR Hornings O & S, NRS DI85/1); servant of Finlayson, 1612–13 (Exchequer Records: Orkney [and Shetland] Rentals and Accs., NRS E41/3).
48 Orkney Record and Antiquarian Soc. Recs, OA D.46, box 1, no. 7.

dangerous seyis', and followed this by a seaborne tour of Whiteness and Weisdale and the southern west coast down to Dunrossness. Then there was a journey to Fair Isle, with similar precautions to those made for Foula. After that, he returned to Orkney and Kirkwall, where he recited his letters of apprising at the mercat cross. Ritchie's exaggeration of the distance involved in his trip to the Skerries was that of a man who preferred to keep his feet on terra firma, and his trip south, like that going north, was made largely overland, changing horses at Elgin. He did not go to Edinburgh, but made his way direct to Dumbarton to denounce the earl himself.

Ritchie returned to Orkney towards the end of 1613 to join Finlayson and his other assistants in the gathering of the rents. Unfortunately, Finlayson's 'evill demeanour' had made him and his administration very unpopular indeed.[49] This may have been because of the money value placed upon arrears of victual, which was in all cases at least double what it had been in Earl Robert's testament 16 years before, aggravated by the zeal with which his men had saturated the islands with proclamations and with which he himself criticised and rejected items in the tackmen's accounts. His comments – 'repellis' and 'referrit to trial' – were to be found all over the returns, particularly those of Holm and Paplay, Firth, Westray and Papa Westray, and South Ronaldsay. In the last of these he repelled the whole allowance made by the tackman for paying the ferrymen of the eastern South Isles. Eventually he was so hated that it was not surprising that in some quarters the new regime became even more unpopular than the old.

This odium makes a convenient starting point from which to examine the support for Patrick and his representatives that now made itself felt. The existence of this support has been the subject of much speculation, running as it does completely counter to the commoner picture of him as hated tyrant and visitor of Scottish misrule on Scandinavian islands. Earlier writers, who tended to see the struggles in the Northern Isles in quasi-nationalistic terms – Scot versus Orcadian and Shetlander – have suggested that perhaps it was Patrick who was seen at the time as the defender of northern traditions rather than his enemies, the Scots lairds represented by Bruce and Monteith.[50] His supporters were therefore motivated by a consciousness that what was left of the old Norse order was being swept away. To those who think this, the most noteworthy of the measures setting up the new administration is that 'discharging the use of foreign laws within Orknay and Shetland'. Yet although the abolition of the old laws has provoked controversy on more than one occasion since,[51] there is little evidence that it was regarded as an issue at the time. It is true that when young Robert Stewart and his followers came to draw up their 'bond of association' in 1614, they included in their statement of aims and motives a reference to 'corruptioun of the lawis'. Yet they were not specific

49 *Criminal Trials*, iii, 289.

50 J. Stewart, 'Udal Law and Government in Shetland', *Viking Congress*, Edinburgh, 1954, 103.

51 Stewart, 'Udal Law and Government in Shetland', 110–11; Smith, 'The Law Relating to the Treasure', *St Ninian's Isle and its Treasure*, Aberdeen, 1973, i, 149–66.

about what they meant by this, nor did they make any mention of the old legal system. It could mean that Law or Aitken or Finlayson had destroyed the lawbook, but there is no evidence that the new courts were unpopular. After a brief hiatus during the rebellion of 1614, they resumed and have continued ever since. Unlike Finlayson, who was in the end hounded out of Orkney, Aitken spent the rest of his life there, dying there as late as 1643.[52]

What then motivated support for Patrick? In part it was detestation, not of Law's courts but of Finlayson's administration. At one point in the course of the 1614 rebellion, the rebels were to discuss shooting Finlayson, walking in the court-yard of the palace, from their vantage point in the steeple; they decided against it, as there was a danger they might hit Aitken, his companion, with whom they had no quarrel.[53] Secondly, there was the government's eventual choice of commander against the forces of rebellion – the earl of Caithness; he was to prove too old an enemy of too many Orcadians to command support in the islands. But there were other, perhaps more positive reasons for supporting Patrick. It must be remembered that he was never wholly without allies in the north outside the circle of his own servants. In Shetland those Sinclairs whom he had backed in the struggle with Bruce of Symbister remained reliable, even if others were willing enough to take the council's commission.[54] In Orkney, Caithness was to find the Sinclairs (presumably apart from those of Eday) untrustworthy. The Halcros were similarly split in their allegiance; Hugh Halcro of Halcro, though a former attendant of Patrick, was one of the commissioners of the peace, but the children of William Halcro of Aikers had established links with the earl's servants. Two of his daughters had married Henry Black and Bernard Stewart, and their brother, Patrick, was to be Robert Stewart's chief lieutenant in the events of 1614.

Patrick's worsening position was to force his friends, and some of his foes also, on to the horns of a dilemma. Were they to co-operate with the crown, or not? For the gentry of Orkney and Patrick's close retainers, some of them also scions of minor landed families, turning against their vindictive and dangerous master was a risky course of action. The position into which Patrick had manoeuvred himself was without precedent and the council itself showed marked reluctance to act decisively against him. He was not without support in Edinburgh, and in the north there seemed no guarantee that he might not yet extricate himself from his troubles; he himself appeared confident that he could still do so. If he did, where would those who had opposed him stand? Different solutions were found to the problem. The allegiance of many of Patrick's immediate servants, often men who had served him for many years, who had lost their offices and had therefore a strong personal interest in preserving the status quo, remained firm, but Bernard Stewart, like Halcro of Halcro, openly joined the new regime, becoming keeper of the Palace

52 O & S Tests, NRS CC17/2/4.
53 *Criminal Trials*, iii, 298.
54 *RPC*, x, 707.

of Birsay under Finlayson. Others, like Thomas Black or Thomas Laing, did so too, but were later induced to return. Some of the Orkney gentry also hedged their bets. Irving of Sebay, another of the commissioners of the peace, was believed to have played a double game between Robert Stewart and the earl of Caithness.[55] While Robert was holding Kirkwall Castle against Caithness, he was visited by Halcro of Halcro, Francis Moodie of Breckness and Henry Stewart, younger of Graemsay, who were all said to have eaten and drunk with him. Only Monteith of Egilsay took any role at all in the gathering of forces to combat Robert's rebellion, and only the distrusted Irving of Sebay was actually present at the action. The others, even the Bruces, kept their heads down.

Francis Moodie, who apparently offered encouragement to Robert Stewart despite his much-vaunted opposition to Patrick, may have been struck by the support that the earl and his son commanded among the people. He had previously complained of being seized by a crowd of the earl's supporters, including 'most of the inhabitants' of Kirkwall, and Caithness too noted the sympathy in the capital for Robert and his rebels, a support that was also to be found among the commons of Birsay and Harray. This was understandable since Birsay and Kirkwall were so important to the earldom, and their inhabitants would be long accustomed to the service of the Stewarts, but their position was also perhaps a difficult one. To whom were they to pay their rents – Finlayson, or Robert Stewart? Should they obey summons to *wappenshaws*? The attitudes of the commons of Sumburgh or Scalloway are unknown, but there is no evidence in either Shetland or Orkney of romantic fictional heroes like Thorvald of Brenister or Thorburn Sigurdson.[56] Instead there was at best a cautious obedience to whoever seemed in control at the time.

Patrick was taken to Dumbarton Castle on 27 February 1612. He remained there for almost two years, until mid-January 1614,[57] while the council continued to pressurise him to resign all his rights in the earldom of Orkney. At length he agreed to do so, and was returned to Edinburgh to complete the formalities.[58] There he sang a quite different song, and kept the council guessing for the next four months. At first he denied that he had agreed to anything; then he declared that the matter was of such weight that needed time to confer with his advisers Lord Blantyre and the earl of Cassillis. He was given a month to consider his position. Exactly one month later, on 1 March 1614, he was brought again before the council. This time he excused himself on the grounds that his friends had been unable to visit him because of bad weather, and asked for a deferral of a further two and a half months, until 15 May. The council gave him till the last day before the courts rose to give his answer.[59] On 10 March he asked for five more days, and, as Blantyre and Cassillis were due in Edinburgh on 15

55 *Criminal Trials*, iii, 288.
56 For the story of these stout, but fictitious souls, see Anderson, *Black Patie*, ch.1.
57 *RPC*, x, 200–1.
58 Balfour of Denmilne Papers, NLS Adv. Ms. 33.1.1 (v, 24).
59 Balfour of Denmilne Papers, NLS Adv. Ms. 33.1.1 (v, 28).

March, this was granted.[60] When they met, he sought their influence in procuring a personal audience with the king. By this means, he felt sure that he would be able to give satisfaction.[61]

Like his opponents, he was trying to outflank the council in the hope of a more sympathetic hearing from the king; in all probability, his undertakings at Dumbarton had been no more than a means of procuring his return to Edinburgh to try and effect this, having been refused the direct access that he had sought. To this end, after two months in the capital, he sent his servant Thomas Laing to London, with a letter of recommendation to his brother Robert. Laing was later interrogated by the council about the trip, in a manner that suggested that they had known nothing of it at the time. His answers were not informative, probably because there was little to say. He had left London empty handed; on his way back he was overhauled at Scarborough by a messenger with two letters to Patrick from Robert, which he had duly passed on.[62] That was all; Patrick's attempts to contact the king had come to nothing – though neither had he made any concession to the council's demand that he resign the earldom. In mid-May, however, news came that his son had broken his undertakings and gone to Orkney. Patrick was ordered to be returned to Dumbarton.[63]

During his time in Dumbarton, Patrick had been looking at other, more desperate remedies for his problems. Some time after his first incarceration there in 1612 he had sent his secretary, Michael Mair, to ask James Lyon, an illegitimate son of Thomas, master of Glamis, and Sir Robert Crichton of Cluny to help in a plan to decamp to Orkney. Both were among Patrick's creditors and Lyon's half-sister Margaret was married to Patrick's brother Master James. Neither was particularly keen on the idea, but influenced by Patrick's 'mony fair promises' and perhaps by the fact that they might never otherwise see their money again, they agreed to assist. Crichton later excused himself, and Lyon and Mair together agreed upon a plan to hoist the earl over the castle wall by means of a rope and an 'instrument of yrne', probably a grapnel. Patrick for his part was to send his three warders on false errands, leaving the coast clear. Horses were brought to the Hill of Dumbuck, about two miles upriver, one of which would then be taken right up to the castle wall. But when Mair and Lyon went to Dumbarton and told the earl that all was ready, Patrick's resolution failed him totally. He shrank from the prospect of physically scaling the wall and decided to try to suborn the porter instead. The porter simply informed the keeper of the castle and the escape attempt was at an end.[64]

Later the same year Mair came again to Lyon at his Canongate lodging with Patrick's request to meet him. Lyon not unnaturally refused, saying that he would

60 RPC, x, 219–20.
61 RPC, x, 224.
62 Criminal Trials, iii, 296–301.
63 Balfour of Denmilne Papers, NLS Adv. Ms. 33.1.1 (v, 24).
64 Criminal Trials, iii, 324.

'*mell* [have dealings with] na forder with the Erll nor in nane of his courses'. Mair
agreed heartily, saying of his master, 'I see this man has not the grace of God in
him; I will lykewayis half no forder dealing with him.' He thereupon left Patrick
and entered government service, in the office of the director of chancery. But this
was not the end of Lyon's dealings with Patrick Stewart; when the earl learned in
early 1613 of his son's capitulation to the bishop, he was furious at what he saw as
Robert's disloyalty, which deprived him of effective influence in the north. When
Robert became aware of his father's reaction, it was Lyon's counsel he sought. Lyon
suggested that he should go to the court in London and try to win the favour of the
king. Robert demurred, saying that he had no funds for such a journey, and made
it plain that he was anxious to regain his father's favour. Instead he prevailed upon
Lyon to accompany him to Dumbarton to help plead his case.

Robert met the full blast of his father's wrath. Patrick would not look at him,
or speak to him except to shout imprecations – 'Feble unworthie beast'; he was
'the wraick of him and his estate'. Robert answered lamely that 'if he had the house
againe he would keep it better'. The long-suffering James Lyon prepared to leave
Dumbarton, but allowed himself to be persuaded to go once more to Patrick on
Robert's behalf and say that his son 'wald tak sum disperat course and go oute of the
cuntrey yf he could not procure his favour'. Patrick's reaction was at first the same,
calling his son a 'fals feble beast' for surrendering the castle, but at length agreed to
receive him. The interview was still an uncomfortable one. The earl believed that
Robert 'had not a spirite nor courage to follow any interprise' and he would grant
him no favours until he had shown his resolution by repairing the wrong he had
done. He would 'prove a prettie manne yf the House come againe in his hands; for
it wald stand him to his lyfe'. Robert undertook to return to Orkney, and Patrick
demanded that Lyon underwrite this promise. Lyon refused, saying that 'Robert
wald speke and promeis for him self'. When Robert had done so Lyon, who had
increasingly little taste for what he had been required to do, left for the burgh of
Dumbarton on the first stage of his journey homewards.

On the way he was pursued by Duncan Mitchell, a messenger for the earl, who
had been sent to persuade him to return to the castle. This Lyon would not do,
since he felt that Patrick's only intention was to involve him directly in Robert's
doings in the north. When he reached Dumbarton, he met James Annand, Patrick's
former servant. Annand asked him 'yf he had aggreit the fader and the sone?' Lyon's
response was, 'Thay wer aggreit . . . Robert must neidis go to Orkney or thair wilbe
no lyffe for him'. Annand replied, 'The Erll is ane unhappie man. He knawis Robert
can do no goode in Orknay. His purpois is to bring him to the scaffolde, and to
bring the sclander of his bloode upon the king'.

Lyon went back to Edinburgh with Mitchell. About three weeks later Patrick's
son again came to the capital, seeking his help in a request to John Smith, a
merchant in St Andrews, for 300 merks for the journey to Orkney. Again attracted
by the possibility of extracting hard cash from the earl, Lyon accompanied Robert

to St Andrews. Smith, however, refused to lend any money without receiving in return a bond in the earl's hand, including previous unpaid debts and interest. All Robert and Lyon received from him was £20 to cover their expenses. While they were in St Andrews, Duncan Mitchell came to Robert with letters from his father. These letters were later to be regarded as of great significance in indicating Patrick's influence on the activities of his son, in particular a long memorandum giving his instructions about what was to be done in the north. It later emerged that Patrick had dictated several versions of this memorial,[65] though all concerned took good care to destroy them, and none survived to aid the council's later investigations. According to Lyon, the document was 'full of injunctiounes how Robert sould carye him self in Orkney, bothe anent the taking of Houssis, the intromissioun with the Erllis rentis, and what men he sould put oute of the cuntrey'. There were also instructions to load the earl's ship with such goods as could be acquired and send it to Bergen, where the money obtained should be used to buy powder and bullets.

The three men, Robert, Lyon and Mitchell, returned to Leith together, then made for Dumbarton. Robert put up at a smith's house outside the town, while Lyon and Mitchell set out for the castle. They were met on the way by John Burn, a servant sent by Patrick. Burn warned Lyon to go back, since his coming was dangerous; the council 'wald be in suspicioun that thay had some purpois for thair going to Orknay'. In any case he would not be allowed access. Lyon was determined to see Patrick, but was forbidden entry by the castle keeper in person, shouting down from the walls. It was now Lyon's turn to lose his temper, since his whole interest in these affairs centred on the money owed to him. He threatened to Burn that he would tell all to the council, and for good measure exaggerated the scale of his own commitment by pretending that he had actually furnished Robert with men for his enterprise. In the end he managed to extort £2 sterling. Mitchell, as a servant, was allowed into the castle, and told Patrick the story of the ill-fortune in St Andrews. Patrick's reaction was predictable; he was 'heichlie commovit' and poured out vituperation against his son – 'Fals feble knave . . . Villaine . . . Pultrone . . . Or he wer not hangit, he sould hang him with his awne hand, because unworthelie he had left his Houssis and has not grace to win thame agane'. When Lyon returned to the smith's house, he told Robert his own conclusion that 'the erll had no uther course but to bring him to the scaffold'. Robert, with a deep sigh, answered, 'I fear it salbe swa.'

The young man's anxieties about his father's plans were shared by another important visitor to Patrick in his prison. This was a man who, unlike James Lyon, would go on to play a very prominent, not to say controversial, part in future events. Patrick Halcro came to Dumbarton in the summer of 1613.[66] Why he was there, and what discussions he had with the former earl, remain a matter for debate. Later Patrick was to deny before the council that they had ever exchanged more than half-a-dozen words. According to Halcro the two had private conversation, in the course

65 *Criminal Trials*, iii, 305.
66 *Criminal Trials*, iii, 307.

of which Patrick asked 'if be ony meanes, he could come be his Houssis againe in Orknay'.

Halcro replied, 'Your Lordship hes been ower lang in starting. Your Lordship had done weele, yf yow had causit keepe thame better quhen your Lordschip had thame.'

'That can not now be mendit. Is it not yitt possible to gett the Houssis agane?'

'It wilbe hard for your Lordship to gett that done, unless your Lordschip has assurance of the cuntrey people to stand be yow and assist yow.'

'Thay ar a cumpanie of fals people. I can not lippin [trust] in one of thame; bot I mynd to send my son thair quha wilbe your pairt. Will yow assist and tak pairt with my son?'

Halcro said that he at first refused, saying that Robert was 'ower feble a capitane to follow in such a purpois', but that at length he was persuaded, the first of several who were induced to come out for this ill-starred cause.

On 11 August 1613 Robert obtained 800 merks from a certain Francis Scott in Edinburgh.[67] This tided him over till the spring, when he set off for Orkney. Two nights before his departure his father, at that time still in Edinburgh, had a bed made for him in his own room in the castle.[68] Patrick later explained this by saying that Robert's landlady was on the point of giving birth and wished him out of the way; but it was clear that in fact his intention was to step up the emotional pressure that compelled the hapless young man, full of misgivings, to make his father's last desperate throw.

---

67 Court of Session Recs: Acts and Decreets, NRS CS7/300, ff. 245v–7v.
68 *Criminal Trials*, iii, 321.

14

Ower Feble a Capitane

R obert Stewart travelled to Orkney in secrecy, and it was not until he had been
there some time that his departure from open ward became generally known.[1]
The council's initial response was to have Stewart of Killeith send Sheriff Finlayson
after him. Robert was in Kirkwall when Finlayson arrived, accompanied by Thomas
Laing, who was to play a part in future events, and Patrick Murray, a Kirkwall man
who brought Robert a letter from his father; the content of this letter was later to
be the subject of much debate.[2] Finlayson made it clear to Robert that his presence
was not welcome, and he decided to leave Kirkwall for Birsay.[3] On the way he called
at the house of Thomas Black, a former chamberlain of Orkney, though for the
moment he failed to persuade Black to accompany him.[4]

His arrival in Birsay was peaceful enough. He came one morning with five
companions – Archibald Murray, Gilbert Gray, Andrew Martin, Robert Sclater and
Patrick Halcro. He was received at the palace with all courtesy by the keeper, Bernard
Stewart, his father's old henchman, and stayed a couple of weeks 'somequhat civilie'.
Then suddenly he attacked Bernard Stewart and expelled him from the palace at
sword point, keeping his wife Jean Halcro as a hostage. He sent to Kirkwall for
reinforcements, muskets, powder and lead. Eighteen armed men arrived, and
victuals were provided from the keeper's stocks. This sudden change of approach
was prompted by another letter from Patrick, dispatched on the eve of his return
from Edinburgh to Dumbarton, and brought by Duncan Mitchell. Like that taken
to Orkney by Patrick Murray, this letter was later to be the subject of painstaking
investigation by the council. Its very existence implicated Patrick in the activities of
his son, and it was said to contain sinister things; Bernard Stewart believed that it
included orders for his death.[5]

Patrick, however, was much too discreet on this occasion to mention such things

1 *RPC*, x, 240, 695.
2 *Criminal Trials*, iii, 301–2; most references to these events are taken from this source, which includes the
   trials of both Robert and Patrick; the lengthy transcriptions of background letters and other papers also
   included are drawn from Denmilne Papers, NLS Adv. Ms. 33.1.1 (v).
3 *Criminal Trials*, iii, 305.
4 Balfour of Denmilne Papers, NLS Adv. Ms. 33.1.1 (v, 91).
5 *Criminal Trials*, iii, 294–6.

on paper and, according to Mitchell, his master's most decisive orders were relayed by word of mouth. Patrick's lack of funds was now so serious that Robert had to take and retain control of the palace, and procure as much income as he could from the tenants. Robert and his followers went much further. In the middle of June they drew up and signed their fateful bond of association.[6] This document, in effect a sort of manifesto to justify their actions, bore the signatures of 17 of the two dozen or so men now involved. It said that 'be the frequent intrance of extranieris in this cuntrie, the estait of the common welth is in danger, and lyk to perische throw the corruptioun of the lawis, partialitie of juges, the greid of officeris, and oppressioun of magistratis, quhilkis dwangs [harass] the puir anes under the yock of servitude and slaverie; consumeing his Majesties rentis in their awin adois, but utilitie or guid service to his majestie'. The signatories, designing themselves 'the gentlemen of Orkney', undertook 'to be in reddines be our persouns . . . in armoure to repress all oppressiouns and iniquities . . . intendit aganes the common welth of this cuntrie . . . sua that bettir ordour may be establisched, quhaireby God eternalle ma be plesit, and our soverane lord obeyit and servit . . .' They agreed to follow Robert as their leader. Recognising the desperate nature of their enterprise, most appended slogans to their signatures – 'to the dethe', or 'with the hart and handis'. Those who could not write swore on their swords.

It was an extraordinary document, wholly at variance with Robert's public reasons for being in Orkney, and a dangerously explicit statement of aims that would inevitably be regarded as treasonable. No references to the service of his majesty or to touching the evangel could render them permissible, in view of Robert's undertaking not to go to Orkney at all, and of the king's displeasure, manifest even at this early stage. Two important signatures were absent, those of Andrew Martin and Archibald Murray. Martin, who actually drew up the document, had serious misgivings from the first, and avoided further contact with it. Murray's good faith was guaranteed in Robert's eyes (as no doubt was Martin's) by his long service to his father. The bond expressed a view of Orkney affairs that was prevalent enough to ensure widespread support for the rebels. The references to strangers, to corruption of the laws, to greedy officers and partial judges, all suggest the activities of Finlayson and his assistants. These had created enough ill-feeling to render Patrick's cause, against all expectation, more attractive to many than that of the crown.

The first test of the bond-brothers' resolution came quite soon. News of the palace's occupation came before the council and Stewart of Killeith's commission to apprehend Robert and his followers, first granted on 17 May, was renewed.[7] About a fortnight after the occupation had begun, Finlayson marched out to Birsay to confront Robert, accompanied by a force of 60–80 men.[8] He demanded

---

6 Justiciary Court Records, NRS JC26/7/115/7; copy in Balfour of Denrnilne Papers (NLS Adv. Ms.33.1.1 (v, 95, 107); printed *Criminal Trials*, iii, 293–4.

7 *RPC*, x, 240, 695.

8 *Criminal Trials*, iii, 295, 306.

Robert's surrender, offering him the chance to remain 14 days in Orkney to uplift his revenues. Robert refused, and was charged formally to surrender the palace. He responded by having his trumpeter sound a call of defiance, and his muskets then exchanged 30 shots or so with those of the sheriff. In the crossfire Downie Lyle, one of Robert's men, was hurt and a dog was killed. The earl's palace, however, for all its luxurious appointments, was too fine a stronghold for attack by a company without artillery, and after spending one night outside, Finlayson and his men departed.

The following day Mitchell the messenger, who had been at Birsay a fortnight, left for the south, carrying with him Robert's report to his father. Robert now spent a month preparing for his next move, a march on Kirkwall. Robert Sclater, bailie of Birsay, one of the original arrivals at the palace and a bond signatory, twice mustered the able-bodied of the parishes of Birsay and Harray, bringing forth 180 armed men who were entertained and feasted. Officers were appointed and vows taken regarding the aims of the enterprise, which looked forward to 'the tyme the lait Erle of Orknay war repossessit to his ancient and former government . . .'[9] Robert was joined by two more of his father's followers, Thomas Black and Thomas Laing. Both had changed sides, having previously accompanied Finlayson to Birsay. Black, who had been won to Robert's cause by Patrick Halcro and William Paterson, may have been swayed by his old allegiance to the earl, but in Laing's case the motive was a dispute with Finlayson over prize money for a captured pirate ship.[10] So strong was the feeling against Finlayson among men like Laing that Patrick was later to suggest that it was they who were truly responsible for the rebellion, and his son was merely their pawn.[11] Certainly Halcro and Black were among those who discussed with Robert the possibility of killing the sheriff.[12]

Duncan Mitchell arrived at Dumbarton Castle at two o'clock on the afternoon of Thursday 30 June.[13] He found the earl walking in the close, gave him Robert's letter and told him what had happened in Birsay. Patrick was greatly displeased, and flared up: 'The Devill stick his foollis head! . . . He might haif mellit with the scheref depute – and yf he had maid him quyte of him, he wald haif had lesse ado!' His son, Patrick reckoned, had set about matters in entirely the wrong way. If Robert had directed his attentions to the castle of Kirkwall the keepers, as the earl's old servants, would have delivered it to him without trouble. This would have robbed Finlayson of his chief base and enabled Robert to take and banish him – to 'mell' and 'make quit' of him. As it was, Finlayson had forced him at Birsay into outright defiance of the law, and still retained control of Orkney's major stronghold.

Despite his discontents, Patrick had no alternative but to offer words of counsel to his son, by means of two letters, one written on his own account, one in the person

---

9 *Criminal Trials*, iii, 275.
10 *Criminal Trials*, iii, 297–8.
11 *Criminal Trials*, iii, 320.
12 *Criminal Trials*, iii, 298.
13 *Criminal Trials*, iii, 295.

of John Sharp, his secretary.[14] Patrick praised the form of his son's letter (which Robert had written himself, having first torn up a draft by Martin),[15] presumably for its judiciously obscure account of what had happened, 'bot I fear it sall do littill goode'. The overriding point was that 'his maiestie thinks littill of theis materis'. Robert should believe neither the bishop ('tak tent that your holy father betray you not, as he did befoir'), nor the word of anyone who sought to offer conditions, since the council would not recognise any. No safe conduct south could be trusted; 'seing ye have proceidit so far as you have done, thair is no being heir for yow'. Sharp's letter was brutally explicit; it stated simply that if Robert came south he would be hanged. With the two letters, Mitchell was to convey verbally Patrick's desire that his son hold the palace and not surrender it, to die with honour rather than capitulate and face 'perpetual ward'. Patrick also wondered what support Robert had received from the commons and 'yf thai resortit to him', and he asked for whatever money his son could procure from the arrears. In the event none of this reached Robert, since Mitchell was arrested in Edinburgh before he had a chance to set out.

Robert made his first approach on Kirkwall on 16 July 1614. It took the form of a raiding-party of about 30 men, led by himself, with Patrick Traill, William Paterson and Archibald Murray, aimed at the sheriff's house. The party mustered at the Bu of Corse, which stands on a hill to the south-west of the town and was to provide a good vantage and mustering point then and later. There they learned that the sheriff, fearing an attack of just this sort, had removed himself to the castle. They transferred their attentions to the house of Bernard Stewart. At the early hour of an Orkney daybreak, they discharged a musket-volley and marched into the town. Robert and a small group of followers prised up the latch of the back *yett* of the house, entered the close and attacked the hall door, using a heavy beam as a battering ram. When they failed to gain entry, they applied the beam to a window. The occupants of the house were waiting for them; Bernard Stewart himself led the defence, hagbut in one hand, rapier in the other. Archibald Murray grabbed the gun, but was wounded in the hand by Stewart's sword.[16]

Beaten off, Robert returned to Birsay and his party resolved, as it had done in 1612, on an assault on the strategic points of the capital – the castle, the cathedral, the palace, the girnel. It was almost certainly Patrick Halcro who planned the deployment of forces. The cathedral and castle were particularly important; the girnel, though robustly constructed, was purely a source of supply rather than any sort of stronghold.[17] The palace, particularly Patrick's gracious additions, was much less easily defensible than the two stronger buildings, though attacks on it

14 *Criminal Trials*, iii, 305.
15 *Criminal Trials*, iii, 303.
16 *Criminal Trials*, iii, 276.
17 The exact site of the girnel at this date appears to be unknown. It was not the building known today as the girnel, which lies on the modern harbour front and was erected in the mid-seventeenth century. It is possible it lay closer to the castle and the Peerie Sea, which served as a harbour in earlier times.

could be severely hindered by marksmen positioned on the commanding height of the steeple, only a few yards to the north. The cathedral had in the past been regarded as of strategic importance for its size and strength.[18] The castle, 50 yards or so to the north-west, was the most formidable obstacle of all. Very strongly built, it consisted of a central keep surrounded by a curtain wall with two turrets set into it and a blockhouse at its gate. Behind this lay a bridge – not a drawbridge but a semi-permanent timber structure that connected directly with the 'iron yett' of the keep, situated half-way up the whole height of the house, at a steep upward angle.[19] The keep itself was battlemented on top, elaborately arranged inside and equipped with seven iron cannon and six of brass.[20]

Eight days after the attack on Bernard Stewart, a band of between ten and 20, led by Patrick Halcro with Black, Murray and Laing in support, took the cathedral tower unopposed. Halcro and one of his men, William Delday, entered by a window and opened the doors from the inside. They set up a position in the tower and left a small force there, led by Black, while Halcro, Laing and Murray departed to join Robert, who was assembling a force of 60–100 at the Bu of Corse. When Robert was ready, he sounded his trumpets, the steeple party blew a horn in response, and with displayed banner and beating drum, he marched on the castle. Finlayson and his men made no more than token resistance; a few shots were fired to no effect and the building was quickly overrun. At night a second and successful attempt was made on the house of Bernard Stewart and he joined the sheriff and Henry Aitken, who had taken refuge in the palace,[21] as a prisoner in the castle. Five days later, they were put on ships bound for the south. In the attack on the Palace of the Yards the defenders of the New Wark suffered the only casualty of the whole operation: Robert Chalmers, a Kirkwall merchant, was hit in the hand by a musket ball.[22] Thomas Laing, Alexander Leggat, and Gilbert Gray (another follower of Finlayson who had changed sides) garrisoned the palace and led the group that broke down the doors of the girnel. Provisions found in these buildings were borne away to the castle.[23] The cathedral party was increased to 12, and a feather bed was sent in for Thomas Black.[24]

The occupation of Kirkwall was now complete, and the rebels consolidated their position. When a suit of sails was found in the castle, Magnus Treb from Sanday

18 P. D. Anderson, 'Birsay in the Sixteenth Century', *Orkney Heritage 2 – Birsay, A Centre of Political and Ecclesiastical Power*, Kirkwall, 1983, 83–4.

19 According to Bishop Law, the keep's door stood 'about the mids of the wholl hight of the house' (*Letters on the Ecclesiastical Affairs of Scotland*, ii, 380). The suggestion that it must have stood well above the level of the outer door was made to me by Dr Raymond Lamb and is the only explanation for its relationship to the door of the keep, in view of the otherwise flat nature of the local terrain.

20 Orkney Record and Antiquarian Soc. Recs, OA D.46, box 1, no. 7; Caithness gives the numbers as eight of brass and six of iron (*Criminal Trials*, iii, 293).

21 *Criminal Trials*, iii, 297.

22 Balfour of Denmilne Papers, NLS Adv. Ms. 33.1.1 (v, 91).

23 O & S Papers, NRS RH9/15/150.

24 *Criminal Trials*, iii, 297; *Letters on the Ecclesiastical Affairs of Scotland*, ii, 401–2.

was sent to the crew of a Dutch *waughter* lying out in Kirkwall Roads to exchange it for gunpowder. The purpose of uplifting Patrick's arrears became that of laying in for the campaign. Malt, meal, butter and bere were brought in from all over the islands. Robert went to Stromness and Stronsay to gather teind fish and salt. Sheep were taken from the pastures on Helliar Holm and cattle from the Bu of Skaill, both from the Bus of Folsetter and Corse. Altogether provisions were amassed to a cash value of £5,000.[25] By late July, Robert's control in Orkney was absolute. He had all the major strongholds, and his uplifting of goods from his father's farms was so thorough that there was little left for the comfort of any invading army. He and his men were visited by 'numbers of people of all ranks', and they did not come to discourage. Francis Moodie told him that '24 rebels would make 500 men' – that the example of 24 stalwarts would bring out substantial support.[26] George Traill provided them with sheep. So far all had been successful; but it must have been plain to the rebels that all they could do in the coming weeks would be to sit and wait for the response of the government.

On 5 July 1614, the same day Stewart of Killeith's commission was renewed, Duncan Mitchell, Patrick's messenger, was arrested in Edinburgh. When Patrick's letters to Robert were found, the council acted swiftly: three members of the guard were dispatched to Dumbarton the same night, with orders to arrest John Sharp and search Patrick's papers.[27] Up to this point the council had given no sign of suspecting collusion between Robert and his father, or of believing that Robert was intending to do more than stir up trouble in the islands. Although Mitchell's letters gave no clue as to either's ultimate intentions, their existence suggested strongly to the unhappy councillors that what was happening in Orkney was no ordinary disturbance. Their promptness of action was in vain. When the guards arrived at the castle gate of Dumbarton at five o'clock the next afternoon, both the keeper and his deputy were out, and through the pettifogging delays of the staff the council's men were not admitted till mid-morning the following day. By then John Sharp had escaped, and nothing of significance was found among Patrick's papers. Despite the failure of the earl's previous attempt to influence his captors, he was clearly not without friends in the castle.

Mitchell was interrogated by members of the council, including the secretary Lord Binning, the former Hamilton of Monklands, who was to be responsible for the government's conduct during the whole episode. The messenger described his previous visits to Patrick in Edinburgh, and to his son in Birsay, the taking of the palace and the confrontation with Finlayson, his most recent interview with the earl, and the part played by Sharp in the framing of the correspondence. At this point, despite the displeasure of king and council, the situation was still not regarded as particularly serious, and it was not discussed again for about three

25 O & S Papers, NRS RH9/l5/122.
26 *Criminal Trials*, iii, 285.
27 *Criminal Trials*, iii, 299.

weeks. Towards the end of July, as Robert and his men continued their 'foolische courses', the council debated what to do.[28] The majority of its members favoured the most obvious solution, which was to send Stewart of Killeith himself, as sheriff and chamberlain, to Orkney. They discussed how he was to go there and what sort of company he should take with him. Some councillors were of the sanguine opinion that the forces available within Orkney itself would be sufficient for him to subdue the rebellion, 'althoght the authoures wer ten tymes mo in number'. Others, perhaps conscious that Stewart's unpopular regime could expect little support in the islands, felt that it would not be safe for Sir James to 'hazard himself with the country people'; he should have a force of 60 paid men. A decision on the matter was deferred until the following day.

Early the very next morning, 29 July, news arrived of the assault on the strongholds of Kirkwall. Shaken, the councillors convened in the over council house. Killeith was there, and was then commissioned to lead an expedition.[29] He was allowed up to 500 men, and Lord Lovat offered more. The proclamations against assisting the rebels were renewed, and ships planning to sail north were ordered to stay in port.[30] Expedition preparations began almost immediately, and trumpet and drum were sent round to advertise for recruits. It was said that Killeith hoped to gather most of his force in three or four days, and leave for the north in less than a week; in reality he had no stomach for the enterprise. Hitherto his sole action in response to the challenge to his authority had been to send Finlayson in an attempt to warn Robert off. Now, when it was obvious that he had to take direct military measures, he elected to travel overland while the bulk of his army would go by sea.[31] This was hardly a practical possibility – the force would in all likelihood arrive without a commander – and when an alternative scheme was put to the council, Stewart stepped down only too willingly.

The earl of Caithness now took a hand. He had other reasons for adopting this cause besides his long-standing hatred of Patrick. He was in Edinburgh that summer to pursue his feuds with the earl of Sutherland and Lord Forbes;[32] he hoped that the credit he might gain from taking charge of the Orkney expedition would enable him on the one hand to escape the litigation of Forbes, and on the other 'to revenge his late quarrel against the house of Sutherland, having left no other means unattempted'.[33] At first he remained in the background, offering support to another candidate for the leadership of the expedition, Robert Monteith of Egilsay. Monteith had the backing of 'some gentlemen' of Orkney who felt that the current plans would be too burdensome, and told the council that local support

28 *Criminal Trials*, iii, 284.
29 *Criminal Trials*, iii, 284.
30 *RPC*, x, 698.
31 *Criminal Trials*, iii, 284.
32 Gordon, *Genealogical History of the Earldom of Sutherland*, 299.
33 Gordon, *Genealogical History of the Earldom of Sutherland*, 299.

would enable him to do the job with only the 60 men originally proposed.[34] The council accepted this, and he received a commission on 3 August, about the time Killeith's men had been due to set off.[35] He was to receive funds for 100 men, with a trumpeter and heralds and their pay for a fortnight. Caithness promised a further 100 under Henry Sinclair, his brother.[36] A ship was prepared – the *Post* of Leith, under John Stewart[37] – and there would be two 'battering pieces' from Edinburgh Castle for laying siege. There was a week to prepare.

Monteith's commission was only three days old when Caithness himself took over command, as the council was said to have 'earnistlie intreatit' him to do.[38] The justification given for a second change of leader was the earl's 'power and forceis and . . . the freindschipe he hes in the cuntrey of Orknay'. Caithness may have used Monteith as a catspaw, fearing that the council might be reluctant to entrust him with its response to the rebellion; in the event he found the councillors much more receptive to the idea than he expected. One likely reason was that, like Monteith, he 'did undertake the same without great charges to the king'. Another was the support of Bishop Law, who had suggested him as a governor in the north as early as June 1612.[39] He was also useful as the only great noble likely to interest himself in the case. As such he might be better able to command obedience from the Orkney gentry than Monteith, who was merely one of their number.

Caithness was advanced to the status of king's lieutenant, with justiciary powers. He had the option of promising pardon to up to six of the rebels, provided they were not 'interprisaris and counsellouris in the affair', and had not taken part in the earlier revolt. He received £800 as pay for the 60 soldiers promised, £300 for equipment and provisions and 100 merks for gunpowder and fuses; additional funds would be available if the expedition took longer than expected. The council formally charged the rebels to surrender, promising pardon for deserters, and issued a commission to some of the Shetland gentry – Bruce of Cultmalindie, Thomas Black of Strom, the Sinclairs of Brough, Houss and Quendale – to apprehend any rebels who might make their way there.[40]

Preparations began in earnest. Robert Windram, the Albany Herald, and his trumpeter John Johnston, were appointed to make proclamations; two cannoneers, two wrights and a smith were to operate and maintain the cannon furnished by Edinburgh Castle's master gunner; and four Leith skippers certified the merits of the *Post*, which was to carry the guns. The boat of Eustace Robertson, of Burntis-land, was to act as pinnace. A report that Robert and his men had 'sett to the sea ane

34 *Criminal Trials*, iii, 285.
35 RPC, x, 700.
36 RPC, x, 261, 701.
37 RPC, x, 262, 701.
38 RPC, x, 701–4.
39 *Letters on the Ecclesiastical Affairs of Scotland*, i, 290.
40 RPC, x, 707.

ship of warre in goode equippage',[41] whether true or not, prompted the council to engage the vessel of Robert Cairncross, another Burntisland man, who for £800 was to take on 20 armed seamen, as well as guns and ammunition. John Skemure was appointed surgeon at £30 a month, with £100 for his 'kist and furnessing of druggis'.[42]

The cannon consisted of a large weapon called *Thrawn Mouth*, weighing about a ton and a half, firing a missile of about 30 pounds from a six and a quarter inch calibre barrel; and a *culverin bastard*, a piece of about four inch bore, throwing iron shot weighing about eight pounds. The maximum range of *Thrawn Mouth* was just under a mile, and of its companion rather less. Both were French, and of some antiquity; *Thrawn Mouth* bore the porcupine badge of Louis XII (d. 1515) and the culverin was cast with the salamander of Louis's successor Francis I (d. 1547). *Thrawn Mouth* had been in Scotland since at least 1547, when she was recorded as being in Dunbar Castle. Both were battering pieces, specifically designed for siege work. In other countries they might have been regarded as less than adequate, and the personnel and ammunition provided for them was meagre; the two gunners had a total of 60 bullets when each piece, well manned, could have been fired 30 or 40 times a day. Even allowing for the inadequacies of the Scottish artillery establishment (guns had frequently to be borrowed from England) and the technological backwardness that meant that ammunition had to be imported at great expense, the artillery provision of the expedition was poor.[43] It reflected the seemingly acute lack of funds that had lain behind the council's whole conduct of events. Accompanying the cannon was a long inventory of the tools and materials for them – two barrels of 'cuttit yron for hailschott', planks, spars and skins for the construction of siege equipment and gun platforms. Butter was used for greasing wheels – almost certainly Orkney butter, which was regularly used by Edinburgh Castle's artillery as a lubricant.[44]

During the two weeks of preparation, there were further developments elsewhere. On 4 August the constable of Dumbarton Castle was ordered to make Patrick a close prisoner, and replace his personal servants with one of his own.[45] A

41 *RPC*, x, 708, 711.
42 *RPC*, x, 707–9.
43 I am very grateful to Dr David Caldwell of the Royal Museum of Scotland for statistics and other details regarding these weapons. The figures he gives are as follows:

	Cannon weight	Shot weight	Barrel diameter	Range
Thrawn Mouth	3,800 lb	33 lb	6 ¼ in	1,700 yds
	1,727.27 kg	15 kg	159 mm	1,554.8 m
Culverin	1,970 lb	8 lb	3 5/6 in	1,600 yds
Bastard	895.45 kg	3.64 kg	97 mm	1463.04 m

44 *RPC*, x, 713–14; the popular idea that Orkney butter was used to grease *Mons Meg* is not merely legend, since there is a reference to it being used for the lubrication of cannon, including *Mons* herself, in the *Accounts of the Master of Works*, ii, 233.
45 *RPC*, x, 262.

week later, Bernard Stewart, the expelled keeper of the Palace of Birsay, arrived in Edinburgh. He was interviewed by Lord Binning and Gideon Murray of Elibank, the treasurer depute, who were more interested in Patrick's part in events than with eliciting information likely to be of use to the expedition. They asked Stewart whether his old master had invited him to join in the rebellion, and he described a conversation he had had in Dumbarton. Hearing that Robert was going to Orkney to take up duties, he went to see Patrick, since he was afraid that his own possessions would suffer. Patrick became very angry and, pulling at his beard with rage, said 'Yf Robert be gone to Orknay, the king and yow will not mend it – and your best wilbe to beholde him.'[46] He claimed to have the support of Mar and Lennox in persuading the king to accept what he had done. This was why Stewart had co-operated with Robert when he arrived in Birsay; but Patrick's ire was not so easily assuaged and may have been part of the reason for his son Robert's sudden attack on him. After his expulsion Stewart had employed Robert Halcro of Cava to persuade Robert to free his wife. During discussions, Halcro said he caught sight of a letter from Patrick urging his son to kill Stewart.

There were other measures, defining more closely the scope of Caithness's duties. He was ordered to 'mak choise of some speciall gentilmen of his awne and of the cuntrey people' whose assistance would enable the invasion to take place with as little 'harme, prejudice and inconvenient to the cuntrey' as possible.[47] Killeith, though he had renounced command of the expedition, was still chamberlain of Orkney and Shetland, and secured a council order that Caithness hand him over Kirkwall and Birsay as soon as they were taken.[48] Much more important was the addition of James Law to the leadership of the expedition. He was very unwilling to undertake this duty and agreed, out of loyalty, only after strong assurances by Binning regarding the conduct of his affairs in his absence.[49]

Caithness's expedition set sail on 20 August, and arrived at Castle Sinclair, his own seat, two days later. There the earl spent the night making ready for Orkney. Thirty Caithness men crossed the Firth with him on 23 August. At six o'clock in the evening they anchored in Elwick, the bay on the south coast of Shapinsay, tucked behind Helliar Holm but commanding a view to the south-west, across the String to Carness, the intended landing point on the Mainland, and the cathedral of Kirkwall, plainly visible beyond.[50] The next day Albany Herald Windram was sent over to make the proclamation against the rebels, accompanied by notaries, messengers

---

46 *Criminal Trials*, iii, 296.

47 *RPC*, x, 710–11.

48 *RPC*, x, 712; Killeith had also received a letter from the earl of Somerset, the Ker of Farniehurst who had become the English lord chamberlain and was acting treasurer of Scotland, 1614–15, stating that it was the king's will that he should lead the expedition (*ibid.*, 714). Somerset is said to have 'succeeded to Dunbar's expectations of [Patrick's] estate' (M. Laing, *The History of Scotland*, vols I–IV, Edinburgh, 1804, i, 65, cited in *Notes*, ed. Peterkin, app., 54).

49 Balfour of Denmilne Papers, NLS ref. Adv. Mss. 33.1.1 (v, 86); *RPC*, x, 710.

50 *Criminal Trials*, iii, 286.

and witnesses. As he entered Kirkwall he was confronted by the cathedral party, led by John Guild, with Gilbert Gray, Patrick Traill and Thomas Black. Robert had ordered them to prevent the herald from discharging his office and bring him to the Yards. Guild, a mysterious character and a rival to Black in his command of the group, was particularly truculent. He grabbed Windram's tabard, tore it, and 'preast to half tane it af him'.[51] The king's men were 'most injuriouslie and dispytfullie abused, bothe in word and deid', taken at gunpoint and kept prisoner until the evening. The same day, over 300 rebels marched out to Carness with ensigns flying in defiance.[52]

Balked of the customary mode of publishing the wishes of king and council, Caithness was compelled to send letters round the islands commanding the support of the gentry and other inhabitants. The results disappointed him – 'for the most part I did not find that reddie willingnes whiche I expected' – and he sent for the rest of his followers from across the Firth. He managed to assemble about 200 islanders, and when his own men arrived on 26 August, led by his kinsmen Sinclair of Mey and Sinclair of Ratter, the expedition finally came over to the Mainland. At ten o'clock in the morning they brought ashore the smaller of the two guns, and laboriously dragged it through deep soil the two miles to Weyland, about three quarters of a mile north-east of Kirkwall Castle. It was set in place about three o'clock. As the earl's infantry marched towards Kirkwall, a force of rebels came out to meet them, shouting that they would fight, even if outnumbered 20 to one. Their companions in the castle, the steeple and the tower of the Yards fired shots in support. About 80 of the rebels confronted Caithness at the Ba' Lea, a tract of recreation ground near Papdale but, according to the earl, fled 'schamefullie' when his men marched directly upon them. Some 'pressed poore menne' deserted. Caithness ordered his gunners to fire on the castle. Their second shot (which in retrospect was shown to be rather fortunate) hit and almost destroyed the turnpyke head – the turret on top of the keep that covered the stair inside. About six o'clock in the evening the earl took possession of the town itself. Whether or not the rebels behaved as ignominiously as Caithness's account suggests, the open show of defiance, both at Carness and the Ba' Lea, was later to be viewed as a very serious matter indeed by the crown.

The earl's forces had now completed their landing, the most hazardous stage of the whole campaign, had the rebels chosen to take advantage. Caithness made much of the rebels' lack of resolution, but both he and the bishop found the situation much less agreeable than they had anticipated. The earl sent ministers to the rebels to 'instruct, admonish and threaten them', but found them 'most obstinate, and maliciouslie resolved to hold out to the deathe'. This strength of feeling was not confined to active rebels; Bishop Law wrote of 'greater contempte and obstinacie in the rebelles, les trust and willing obedience in the people then we could foresie or did expect . . . gif God doe not subdue the pryde of the villanous knaves, thare

51 *Criminal Trials*, iii, 278, 287, 300.
52 *Criminal Trials*, iii, 286–7; *State Papers of Melros*, i, 143–5.

is great appeirance of much blood schadding before the houss and haulds can be takin'.

The result was an extreme shortage of virtually every necessary. 'Thair is heir no bread, nor drink, nor uther victuallis to be had for pryce, prayer or command,' wrote the earl; if he and his men were not to starve they had to be supplied from the country of Caithness, and if the rebels held out for any length of time at all, 'thair will be not be pouder, leid, billettis nor matche to serve for this service'. Further supplies might have to be sent up from Edinburgh. Conscious of the council's parsimony, the earl suggested that necessaries might be sold to his men so that there would be 'litle or no hurt to his Majesties money'! Even ink was in short supply; the earl and the bishop had hardly enough for the letters they wrote from Weyland.[53] In these, both boasted of the hardships they shared with their men. The earl had spent the previous night 'ludged about the Ordinance', and according to the bishop he 'and all of us, leives lyke souldiours withe verrie temperat dyet; out in the daye and nicht lying about dykes or within houses no better then croffes . . .'[54] The spectre of Summerdale remained ever before the earl. Rather than forsake his duty he had 'willed rather to be buried in his grandsire's grave . . .'

The positions were now ready for the start of the siege proper. On 27 August, as the bishop was writing his letter, the cannon was firing from Weyland towards the castle. The next day, a Sunday, it was moved to Newbigging 'within ane muscatt schott' of the New Wark, on whose Chapel Tower it was trained. The early success of the bastard in striking one of the vulnerable parts of the castle from the outer limit of its range had not been repeated, while the Chapel Tower was proving an uncomfortably effective vantage-point for Robert's musketeers. Robert, moreover, following to the letter his father's instructions about keeping his houses, had billeted himself in the palace rather than the castle. All day until midnight on Monday 29 August the earl's guns and his muskets, stationed behind the dykes of the palace garden and in nearby houses, fired on the buildings. The results were not impressive. The earl reported that his bombardment managed to 'noy thame much', but in fact the only casualties among the defenders were Robert's mother, Marjorie Sinclair, who was shot through the hand, and a boy attendant wounded in the thigh. Nothing in the surviving ruins of the building (which continued in use after Patrick's time) shows that it ever suffered from attack by gunfire.

The same afternoon *Thrawn Mouth* was landed and brought directly into town, a distance of four miles. She was positioned to fire on the massive oriel windows of the great hall, on the east side of the building. Ladders were prepared for storming. Before she could go into action the following morning, Robert made the first of his moves to come to terms with the earl. He had realised that his father's house could

---

53 *State Papers of Melros*, i, 145–7, *Letters on the Ecclesiastical Affairs of Scotland*, ii, 369–70.

54 *Sic* – the use of the word 'croffes' appears to be a very early example of the common mistake of thus describing the croft house, rather than the smallholding to which the term properly refers (G. Donaldson, *Isles of Home*, Edinburgh, 1983, 114–15).

not be defended against heavy cannon, but his negotiations went well beyond the simple question of surrender of the building. Robert offered to yield all his positions in return for pardon and mercy for himself and his companions. This was impossible; he must surrender unconditionally to the clemency of the king, or suffer the worst. Negotiations continued during the last day of August while, Caithness said, Robert and his men 'so spoiled [the palace] . . . that thare was not above thrie or four lockes left upoun dorres, in all the place'. Robert and his men were allowed to leave for the castle, and at three that afternoon Caithness took possession of the palace. The first of Robert's strongholds had fallen.[55]

As an alternative to Robert's unrealistic demand for clemency, Andrew Martin had suggested he offer Caithness a guarantee to appear before the council. Robert refused, beset as he now was by indecision and fear. His close servants had observed his weakness for some time. According to Patrick Halcro, he had been in bed when Caithness's cannon first began to fire, and remained there while the cumbrous and undermanned weapon fired six shots. When taxed by Halcro about this, he remained silent; Halcro then asked him 'how he thoght this mater wald lest'. Robert dodged the question and replied: 'I will not tak me to the sea; my fader will then say I haif feblie gevin over his Houss. I will rather hald oute quhill the house be dung downe abone my heade, or I rander my self to the erll of Caithness, or yitt to the Counsell, to be tortourit, quhill I confes aganis my fader, the thing that may be his wrack and myne.'[56] He maintained, pathetically, his 'expectatioun' that his father would break ward and come north. Events were to show that there was still plenty of spirit left in Robert's supporters, but the youth himself was a poor hunted creature, terrified of the cannon, afraid of the retribution of the government, and yet forced by his abject regard for his father into a hopeless enterprise for which he had no appetite or aptitude at all.

As his unhappy demeanour became apparent, some of his followers began to make alternative arrangements. On the day Robert gave up his father's house, he also lost his most important vantage-point outside the castle. John Guild, 'the gildest [cleverest] knave of all other', yielded control of the steeple, on promise of life and pardon. Guild's outrageous conduct towards the herald made this a heavy price to pay, but there is no doubt as to why Caithness complied. The steeple was 'the rebels strongest hauld'; his forces 'could have no angle in all the place of the Yairdis, frie from the danger of the schottes from the stiple'. This was the reason for the ineffectiveness of the attack on the Yards. Guild wisely made himself scarce and disappeared forever; Thomas Black, the ostensible leader of the cathedral party, was not so fortunate. By his account, he was himself negotiating terms with the earl for the surrender of St Magnus when Guild gave it up on conditions agreed behind his back. Black was left stranded in the earl's power.[57] For Robert the surrender was a

55 *State Papers of Melros*, i, 147–50.
56 *Criminal Trials*, iii, 307.
57 *Criminal Trials*, iii, 297.

major setback. Without it, the only alternative open to the king's lieutenant would have been to turn his cannon on the cathedral itself 'with much travell, coist and danger'.

On 2 September the Palace of Birsay surrendered to forces under Adam Bellenden of Stenness, leaving only the castle in Robert's control. The earl had hopes that his luck would continue, ending in a negotiated surrender, and continued to treat with Robert and Patrick Halcro. He believed, quite erroneously, that Robert's soldiers were quite ready to yield 'bot they are keipit in, and cannot escape'. Halcro offered to surrender himself into Caithness's hands, if he would pardon Robert; the earl could not grant such a condition, while Robert himself was 'so affrayed that he will suffer all that may befall him, [that he would not] rander himself, without promeis and band for his lyffe'. The result was deadlock, and at midnight on Sunday 4 September, the truce came to an end. In its last hours the earl, hoping to impress upon Robert the strength of his position, redeployed his forces; the cannon were positioned to fire on the castle, musketeers placed in surrounding houses, and 16 men sent into the cathedral to fire down on the castle's cannon. Gabions – wickerwork forerunners of the sandbag – were set at the east end of the kirkyard and against the long side of the castle facing across Broad Street. Musket-fire began immediately on expiry of the truce and continued all night. The earl's forces suffered their first fatality; a man filling an empty gabion was shot through the left side, and died some hours later.

In the morning, Caithness brought his cannon into action against the ramparts of the castle, where they inflicted some damage. Briefly, Caithness had some expectation of a quick military solution. Writing from the Yards on 5 September, the king's lieutenant described what had happened since his landing. Just as he was bringing matters up to date the guns opened up and pierced the castle battlements – 'by Gods grace we sail this day beat it doune and dismunt thair ordnance'. Before the letter was finished he had changed his mind. Like the initial hit on the turnpyke-head, the destruction of the relatively flimsy stonework of the battlements gave no idea of the strength of the walls and vaults of the building, on which the cannon had no effect.[58] The earl was later to speak of the castle as 'one of the strongest houssis in Breitane; for I will bring with me . . . cannone billetis, both brokkin lyke goulfe bails upoune the Castelle and clovin in twa halffis'. Nor was he then speaking purely out of frustration. Examining the building closely after all was over he was to add: 'I protest to God the House hes nevir bene biggit by [without] the consent of the divile.'[59]

In response to Caithness's complaints Binning sent him the first of two consignments of ammunition and supplies.[60] Thus fortified, the earl persevered with his bombardment, which succeeded in putting Robert's cannon out of action. The turnpyke of the keep, an already noted weakness, had 'ane grite breatche' made in

58 *State Papers of Melros*, i, 147–50.
59 *Criminal Trials*, iii, 289, 291; *State Papers of Melros*, i, 174–7.
60 *Criminal Trials*, iii, 293.

it, and much damage had been done to the *block-house*. Means had also been found to fire at the iron gate of the keep itself, presumably through the outer gate in the curtain walls – and a possible route of assault had been prepared. Nevertheless by mid-September the besiegers were beset by problems. They had expended 56 shots from one cannon and 57 from the other, using a quarter of a ton of gunpowder, of which only half a barrel was left, with nine cannonballs. The earl commandeered some powder from a passing ship but it was clear that this was far from enough.

In spite of Robert's own irresolution, the morale of the rebels remained high, and the morning after the earl's guns were finally silenced by scarcity they were on the walls asking why the cannon 'did sleip so lang'. This was the more galling since Caithness had tried hard to keep his problem a secret. Bishop Law, relaying these details to Lord Binning, felt that only promises of life to Robert and Patrick Halcro would induce the defenders to surrender,[61] since otherwise 'thair is no thing bot force to constrain them'. The rebels had had their own successes: Martin Sheill, the earl's English smith, had been shot in the arm as he stood by the cannon, and James Ritchesoun, a soldier, had received a fatal wound through the body – delivered, it was said, while he was drinking a health and scoffing at the defenders.[62]

For a time Caithness shifted his attention to the consolidation of his gains. He began by interviewing his prisoners. On 9 September Archibald Murray, who had surrendered Birsay, Thomas Black from the cathedral, and Thomas Laing and Alexander Leggat, defenders of the Yards, were asked about the assault on the Orkney strongholds.[63] Black and Leggat emphasised that they were not members of the inner council of the rebels – that, both agreed, consisted of Murray, Andrew Martin, Gilbert Gray and Robert Sclater. Black conceded that he had assisted Robert Stewart with his tackmen's accounts, but he had joined the rebels unwillingly and in ignorance of their intentions. He had spent the first night in the cathedral after its capture only because he was weary; he was compelled under duress to remain there as captain. His uneasy relationship with his difficult subordinate John Guild suggests he may have been telling the truth. He was a reluctant witness to Guild's abuse of the herald, and Windram himself absolved him from any blame in it. Leggat had gone to Carness, but otherwise had been concerned only with the defence of the Yards. Black and Leggat were asked only about their part in recent events, while Laing was interrogated about his trip to London the previous spring.[64]

The following day, in the great hall of the Yards, the king's lieutenant held the first of a series of justice courts to try some lesser fry. Magnus Treb, who had bartered for gunpowder the sails found in the castle, was also accused of dissuading the commons of Sanday from joining the earl's forces, telling them 'that they wer but fooles to cum over to my Lord and that nane of thame wald cum hame agane unslaine'. He was

61 Balfour of Denmilne Papers, NLS ref. Adv Ms 33.1.1. (v, 81).
62 Gordon, *Genealogical History of the Earldom of Sutherland*, 300–1.
63 Balfour of Denmilne Papers, NLS Adv. Ms. 33.1.1 (v, 90–2).
64 *Criminal Trials*, iii, 296–301.

tried with Thomas Dawson and William Willox, who had used events to indulge in thievery of their own. Treb and Willox were executed; Dawson was spared on the grounds of youth, but also had to act as hangman. The assize that delivered these verdicts consisted in roughly equal measure of Caithness men; Kirkwall merchants and burgesses, including Patrick's old captain, Thomas Lentroun; and members of the gentry who had proved so reluctant to involve themselves in the suppression of the rebellion – Scollay of Strynie, Bannatyne of Gairsay, Henderson of Holland, Balfour of Garth, Craigie of Brough, Sinclair of Tuquoy.[65]

Four days later, shortly after Black and his companions were sent south to the council, Andrew Martin gave himself up. Interviewed by Caithness and the bishop, he painted a picture of fear and dissension among the occupants of the castle. Robert's nerve was no stronger than it had been when he kept his bed. One night Caithness's cannon had fired twice at the yett of the keep, striking fear in the hearts of all. In the morning Robert had asked Martin for counsel. Martin said that 'all was lyk to go wrong', and Robert railed bitterly against his father: 'thair was nevir thing lukkit weill yit quhilk he devysit. God gif I had nevir kend his turnis!' Robert was sustained only by the most slender and unrealistic hopes, put in his head by his desperate sire. When Martin, as fearful himself, asked leave to depart, Robert sought to dissuade him, speaking first of Caithness's cruelty, then of the many changes that could occur to improve their fortunes 'as namelie, the comeing of Spanyeirdis, the practises of Papistis, and the truble whairin the Count Pallatyne wes'.[66] In his correspondence, Patrick had suggested to his son that the difficulties of the international scene – the religious tension in Europe between Calvinist and Catholic, the problems this created for James's foreign and religious policies, into which his own daughter Elizabeth was being drawn as wife of the Elector of the Palatinate – could well deflect the wrath of the king from the comparatively minor matter of the Northern Isles. Martin did not believe a word of it, and departed into the hands of Caithness.

The rebels had lost all but one of their strongholds, several of their major figures, and now one of Patrick's oldest and most trusted counsellors. But Caithness himself was in difficulties. His artillery was out of action, and the only alternative proved a disaster. An attempt was made to assault the castle block-house directly and scale the curtain walls at a number of different places. This left two men dead, others wounded 'and all terrified'. Next an 'instrument of timber' was employed – probably a 'sow' or wheeled shelter for protecting soldiers and pioneers from shots and stones as they endeavoured to attack the walls. The rebels set it on fire before it could be used effectively. To this annoyance was added the realisation that such a strategy was probably futile; deserters from the castle said that the defenders intended to fall back from the curtain walls and block-house into the keep.[67]

---

65 O & S Papers, NRS RH9/15/150.
66 O & S Papers, NRS RH9/15/150.
67 *Criminal Trials*, iii, 303.

The siege was reduced to an exchange of musketry. At two o'clock on 19 September, William Irving of Sebay was killed, picked off 'among us all standing by', a soldier was fatally wounded in the back and another hit in the arm. One of the castle company was killed. Irving's death was in the earl's view a judgment, since he believed he had been 'ane moyenour [agent] and ane greit freind to the Traitour'. This strengthened Caithness's view of the Orcadians (ironically similar to Patrick's) as being thoroughly untrustworthy. He had never been able to stop them from supplying the rebels with food and drink and telling them what he was doing. 'I protest to God I . . . nevir sall cum to ane cuntrie that may be compairitt in falsett to this cuntrie people! I use thame baith with lenitie and fair forms . . . and for all that I can do, they have thair secret moyen and traffecke with the traitors.' He had got wind of the bond among the rebels, and rumour – or his imagination – had swelled the number of its signatories to 'sevin hundred of this cuntrie men'. In his letters, his references to the enemy bore increasing signs of exasperation – 'thir most bluidie and barbarous Rebeles and Traitouris . . . desperat and cruell Tratours . . . bluidie Tratoures that is within this divilisch Castle . . . give God grant me that gud fortune to get on lyve Robert Stewart or Patrik Halcro, his Maiestie will hear of good sporte'.[68]

As September advanced, the earl became increasingly convinced that negotiation was the only answer. On 9 September, the day he interrogated Thomas Black, he wrote to the council, asking how he should deal with his prisoners, and how far he could reasonably go in promising mercy. He was told to try them in Orkney and impose 'exemplar' punishments, unless there was a pressing reason for doing otherwise, for example if they held important information. Regarding mercy, there was little comfort for Robert Stewart. Any such concession to him 'would seem very strange to his majesty', in view of the trouble and expense already incurred. He might offer pardon to 'assistaris' in order to isolate or betray the principals, provided they told all they knew; but the only encouragement for Stewart or Halcro was that if they surrendered there were many reasons 'quhy thay sould not dispair to find grace with his maiestie quhois great mercie and clemencie is notour to the world in infinit pruiffes'.[69]

The supply ships arrived again on 19 September, the last day of action in the siege. With them came the council's advice, though it was of little assistance to Caithness, who now seemed uncertain what to do next. He began another letter to Secretary Binning. He had little to report except his complaints against the Orcadians, and his belief that his commission would probably need to be extended. 'Hoping evir upon betir news', he postponed its dispatch for so long that it became a kind of journal, which was not finally sent until all was over. Binning, anxious for progress and with other worries besides, began to grow restive.[70] On 22 September the earl held

68 *Letters on the Ecclesiastical Affairs of Scotland*, ii, 380.
69 *Criminal Trials*, iii, 288–9; *State Papers of Melros*, i, 174–7.
70 *State Papers of Melros*, i, 154.

the second of his courts. Janet Whyte was tried for that offence of which he had complained so bitterly – helping and communicating with the rebels. Her husband, William Paterson, was among them, and she was said to have visited him with food and other necessaries; in exchange she had received 'his maiesties fish' – dried fish from the earldom rents taken to the castle. She was absolved by the Orkney jury, two-thirds of them from Kirkwall, who found that she had given nothing, and had received fish only as a necessity for herself and her child.[71]

Caithness abandoned all hope of a military solution. He approached the rebels and asked them directly if they would leave the castle and place themselves in the king's hands, promising Robert that he would be kept safe 'from everie danger of my folkis', till the king's pleasure was known. Fearing torture at the council's hands, Robert wished this protection to be extended until he could be brought into the presence of the king himself. Caithness was in no position to grant this, and refused. By this time, all that was left to Patrick's son was a kind of weak stubbornness, a hopeless determination to make no concession, fortified in the knowledge of the castle's strength. But now the earl was informed of a weakness in his position – the growing dissatisfaction of Patrick Halcro, who was said to have told Robert plainly that he intended to hand over the castle. Caithness had more than once expressed bitter words about Halcro, whose disposition of Robert's men had been so trouble-some, and he had serious misgivings about making important concessions to him. However, if we are to believe the earl, Halcro had already been turning over in his mind his response to any concession. The result was a series of discussions with Robert and Halcro separately. The exact nature of these is debatable, as is the responsibility for the outcome, but in the end, on 29 September, Robert Stewart surrendered.[72]

71 *State Papers of Melros Papers*, i, 169.
72 O & S Papers, NRS RH9/15/50.

15

Of your Speciall Causeing, Sending, Hounding out, Command, Counsell, Devyse and only Directioun

The bishop of Orkney and the earl of Caithness disagree over the details of how the rebellion in Orkney was brought to a peaceful conclusion. In the earlier stages their accounts of events roughly coincide, though there is some discrepancy about who should take credit for what, and Caithness in particular makes little mention of his companion's contribution. As the siege moves towards its close the two narratives diverge, in both the timing of events and the estimation of their relative importance. Caithness states that, having reached an impasse with Robert, he asked the young man if he would allow Patrick Halcro to negotiate on his behalf. Robert rejected this. Feigning acceptance, Caithness sent secret word to Halcro asking him if he would come out the following day 'upone plaidges', and speak with him in the cathedral. The two had 'four houres conferens, he and I hand to hand'. Halcro agreed to give up the castle in return for his life.[1] To avoid the suspicion of treachery, at least until the majority of the defenders had been persuaded to leave, he asked for a minister to be sent in to preach to the rebels and put his case for surrender. The earl for his part was to give 'fair countenance' to any who left the castle. These manipulations took over a week to achieve their aim, but in the end they were successful; Robert's support among the defenders crumbled away behind his back, and, with the last of his companions, he gave himself up.

The chief outside source of information for this episode is Sir Robert Gordon, whose account of the siege is the most detailed written before the modern period. Ironically for one who hated Caithness, he supports the earl's version, and it is through basing their work on his that later writers have given Patrick Halcro such a bad press.[2] According to Gordon, Robert remained determined to hold out but Halcro 'persuaded him to the contrary; whereupon Robert Stuart yeilded at last, haveing discovered Patrick Hacro his treasone, by meanes whereof he culd hold out no longer nor yit save himselff; which when Robert Stuart perceaved, though too late, he issued out the nixt morning with such as wold follow him; choosing rather to render himself then to be delyvered by Patrick Hacro'.[3] Caithness himself said

1 *Criminal Trials*, iii, 292; *State Papers of Melros*, i, 183.
2 See e.g. Clouston, *History of Orkney*, 326.
3 Gordon, *Genealogical History of the Earldom of Sutherland*, 301.

he 'maid Patrick Halcro to faill' his comrades;[4] and Halcro was indeed to ensure his own survival by bearing witness against his master. In Gordon's words, he was 'afterward in great favor with Earle George and weill interteyned by him for this service'.[5]

The bishop's story of what happened makes no mention of treachery on Patrick Halcro's part. Adopting a somewhat clerical tone, he paints a different picture of the proceedings. The rebels wanted to hear a minister, prompted as much by 'the sting of their owne consciences', as by their fear of the king and the 'valorous resolutione' of Caithness. Robert Stewart, minister of Hoy and Graemsay, was sent to preach two or three sermons to the rebels 'with effectuall prayers', which 'made for instructione and conversione of their minds and harts'. After two or three days, first Robert, then Patrick Halcro, came out, successively and separately, and conferred with their adversaries. Robert had a second conference with the bishop alone, on Michaelmas Eve (28 September), at which he agreed to abandon the castle, and was escorted by Law into the custody of the earl. It was Halcro who finally surrendered the castle, the following day at about four in the afternoon, after further discussions with Law.[6]

Law's story puts Halcro in a rather different light. He is the one determined to hold out to the bitter end; it is Robert who fails his followers. This version is supported to some extent by Halcro's previous record, which suggests a courageous and capable man. Until the final days, he had shown exemplary devotion to his uninspiring chief. He had made his position clear at the outset by signing the bond. He planned and executed the successful assault on Kirkwall. The ultimate failure of his plans lay at the vacillating and incompetent Robert's door. And Caithness himself testified in one of his letters that Halcro had 'offered . . . to put himselfe in my hands, to be disposed upoune at my plesour, if pardone wer grantit to Robert'.[7] On the other hand, Halcro may have remained in the castle after Robert's surrender simply to divert suspicion from himself. The bishop does not explain why he was promised his life. If at the end a direct approach by the earl persuaded Halcro that his efforts had been in vain, that he owed Robert very little, and that the whole enterprise had now no future except privation and death, one might find some justification, if not excuse, for his actions.

Whatever the truth, the feelings of relief among the earl's forces were enormous. A public service of thanksgiving was held, while a new bridge was built between the castle's inner and outer entrances. The earl and his company then entered the building, inspected it and ran up the royal colours 'in the most solemn and joyful manner', with the sounding of trumpets and the firing of guns by land and sea. Then they 'carussed efter the Orknay fashion' to the king's health and toasted Secretary

4 *Criminal Trials*, iii, 292; *State Papers of Melros*, i, 182.
5 Gordon, *Genealogical History of the Earldom of Sutherland*, 301.
6 *Letters on the Ecclesiastical Affairs of Scotland*, ii, 379.
7 *State Papers of Melros*, i, 148.

Binning and Treasurer Dunbar in wine. For the soldiers there was 'Scapa aill'; imbibing this in the Orkney fashion led to 'jarris' among them that required the mollifying attentions of the bishop.[8]

There is one story concerning the aftermath of the siege that requires notice. According to Robert Gordon, it was with some difficulty that Bishop Law prevailed over the earl's intention to demolish St Magnus after it had been surrendered.[9] In fact there is no contemporary reference to any such aim on the earl's part, and this unlikely story is probably a garbled combination of two elements – on the one hand the earl's feeling that he might have to use his guns against the cathedral as a military hazard, and on the other the actual partial demolition of the castle that followed the end of the siege. Alternatively, the earl's tactical problems may have been compounded by a refusal by the bishop to permit significant damage to the cathedral, though there are musketry pockmarks in evidence on outer walls. Perhaps it was the earl who opened negotiations with Black, and was later able to exploit Guild's treachery. But this is speculation; what can be said is that, whatever Caithness's faults, a desire for the wilful destruction of St Magnus does not appear to have been one of them.

The pleasure of earl and bishop was shared by their masters in Edinburgh, who had become very anxious for news. At the time the castle surrendered, Lord Binning had heard nothing from the north for more than a fortnight. On 15 September, he had written to his brother, Patrick Hamilton, at court in London, seeking royal approval of the council's letter of guidance to Caithness.[10] By 23 September, when he next wrote, he had heard nothing, and by 28 September he was becoming distinctly irritated – 'the attendance upon advertisement from Orknay still deteanis me prisoner in this towne'. He was awaiting word 'everie hour'. His own letters to Orkney had been sent overland 'becaus my messages be sea ar so incertane as misluk may delay thame verie long be the way'. He had strongly reproached Law and Caithness for not doing likewise.[11]

Binning's patience was being further tested by two other important problems outside Orkney. He had persuaded Law to accompany the expedition on condition that he took care of the bishop's financial affairs in his absence.[12] Despite events in Orkney, the reorganisation of the estates had continued, and during July 1614, even as Robert's men were ransacking the barns and pastures of the islands, Law's appointees were putting the final touches to a rental of the new bishopric

8 *Letters on the Ecclesiastical Affairs of Scotland*, ii, 381.
9 Gordon, *Genealogical History of the Earldom of Sutherland*, 300.
10 *State Papers of Melros*, i, 154–8.
11 *State Papers of Melros*, i, 168–9; Caithness's questions to Binning on the disposal of the castle and other matters are undated, but seem likely to have accompanied his letter of 30 September; they were received on 10 October (*Criminal Trials*, 292–3; *State Papers of Melros*, i, 185–6). Binning's letter, conveying the king's views on the treatment of prisoners, was sent north about 27 September and replied to on 6 October; Binning received the reply on 15 October (*Criminal Trials*, 290–1; *State Papers of Melros*, i, 180–1).
12 Balfour of Denmilne Papers, NLS Adv. 33.1.1 (v, 86–8).

parishes;[13] this was then placed before the lords of council and exchequer, with a view to granting a charter. The bishop's letters south (when they arrived) contained pointed allusions to this, and Binning and his brother had indeed been busy expediting the charter's passage through the seals.[14]

The other concern was of more political moment. The government of Scotland had not one but two rebellions on its hands. The Clan Donald had risen against the crown in Islay, in a dispute over titles to their lands 'which they heard some were seeking from the king'. Led by Angus Oig Macdonald, they had taken the castle of 'Dunyveg' and expelled the bishop of the Isles, Andrew Knox. Dunyvaig Castle was at length recaptured by Archibald Campbell of Cawdor, and its defenders executed in Edinburgh. For the Islay Macdonalds, whose lands were duly confiscated and granted to Campbell, events ended hardly more happily than for Robert and his father.[15] The leader of the Macdonalds, however, lived on into old age, albeit in exile; he was the rumbustious Sir James of Islay, who had previously been warded with Patrick in Edinburgh Castle, and had spoken to him of their respective plights. According to Andrew Martin, Sir James had 'wissit him selffe to be at hame, and the Erle of Orknay to have bein in Orknay, to do for thame selves; the ane in the west and the uther in the north'.[16]

The earl of Caithness was busy in the days after the surrender. The soldiers had received pay till 8 October, and the decision was made to embark them on 2 October. The ships were also to carry the cannon – those brought from Edinburgh, Kirkwall Castle's own[17] and another government weapon, brought from Thurso, which had seen service in Lewis. The herald and his men were to take with them Andrew Martin and another servant John Burn, former keeper of Scalloway Castle (who was gravely ill and in the event unable to travel), as well as the long-delayed dispatches to the council. The bishop said, 'It was nather of cairlessnes, negligence, nor oblavioune, that my lord and I did not wryte so frequentlie, bot our instante cair and diligence to bring the service to sum happie end, did hauld us from wryting, till we did sie the expectit fruit of laubours which we knew wauld not be unpleasing to his Maiestie and your honouris.'[18]

Caithness sent three letters – to the king, the secretary and Murray of Elibank the treasurer-depute, giving his version of events in varying degrees of detail.[19] The secretary received his lengthy description of the surrender and the dealings with Halcro that had brought it about. Anxious perhaps that he had gone too far in pardoning Halcro, he made the disreputable remark that 'I luik that my word and promeis gevin to Patrik Halcro sall not be fulfillit. Befoir it wer, I had rather be in

13 Rentals, ii, 116–49.
14 RMS, vii, no. 119.
15 D. Gregory, The History of the Western Highlands and Isles of Scotland, Edinburgh, 1836, 349–91.
16 Criminal Trials, iii, 303–4; State Papers of Melros, i, 184–5.
17 Letters on the Ecclesiastical Affairs of Scotland, ii, 382.
18 Criminal Trials, iii, 290.
19 Criminal Trials, iii, 288–90; State Papers of Melros, i, 174–7.

my grave.' He put to the secretary a series of administrative questions. What was to be done with the castle? It could be repaired and kept as a place of refuge in the case of foreign invasion, or demolished as 'nather necessar for any ordinary service of the king, nor a fit habitation for his officers', and which 'may be mor easilie takin be forren foes . . . then recovered agane from them'. Similarly the Palace of Birsay might be razed as 'the place whence the trubles did spring' or 'keiped with some allowance'. What of the government of the islands? Finlayson the sheriff depute was unfit for his office, 'hated to the death' by all, was of 'no sufficient qualities for such a place', and 'by his former evill demanor, is so contemned of the basest that he sall nevere . . . recover credit, authoritie and regard hier'. Indeed if he were to remain after the earl's departure he would be in danger of his life (there had already been several attempts to kill him) 'and some new broyl may arise'.[20] Caithness had come to detest the islands and their inhabitants; not only was the weather 'evill and varient' but 'so is the people; for he that wald rewle heir hes both neid of wit and manneheid, and manie earis and eis'. He wanted to leave, and sought 'ony service of grittar importance' from the king.[21]

James Law's letter to Binning on 29 September, though not written piecemeal like the earl's, was a parallel to it, giving his alternative account of events; it included also a tart reference to his own financial affairs and Binning's responsibilities – 'If his Maiestie salbe moved to convert ane Bischope in ane beggar, I sall never ascryve it to any aversenes of his Royall hart, bot to the perversnes of those who worships his purpure and loves not himselfe . . .'[22] Like Caithness too, the bishop wrote to the treasurer-depute, outlining his and the earl's intentions, speaking favourably of Caithness's performance in the enterprise – 'I will not write his dew praises leist I suld seme to flatter or faine. This onlie I must say that in all his cariage he hes schewed him self nobill, liberall, modest, valerous and zelous . . .' The rebels themselves had confessed that if the council had appointed Sir James Stewart of Killeith or 'gud Robert Menteyth' as leader of the government forces, this would have 'done thame greit plesour' .[23]

A week later the two wrote again. Law had now received assurances regarding his affairs, for which he was grateful.[24] The weather continued dreadful. 'The winds, hailes, snaws, raines ar so extraordinarie in thir places, that all had bene done and accompleissed befor this day [6 October] give it had bene possible.' The business of winding up nevertheless proceeded. Andrew Martin left for Edinburgh with Windram and the soldiers. Robert and Patrick Halcro were sent to Castle Sinclair to await the earl. The remainder of the rebels were kept in the castle until their trial on 7

---

20 *Criminal Trials*, iii, 292–3.
21 *Criminal Trials*, iii, 292; *State Papers of Melros*, 182–4.
22 *Letters on the Ecclesiastical Affairs of Scotland*, ii, 380.
23 *Letters on the Ecclesiastical Affairs of Scotland*, ii, 380–2.
24 *Letters on the Ecclesiastical Affairs of Scotland*, ii, 392–3; *Criminal Trials*, iii, 290–1; *State Papers of Melros*, i, 180–1.

October, nine days after their surrender.[25] They were Gilbert Gray, William Kirkness, Thomas McCulloch, Thomas and Patrick Taylor, William Paterson, Patrick Traill, Donald Fiddes, Magnus Delday, William Donaldson and John Stewart. Gilbert Gray, from Birsay, was a bond signatory and one of Robert's most active supporters throughout the rebellion. As such, he was the subject of a separate indictment which detailed his crimes – taking the castle, cutting the bridge, attacking and looting the girnel, being at Carness and the Ba' Lea, keeping the Yards and shooting from it, and being in the party that assaulted the herald. Not surprisingly, he was sentenced to death, to be led to his doom 'backwards, as a traitor', and his body to hang on the gallows at the castle gate for 24 hours afterwards.

The others had been Robert's companions in the castle. William Paterson was the husband of Janet Whyte who had faced the charge of aiding the rebels, and he and his companions were jointly accused of besieging Sheriff Finlayson in the castle, taking and holding the building, attacking the herald and sharing responsibility for the deaths and injuries that had occurred among the earl's party. Paterson and Thomas Taylor confessed to being at the Ba' Lea and Carness; Kirkness and McCulloch both admitted to discharging hagbuts at the government forces; and Patrick Taylor had been with Robert Stewart in Stronsay and Birsay. On these charges, all shared the fate of Gilbert Gray except William Donaldson and John Stewart. Donaldson acted as hangman to all his companions and was to continue to perform this office for the rest of his life, on pain of being hanged himself. John Stewart was a mere boy and there was doubt as to whether he had borne arms, or was even capable of doing so. He was flogged through the whole length of Kirkwall and banished from Orkney forever on pain of death.

The earl then went to Birsay, source of much of Robert's rank and file support. Forty-nine men of the parish and 47 from Harray were summoned to the palace to find caution in 500 merks. Only eleven of these faced specific charges, but virtually all had gone with Robert on expeditions to take up revenues. The accused and their cautioners were a close-knit group of fencible men. Many provided surety for each other – the Birsay pair Thomas and Edward Allan for example, and James and William Sinclair from Harray. Some, presumably the better-off, stood caution for two and even three of their fellows. Robert Sclater, the bailie of Birsay and a major figure, became surety for Alexander Hammer in Greeny, Thomas Moar in Marwick and Oliver Fea. Some on the other hand had to find their guarantors outside the parish. Adam Bellenden of Stenness did service for Robert Langskaill in Marwick, Magnus Pow in Flett and David Moir in Birsay Besouth. William Hannay, a kenspeckle figure in Kirkwall, stood for no fewer than seven individuals, including a half-share in Robert Sclater.

Among those who faced particular charges, Sclater had signed the original bond and in his capacity as bailie had convened wappenshaws at Robert's command. Robert Linklater in Garsetter had also signed the bond, and had been at the Ba'

Lea with Oliver Linklater in Housbey, Alexander Hammer, William Harvie and Alexander Fea. Fea, Harvie and the Linklaters had also been at Carness. Harvie and Oliver Linklater had helped to take the Yards. Oliver Hammer had gone no further than the Bu of Corse, but John Sclater had been 'in array' with Robert when the herald arrived in Kirkwall. George Hammer and David Moir confessed that they had pursued and shot at Adam Bellenden of Stenness who, curiously, was Moir's cautioner. No mention was made of Sclater or Robert Linklater's signing of the bond, whose full significance was perhaps not yet manifest. Of all these individuals only one, George Hammer, suffered further, though the confessed actions of several certainly rendered them liable to punishment and, in Robert Sclater's case, to the severest penalties.

George Hammer was tried in Kirkwall on 24 October, before the fourth and final of Caithness's courts. With him were William Henderson, William Craigie, Oliver Ingsay, John Brown and David Kennedy. Hammer and William Henderson were hanged. Hammer had participated in the campaign from Birsay to the Ba' Lea. William Henderson had borne Robert's trumpet and drum, but was 'Na ordiner trumpetir' who 'mycht easilie half eschewit sic proceidingis were nocht that he wes so rebelliouslie and traiterouslie disposit'. He had been at Cairston where Robert was taking up fish, and had sounded his trumpet, 'alluring thairby utheris for stuffing of his majesties house of Birsay'. It was he who sounded the call at Birsay 'in sign of derisioun'. He had then made his way to Kirkwall at night to fetch his drum, and accompanied Robert's men as they marched for Corse 'with sound of trumpet and drum successive'. He had been in the cathedral and the castle, at Carness and the Ba' Lea. His whole demeanour had been one of immoderate and aggressive devotion to the rebels' cause. He had charged the inhabitants of Kirkwall to rise with them, at first on pain of death, then under threat of 'burning of man, wyffe and bairne and taking the first spuilyie', saying to them that he 'hoipit to dwell in some of their houssis'. During these activities he wore 'Robertis cognisance on his foirheid to avow his contempt and treassonous rebellion.'

The others were luckier. David Kennedy was largely exonerated through John Finlayson's testimony, and banished to Caithness until he received licence to return. William Craigie in Kirkwall had broken a promise of obedience to Finlayson, and had been present at most of the major incidents in Kirkwall, but his excuse of impressment was accepted and he was merely banished. Oliver Ingsay alias Seatter was similarly treated, his chief crime being that of arranging a meeting between Robert Stewart and George Traill, who had supplied the rebels with sheep; although he had been at Birsay, Corse and the taking of the Yards, there was no evidence that he had borne arms or marched under displayed banner. Finally John Brown, a messenger (who had been busy in Orkney since 1611 helping to establish the new administration) was arraigned upon several charges. He had apparently been at Carness and the Ba' Lea, as well as in Stronsay for the collection of fish. He had kept the rebels apprised of the earl's activities, and eaten and drunk with them; and he had refused to execute royal letters presented to him by Finlayson. This latter charge might have been a serious one, but neither it nor any of the others was thought to render him 'worthy of death', and he was banished until he could obtain a fresh warrant from the Lord Lyon. This leniency suggests that Brown had had little choice in what he did, and that Finlayson's unpopularity was such that defiance of him was best treated tactfully.

These trials indicate two important points: firstly, the formal importance of specific incidents and actions in deciding serious guilt, and secondly the need for understanding of the conflict of loyalty that ordinary people had faced during the rebellion. On the first point, certain incidents recurred again and again in the indictments. Carness and the Ba' Lea, though of little military importance, involved definite and recognised forms of treasonable defiance – bearing of arms, wearing of 'battle array', displaying of banners, beating of drums; similar was the assembly at Corse where the trumpet was sounded. These demonstrations are cited as equally culpable with direct forms of aggression, such as assaulting the herald, defying orders to surrender, or firing on the earl's forces. Involvement in any of them was a most serious matter, receiving mercy only in the case of lack of evidence or convincing excuse. A distinction was observed between those who followed Robert in uplifting rents on the one hand, and on the other those who stayed in his company after the taking of Birsay or who, like William Henderson, expressed their defiance to an extreme degree. It was said that 'nane, at least few' of the Harray men 'culd freith or purge thameselffis of accumpaneing Robert in armes to Essinquoy, Campstane and Holme' yet nothing more than caution was required of them. The Birsay men 'all in ane voce' declared that what they had done 'was be . . . Robert and Andro Martyne thair subtill persuasiounis', on one hand claiming warrant from the privy council, on the other 'manassing' that they would 'dispossess them ower the gavill of thair howssis'.[26]

In early November, Caithness left Orkney, leaving his executive functions in the hands of Sinclair of Ratter.[27] On 15 November he took the oath in Edinburgh as a member of the privy council and sat with others to interrogate Patrick, Robert and Patrick Halcro.[28] The following day, he wrote to the king, telling of his return from Orkney and confessing 'my skille . . . was not correspondent to my wille, bot praisit be to God he of his mersie hes maid all thingis cum, by your Maiesteis gud luk and not by my guid Gyiding . . . that now all is provine upone the only authore of this wyld and onnaturall rebellioune . . .'[29] A week later, he was granted his triumph. Amid much rejoicing, the sound of drums and trumpets and salutes from the castle, *Thrawn Mouth* and her companion were drawn through the streets of the capital

26 O & S Papers, NRS RH9/15/150–1.
27 *Criminal Trials*, iii, 286.
28 *Criminal Trials*, iii, 322–3.
29 *Letters on the Ecclesiastical Affairs of Scotland*, ii, 401–2.

with the keys of Kirkwall Castle hung round their mouths.[30] The following day the council's approval of Caithness's achievement was placed on the register,[31] and in January he was summoned south to receive the king's thanks – an annuity and remission of his past offences.[32]

In the days after the surrender of Kirkwall Castle, Bishop Law began to investigate the background to what had happened, and in particular just what responsibility lay with the disgraced prisoner in Dumbarton. He interviewed John Burn, who was to have been sent south, but whose illness was now so serious that he was clearly dying. Burn said that he had accompanied Robert north on Patrick's orders to collect arrears for the years 1609–10, with the promise of a fee of 1,000 merks. When he had asked the earl why he was sending Robert, 'sieing he wes ane young man who appeirandlie wald trouble the countrie', the earl had replied that 'it was not ane matter for him to know', and that he would 'heare other newes or it wes long'. Law asked him whether Patrick had given any instructions to Robert about taking the Kirkwall strongholds. Burn said that the first letter sent by Patrick to his son, that taken north by Patrick Murray, had advised Robert that if he and Patrick Halcro could not 'take the houses', they should 'go over quietlie' to Caithness, to the home of Patrick's brother-in-law, James Sinclair of Murkle, 'untill they fand fitt tyme and occasion'. This letter, though it had since disappeared, seemed a clear reference to Robert's hidden motives, but it raised certain questions. Robert did not go to Caithness, but nor did he take the houses when he first arrived in Kirkwall, even though 'by his own confession' (and in the opinion of his father) the castle garrison would simply have handed the building over. When asked why Robert did not strike earlier, Burn could only say that 'he thoght not the tyme fitt and that thingis were not prepaired'.[33]

At the beginning of November, the bishop cross-examined Patrick Halcro's mistress, Margaret Bichan.[34] She 'revealit and confessit to me more than any other' about the rebels. His report on their conversation was confined to just one illuminating episode. One day during the siege the company in the castle discovered that one of the earl's letters to his son had gone missing. This caused great alarm, and a boy was sent to Halcro's mother's house in the town, carrying the key to a chest there, with instructions to Bichan to bring Robert the writs and letters she would find in it. Inside were only two documents; one was a bond and warrant to Patrick Halcro to take and keep the castle when he could, granting him double the allowance of previous constables; the other contained names of 'associatis and assisteris'

30 Calderwood, *History*, vii, 122; *RPC*, x, 286n.

31 *RPC*, x, 289–91.

32 J. T. Calder, *Sketch of the Civil and Traditional History of Caithness*, Wick, 1887, 43.

33 *Criminal Trials*, iii, 296–301.

34 The lady's name is rendered as both Bicchane (*Criminal Trials*, iii, 291) and Buchanane (Balfour of Denmilne Papers, NLS Adv. Ms. 33.1.1 (v, 114)); the Orcadian surname has been preferred to the Scottish. She was the wife of one Simon Stewart, but had borne Halcro a daughter. Law had another reason for interrogating her, since he intended to banish her from Orkney as an adulteress.

in the scheme. Both papers were signed by Patrick. Mistress Bichan brought the documents to Halcro, who read over the bond, then handed it to Robert who tore it to pieces and stamped on it. The woman remonstrated with them – 'Fye upon you Sir! Why have yee done that? It had bene better to have keipte it.' Both men replied 'that that band should not do hurt in tyme coming' and that 'the Earle of Orknay should not want his head for it'.[35]

This was among the matters discussed by the council when Andrew Martin was brought before them. The incident had taken place on the day after the fall of the Yards. Martin's account was that he had seen Robert and Patrick Halcro tearing off Patrick's signature from a document, which he presumed to be some sort of agreement between the three. It was then realised that there were further papers bearing the earl's subscription, and a boy was dispatched for them. Martin personally lowered him from a castle window on a rope, but of what happened later he knew nothing. He had already told Caithness of Robert's commission from his father to uplift all arrears of rents and duties.[36] When he had first seen this, he asked if there were any other tasks Robert had to perform; the young man answered that he had, but would not give details. On the question of the earl's letter carried by Patrick Murray, all he had heard was Robert saying angrily that he would not go to Caithness, but would stay in Orkney.[37] He had written a reply for Robert to the letter brought by Duncan Mitchell to Birsay, stating that he had arrived in Orkney to uplift arrears, but that Finlayson had compelled him to leave Kirkwall for Birsay, and he intended to resist him there. Robert did not find this account acceptable – it was possibly too explicit; he tore up Martin's draft and wrote his own version.[38] There was little in the way of written evidence, therefore, that could incriminate Patrick, but there was one document whose continued existence boded ill for the remaining rebels. Martin was shown a copy of the bond of association, and hesitantly agreed that he had written it, though he had not signed it nor looked at it since it left his hand.

Martin cut a sorry figure. Immediately after this interrogation, he wrote a rambling letter to Binning with additional information which he said he had forgotten at the time and which he felt he ought to tell 'for saiftie of my aithe', and because Binning had 'gart me sweare to be plaine'. In conversation with Martin, Robert had once stated that his father could have made his way to Orkney in person if he had wanted, and many men would have accompanied him, but he dared not break ward. When Martin had asked Robert how many followers Patrick might have looked for, he replied 'four or fyve thowsand give he had pleasit', although he did not say who such men might be. Later in the letter Martin mentioned the conversation between Patrick and Sir James Macdonald of Islay, bemoaning their situation together in ward in Edinburgh Castle; in between he threw himself abjectly

35 *Criminal Trials*, iii, 304.
36 *Criminal Trials*, iii, 301.
37 *Criminal Trials*, iii, 301–2.
38 *Criminal Trials*, iii, 303.

on Binning's mercy, seeking his intercession with the king 'in this unhappie tyme of miserie'. He had had no choice but to join Robert, being 'aged and depauperat, able to die of hungar, give I had not gottin helpe be him in meit and drink'. He had never borne arms, made musters, nor stood watch against Caithness 'eftir I hard of his purpose'. He undertook to inform Binning of anything else of relevance that might have occurred to him – 'So confeiding in his Majesties clemencie and your lordschips affectioun towards me'.[39]

By now Patrick himself had been brought back to Edinburgh. Binning and the king's advocate interrogated him in the castle on 22 October. He denied all knowledge of what had happened. It had been Stewart of Killeith who had first told him of Robert's departure for Orkney, pointing out the dangerous offence this might give to the king. Patrick had explained that Robert was so short of money that he had gone north to collect arrears in order to supply his own and his father's wants; since it was 'evill tane', he would write personally to Robert, bidding him leave for Caithness. He asked Sir James to ensure that the letter was sent to his son, and that his servants assist him to cross the Firth. This was, he said, the only letter he had written during the whole time Robert was in Orkney. The councillors shifted their attention to the letters written for him by John Sharp, and found in the possession of Duncan Mitchell. Patrick denied being a party to them. Sharp had indeed intended to write, but he had forbidden it. Both Sharp and Mitchell were brought into Patrick's presence, but neither would contradict this. Patrick's view was that the responsibility for the rebellion lay neither with him nor his son, but with the 'cuntriemen', whose treatment at the hands of Finlayson had 'disponit thame to rebellion'. It was they who had persuaded Robert to assist them and act as their head. He denied knowing Patrick Halcro at all or ever having had anything to do with him. As far as he knew, Halcro's sole motive in assisting Robert was that of affection. He was confident that Sharp, Mitchell and Robert himself would bear this out.[40]

It was proving extremely difficult to build up a case against Patrick as instigator of the rebellion. Admittedly, it strained credulity to accept that he knew nothing of what his son had done. His fury at Robert's surrender of the strongholds in 1612; his refusal to abandon his claims to the earldom; his extravagant and tempestuous nature – all these must have made the council deeply suspicious. Yet his tracks, if tracks there were, had been well hidden. The tenor of the Patrick Murray letter, existing now only in the minds of those who had seen it, could have meant that Robert went only to uplift revenues to which he was entitled, or that he went to await a time when he could lawfully resume control of the Orkney houses, or that he went to raise rebellion. That he did indeed rise against the king still did not mean that the main impulse came from Patrick. He might well have refused to go over to Caithness because he feared his father, who would interpret it as a further sign of

39 *Criminal Trials*, iii, 303–4; *State Papers of Melros*, i, 184–5.
40 *State Papers of Melros*, i, 188–9.

weakness; and more and perhaps greater pressure could have come from determined individuals like Halcro and Laing who wished to revenge themselves on Finlayson. The bond's terms could hardly be expected to mention Patrick, but concentrated on alleged oppression by the new administration in the Northern Isles.

John Sharp was examined before the council on 1 November. He had been in Patrick's service since the summer of the previous year, in succession to Michael Mair. About six weeks after he had joined his new master in Dumbarton, he had taken down a memorial instructing Robert to go to Orkney, set tacks and rule the country 'as yow did before', and send to Norway for supplies, particularly gunpowder. Patrick then put the document in his pocket and Sharp never saw it again. Robert himself arrived less than a fortnight later. After Patrick had been transferred to Edinburgh in January 1614 he dictated a second memorial in the same terms, with the addition that Robert should 'put furth of the countrey of Orkney suche as hes nothing to do in it'. A third in similar terms was written when Robert departed for the north, accompanied by a letter urging him to follow it scrupulously; this Patrick would not subscribe for fear of interception. At about the same time, Sharp also wrote out the Patrick Murray letter. This said something to the effect that 'yow shall speak the countreymenne and try yf thay will tak your pairte; and yf the countrey men will tak your pairte, yow shall reteir your self to Caithnes and stay there and proceede no thing whill I send yow worde'. Finally, in response to Robert's letter after the taking of Birsay, Patrick dictated the one intercepted in Mitchell's hands, with another in Sharp's own name, warning Robert bluntly not to come south. The earl ordered Sharp himself to go north to join Robert who 'would not let him want'. When Sharp asked if he was to take a letter with him, Patrick demurred, fearing that he might be taken in possession of it on the way.[41]

Though it contained some sinister allegations against Patrick, none of Sharp's testimony gave the council convincing proof of Patrick's involvement in the rebellion. Sharp had heard neither Patrick nor Robert say anything explicit about the rising, though he recalled Patrick's caustic comments about his son's first surrender to the bishop. Robert's letter to his father repeated the story of how, while in Orkney to uplift his father's revenues, he had been 'persewed' by the sheriff and compelled to leave Kirkwall for Birsay; Sharp believed that this was merely an excuse, and the way that Robert put it to his father – 'it will please your lordschip to tell the counsale in my name that . . .' – suggested the concocting of a story to justify his action. Nevertheless, there was no proof of a direct link between Patrick and his son's actions in Orkney. His instructions had been written months before and could easily be interpreted as general observations about what Robert should do given a legitimate opportunity. In any case all the versions of these instructions had disappeared; all that remained were the differing recollections of Sharp and the others.

The following day, 2 November, Patrick was again examined, with little result. Questioned about Thomas Laing, he recalled him as a former servant but had no memory of whether he had brought letters from England. He had never intended to break ward, nor had he ever given his son instructions regarding rebellion. His anger with Robert had not been because he had handed the houses to the bishop, but because he had not inventoried the contents before doing so. He admitted meeting Patrick Halcro, but denied having much conversation with him. He had sent a letter north with Patrick Murray, but only telling Robert to betake himself to Caithness. He could not remember the contents of the letter sent to Robert with Duncan Mitchell nor whether he had signed it. He could not recall dictating memorials to Sharp for his son, nor had he asked Sharp to warn Robert that he would be hanged if he came south. He conceded that Mitchell had brought Robert's letter saying that he had been forced to go to Birsay, but denied discussing this with the messenger, or giving him any instructions to pass on. Similarly he had given no directions to Sharp to carry to Orkney; in fact he had not sent him to Orkney at all, but to the privy council in Edinburgh, with a letter to the chancellor, the earl of Glencairn. Sharp was then re-examined before Patrick. He said that Patrick had told him 'in plain terms' to go to Orkney but, aware that the council was looking for him, they used the letter to Glencairn as a cover against any awkward questions from the soldiers of Dumbarton Castle. On hearing of the arrest of Mitchell, Sharp had gone to Edinburgh and given himself up.[42] His previous deposition was read out, and also that made by Duncan Mitchell at the time of his arrest. Patrick denied everything except for such concessions as he had already made.[43]

Questions were put concerning the one letter from Patrick to Robert that did survive, the one found in Mitchell's possession. What had he meant when he said that he 'allowit of the forme and tennour of Robertis letter written to him'? To this, apparently a reference to his suspicious remark that his son had done 'verie weill in wrytting your letter in the form ye do', Patrick said that he had meant nothing more than that his son had written the simple truth. What had been the significance of his statement that 'thair is uther materis heir to think upoun . . . as that I believe his maiestie thinkis littill of theis materis'? This looked like a reference to the king's extreme displeasure at what was happening, but to Patrick it meant that the king had other, more important preoccupations, such as the death of his eldest son, and the problems of the Elector Palatine (Robert had of course mentioned the latter to Andrew Martin). As for his remark that 'Gif yow cum in this cuntrie upone onie conditioun, the Tolbuithe will be your best', all he meant was that Robert would be imprisoned, both for debt and for his assault on the house of Birsay.

Some days later Robert Stewart himself was brought to Edinburgh, and on 13 November he and Halcro were examined. 'Humblit on his knees and deiplie sworn', Robert provided a somewhat confused picture of what he had tried to do. First he said that his father, angry at his capitulation to the bishop, had refused him

42 *Criminal Trials*, iii, 322–3.
43 *Criminal Trials*, iii, 322–3.

recognition or allowance and he could no longer maintain himself in Edinburgh; for this reason he had gone to Orkney to uplift old arrears. Then he suggested that he had done this on his father's orders, and that before he departed, his father dictated memorials to him in the same terms as those drafted with John Sharp. He was to seek to repair the wrongs he had done, and if he could regain possession of the castle 'by any means', he should do so and send to Norway for provisions. While in Orkney he had received two or three letters from his father, through Murray and Mitchell. One of the Murray letters told him to take the house of Birsay, but if he could not keep it he should retire across the Firth. The Mitchell letter concerned the taking and holding of houses 'if he could come by them'. His father also told him several times that he would escape from ward and join him; Halcro confirmed his hopes of this.

Halcro's relationship to Patrick and his son was of clear interest to the council. Robert himself sought to exonerate Halcro from the charge of leading him from behind, saying that he had not been told of the intention to take Kirkwall Castle until after the confrontation at Birsay. Only when Robert showed him the Mitchell letter did he agree to take part. Halcro himself received no letters from Patrick, but he did speak of his interview at Dumbarton the previous summer, in which he had expressed his low opinion of Robert's leadership qualities. This supported the view that Halcro was intended to be the intelligence behind the revolt – and out of support for Patrick rather than antipathy to John Finlayson. On the other hand these discussions had been exploratory, and had taken place long before the event. Halcro did make two points that suggested a link between Patrick and his son's activities. He confirmed that it was on Patrick's orders that a ship had been sent to Norway (it had arrived after all was over, with 60 barrels of gunpowder); and he mentioned Robert's fear that torture by the council might make him 'confes aganis' his father.[44] This was not enough. Two days later Patrick was confronted by his son and Halcro, but denied any direction to the former or discussion with the latter regarding the rising in the north.[45]

The council shifted their attention to the events at Dumbarton the previous year, by taking the depositions of James Lyon and Michael Mair, and re-examining Mitchell the postman. Lyon told his story of the abortive plot to help Patrick escape, and of his difficult position regarding the bad blood between father and son. Mair confirmed this. Mitchell had been concerned solely with the abortive money-raising visit to St Andrews. Patrick, faced with these men and their depositions, maintained his denials; the idea of his breaking ward had been Lyon's, and he had refused to listen. His displeasure with Robert in Lyon's presence was over the excessive amount of time Robert spent in the man's company.[46]

On 5 January 1615, Robert and his lieutenants – Thomas Black, Archibald Murray,

44 *Criminal Trials*, iii, 306–7.
45 *Criminal Trials*, iii, 322–3.
46 *Criminal Trials*, iii, 327.

Andrew Martin, Thomas Laing, Alexander Leggat – were tried in Edinburgh. They had no counsel 'but God'. Their objections to Caithness men on the assize were rejected on the dubious grounds that the earl had no particular feud with them, but had only acted as commissioner, and had knowledge, but not interest in the matter.[47] Other assizemen included Robert Henderson of Holland and Edward Scollay of Strynie. The confessions of the accused were read out, and the assize, with Henderson of Holland as chancellor, declared them all guilty.[48]

Clearly doomed, Robert was anxious to make his peace with all concerned. He conceded that he had grievously offended God and king by his actions, and agreed to repeat his acceptance of wrongdoing on the scaffold itself as a warning to others. This he did at the mercat cross of Edinburgh the following day, repeating a prepared formula at the four corners of the platform.[49] He was asked publicly by the ministers who had caused him to act as he did. He replied 'that his fader was the intysair and induceair of him, and that no uther persone in the warld could haif induceit him to this rebellion', though he also said that his father had given him a 'contraremand before he entered in execution'. Then, with his followers, he submitted to the noose, exciting much public sympathy for his 'tall stature and comelie countenance'.[50]

But the trial and punishment of his father was another matter. After all their inquiries and cross-examinations, the council at the end of 1614 was still no nearer the confident proof of treason that would justify prosecution, and execution, of the king's cousin. Patrick's capacity to mask his real intentions, and to provide plausible justifications for every seemingly treasonable act, seemed inexhaustible. So much so, that it was thought he might well have escaped altogether, had he not, in the second week of the new year, done something quite unexpected. He confessed. We can only guess at why he did so, though the timing is perhaps suggestive; it happened on 12 January, five days after Robert's execution. His son's death, alongside poor Andrew Martin, his oldest and most faithful servant, could have sapped his morale. Perhaps too that tendency to loss of nerve that had paralysed him in his planned flight from Dumbarton had afflicted him again, and made him throw himself on the mercy of the authorities. Perhaps he felt that he might still rely after all on the favour of the king.

On 1 February Patrick was tried before assessors, who comprised most of the prominent members of the privy council and the session. The indictment showed the council's confidence that they could at last place their own rather than Patrick's construction on his actions. Mention was made of his 'former tirranie and opressioun', and he was accused of plotting to escape from Dumbarton Castle, though 'skarrit and hindreit' from doing so. He had incited the rebellion by the 'mony thraitningis and minatorie speiches' uttered against his son for surrendering the

47 *Criminal Trials*, iii, 280n.
48 *Criminal Trials*, iii, 282–3.
49 *RPC*, x, 829–30.
50 Calderwood, *History*, vii, 194.

castle of Kirkwall to James Law, and directed it by means of letters to Robert and
the influence of Patrick Halcro. His guilt was clearly shown by the depositions of
Robert and his followers, as well as by Lyon, Sharp, Mitchell and Halcro. Robert's
actions were 'of your speciall causeing, sending, hounding out, command, counsell,
devyse and only directioun'. But most important of all was Patrick's own deposition,
subscribed before the council, in which he confessed his directing of the rebellion,
craved the king's pardon and submitted to his will.

Patrick had four advocates in his defence, including James and Alexander
King. Despite many years of service, which had made them well acquainted with
the defence of the indefensible, they had an impossible task. Their strategy was
largely procedural – alleging that many points in the indictment were unknown to
their client, that they had received no copy of it with which to prepare a defence,
and that the charges were not the ones for which Patrick had been warded. After
a half-hour recess, they accepted the indictment, disputing only Patrick's motive
in sending his son to Orkney, which was 'to . . . intromit with his houses goods
and gair upone mere ignorance and simplicitie', not realising that it might suggest
treason. Patrick had not given him orders to do this or anything else. This was much
less of a concession than Patrick had previously offered the council, suggesting that
he had recovered his nerve. But it was too late. He had no alternative now but to
throw himself on the mercy of the court – 'and thairfor, fleeing fra all forder defence
of his awin innocencie, hes his refudge to his Maiesteis grace and mercie; And as
of befoir craves God and his Maiestie pardoun for his oversight and negligence
on this poynt; and in all humilitie and submissioun cumis in [his] hienes will . . .'
In reply the prosecution produced a long series of documents – depositions, the
commissions to Caithness and the bishop, the letters taken from Duncan Mitchell,
the bond, the process against Robert. With them was Patrick's confession that the
taking of Kirkwall Castle was carried out on his instructions; it was accompanied
by certifications of his submission to the will of the king, both on 12 January and
that same day. Faced with all this the assize could return only one verdict, and there
could be only one sentence. Patrick was unanimously found guilty, and sentenced
to be executed in two days' time.[51]

There now followed a pathetic coda to the career of Patrick Stewart. He took
his sentence 'impatiently', to such a degree that when he was visited by clergy to
prepare him for death, they found him 'irresolute' and successfully pleaded for three
days' stay.[52] A more famous account says that the delay was because Patrick was
so ignorant that he could not recite the Lord's Prayer.[53] This is extremely implau-
sible. There is no reason at all to suppose that the foster son of Waus of Barnbarroch
and the patron of the finest architect of his time was unfamiliar with elementary
religious texts. It is more probable that a combination of his passionate nature and

51 *Criminal Trials*, iii, 312–18.
52 Spottiswoode, *Historie*, iii, 221–2.
53 Calderwood, *History*, vii, 194–5.

the fear of death made it for a time impossible to hold conversation with him, and unlikely that he would cut a seemly figure on the scaffold. Under the influence of the ministers, he was eventually reconciled to his fate and on Sunday he took communion. On Monday 6 February 1615, he was escorted to the mercat cross by the magistrates of Edinburgh and, between two and three o'clock in the afternoon before a great crowd, his life came to an end under the blade of the Maiden.[54]

54 McCulloch, 'History of the "Maiden" or Scottish Beheading Machine, with Notices of the Criminals who Suffered by it', PSAS, vii (1870), 553–4.

16

Jarris and Discontentmentis

Execution of a nobleman of such eminence as Patrick Stewart, an event that council and king had gone to such pains to avoid, was the subject of some remark. The English diplomat John Chamberlain spoke of it in a letter to his colleague Sir Dudley Carleton; Lord Carew mentioned it to Sir Thomas Roe, ambassador to the great mogul; and it was noted in a number of the histories of the period.[1] It brought to an end a career that was virtually unique. Not since the execution of Murdoch, duke of Albany, in 1424, under very different circumstances, had anyone as close to the king suffered the supreme penalty. Perhaps the nearest parallel to Patrick's story is that of Francis Stewart, earl of Bothwell, his cousin. The latter's career ended in disgrace and exile rather than death, but he was of the same rank, approximately the same age, he stood in exactly the same relationship to the king, and like Patrick, he combined civilised tastes, especially in architecture, with a curiously total lack of judgment.[2]

Like that of Bothwell, Patrick's departure from the scene had few repercussions at court. Francis Stewart's activities, vigorous though they were, had little political rationale, and none of the factions mourned his passing. Patrick had taken little part in court affairs for some years; his attitude to authority had something of the same unreasoning contempt, but none of the almost inspired madness of Bothwell's attacks on the king. King James, at least for a time, 'seems to have admired his cousin [Bothwell]'s dash and verve too much to take effective action against him.'[3] Patrick's madness on the other hand combined a continual grasping search for money that stopped at nothing, with the overweening conceit of a sprig of the royal house who recognised no boundaries to his freedom of action. This excited no admiration in his cousin, or anyone else. Moreover, while Bothwell's curious operations were conducted within the old kingdom of the Scots, Patrick's carried on into the wholly new dispensation of James's Great Britain. Even before his death Patrick was, in Scottish terms, something of an anachronism at a time when the king, on a wealthier and more powerful throne, was increasingly less indulgent of the old troublemakers of Scotland. This is perhaps best illustrated by Patrick's conflict

---

1 *CSP Domestic* (1611–18), 275, 284; *The Historie and Life of King James the Sext*, 386.

2 RCAHMS, *Inv.*, Midlothian, 47–51.

3 G. Donaldson and R. S. Morpeth, *Who's Who in Scottish History*, Edinburgh, 1977, 102–3.

with Binning, 'Tam o' the Cowgate', a man of relatively humble origin who was ultimately to attain Patrick's own rank through the increasing opportunities that the age provided for the able.

But if Patrick was remembered in Scotland chiefly for the manner of his death, it was some time before his shadow passed from Northern Isles. At first, it seemed as though the transition to the new rule would be a peaceful one. The transfer of the lands of Orkney from Sir John Arnot to the crown went forward.[4] John Finlayson delivered his final account on 15 June 1615.[5] The earl of Caithness had left Sir John Sinclair of Ratter in Orkney, with orders to demolish Kirkwall Castle, that 'starting-hoill and place of retreat for tratouris and rebellis'. Though its demolition took some time and was incomplete, the building was reduced to shapeless lumps of masonry.[6] Bishop Law continued in Orkney as chamberlain, commissioner of justiciary and sheriff principal, while trying to gather together as much as he could of Patrick's personal effects, dispersed by Robert and his men.[7] The bishop's responsibility for civil, as opposed to ecclesiastical, matters was superseded by Henry Stewart of Carlongyie and Master William Livingston, who reaffirmed Henry Aitken and Robert Coltart in their posts and began holding justiciary courts in Orkney and Shetland.[8] The following year, on the death of Archbishop Spottiswoode, Law was advanced to the see of Glasgow, and was succeeded in Orkney by George Graham.[9]

There also followed a number of measures to punish, excuse or compensate those who had been involved in the events of the past few years. Henry Stewart, Patrick's page, who had been imprisoned in the Edinburgh tolbooth, in the general panic that followed the news of the rebellion, secured his freedom.[10] Patrick Halcro received remission for his part in events, with Caithness as his surety.[11] Robert Stewart's escheat was granted to his mother, Marjorie Sinclair.[12] Master James Stewart, who had stood surety for his brother for £600 with £50 in costs, had his goods attached for the amount.[13] He had proved himself an enthusiastic supporter of his brother, and had been responsible for disturbances in Orkney; others who had suffered financially in Patrick's service fared better. Thomas Livingston of Ballintone,[14] who had lost much by sureties he had put up, received a charter from

---

4 O & S Papers, NRS RH9/15/123; *RPC*, x, 354–5; Arnot did not live long to enjoy the settlement, dying in 1616.

5 O & S Papers, NRS RH9/15/194.

6 *RPC*, x, 319–21, 322–3.

7 *RPC*, x, 313–15.

8 *Ct Bk of O & S, 1614-15*, 11.

9 *Fasti*, ed. Watt and Murray, 329.

10 *RPC*, x, 403.

11 *RPC*, x, 318.

12 *RSS*, NRS PS1/85, f. 119r and v.

13 *RPC*, x, 372.

14 Sometimes referred to as 'of Bantone', this may refer to the common pronunciation of the name and may also locate the designation, otherwise unknown, to the area of Banton, east of Kilsyth.

the king of lands in Stenness.[15] Robert Monteith of Egilsay received a new charter of his Egilsay and St Ola lands.[16] William Veitch of Davach (Davact) received the escheat of Patrick's movables – the pots and pans, the compass, the watch-chain with no watch.[17] Patrick's creditors were identified and ranked. Included were Livingston of Ballintone, and previously unknown figures such as Master James Seton and the widow of Mr Robert Pont.[18] A letter was drafted for sending in the king's name to Bergen regarding a ship of Patrick's that had been impounded there.[19]

Perhaps the most unfortunate victim of events was Margaret Livingston, countess of Orkney, left with debts to Edinburgh merchants and moneylenders, after a long history of being caught up in her husband's financial troubles.[20] She also owed money to her brother, Lord Livingston, and had already written to him from Kirkwall in May 1600 about the difficulties of drawing funds together to pay him.[21] In 1603 Sir John Arnot had paid out £2,618 on her behalf for provisions including wine, ale, meat, fruit, bread and coal.[22] By July 1609 the tradesmen's complaints against Patrick also named her, and she had lost the income of her widow's liferent lands to Robert, Lord Roxburghe, her son-in-law.[23] She was in dispute with Mr Adam Bellenden of Kilconquhar (who had officiated at her marriage) over a black velvet gown and cloak.[24] In June 1611 Arnot raised an action to recover 7,000 merks that he had lent her over the previous three years for upkeep of her household.[25] She complained that her husband had deserted her and deprived her of maintenance, and raised an action in the commissary court of Edinburgh to compel Patrick to return to her and provide her with income. She was successful, securing the sum of 1,000 merks annually,[26] but it was a hollow victory. Patrick, imprisoned and penniless, was clearly unable to be a husband to her, financially or in any other way. After his death she received a yearly pension of 2,000 merks to assist her in her 'poir

---

15 *RMS*, vi, no. 1345.

16 O & S Papers, NRS RH9/15/11.

17 *RSS*, NRS PS1/85, ff. 96v–8r.

18 Mar and Kellie Papers,, NRS GD124, 76–82; the last of these was probably owed arrears of pension granted to her husband in 1602 for his visitation to the kirks of Orkney in 1596 (Craven, *History of the Church in Orkney*, 75; Church Recs: Reg. Pres., NRS CH4/1/3, f. 66).

19 Balfour of Denmilne Papers, NLS Adv. Mss 33.1.1 (xv, 56); this action was still in progress in June 1618 (*RPC*, xi, 630).

20 Misc. Papers, NRS RH15/12/11, 17; Reg. Deeds, NRS RD1/29, ff. 32v–3r, RD1/71, ff. 317r and v.

21 Misc. Papers, NRS RH15/12/7.

22 O & S Papers, NRS RH9/15/109.

23 Court of Session Recs: Acts and Decreets, NRS CS7/248, ff. 231r–3r, CS7/253, ff. 109v–13v; Roxburghe's case cited among other things Patrick's denunciation at the instance of Monteith of Egilsay. The lands, ironically, included those that the previous countess had enjoyed – those of the Kerse, round modern Grangemouth.

24 O & S Papers, NRS RH9/15/116a.

25 Court of Session Recs: Acts and Decreets, NRS CS7/261, ff. 286r–7r.

26 Edin. Comm. Ct Recs: Acts and Decreets, NRS CC8/2/41, 42; Court of Session Recs: Acts and Decreets, NRS CS7/273, ff. 59r–63v.

and distressit estait'.[27] This may have relieved her, but she was still being pursued in March 1619 by Janet Forrest, widow of Robert Stewart, provost of Linlithgow, for over £500.[28] Patrick's daughter Mary was also in financial trouble. She was one of the two illegitimate siblings of Robert (the other was Katherine, said to have married John Sinclair of Ulbster), and since 1614 had been in the care of Katherine Paterson, daughter of a deceased burgess of Kirkcaldy. With Patrick's fall, her means had disappeared and she appealed to the privy council for help.[29]

Despite the execution of Patrick and his son, the complete reorganisation of his estates, and all the efforts of Caithness, the bishop and the king, there was still unrest in Orkney. On 25 January 1616 a proclamation was ordered to scotch rumours, said to be circulating in the islands, that the offices of justiciar, sheriff, admiral and chamberlain were to be granted to some of the earl's brothers.[30] This had caused such disquiet that there was widespread refusal to hand over duties to the crown. These difficulties, which were apparently in Orkney and not Shetland, did not derive, as one might have expected, from fear of the restoration of Stewart tyranny; quite the reverse. What worried the crown was the possibility of another revolt, this time in the name of John Stewart. The rumours, said the proclamation, had been spread by 'some factious, seditious and restles personis, lovearis of trouble and unquietnes . . . grevit' by the failure of the rebellion. They wished to encourage the commons to take up arms again, to 'thair wraick, ruyne and distructioun, by intyseing of thame to imbrace and follow oute suche foolische courses as in the end will involve thame under the guylt of heich treasoun'. The crown's proclamations made it clear that the rumours were false and payment of duties had to be made, on pain of the highest penalties.

In fact, both John Stewart and his brother Robert spent much of their time in England attending upon the king. Both were arrogant and difficult courtiers, and John showed the same dangerous turbulence for which he had had a name in Edinburgh. In December 1604 for example, he was involved in a fracas over precedence with Sir Thomas Somerset, and was placed for a time under house arrest.[31] Nevertheless he was to retain the king's favour throughout his life. Already created Lord Kinclaven under James VI, he was later to be advanced by Charles I to the earldom of Carrick, not Robert Bruce's old title but said to derive from Carrick in Eday.[32] This curious dignity, which died with him, was the nearest he came to his ambition of succeeding his brother, though for years after Patrick's death, John Stewart retained a lively interest in this possibility.

The career of Sir Robert Stewart was less successful. The king granted him the keepership of the royal park of Bewdley, but on 20 September 1606 he was relieved

27 RSS, NRS PS1/85, f. 107r and v.
28 RPC, xi, 560.
29 Scots Peerage, vi, 577; RPC, viii, 344–5.
30 RPC, x, 449–50.
31 Salisbury Papers, xvi, 391–3.
32 Scots Peerage, ii, 441.

of it because he had treated it as a sinecure and assigned it to 'certain townsmen, whereby inconvenience grows to our service'.[33] He fell deeply in debt and had to be rescued from custody at the hands of one Goodall, a barber, by his brother John, his brother-in-law Lord Lindores, and the earl of Roxburghe. Lindores by his own account suffered considerably as a result of this, since the discharging of Stewart's debt caused his own creditors to press him.[34] This did not end Sir Robert's money troubles, and three years later, in December 1609, he is found imprisoned in the bailie's house in the Strand.[35]

John Stewart, Lord Kinclaven, had possessions of his own in Orkney, with an estimated value of £30,000.[36] Monteith of Egilsay was his agent for many years, and Bannatyne of Gairsay was among his dependers.[37] In July 1615 he conducted a detailed examination of the contents of Patrick's charter chests, at that time still held by Livingston of Ballintone.[38] His hopes of power in the north had direct repercussions in Orkney. There was a feud between Monteith of Egilsay as his representative, and his sworn enemies William, John and James Colville, sons of the murdered Henry Colville and stepsons of John's own illegitimate brother, the now deceased William Stewart.[39] Besides the old grievance of Henry Colville's murder, this had concerned a long-standing dispute with William Stewart over Monteith's estates in Egilsay. Also involved were other persons of 'a turbulent humour and dispositioun' who had been required after the rebellion to find surety for their good behaviour. These included Patrick Stewart, son of Monteith's brother-in-law James Stewart of Graemsay, who in September 1618 attacked Robert Halcro of Cava's house in Stenness, apparently because Halcro was engaged in collecting the king's rents.[40] Stewart was probably supported by his father, who had long been a supporter of the former master of Orkney.

These activities may well have helped to bring about the ruin of the tacksman, Sir James Stewart of Killeith. After the forfeiture of Patrick and the erection of the islands into a stewartry, Killeith, now Lord Ochiltree, continued to hold the tack of the revenues that he had been granted in 1613. In 1622, this tack was terminated, and he fled abroad to escape his creditors. George, Lord Gordon, heir to the earl of Huntly, made an unsuccessful bid to succeed him,[41] perhaps as part of his attempt to pick a fight with the earl of Caithness, but the following year, two more

33 *CSP Domestic* (*addenda, 1580–1625*).

34 *Salisbury Papers*, xix, 193–4.

35 *Salisbury Papers*, xxi, 164–5.

36 *Letters and State Papers during the Reign of King James the Sixth* (Abbotsford Club), Edinburgh, 1838, 371.

37 In August 1611 he had received a charter from Bannatyne of Gairsay of lands in South Ronaldsay (*RMS*, vii, no. 558) and he also held the duties of the parsonage of Orphir, the former living of Henry Colville (Court of Session Recs: Process Papers, NRS CS15/158). He lent 6,000 merks to Robert Monteith of Egilsay (Reg. Deeds, NRS RD1/340, f. 116r and v).

38 *Salisbury Papers*, xvi, 391–3.

39 *RPC*, xi, 544–6; the mother of the three Colvilles was Katherine Douglas (*O & S. Ct Bks 1614–15*, 49).

40 Court of Session Recs: Acts and Decreets, NRS CS7/325, f. 306r and v.

41 *RPC*, xi, 535–7; George Gordon, second marquess of Huntly (c. 1590–1649) (ODNB).

serious candidates were put forward, Monteith of Egilsay and Sir John Buchanan of Scotscraig. Monteith's claim was based on debts owed him from Patrick's estate amounting, he claimed, to £40,000. In payment he offered the king 40,000 merks annually in tack duty in exchange for writing off the debt.[42] The council advised rejection, partly on the grounds that his claims would be better pursued in a court of law, but more importantly because debts from within the islands cast doubt on his ability to give impartial justice to the inhabitants 'upoun occasioun of ony jarris or discontentmentis betuix thame' – on this point 'the said Robert cannot cleir him self'. This also sounds like a veiled reference to Monteith's relationship with Kinclaven.

Buchanan's claim was superior, both because of a larger promised yearly payment of 45,000 merks and because of the better reputation he enjoyed in the islands.[43] He and his wife Margaret Hartsyde were granted a five-year tack of the lands of Orkney and Shetland from 1622.[44] He was a curious choice; the appointment, coupled with confirmation of his grant of the lands of Scotscraig, marked his final rehabilitation after about 15 years of disgrace and internal exile. He and his wife had been banished to Orkney after she was convicted in August 1608, in mysterious circumstances, of theft of the queen's jewels. Whether this mysterious affair had anything to do with the queen's quest for control of her son is anyone's guess.[45] At any rate, it was only after 1611 that Buchanan had been allowed to travel out of Orkney, and even then under strict conditions.[46] During the rebellion, his wife's pleas to be allowed to leave fell on deaf ears.[47] In the strictness of their banishment, they began to put down roots, acquiring property in Kirkwall and elsewhere, and making Orkney their home.[48]

Buchanan's appointment did not stop Kinclaven from continuing to pursue what he regarded as his rights, which were to a limited extent recognised by the crown. In December 1621 he obtained a pension of £3,600 from the island revenues, even though the council objected to such an impoverishment of the royal patrimony.[49] This was as far, however, as the king was prepared to go. At the end of 1623, hoping to raise more money from the island estates than could be provided by a tacksman,

42 *State Papers of Melros*, ii, 365–6.

43 *State Papers of Melros*, ii, 439–40.

44 *State Papers of Melros*, ii, 439–40.

45 *State Papers of Melros*, ii, 439–40: Buchanan also held a subtack from Killeith of the royal estates in Shetland (Exchequer Act Books or Register, NRS E4/4/321).

46 *Criminal Trials*, ii, 544–57; RPC, viii, 148, 517n, 544–5; theft was the ostensible reason for Hartsyde and her husband's disgrace, but according to Sir James Balfour, 'the Courtiers talked, that it was for reuelling [revealing] some of the Queinis secretts to the king, wich a wysse chambermaide would not have done'. It seems to have been about this time that King James began to use the north of Scotland as a place of banishment. In September 1606 three ministers were banished for holding conventicles, James Irving to Orkney, William Forbes to Shetland and James Greg to Caithness (RPC, vii, 261).

47 RPC, ix, 600.

48 Balfour of Denmilne Papers, NLS Adv. Ms. 33.1.1 (v, 70).

49 *State Papers of* Melros, ii, 441–2.

James began to think of feuing them again. On hearing of this, Kinclaven spoke to Chancellor Hay about his rights in the matter, saying that 'he could hardlie believe that [Hay] would seik the overthrow of his house' by feuing the estates to anyone but himself. Hay thought it unlikely that he or indeed anyone else would be made earl of Orkney. Kinclaven was not pleased, but was realistic enough in later meetings with the chancellor to switch his discussions from the Orkney estates to the lands from which he took his title as lord – those of Kinclaven and Innernytie. These were still held by the chancellor, though the latter was perfectly willing to sell them.[50] Even this did not end John Stewart's interest in Orkney, but it probably marked the end of any possible revival of the Stewart earldom.

This work, whose history is sketched out in the preface, has sought to disentangle the actual story of Robert and Patrick Stewart, earls of Orkney, from the fictions, extravagant and sometimes fantastical, that have surrounded them – insofar as this can be done. Both the previous books on the subject have contained examinations both of modern attitudes to the Stewart earls in the islands of Orkney and Shetland, and of the extraordinary legends and stories that have grown up around them, particularly Patrick. The reader is referred to these works for an analysis of them, but now that an attempt has been made at a final account of the real story, it is important to look back in the light of new knowledge and see where the legends may contain echoes, if not more than that, of truth. Certain images are common to both legend and historical record. Imprisonment, torture and the threat of torture undoubtedly took place in the cellars of Kirkwall Castle, though there is a great deal more information on this for Patrick than for Robert. There is no reason to doubt that Scalloway Castle was built by forced labour, though the more skilled workers were undoubtedly paid for their efforts. The lands of some small udallers were acquired in both Orkney and Shetland by both earls, though to what extent this was oppressive is difficult to say.

Perhaps the most significant difference between the legends and the true stories concerns the nature of the opposition to Patrick. It is here that the legends surrounding Bruce of Cultmalindie are closer to the reality of the situation than those concerning Patrick alone. Bruce is central to an understanding of why Patrick is particularly notorious in the history of Shetland. Bruce was a udaller; he may have acquired his lands by the oppressive methods the legend associates with Patrick, but that did not make him a feudatory of the earl, like the gentry of Orkney. Popular perception – though that alone – has to that extent made him a true representative of the Shetland opposition to Earl Patrick, though it is plain that he was at the same time no champion of the natives – a Scot, a land-grabber, a tyrant himself given the opportunity, and a man whose opinion of local culture was no higher than Patrick's own. The Sinclairs – a native family, or at least the assimilated descendants of an earlier Scottish influx – were too divided among themselves to offer any united front against Patrick, but it was they and the Bruces who interested Patrick most, because of their relative wealth. Although Patrick did acquire small estates on occasion, his major purpose was not served by the oppression of small landholders. Perhaps the nearest equivalent in reality to the legendary, or fictional, actions of such figures as Thorvald of Brenister and Thorburn Sigurdson of Dalsetter[51] are the more passive but courageous actions of such as Sinclair of Aith and Mouat of Heogaland in refusing to convict Henry Wardlaw despite Patrick's clear wish that they do so, ordering an immediate retrial when the first verdict proved not to his liking.

In Orkney the picture is even more at variance with legend and fiction. George Mackay Brown's vision of the earl's men torturing a udaller in Birsay[52] contains some semblance of real events, but plainly it was not minor udallers who caught Patrick's interest. His chief targets were his own wealthier vassals. The hapless 'witch' Alison Balfour and her family are a special case, and it was not their lands that Patrick's men were after. The fact is that in Orkney there were quite sizeable sections of the populace, in Birsay, Harray and Kirkwall, who were prepared to take up arms in support of the Stewart earldom, and elements who would even have contemplated its restoration.

What of the characters of these men – Robert and Patrick Stewart? Of the two, Patrick may seem to be the more interesting and complex, and it is clear that he left a great deal of well attested material and excited remark behind him, descriptive of his personality. But Robert offers his subtleties too, though he can hardly be described as a subtle character. As has already been touched on, it seems strange that someone who gives such meagre evidence of ability, is generally described as of little account and as being utterly untrustworthy, should have had the breadth of vision to achieve what he did in Orkney and Shetland, albeit for a brief period, leaving the likes of Bellenden and Bothwell, seemingly much abler men, fuming in frustration.

Father and son were both dispiriting villains; but Patrick Stewart was in some ways a curiously vulnerable one, whose character was long recognised as carrying the seeds of his own destruction. Where his own father generally seemed to know which way contrary winds were blowing, Patrick was oblivious to anything other than his own desires. Throughout the melancholy story of his decline and fall, clues to his nature emerge from the midst of complex events. There is little doubt that by the standards of his time as well as ours he was a very strange man indeed. His most striking characteristic was extravagance, in big things and in small. His style of living; the livery, equipment and the numbers of his followers; the colossal debts he ran up; the money he carried about with him; the marriage aspirations; the guns he collected; the curious assemblage of precious bits and pieces he kept with him in captivity; and his one monument, the architecture he inspired, all testify to this.

There seems a corresponding extravagance of character: a total lack of scruple

---

51 See Anderson, *Black Patie*, ch. 1, 'Patrick Smokes His Pipe'.
52 See Anderson, *Black Patie*, ch. 1, 'Patrick Smokes His Pipe'.

in maintaining his vainglorious establishment at the expense of all with whom he came into contact; obduracy in responding to advice on wiser courses; beard-tugging fury at the thwarting of his wishes. His son's claim that nothing he ever did turned out right might be attributed to exasperation, but John Stewart's suggestion that Patrick's activities might be ascribed to 'simplicity' rather than 'malice' suggests that the more charitable felt Patrick's judgment to be seriously disturbed. Michael Mair, undeterred by family obligations, long service, or money owed, recognised the signs of a loser and departed his service. Perhaps this was another reason why Patrick, as an intimate of the king, was denied infeftment in his lands for so long, and why there were repeated and increasingly determined attempts to ensure that he was provided with good advice.

Another characteristic is a curious combination of naivety and, perhaps, something of his father's slipperiness. His continued belief in his influence on the king, in the face of both evidence and wiser counsel, lasted long after all possible credibility had been exhausted; indeed his belief that he could behave as he did without penalty indicates a curious unworldliness. His capacity to defend his actions against criticism was, however, considerable. Though it is necessarily difficult to distinguish Patrick's own thoughts from those of his legal advisers, there is in his answers a consistent vein of skilful self-justification, both in shifting the blame and in providing alternative interpretations of his actions and statements. His ability to parry awkward questions from all angles meant that everything he wrote or said was capable of more than one interpretation, and on the most important point of all – his part in his son's revolt – nothing was proved until he finally yielded and himself gave the game away.

This loss of nerve at the end – for that is what it appears to have been – highlights the negative side to Patrick's extravagant temperament, and the arrogance and groundless optimism that went with it. Each high had its corresponding low. In the 1590s there was the great plan for marriage in the Netherlands, then conspicuous disgust at its failure, and retiral to Orkney to lick the wounds to his pride. There was the wilful disregard for the courts leading to heavy fines, followed by desperate attempts to pick up tiny rooms in Orkney and Shetland to eke out income. In 1613 there was the daring plan to escape from Dumbarton, an adventure worthy of the swashbuckling earl of Bothwell himself – followed by the humiliating decision, with the grappling-hook ready to throw and the horses saddled and waiting, that perhaps it was not such a good idea after all. This was not even the end of the matter. He recovered from this personal reverse and continued to boast to his son of the possibility of his coming north; Robert spoke naively of this on a number of occasions. Most significant of all was the total collapse that followed on Robert's execution, which led to Patrick's trial and condemnation, and the last terrified days waiting for death. His response to the churchmen who visited him might conceivably have been one of arrogant disregard, but the reference to his 'irresolution' rather suggests a metaphorical pulling of the bedclothes over his head to shut out reality, after the fashion of his son.

One is tempted to ask if these swings of mood and attitude were pathological in origin, whether those who spoke of him as a maniac[53] were perhaps closer to the truth than they knew. If Patrick did suffer from some kind of psychological malaise – bi-polarism for example – it was not sufficient to warrant his being declared altogether incompetent, since his own assent to his forfeiture of Orkney and Shetland was clearly desired. It is an intriguing speculation, but in the end we cannot know the truth of such a matter, and are compelled to take Patrick on his own terms, without special excuse. When we do, we find an extraordinary, difficult and fascinating character, whose activities strained the ingenuity of king, officers of state, councillors, lords of session, lawyers and friends. The picture the session records provide of the chronic concurrent streams of litigation illustrates what Sir Lawrence Gowing once described as 'the inconceivable strangeness of the past for which one is never quite prepared.'[54]

What is absent from the legends surrounding the Stewart earls when compared with the historical record is the latter's sheer complexity. In Robert's case, he had to deal throughout his life with ground shifting under his feet, as queen, regents and king all required urgent responses, never ultimately satisfied, if he was to achieve his aims in a political environment already tortuously unusual. In Patrick's case, it was his character that was central to events. His fall is sometimes seen as part of that policy of pacification in the Highlands and the Borders that is generally regarded as one of James VI's most enduring achievements.[55] Yet the turbulence in these areas had been endemic for centuries. The political and social structure of the Northern Isles on the other hand, though an intricate one which had seen great changes in the past century and a half, had not previously given rise to the chronic unrest to be found elsewhere. That among the Sinclairs, and between Sinclair and Bruce, were small beer compared with the west, and could easily have been contained by a stronger, more sensible Patrick. What happened instead was almost entirely his responsibility.

Patrick Stewart is altogether more interesting than his father Earl Robert, who began that half-century interlude in the history of Orkney and Shetland that Patrick brought to such a disastrous close. We know more about him; we have more insight into his character; we can even, on occasion, hear him speak. His failings were perhaps those of his father, but they were on a grander, perhaps even paranoid scale, and the word paranoid can be suggested with something approaching its true meaning, instead of its modern loose sense, filched from psychiatry and made a synonym for mere touchiness or oversensitivity. It is little wonder that his person-ality, long after most of the true details of it were lost to view, should continue

53 F. T. Wainwright, 'The Golden Age and After', *The Northern Isles*, Edinburgh, 1962, 188–92.

54 Gowing, review of John Michael Montias, Vermeer and his Milieu: a Web of Social History, *TLS*, 16–22 March 1990 (no. 4533), 159.

55 J. D. Mackie, *A History of Scotland*, Middlesex, 1964, 193–5; Willson, *James VI and I*, 320–1.

to be felt brooding over the Northern Isles, with that of his father lurking in the background. This book is not intended to exorcise the ghost of either, but to bring back from the shadows characters, undeniably unpleasant, but yet a great deal more interesting than their reputation in the islands has hitherto suggested.

Glossary

acquittance – action of clearing of debt or other obligation

ad perpetuam remanentiam – permanently; phrase used when vassal so surrenders his estate to superior

aithe – oath

Alhallo – Orkney head-court, held in November of each year

allanerlie – only

angel noble – English gold coin, equal to ten shillings sterling

apprising – legal process whereby lands or other heritable rights of debtor were sold (subject to limited right of redemption) to pay debt due to creditor

arbitral – see *decreet arbitral*

art and part (*airt and pairt*) – acting as accessory or accomplice

assythement – sum given to relatives of persons killed, by way of damages and indemnification, when the killing amounted to a crime

augmentation – increase in feu duty

auld earldom land – land originally granted by Earl Paul to his follower Sigurd of Westness

awand – owing

baable – bauble, child's toy

bailiary office – office of bailie or local magistrate in the parishes of Orkney

balk – unploughed length of land in open field

bawbee – small coin, worth a halfpenny Scots

bere (*beir*) – four-rowed barley, once very common throughout Scotland, though rare today

bismar and pundlar (in Shetland *punder*) – wooden instruments used as form of beam balance in measuring of various commodities, notably in connection with payment of rent, *skat*, etc. in kind. In Orkney, the bismar was used for small quantities, the pundlar for large; in Shetland this was reversed.

blenche ferme – feudal holding where *reddendo* is purely nominal

block-house – a protruding tower built into the wall of a castle for defensive purposes

boistis – threatens

bond – written obligation to pay money or do some act. Sometimes used of mutual undertakings between persons for mutual assistance – old form *band*. A general bond or band was an obligation imposed on parties to a feud obliging them to keep the peace See also *friendship, maintenance, manrent*

booth – storage facility and trading post

boots, buittis – an instrument of torture in which the feet of the victim were placed and then wedges driven in

bordland – early on, land requiring work by slave labour; later, a generic term for earl's original estates, as opposed to *conquest land* acquired later

bruk, bruik – possess

brute – report

bu (bow, bull) – head farm of *udal* estate

bull – measuring container (and measure) of fish–oil or butter, amounting to two imperial quarts, or four *cans*

can – measuring container (and measure) of fish-oil or butter, amounting to two imperial quarts

caschielawis – instrument of torture; how it operated is unknown. For discussion of its possible nature, see Anderson, *Black Patie*, app. 4.

casualties – payments falling to feudal superior on happening of uncertain date or occurrence. See also *wardship*

caution – legal security in civil matters; a *bond of caution* obliged its granter to find surety in a given sum

cautioner – one who provides security in the matter of *caution*

chalder – unit of Scottish grain measure, equivalent to approximately 4–6 English bushels

chalmerchield – valet or groom of the chamber

chalmerlane – chamberlain, factor

chantor – equivalent of English and Latin *precentor* superintending music of cathedral and its song school

co-adjutor – person appointed to assist holder of high ecclesiastical office

cois – exchange

commendator – person (usually layman) holding revenues of benefice, usually for life

commissary court – court taking the place of the former ecclesiastical courts concerned with consistorial and testamentary matters. The presiding judge was called the *commissary*

compearance – formal appearance before a court

compt – account

comptroller – royal official, responsible with treasurer for financial administration

conding – condign

conquest land – land acquired rather than inherited

consuetudes – customs

cordiner – shoemaker

cost – combination of two thirds malt and one third meal, used in Orkney in paying of victual rents

cowp bill – licence granted to merchants in Shetland, laying down conditions of trade

craar (crair) – small trading vessel

culverin bastard – cannon; the name given to the middle size of culverin, between grand culverin and medium culverin

curator – guardian

cuttell – unit of Shetland cloth measure, also rod used for measuring cuttells in length. 60 cuttells = 1 *pack*. Equivalent to Scots *ell*

dag – pistol

deal – a plank

decreet arbitral – final decision by an arbiter

demission – resignation of office

Dens – Danish

dispone – convey (of land)

doer – a lawyer, factor or other representative or adviser

dogger, dogger boat – two-masted fishing vessel

double fly-boat – see *fly-boat*

dredour (dreaddour) – fear or dread of

dwang – harass

ell – unit of Scots cloth measure, equivalent to approximately 37 English inches

entail – destination of heritable property to specified line of heirs

entres silver – money paid on entry into tenure of land

escheat – forfeiture of estate

excambion – contract in which one piece of land is exchanged for another

extraniers – strangers

falcon – a light cannon

fasheous – troublesome

fathom – measure of volume of peat.

feallis – liege-men, adherents

fee – full right of property in heritage, as distinct from liferent

ferd – fourth; ferd of kyne – in the fourth degree of relationship

feu, feuferme, feuar – feudal holding, one who holds thus

flit and fure – Orkney and Shetland term meaning to render transport service to landlord, superior or holder of crown lands

fly-boat – small, fast-sailing vessel

foud (fold), foudry – senior legal official in Shetland (name also given to local magistrates, who are alternatively styled underfouds); the name of the post. Equivalent position in Orkney was lawman before 1541 and sheriff thereafter

four forms, letters of – first step in execution against the person for debt, consisting of four charges, last being to debtor to enter prison on pain of denunciation

friendship, bond of – bond entered into by two or more men of equal rank for their mutual assistance

fure – see flit and fure

fustian – thick-twilled, short-napped cloth, dyed dark

gainstowd – opposed

galleass – vessel powered by both sails and oars

general band – see bond

gerssumes – see grassum

girnel – granary

grandrie – 'septennial court to abate nuisances and punish local abuses'; see also *sculding*

grassum – entry fee paid by holder of *tack*

grieve – farm overseer

gudling – unit of Shetland measure in various commodities. In cloth, it was equivalent to six *cuttells* of *wadmel*, at least before Bruce's time

Gulathinglaw – the legal system of western Norway from the mediaeval period onwards, and said to have influenced the legal systems of Orkney and Shetland

hagbut – early form of portable firearm, so called from hook cast on gun by which it was attached to support

Hanse – a powerful mercantile league of north German cities, such as Bremen, Hamburg and Lübeck

head bu (*heid bull*) – see *bu*

Herdmanstein – Orkney head-court, held in January of each year

hereit – harried

heritable (*property*) – property capable of being inherited, notable house and lands

holmganga – 'island-going', reference to Norse practice of opponents in single combat repairing to small island to hold their contest

horning – judicial outlawry for debt, so termed because it was signalled by three blasts on the horn at the mercat cross; *horn, put to the* – outlaw for non-payment of debt, so termed because failure to make payment was signalled by law officer making three blasts on horn at the mercat cross. *Unrelaxed at the horn* – continuing in state of outlawry for debt. *Register of hornings* – register of those put to the horn.

hoy – small vessel, used for carrying passengers and goods, usually for short distances

impignoration – pledging

incuntreyis – in the instance cited in the text, probably the Scottish Lowlands, thought of as an example of a stable law-abiding area.

infeftment – act of putting in possession of land or other heritable property; also legal deed by which this was done

instrument – document testifying to completion of act of e.g. sasine, putting in possession of land. See also precept

intromit (*intromitter, intromission*) – to handle or deal with (funds or other property)

justice-ayre – circuit followed by justices of Justiciary Court

justice clerk – clerk to the High Court of Justiciary, or supreme criminal court

kail – form of cabbage with open curled leaves

kindly – (of land tenure) quasi-hereditary, based on long possession by same family

kingsland – land in Orkney or Shetland formerly held by the kings of Norway

kirkland – land not forming part of bishopric land, but settled on some local kirks or prebends of the diocese

lach (*laich*) – low

landmail – rent paid by tenants

larrett – coarse linen cloth

last – Orkney measure of weight or capacity, equal to twenty-four meils

laver – water scoop

lawburrows – legal security required from or given by a person that he will not injure
   another

lawman – judge and legal adviser in courts in Shetland prior to 1550

lawrightman – local magistrate and overseer of standards of weights and measures

Lawting – head court in Northern Isles in Norse times

leanger – final duty paid in Shetland in wadmel on the complete payment of all other
   duties

letter of marque – commission to individual who has suffered wrong at hands of member
   of foreign state and been denied justice by that state, to recover his loss by direct
   action against other members of that state (maritime procedure)

ley – fallow

liferent – right to receive till death the revenue of a property, without the right to dispose
   of the capital

ling – fish related to the cod

lippin – trust

lispund – measure of weight used in Northern Isles mainly for butter and sometimes oil;
   divided into 24 merks and equal to one setting grain weight

mails – feu duties, rents

maintenance, bond of – bond granted to man of lesser rank by his patron, in exchange for
   his *bond of manrent*

manrent, bond of – bond by which free man became client of his patron, bound to assist
   him

marque – see *letter of marque*

mart – cured carcase of beef

meil – measure of Northern Isles grain weight, equal to six settings or one twenty-fourth
   of a last

mell – have dealings with

merk – mark Scots, worth 13s 4d Scots; also measure of weight in Northern Isles, equal
   to 1/24 *lispund*, and a measure of extent in Shetland

mes, mess – mass (religious observance)

messuage – principal dwelling-house of barony

moyane – influence, power to exert influence

multures – duties payable in kind for having grain ground at local mill

neg (naig) – a small horse or pony

Negative Confession – confession drawn up in 1581 during 'popish scare' and denouncing
   all kinds of papistry

newel – upright round which steps of a circular staircase wind

nonentry – failure of an heir of a deceased vassal to obtain entry to a feudal property

Octavians – eight administrators employed by James VI to reorganise royal finances

odal – see udal

ogang, owgang – court of perambulation held to settle disputes about land boundaries

outbrecks – barren land, thinly coated with earth and hardly worth cultivating

pack – unit of Shetland cloth measure, consisting of 60 *cuttells*

parteikis – practicks; legal precedent or usual practice

passments – strips of precious material, used as trimming for garments

peitstane – coping stone – stone shaped to provide top covering of a wall

pend – covered walkway. In cathedral terms it is more commonly referred to as the *triforium*, running alongside the cathedral at an upper level

pennyland – measure of extent in Orkney

perambulation – judicial proceeding for deciding questions of disputed marches. See *ogang*

pilliewinkis – thumbscrews

pinnace – a small vessel acting as a tender for a larger one lying off

plak (plack) – coin worth four pence Scots

poind (poynd) – seize and sell the goods of a debtor

prebendary – member of cathedral chapter, holding prebend (*stouk, stallery*) or stipend

precentor – cathedral dignitary superintending music of cathedral and its song school

precept – writ commanding officer or deputy to take legal action, such as to give actual possession of heritable property

Premonstratensian – strict form of the rule of St Augustine, founded by St Norbert at Premontre in 1120

pro rege – see *kingsland*

protocol book – notary's copy-book of instruments recording legal transactions, especially conveyances of land

pundlar, punder – see *bismar and pundlar*

quitclaim – renounce

quoin – stone shaped for use in an angle or corner

quot – the share of the movable estate of a deceased person due to the commissary court on registration of a testament

quoy, quoyland – enclosure, or piece of land originally taken into cultivation from outside hill dyke; also a form of *quey*, a heifer

rabbet – stone tongued and grooved for use in a series of joints

reddendo – duty or service to be paid or rendered by vassal to superior in accordance with feu charter

regality – jurisdiction of high power, largely independent of the crown, trying all cases except treason

remainder – interest in estate which operates only on termination of a prior interest

resset (reset) – receiving, usually of stolen goods, but also the hiding of a fugitive

rests – arrears

rig and rendell – see *runrig*

roithmen – Orkney legal term for the 'best landed men' who composed head courts up to early sixteenth century

rooing – shearing by plucking wool by handrig and Rendell

room – parcel of land

rowme – see *room*

running at the ring – a game in which each of a number of riders endeavours to carry off on the point of his lance a circle of metal suspended from a post

runrig – system of cultivation in which separate ridges in fields were cultivated by different occupiers

sasine, sesing – act of giving legal possession of landed property in Scotland; the legal deed by which such possession is given

scaff boit – light boat or skiff

scattald – land attached to township or group of townships

schound – meeting to partition inheritance among heirs; *schound bill* – record of *schound*

sculding – part of *grandrie* procedure, whereby whole population of a scattald might be put to probation in case where crime had been committed by unknown person

sellar – cellar

servitor – male servant; in this context usually one occupying a major position in respect of his master, rather than a humble servant

setting – measure of Northern Isles grain weight, equal to six meils

sewar – honorary server at royal banquets

sheep holm – an islet, uninhabited, but used for grazing sheep

sheriff in that part – in Scots law, messenger-at-arms, appointed by crown to supply place of sheriff in executing process

sixern (*sixareen*) – six-oared boat of distinctive Shetland design

skat – land tax of Norse origin, divided into various types, e.g. malt skat, butter skat, forcop, leanger, wattle, etc.

skatheles – free from harm

sklent – crooked

souertie – surety

Spanze – Spanish

sparsim – scattered

spiritualities – income, consisting mainly of teinds, derived by bishopric or abbey from parish churches appropriated to it

spuilyie – taking movables from another's possession against his will

staller, stallery – see *prebendary*

stouk – see *prebendary*

strenye – distrain, seize goods to ensure payment

subchantry – post of under *precentor* superintending music of cathedral and its song school, with lands and income pertaining thereto

sucken – power of an estate to compel tenants to use a certain mill

suddart – soldier

suffragan – subject or subordinate to a metropolitan

Sumburgh Roost – a strong and potentially perilous current that swirls around Sumburgh Head at the southern tip of mainland Shetland

swine-rooting – practice of pigs turning up ground with snout; Norse law made provision for redress of damage caused to neighbouring crops by pigs in this way

tack – lease, customarily renewable every 19 years in Scotland, every three years in Shetland

tackman – functionary responsible for the ingathering of each parish's rental and other payments. Unique to Orkney, and not to be confused with *tacksman*

tacksman – holder or a *tack* or lease

teinds, teindsheaves – tenth part of annual produce of land, due to the church

temporalities – ecclesiastical revenues from lands and their rents, as opposed to spiritualities

tenement – piece of land the subject of tenure

tenendas – clause in charter expressing nature of tenure by which lands are to be held; see also *entail, remainder*

terce – liferent of one third of husband's heritage given by law to widow

thingholm – holm in Loch of Tingwall, Shetland, close to northern shore where formerly chief annual assize is said to have taken place

thirds (of benefices) – third of benefice revenues uplifted by crown from 1562 to early seventeenth century for its own use and for payment of stipends of reformed clergy

thirlage – obligation of tenants on an estate to use a certain mill

timmer – driftwood

tinsel – forfeiture

tocher, tochergudis – dowry, items making up dowry

tonsure – the act of shaving the hair from the top of a monk's or priest's head as a sign of entering holy orders

triforium – see *pend*

tron stone – unit of weight in Scotland, originally derived from the weights of Lanark, although it varied from place to place

tulchan – literally, calf-skin stuffed with straw, used to induce cow to give milk, used figuratively of bishops appointed in sixteenth century in order to divert bishopric revenues into lay hands in form of pensions

tulyie – brawl

tystour – box, case

udal, uthell, udaller – (of land) owned outright without a superior; one owning land thus

umboth duties – name given in Shetland to dues payable to bishop of Orkney

unblicht – unbleached

underfoud – see *foud*

unrelayed at the horn – undischarged as outlaw or bankrupt

victual – goods in kind

volt – vault

wadmel – coarse woollen cloth, used in Shetland in part-payment of rent

wadset – pledge of lands in security for debt

wafting – protecting

wand-bed – *wicker* bed

wappenshaws – muster of men under arms

Wappenstein – Norse court held in Orkney; formerly 'weapon-court' or assembly for reviewing weapons and equipment for war, but court held by Robert 6 Feb. 1580 is only example known

ward(ship) – guardianship of infant heir; also restriction of liberty, whether 'open' or 'close'

warrandice – clause in disposition guaranteeing that right conveyed shall take effect

water-kail – broth made without meat

warrender – keeper of a rabbit warren

wattle – originally hospitality exacted by travelling officials in the Northern Isles, later an assessed tax

waughter – a guard ship, employed as a convoy for the Dutch fishing fleet in northern waters.

wecht – weight

wether (*wedder*) – castrated ram

whinger – short dagger

wirry (*worry*) – strangle

wrack and waith – rights to wrecks and goods cast up upon the shore

yconomus – general administrator of an ecclesiastical foundation during a vacancy

yett – gate

yoill (*yole*) – Shetland boat rather shallower and lighter than the *sixern*

yopindale – silver coin, originally worth 15 shillings Scots

Bibliography

PRIMARY SOURCES – PRINTED

A Chronicle of the Kings of Scotland (Maitland Club), Glasgow, 1830.

A Diurnal of Remarkable Occurrents that have passed within the Country of Scotland since the Death of King James the Fourth till the year 1575 (Bannatyne and Maitland Clubs), 1833.

Accounts of the (Lord High) Treasurer of Scotland, 1473–1574, vols I–XII, eds T. Dickson, J. B. Paul and C. T. McInnes, 1877–1970.

Accounts of the Collectors of Thirds of Benefices, 1561–2, ed. G. Donaldson (SHS), 1949.

Accounts of the Master of Works, vol. I, *1529–1615*, ed. H. M. Paton, 1957.

Acta Curiae Admirallatus Scotiae, 1557–62, ed. T. C. Wade (Stair Soc.), 1943.

Acts of the Lords of Council in Public Affairs, 1501–54, ed. R. K. Hannay, 1932.

Balcarres Papers (Foreign Correspondence with Marie de Lorraine, Queen of Scotland), ed. M. Wood (SHS), 1925.

Bannatyne Miscellany, vols I–III (Bannatyne Club), 1827–55.

Book of Records of the Ancient Privileges of the Canongate, ed. Marguerite Wood (SRS), 1955.

Book of the Universall Kirk of Scotland (Acts and Proceedings of the General Assemblies of the Kirk of Scotland), vols I–III (Bannatyne Club), 1839–45.

Buchanan, G., *Rerum Scoticarum Historica*, Edinburgh, 1582, trans. A Constable, as *A History of Great Britain, England as well as Scotland* (SHS), Edinburgh, 1982.

Calderwood, D., *The History of the Kirk of Scotland*, vols I–IV, ed. T. Thomson (Wodrow Soc.), 1842–3.

Calendar of Border Papers, ed. J. Bain, vols I–II, Edinburgh, 1896.

Calendar of State Papers relating to Scotland and Mary, Queen of Scots, 1547–1603, vols I–XIII, ed. J. Bain et al., 1898–1969.

Calendar of State Papers, Domestic, 1603–1625, vols VIII–IX, XII, ed. Mrs E. Green, 1857–8, 1872.

Calendar of State Papers, Foreign, 1863–1950, vols I–XXIII, various eds.

Calendar of State Papers, Spanish, 1580–1603 (Calendar of Letters and State Papers relating to English Affairs, preserved principally in the Archives of Simancas), vols III–IV, ed. M. A. S. Hume, 1896–9.

Calendar of State Papers, Venetian, 1603–7, vol. X, ed. H. F. Brown, 1900.

Calendar of the Laing Charters, ed. J. Anderson, Edinburgh, 1899.

Charters and other Records of the City and Royal Burgh of Kirkwall, ed. J. Mooney (Spalding Club), 1952, Kirkwall, n.d.

Charters of Holyrood (*Liber Cartarum Sancte Crucis*), ed. F. Egerton (Bannatyne Club), 1840.

Commentary on the Rule of St Augustine by Robertus Richardinus, ed. G. G. Coulton (SHS), 1935.

Correspondence of Sir Patrick Waus of Barnbarroch, vols I–II, ed. R. Vans Agnew, (Ayr and Wigton Historical Society), Edinburgh, 1887.

Courcelles's Negotiations in Scotland, 1586–7 (Bannatyne Club), 1828.

Court Book of the Regality of Broughton and the Burgh of the Canongate, 1569–73, ed. M. Wood, Edinburgh and London, 1937.

Criminal Trials in Scotland, vols I–III, ed. R. Pitcairn, Edinburgh, 1833.

'Daemonologie', *King James VI and I: Selected Writings*, ed. N. Rhodes, J. Richards and J, Marshall, Aldershot, 2003, 149–97.

Diary of the Rev. John Mill, Minister in Shetland 1740–1803, ed. G. Goudie (SHS), Edinburgh, 1889.

Early Records of the University of St Andrews, 1413–1579, ed. J. Maitland Anderson (SHS), 1926.

Early Scottish Charters prior to AD 1153, ed. A. Lawrie, Glasgow, 1905.

Extracts from the Records of the Burgh of Edinburgh, 1589–1603, 1573–89, 1604–1626 (Scottish Burgh Record Society), ed., R. K. Hannay, M. Wood, 1927, 1931.

Gordon, R., *Genealogical History of the Earldom of Sutherland*, Edinburgh, 1813.

Holinshed, R. *Chronicles*, ii, 439 (Holinshed Project Website – 1577 and 1587 editions comparative text), Oxford, in progress (online edition).

(*Inquisitiones Generales*) *Inquisitionum ad Capellam Regis Retornatarum quae in Publicis Archivis Scotiae adhuc Servantur*, vols I–III, ed. T. Thomson, Edinburgh, 1811–16.

Keith, R., *History of the Affairs of Church and State in Scotland*, vols I–II, ed. J. P. L. (Spottiswoode Soc.), 1844.

Knox, J., *History of the Reformation in Scotland*, vols I–II, ed. D. Laing, 1846–8; W. Croft Dickinson, 1949.

Kolsrud, O. *Den norske Kirkes Erkebiskoper og Biskoper indtil Reformationen, Diplomatarium Norvegicum*, xviib, Christiania (Oslo), 1913.

Laing, D. A., 'Decreit of Spuilzie, granted by the Lords of Council to William Bruce of Symbister in Zetland, against Patrick, Earl of Orkney, 4th October 1609', *Archaeologia Scotica* (Proceedings of the Society of Antiquaries of Scotland), iv, 385–98.

Letters and State Papers during the Reign of King James the Sixth (Abbotsford Club), Edinburgh, 1838.

Letters of James V, ed. R. K. Hannay and D. Hay, Edinburgh, 1954.

Letters on the Ecclesiastical Affairs of Scotland, vols I–II (Bannatyne Club), 1841.

Lindsay of Pitscottie, R., *The Historie of Scotland* (STS), 1899.

Lord Henry Sinclair's 1492 Rental of Orkney, ed. W. P. L. Thomson, Edinburgh, 1996.

Melville of Halhill, Sir James, *Memorials of His Own Life* (Bannatyne Club), Edinburgh, 1827.

Monteith, R., *Description of the Isles of Orknay and Zetland*, Edinburgh, 1711.

Moysie, D., *Memoirs of the Affairs of Scotland* (Bannatyne Club), Edinburgh, 1830.

Notes on Orkney and Zetland, ed. A. Peterkin, Edinburgh, 1822.

Oppressions of the Sixteenth Century in the Islands of Orkney and Zetland, ed. David Balfour (Maitland Club), 1859.

Original Letters of Mr John Colville (Bannatyne Club), 1858.

Orkney and Shetland Records, ed. A. W. and A. Johnston (Viking Soc.), 1907.

Orkney Testaments and Inventories, ed. R. S. Barday (SRS), Edinburgh, 1977.

Papiers d'état relatif a l'histoire de l'Écosse au XVIe siècle, vols I–II, ed. A. Teulet (Bannatyne Club), Edinburgh, 1851.

Pococke, R., *Tours in Scotland* (SHS), Edinburgh, 1887.

Prot. Bk Gilbert Grote 1552–73, ed. William Angus (SHS), Edinburgh, 1914.

Records of the Earldom of Orkney, ed. J. Storer Crouston (SHS), 1914.

Records of Elgin 1234–1800, ed. William Cramond, vol. 2, (New Spalding Club), Aberdeen, 1908.

Records of the Parliaments of Scotland to 1707, St Andrews, 2007–2011 (online edition).

Regesta Regum Scottorum, vol. I, ed. G. W. S. Barrow, 1960.

Register of the Privy Council of Scotland, 1585–1625, vols IV–IX, XIV, (second series), VIII, ed. D. Masson, 1881–98.

Registrum Magni Sigilli Regum Scotorum, 1488–1584, vols V–VIII, ed. J. M. Thomson, Edinburgh, 1888–94.

Registrum Secreti Sigilli Regum Scotorum, 1567–84, vols VI–VIII, ed. G. Donaldson, 1966–82.

Rentals of the Ancient Earldom and Bishoprick of Orkney, ed. A. Peterkin, Edinburgh, 1820.

Report by de la Brosse and d'Oysel on Conditions in Scotland 1559–60, ed. G. Dickinson (SHS Misc. IX), 1958.

Reports on the Royal Archives of Denmark, and Report on the Royal Library at Copenhagen (45th and 46th Reports of the Deputy Keeper of the Public Records, 1884–5), ed. W. D. Macray.

Salisbury Papers (HMC), vols I–XXIV, London, 1889.

Selections Illustrative of the History of Scotland, mdxliii–mdlxviii (Maitland Club), 1837.

Shetland Documents, 1195–1579, ed. B. Smith and J. Ballantyne, Lerwick, 1999.

Shetland Documents, 1580–1611, ed. B. Smith and J. Ballantyne, Lerwick, 1994.

Skene, W. F., *Memorials of the Family of Skene of Skene from the family papers with other illustrative documents* (New Spalding Club), Aberdeen, 1887.

Spottiswoode, J., *History of the Church of Scotland* (Bannatyne Club), vols I–III, Edinburgh, 1851.

State Papers and Miscellaneous Correspondence of Thomas, Earl of Melros, vols I–II (Abbotsford Club), Edinburgh, 1837.

Statutes of the Scottish Church, 1225–1559 (SHS), trans. and ed. D. Patrick, Edinburgh, 1907.

The Autobiography and Diary of James Melvill (Wodrow Soc.), 1842.

The Court Book of Shetland, 1602–4, ed. G. Donaldson (SRS), 1954.

The Court Books of Orkney and Shetland, 1612–13, ed. R. S. Barclay, Kirkwall, 1962.

The Court Books of Orkney and Shetland, 1614–1615, ed. R. S. Barclay (SHS), Edinburgh, 1967.

The Exchequer Rolls of Scotland (Rotuli Scaccarii Regum Scotorum), 1580–1600, vols XXI–
    XXIII, ed. G. P. McNei1, 1901–8.
The Historie and Life of King James the Sext, 1565–96 (Bannatyne Club), 1825.
The Scottish Correspondence of Mary of Lorraine, ed. A. Cameron (SHS), 1927.
The Works of Sir David Lindsay of the Mount, ed. D. Hamer (STS), 1931.
Wallace, J., *A Description of the Isles of Orkney,* Edinburgh, 1883.

PRIMARY SOURCES – MANUSCRIPT

Acta Dominorum, NRS CS5.
Acta Dominorum et Sessionis, NRS CS6.
Baikie of Tankerness Mss, OA D.24.
Balfour (of Balfour and Trenabie) Papers, OA D.2.
Balfour of Denmilne Papers, NLS Adv. Ms. 33.1.1.
Balfour of Pilrig Muniments, NRS GD69.
Bellenden Papers, NLS Adv. Ms. 22.3.14.
Breadalbane Muniments, NRS GD112.
Bruce of Sumburgh Papers, SA D.8.
Bruce of Symbister Papers, SA GD144.
Church Records: Register of Presentations, NRS CH4.
Court of Session Records: Register of Acts and Decreets, NRS CS7; Process Papers,
    CS15; Register of Cautions in Suspensions, CS290; Register of Cautions in Lawbur-
    rows, CS295.
Craven Bequest, NRS GD106.
Cunningham of Caprington Muniments NRS GD149.
Diligence Records: General Register of Hornings, Inhibitions, etc., NRS DI3; Partic-
    ular Register of Hornings for Edinburgh, DI47; Orkney, DI85.
Earldom of Orkney Papers, OA D.13.
Edinburgh Commissary Court Records: Register of Acts and Decreets, NRS CC8/2;
    Register of Testaments, CC8/8; Register of Deeds and Protests, CC8/17.
E. S. Reid Tait Papers, SA D.6/194.
Exchequer Records: Abbreviates of Charters of Kirklands, NRS E14/1–2; Orkney
    Rentals and Accounts, NRS E41, E108; Buildings and Works Papers, E342.
Fea of Clestrain Muniments, NRS GD31.
Gardie House Papers.
Gordon Castle Muniments, NRS GD44.
Hugh Marwick Papers, NRS GD1/236.
Irvine of Midbrake Papers, SA D.13; NRS (microf.) RH4/35/388/41.
Justiciary Court Records: Books of Adjournal, NRS JC2; Register of Cautions, JC19;
    Small Papers, Main Series, JC26.
Kinfauns Muniments (Lord Gray's Papers).
King James VI Hospital, Perth, Muniments, NRS GD79.
Kinross House Papers, NRS GD29.
Mar and Kellie Papers,, NRS GD124.
Miscellaneous Microfilms, NRS RH4/35/388/32 and 41.

Miscellaneous Papers, NRS RH15.

Miscellaneous Photocopies and Transcripts, SA SA2.

Moray Muniments (HMC).

Morton Papers, OA D.38 (formerly Orkney Archive NRS GD150).

Orkney and Shetland Papers, NRS RH9/15.

Orkney Record and Antiquarian Soc. Recs, OA D.46.

Orkney Testaments, NRS CC17/2/1.

Particular Register of Sasines for the Sheriffdom of Orkney, NRS RS43.

Pittenweem Writs, NRS GD62/158.

Protocol Books of: Thomas Auchinleck, NP1/36; William Stewart, NRS NP1/62.

R. K. Hannay Papers, NRS GD214.

Register House Charters, NRS RH6 and supplementary.

Register of Deeds (Books of Council and Session): 1st series, NRS RD1; Deeds
    Warrants, RD11.

Register of the Privy Seal, NRS PS1.

Rose Papers, NLS Adv. Ms. 49.7.19

Roxburghe Muniments (Floors Castle; NRA(S) survey no. 1100).

Scarth of Breckness Muniments, NRS GD217.

Shand of Broughty Ferry scrapbooks, SA ref. D1/135.

Sheriff Court Records: Orkney and Shetland, SA SC12.

Sheriff G. H. M. Thom's Papers, NRS GD1/212.

Shetland Library Collection, SA D11/189.

Sinclair of Mey Muniments, NRS GD96.

Smyth of Methven Papers, NRS GD190.

State Papers, NRS SP.

Storer Clouston Papers, OA D.23.

Strathmore Papers, Bowes letter books, Glamis Castle; NRA(S) Survey no. 885.

Traill Dennison Papers, OA D.14.

Tulloch of Tannachie Muniments, NRS GD107.

Vaila Papers, SA D10.

Wodrow Robert, Ms. life of James Law, GUL Mss Gen.1198, 1207.

SECONDARY WORKS

Anderson, M. O., *Early Sources of Scottish History, AD500 to 1286*, [1922] (1999).

Anderson, P. D., *Robert Stewart, Earl of Orkney, Lord of Shetland*, Edinburgh, 1982.

Anderson, P. D., *Black Patie: the Life and Times of Patrick Stewart, Earl of Orkney, Lord of
    Shetland*, Edinburgh, 1992.

Armstrong, W. Bruce, *The Bruces of Airth and their Cadets*, Edinburgh, 1892.

Arnott, J., *The House of Arnot and some of its Branches: a Family History*, Edinburgh, 1918.

Bingham, C., *James V, King of Scots*, London, 1971.

Brand, J., *A Brief Description of Orkney, Zetland, Pightland Firth and Caithness*, Edinburgh,
    1701–3.

Brøgger, A. W., *Ancient Emigrants. A History of the Norse Settlements of Scotland*, Oxford,
    1929.

Burrows, E. H., *The Moodies of Melsetter*, Cape Town, 1954.

Calder, J. T., *Sketch of the Civil and Traditional History of Caithness*, Wick, 1887.

Cameron, J. *James V: the Personal Rule 1528–1542*, East Linton, 1998.

Catton, J., *History of the Shetland Islands*, Wainfleet, 1838.

Clark, J., *Genealogy of the Fordyce, Bruce and Clark Families*, Falkirk, 1899.

Clouston, J. S., *History of Orkney*, Kirkwall, 1932.

Clowes, W. L., *The Royal Navy: a History from the Earliest Times to the Present*, London, vols I–VII, 1901.

Cluness, A. T., *The Shetland Isles*, London, 1951.

Craven, J. B., *A History of the Church in Orkney, 1558–1662*, Kirkwall, 1897.

Craven, J. B., *Church Life in South Ronaldshay and Burray in the Seventeenth Century*, Kirkwall, 1911.

Craven, J. B., *Sir John Arnot of Barswick and the Family of Arnot in South Ronaldsay*, Kirkwall, 1913.

Cuthbert, O. D., *A Flame in the Shadows: Robert Reid, Bishop of Orkney, 1541–1558*, Kirkwall, 1998.

Donaldson, G., *Shetland Life under Earl Patrick*, Edinburgh, 1958.

Donaldson, G., *The Scottish Reformation*, Cambridge, 1960.

Donaldson, G., *The First Trial of Mary, Queen of Scots*, London, 1969.

Donaldson, G., *Scotland, James V – James VII*, Edinburgh, 1971.

Donaldson, G., *Isles of Home*, Edinburgh, 1983.

Dow, J., *Ruthven's Army in Sweden and Esthonia*, Stockholm, 1965.

Edmondston, A., *View of the Ancient and Present State of the Zetland Islands*, Edinburgh, 1809.

Elder, J. R., *Spanish Influences on Scottish History*, Glasgow, 1920.

Elliot, J. H., *Europe Divided*, London, 1968.

Fenton, A., *The Northern Isles: Orkney and Shetland*, Edinburgh, 1978.

Fischer, T. A., *The Scots in Sweden*, Edinburgh, 1907.

Fraser, A., *Mary, Queen of Scots*, London, 1969.

Fraser, W., *The Lennox Book*, vols I–II, Edinburgh, 1874.

Fraser, W., *The Elphinstone Family Book of the Lords Elphinstone, Balmerino and Coupar*, vols I–II, Edinburgh, 1897.

Fraser, W., *Memorials of the Earls of Haddington*, vols I–II, privately printed, Edinburgh, 1889.

Gjerset, K., *History of the Norwegian People*, vols I–II, New York, 1927.

Gore-Browne, R., *Lord Bothwell*, London, 1937.

Goudie, G., *The Celtic and Scandinavian Antiquities of Shetland*, Edinburgh, 1904.

Grant, F., *The County Families of the Zetland Islands*, Lerwick, 1893.

Grant, F., *Zetland Family Histories*, Lerwick, 1893.

Grant, J. *Cassell's Old and New Edinburgh: its History, its People and its Places*, vols I–III, London, 1885–7.

Gregory, D., *The History of the Western Highlands and Isles of Scotland*, Edinburgh, 1836.

Hay Fleming, D., *Mary Queen of Scots*, London, 1898.

Hay Fleming, D., *The Reformation in Scotland*, London, 1910.

Hibbert, S., *Description of the Shetland Islands*, Edinburgh, 1822.

Holbourn, I. B. S., *The Isle of Foula*, Lerwick, 1938.

Hossack, B. H., *Kirkwall in the Orkneys*, Kirkwall, 1900.

Laing, M., *The History of Scotland*, vols I–IV, Edinburgh, 1804.

Lang, A., *The Mystery of Mary Stewart*, London, 1901.

Lee, M., *James Stewart, Earl of Moray*, New York, 1953.

Lee, M., *John Maitland of Thirlestane*, Princeton, 1959.

Low, G., *A Tour through the Islands of Orkney and Schetland*, Kirkwall, 1879.

Lynch, M., *Scotland: a New History*, London, 1991.

Lyon, C. J., *History of St Andrews*, vols I–II, St Andrews, 1843.

Mackenzie, J., *The General Grievances and Oppressions of the Isles of Orkney and Shetland*, Edinburgh, 1836.

Mackie, J. D., *A History of Scotland*, Middlesex, 1964.

Mackie, R. L., *King James IV of Scotland*, Edinburgh, 1958.

Marshall, R., *Mary of Guise*, London, 1977.

Marwick, E. W., *The Folklore of Orkney and Shetland*, London, 1975.

Mooney, J., *The Cathedral and Royal Burgh of Kirkwall*, Kirkwall, 1943.

Napier, M., *Memoirs of Napier of Merchiston* (Letters of Adam Bothwell), Edinburgh and London, 1834.

Nau, C., *The History of Mary Stewart*, ed. J. Stevenson, Edinburgh, 1883.

Nicolson, J. R., *Shetland*, London, 1979.

Pettifer, E. W., *Punishments of Former Days*, Bradford, 1939.

Ridpath, G., *The Border-History of England and Scotland*, London, 1776.

Ruvigny, M. A. H. D. H. de la de M. de, *The Moodie Book*, privately printed, 1906.

Sanderson, M. H. B., *Mary Stewart's People: Life in Mary Stewart's Scotland*, Edinburgh, 1987.

Sandison, C., *Unst – My Island Home and its Story*, Lerwick, 1968.

Scott, W., *Northern Lights*, Hawick, 1982.

Simpson, D. *The Castle of Bergen and Bishop's Palace at Kirkwall. A Study of Early Norse Architecture*, Edinburgh, 1961.

Simpson, D., *Bishop's Palace and Earl's Palace*, successive edns, Edinburgh, 1965–2006, revisions by D. Pringle, 1991 and C. Tabraham, 2006.

Skene, W. F., *The Chronicles of the Picts and the Scots*, Edinburgh, 1867.

Smith, H. D., *Shetland Life and Trade*, Edinburgh, 1984.

Smith, J., *Annals of the Church of Scotland in Orkney from 1560*, Kirkwall, 1907.

Smith, T. B., *St Ninian's Isle and its Treasure*, Aberdeen, 1973.

Stafford, H. G., *James VI of Scotland and the Throne of England*, New York and London, 1940.

Thomson, W. P. L., *(The New) History of Orkney*, Edinburgh, 1987, 2001.

Tudor, J. R., *The Orkneys and Shetland*, London, 1883.

Willson, D. H., *James VI and I*, London, 1956.

Withrington, D. J., *Shetland and the Outside World, 1469–1969*, Oxford, 1982.

Wormald, J., *Lords and Men in Scotland: Bonds of Manrent, 1442–1603*, Edinburgh, 1985.

ARTICLES

Anderson, I. J. D., 'Anderson's Ambles: the West Coast Walk', *Shetland Life*, xvii (March 1982), 26–8.

Anderson, M. O., 'The Celtic Church in Kinrimund', *IR*, xxxvii (1976), 3–4.

Anderson, P. D., 'Alison Balfour', *Biographical Dictionary of Scottish Women*, ed. R. Pipes and E. Innes, Edinburgh, 2006, 23–4.

Anderson, P. D., 'Cathedral, Palace and Castle: the Strongholds of Kirkwall', in *The Faces of Orkney: Stones, Skalds and Saints*, ed. D. J. Waugh, Scottish Society for Northern Studies, Edinburgh, 2003, 81–93.

Anderson, P. D., 'Oliver Sinclair of Pitcairns', in *Who was Who in Orkney*, ed. W. S. Hewison, Kirkwall, 1998, 143.

Anderson, P. D., 'Robert Stewart, Earl of Orkney', 'Patrick Stewart, Earl of Orkney' and 'Mistresses and Children of James V', *Oxford Dictionary of National Biography*, 2004, online.

Anderson, P. D., 'Birsay in the Sixteenth Century', in *Orkney Heritage 2 – Birsay, A Centre of Political and Ecclesiastical Power*, ed. W. Thomson, Kirkwall, 1983, 82–96.

Anderson, P. D., 'Earl Patrick and his Enemies', *New Orkney Antiquarian Journal*, i (1999), 174–85.

Anderson, P. D., 'Earl William to Earl Patrick: a Survey of the History of Orkney and Shetland from 1468 to 1615', in *Shetland's Northern Links: Language and History*, Scottish Society for Northern Studies, ed. D. J. Waugh, Edinburgh, 1996, 174–85.

Anderson, P. D., 'The Armada and the Northern Isles', *Northern Studies*, xxv (1988), 42–57.

Anderson, P. D., 'The Stewart Earls of Orkney and the History of Orkney and Shetland', *Northern Studies*, xxix (1996), 43–52.

Begg, J., 'The Early Orkney Justiciary', *POAS*, viii (1929–30), 17.

Begg, J., 'The Orkney Bailie Courts', *POAS*, ii–iv (1923–6), 69–76; iii, 55–64; iv, 37–43.

Clouston, J. S, 'James Sinclair of Brecks', *POAS*, xv (1937–9), 61.

Clouston, J. S, 'The Battle of Summerdale', *Old Lore Miscellany*, ii (1909), 95.

Cowan, E. J., 'The Darker Vision of the Scottish Renaissance: the Devil and Francis Stewart', in *The Renaissance and Reformation in Scotland*, ed. I. B. Cowan and B. Shaw, Edinburgh, 1983, 124–40.

Cowan, I., 'The Appropriation of Parish Churches', in *An Historical Atlas of Scotland c. 400–c. 1600*, ed. P. G. B. McNeill and R. Nicholson, St Andrews, 1975, 37–8, 144–7.

Crawford, B. E., 'The Earldom of Orkney and Lordship of Shetland; a Reinterpetation of their Pledging to Scotland in 1468–70', *Saga Book* (Viking Soc.), 1969, xvii, 156–76.

Crawford, B. E., 'The Pawning of Orkney and Shetland: a Reconsideration of the Events of 1460–9', *SHR*, xlviii (1969), 35.

Crawford, B. E., 'The Fifteenth-century "Genealogy of the Earls of Orkney" and its Reflection of the Contemporary Political and Cultural Situation in the Earldom', *Mediaeval Scandinavia*, x (1976), 163.

Crawford, B. E., 'David Sinclair of Sumburgh', *Scandinavian Shetland: an Ongoing*

Tradition?, ed. J. R. Baldwin (Scottish Society for Northern Studies), Edinburgh, 1978, 1–11.

Crawford, B. E., 'William Sinclair, Earl of Orkney, and his Family: a Study in the Politics of Survival', in *Essays on the Nobility of Medieval Scotland*, ed. K. J. Stringer, Edinburgh, 2007, app., 252.

Dickinson, W. C., 'Odal Rights and Feudal Wrongs', *Viking Congress*, Edinburgh, 1954, 142.

Dilworth, M., 'Coldingham Priory and the Reformation', *JR*, xxiii (1972), 126.

Dobie, W. J., 'Udal Law', in *The Sources and Literature of Scots Law*, ed. H. Mackechnie and J. C. Brown (Stair Soc.), Edinburgh, 1936, 445-60.

Dobie, W. J., 'A Shetland Decree', *JR*, li (1939), 1.

Donaldson, G., 'The Early Ministers of Shetland', *Shetland News*, 9 Sept. 1943.

Donaldson, G., 'The Bishops and Priors of Whithorn', *TDGNHAS*, 3rd series, xxvii (1950), 147.

Donaldson, G., 'Bishop Adam Bothwell and the Reformation in Orkney', *SCHS*, xiii (1959), 85 *et seq.*

Donaldson, G., 'Stewart Builders: the Descendants of James V', *The Stewarts*, xiv (1974), 116.

Donaldson, G., 'The Income of Scottish Religious Houses', in *Mediaeval Religious Houses*, ed. I. B. Cowan, London, 1976, 199–200.

Doughty, D. W., 'The Library of James Stewart, Earl of Moray, 1531–70', *IR*, xxi (1970), 18.

Drever, W. P., 'Udal Law', in *Encyclopaedia of the Laws of Scotland*, vols I–XVI, ed. A. C. Black, Edinburgh, 1933, xv, 321–36.

Forte, A. D. M. 'Black Patie and Andro Umfra: a Prosopograpical Study of "Just Feir or Dredour" in Early Seventeenth-century Shetland', *Stair Society Miscellany*, v, (2006), 89–191.

Gould, J. A., 'Alexander Myln of Cambuskenneth', ODNB, online.

Hamilton, J. R. C., 'The Old House of Sumburgh – "Jarlshof"', *Excavations at Jarlshof, Shetland*, Edinburgh, 1956.

Hogg, A., 'Sidelights on the Perth Charterhouse', *JR*, xix (1968), 168.

Irvine, F., 'Profiles from the Past, No. XXIII; Earl Patrick Stewart', *New Shetlander*, lxix (1964), 8.

Irvine, J. T., 'The Bruces of Muness', *Shetland News*, 20 April 1895.

Jo. Ben., 'Descriptio Insularum Orchadia', *Macfarlane's Geographical Collections* (SHS), iii (1908), 309–20.

Leith, P., 'The Bellendens and the Palace of Stenness', *POAS*, xiv (1936-7), 41-4.

Leith, P., 'The Kirk and Palace of Stenness', privately printed, c. 1956.

Leith, P. [Jr], and Leonard, S., 'The Kirk and Parish of Stenness', privately printed, 2007

Macmaster, A., 'Alexander Myln of Cambuskenneth', DNB, London, 1885–1900, xiv, 2.

Manson, T. M. Y., 'The Fair Isle Armada Shipwreck', *The Scottish Tradition* (1974), 121–31.

McCulloch, W. T., 'History of the "Maiden" or Scottish Beheading Machine, with Notices of the Criminals who Suffered by it', *PSAS*, vii (1870), 553-4.

McGavin, N. A., 'Excavations in Kirkwall, 1978', *PSAS*, cxii (1982), 392–436.

McKerral, A., 'The Kintyre Properties of Whithorn and the Bishopric of Galloway', *TDGNHAS*, 3rd series, xxvii (1948–9), 183–92.

McNeill, P., 'Sir James Balfour of Pittendreich', *JR*, v (1960), 6.

Megaw, B., 'The Barony of St Trinian's in the Isle of Man'; *TDGNHAS*, 3rd ser., xxvii (1948–9), 173–82.

Melville, R. D., 'The Use and Forms of Judicial Torture in England and Scotland', *SHR*, ii, no. 7 (1905), 232–48.

Mitchison, N., 'Meeting Earl Patrick', *New Shetlander*, cxciii (1970), 9.

Mooney, J., 'Kennedys in Orkney and Caithness', *POAS*, x (1931–2), 17–20.

Murray, A. L., 'Sir John Skene and the Exchequer', 1594–1612, *Stair Society Miscellany One* (1971), 141–2.

Rendall, R., 'Birsay's Forgotten Palace', *Orkney Herald*, 21 April 1959.

Renwanz, M. E., 'From Crofters to Shetlanders', unpublished PhD thesis, Stanford, 1980.

Robberstad, K., 'Udal Law', in *Shetland and the Outside World, 1469–1969*, ed. D. J. Withrington, Oxford, 1996, 49.

Ryder, J. 'Udal Law', *The Laws of Scotland: Stair Memorial Encyclopaedia*, vols I–XXV, Edinburgh, 1987–9, xxiv, paras 301–16. Editorial excursus paras 317–29.

Scott, D., 'The Dons: Legends of the Armada', *The Orcadian*, 19 Nov. 1970.

Sellar, D., 'Udal Law', *The Laws of Scotland: Stair Memorial Encyclopaedia*, vols I–XXV, Edinburgh, 1987–9, xxiv, 193–230.

Simpson, W. D., 'Noltland Castle, Westray: a Critical Study', in *Charters and Other Records of the City and Royal Burgh of* Kirkwall, ed. J. Mooney (Spalding Club), Aberdeen, 1952.

Simpson, W. D., 'The Castles of Shetland', *Viking Congress*, Edinburgh, 1954.

Simpson, W. D., 'The Northernmost Castle of Britain', *SHR*, xxxviii, no. 25 (1959), 3.

Smith, B., 'Bismars and Pundars', *New Shetlander*, clxvi (Yule 1988), 6–7.

Smith, B., 'Shetland in the Saga-Time; Re-reading the *Orkneyinga Saga*', *Northern Studies*, xxv (1988), 21–41.

Smith, B., 'In the Tracks of Bishop Andrew Pictoris of Orkney, and Henry Phankouth, Archdeacon of Shetland', *IR*, xl (1989), 92–3.

Smith, B., 'What is a Scattald?', in *Essays in Shetland History*, ed. B. E. Crawford, Lerwick, 1984; *Toons and Tenants*, Lerwick, 2000, 99–124.

Smith, B., 'A Note on Waithing and Waith', *Toons and Tenants*, Lerwick, 2000, 58–60.

Smith, B., 'When did Orkney and Shetland become Part of Scotland?', *New Orkney Antiquarian Journal*, v (2011), 45–62.

Smith, T. B., 'The Law Relating to the Treasure', in *St Ninian's Isle and its Treasure*, vols I–II, ed. A. Small, Oxford, 1973, i, 149–66.

Steuart, A. F., 'Gilbert Balfour of Westray', *Old Lore Miscellany*, iv (1911), 148.

Stewart, A. M., 'The Final Folios of Adam Abell's "Roit or Quheill of Tyme": an Observantine Friar's Reflections on the 1520s and 30s', in *Stewart Style 1513–1542*, ed. H. M. Shire, East Lothian, 1996, 233–4.

Stewart, J., 'Udal Law and Government in Shetland', *Viking Congress*, Aberdeen, 1954, 84–111.

Stylegar, F-A. and Kjorsvik Schei, L., '"Lords of Norroway". The Shetland Estate of Herdis Thorvaldsdatter', in *West over Sea: Studies in Scandinavian Sea-borne Expansion and Settlement before 1300*, ed. B. B. Smith, S. Taylor and Gareth Williams, Leiden, Boston, 2007, 111–28.

Thomson, W. P. L., 'Fifteenth Century Depression in Orkney: the Evidence of Lord Henry Sinclair's Rentals', in *Essays in Shetland History*, ed. B. A. Crawford, Lerwick, 1984, 125–42.

Traill Dennison, W., 'Armada Traditions', *Orkney Herald*, 8 May 1889; *Northern Notes and Queries*, iv (1890), 120 (no. 236).

Tyrell, E., 'Birsay Palace, Orkney', *The Antiquary*, xlvii (1911), 183.

Wainwright, F. T., 'The Golden Age and After', *The Northern Isles*, London, 1964, 188–92.

Watt, D. E. R., 'Appropriations of some Parish Churches by 1560', in *Atlas of Scottish History to 1707*, ed. P. G. B. McNeill and H. L. MacQueen, Edinburgh, 1996, 368–9.

WORKS OF REFERENCE

An Historical Atlas of Scottish History c. 400–c. 1600, ed. P. McNeill and R. Nicholson, St Andrews, 1975.

Atlas of Scottish History to 1707, ed. P. McNeill and H. MacQueen, Edinburgh, 1996.

Cowan, I. and Easson, D. E., *Mediaeval Religious Houses*, London, 1976.

Dictionary of the Older Scottish Tongue, ed. W. Craigie et al., London and Chicago, 1937–2001.

Donaldson G. and Morpeth, R. S., *Who's Who in Scottish History*, Edinburgh, 1977.

Dowden, J., *The Bishops of Scotland*, Glasgow, 1912.

Encyclopaedia of the Law of Scotland, vols I–XVI, Edinburgh, 1926–33.

Fasti Ecclesiae Scoticanae Medii Aevi (SRS), ed. D. E. R. Watt and A. Murray, Edinburgh, 2003.

Inventory of Ancient Monuments. The Royal Commission on the Ancient Monuments of Scotland. *Twelfth Report with an Inventory of the Ancient Monuments of Orkney and Shetland*, vols I–III, 1946.

Jakobsen, J., *An Etymological Dictionary of the Norn Language in Shetland*, vols I–II, London and Copenhagen, 1928–32.

Jakobsen, J., *The Dialect and Place-names of Shetland*, Lerwick, 1897.

Marwick, H., *The Orkney Norn*, Oxford, 1926.

Marwick, H., *Orkney Farm-names*, Kirkwall, 1952.

Marwick, H., *The Place-names of Birsay*, Aberdeen, 1970.

McGibbon, D. and Ross, T., *The Domestic and Castellated Architecture of Scotland*, vols I–II, Edinburgh, 1887–92.

Morison, W., *The Decisions of the Court of Session*, Edinburgh, 1804.

Scots Peerage, vols I–IX, ed. J. Balfour Paul, Edinburgh, 1904–14.

Scott, H., *Fasti Ecclesiae Scoticanae*, vols I–VII, Edinburgh, 1915–28.

Scottish National Dictionary, ed. W. Grant, David Murison, Edinburgh, 1941–76.

Stewart, J., *Shetland Place-names*, Lerwick, 1987.

The Concise Scots Dictionary, Aberdeen, 1985.

Index